HENRI THEIL'S CONTRIBUTIONS TO ECONOMICS AND ECONOMETRICS

Advanced Studies in Theoretical and Applied Econometrics

Volume 25

The titles published in this series are listed at the end of this volume.

Henri Theil's Contributions to Economics and Econometrics

Volume III:

Economic Policy and Forecasts, and Management Science

Edited by

Baldev Raj
Wilfrid Laurier University, Waterloo, Ontario, Canada

and

Johan Koerts
Erasmus University, Rotterdam, The Netherlands

SPRINGER SCIENCE+BUSINESS MEDIA, B.V.

Library of Congress Cataloging-in-Publication Data

(Revised for vol. 3)
Henri Theil's contribution to economics and econometrics / edited by
Baldev Raj, J. Koerts.
p. cm. - (Advanced studies in theoretical and applied
econometrics: v. 23, 24, 25)
Includes index.
Contents: v. 1. Econometric theory and methodology. - v. 2.
Consumer demand analysis and information theory. - v. 3. Economic
policy and forecasts and management science.
ISBN 978-94-010-5063-0 ISBN 978-94-011-2410-2 (eBook)
DOI 10.1007/978-94-011-2410-2
1. Theil, Henri - Contributions to Econometrics. I. Theil, Henri.
II. Raj, Baldev, 1941- . III. Koerts, J. IV. Series.
HB139.H46 1991 330'01'5195 91-38183

ISBN 978-94-010-5063-0

Printed on acid-free paper

DEDICATION

To

Eleonore Theil

Balbeer Raj

and

Maria Koerts

CONTENTS OF THE COLLECTION

VOLUME I

PART TWO: ECONOMETRIC THEORY AND METHODOLOGY

Section 2.1 Structural Equations

Section 2.2 Systems of Equations

VOLUME II

Section 4.2 Economic Inequality and International Comparisons

Section 4.3 Applications in Econometrics

Section 4.4 Input-Output Analysis

PREFACE TO THE COLLECTION

PREAMBLE

The editors are pleased to present a selection of Henri Theil's contributions to economics and econometrics in three volumes. In Volume I we have provided an overview of Theil's contributions, a brief biography, an annotated bibliography of his research, and a selection of published and unpublished articles and chapters in books dealing with topics in econometrics. Volume II contains Theil's contributions to demand analysis and information theory. Volume III includes Theil's contributions in economic policy and forecasting, and management science.

The selection of articles is intended to provide examples of Theil's many seminal and pathbreaking contributions to economics in such areas as econometrics, statistics, demand analysis, information theory, economic policy analysis, aggregation theory, forecasting, index numbers, management science, sociology, operations research, higher education and much more. The collection is also intended to serve as a tribute to him on the occasion of his 67th birthday.[1] These three volumes also highlight some of Theil's contributions and service to the profession as a leader, advisor, administrator, teacher, and researcher.

Theil's contributions, which encompass many disciplines, have been extensively cited both in scientific and professional journals. These citations often place Theil among the top 10 researchers (ranked according to number of times cited) in the world in various disciplines.

This collection is not intended to provide a normative assessment of his pioneering and influential contributions or serve as a definitive statement on his lifetime of contributions. Furthermore, no attempt is made to provide a documented history of Theil's contribution to the development of the theory and application of econometrics or other disciplines. The collection merely provides the basic building blocks for a more detailed historical inquiry into his influence on the development of these disciplines.

While we have made every attempt to include a significant number of his important contributions, some key contributions could not be included in the three volumes for a variety of reasons. Firstly, we were faced with budget constraints; secondly some of Theil's contributions are contained in books and reprinting them would have been impractical and expensive. The exclusion of some of these contributions is regrettable but could not be avoided.

---

[1] Theil's Festschrift will also be published in 1991. It is entitled, *Contributions to Consumer Demand and Econometrics* and is jointly edited by R.F. Bewley and Tran Van Hoa (MacMillan Press).

ACKNOWLEDGEMENTS

The collection has benefited from the insights and comments of a large number of individuals. In addition, a number of our colleagues and friends have provided helpful suggestions and encouragement which made the task of editing these volumes (which took about two years to complete) quite enjoyable. We extend special thanks to Anton P. Barten, Kenneth W. Clements, Denzil G. Fiebig, Arthur S. Goldberger, Esfandiar Maasoumi, and Roy Radner who shared with us background material on Theil or commented on our initial selection. Helpful comments from Professor Henri Theil and two anonymous referees on our initial proposal led to additions and deletions to the list of included contributions. Their help is also gratefully acknowledged.

We are also grateful to Peter Kennedy and Adolf Buse for their help in refereeing one of the unpublished articles and A.P. Barten and William E. Griffiths for supplying us with an English version of a paper from their personal libraries. In addition, it is a pleasure to thank all those who contributed in other ways to the completion of this project. This list includes Ronald Bewley, Jack Gould, John Kraft, Barry McPherson, Frank Millerd, Alex J. Murray, A.L. Nagar, Russell Muncaster, Tran Van Hoa, Alan Powell and John Weir.

The editors are grateful to the following societies, associations, publishers, and individuals for their permission to reprint articles and chapters from journals and books.

American Economic Association
American Political Science Association
American Statistical Association
Cambridge University Press
Econometric Society
De Economist
Elsevier Science Publishers and North Holland Publishers
Gordon and Breach Science Publishers, Inc.
H.E. Stenfert Kroese B.V.
International Economic Review
Institut de Statistique, Université de Paris
International Federation of Operational Research Societies
Institute for Scientific Information
Institute of Management Sciences
International Statistical Institute
JAI Press
Journal of Accounting Research
MacMillan Publishing Co.
Maandschrift Economie
Metroeconomica
Netherlands Organization for International Co-operation in Higher Education
Pergamon Press Ltd.
Sage Publications Inc.
Roy Radner
Royal Netherlands Academy of Arts and Science
Sloan Management Review Association

Henri Theil
Weltwirtschaftliches Archiv

FINANCIAL SUPPORT

This project was made possible by financial support or research assistance from a number of institutions which are listed below:

- Erasmus University (Faculty Development Fund)
- Wilfrid Laurier University (Academic Development Fund, Laurier Institute, and Research Office)
- McKethan-Matherly Chair of the University of Florida
- University of Chicago (Graduate School of Business)
- Inter-library Loans, Erasmus University and Wilfrid Laurier University Libraries
- Society of Management Accountants of Ontario

RESEARCH ASSISTANCE

The typing work was skilfully performed by the following individuals:

- Elli Hoek Van Dijke (Erasmus University)
- Elsie Grogan and Lori Kapshey (Word Processing Department, Wilfrid Laurier University)
- Andrew and Joan Zador (Science Scribe, Waterloo, Ontario)

In addition, Trudy Trudel helped us with the typing of a few papers. The professional copy-editing of the manuscript (to bring it to a uniform style) as well as proof-reading was performed by Dave Kroeker and Maura Brown. Margaret Forsyth, Tim Kuehn, Ildiko Tiszovszky, and Dr. C. Dubbelman provided competent research assistance including proofreading the retyped material. Gerry Anderson, Abby Brubacher and Chantel Thiel helped with library and secretarial tasks. The help of all these individuals is gratefully acknowledged.

The acquisitions editor, Marie M. Stratta and her assistant Lorraine Jordens from Kluwer Academic Publishers were very helpful throughout the project; it has been a pleasure to work with them. This project would not have been completed without the support of Professor Henri Theil and our spouses Balbeer Raj and Maria Koerts. We thank them sincerely for their moral support.

Baldev Raj,
Wilfrid Laurier University
Waterloo, Ontario, Canada

Johan Koerts,
Erasmus University,
Rotterdam, The Netherlands

CONTENTS OF VOLUME III

PART FIVE: ECONOMIC POLICY AND FORECASTS

SECTION 5.1: ECONOMIC POLICY

CHAPTER 62

ECONOMETRIC MODELS AND WELFARE MAXIMIZATION*

HENRI THEIL
Central Planning Bureau
The Hague, The Netherlands

I. Introductory Survey

1. ECONOMIC POLICY AS A CHOICE PROBLEM

The problem of economic policy for Central and Local Governments is, to find out and to realize the "best" future configuration of the economy that can be attained. Such a configuration can often be described in terms of values assumed by certain variables. For instance, the Government may choose between two alternative configurations for next year, the first of which is characterized by a deficit of the balance of payments of 200 million guilders and 5 per cent unemployment, the second by a deficit of 100 million guilders and 8 per cent unemployment. In general the number of configurations attainable is of course larger than two, and so is the number of variables characterizing the configurations. These variables need moreover not all be quantitative; neither is it necessary that they are all "economic" in the sense that they belong to the field which is generally considered to be economic.

It is the purpose of this paper to deal with some aspects of the use of econometric models, the most well-known "producers" of alternative configurations, for political decision-taking; the aspects especially considered are those of the uncertainty due to the deviations between model and reality. The analysis is rather general and may be applied to decision-taking in other fields, but Government policy has been chosen here for the sake of concreteness.

2. PREFERENCES AND THEIR INTERPRETATION

The choice problem of economic policy is characterized by several difficulties, and the remainder of this section I is devoted to an exposition of some of them. First, we have the question how to interpret criteria like "to choose the best among all attainable configurations." The doctrine of welfare economics is very much concerned with the word "best," and in recent years Professor K.J. Arrow[1] obtained a very interesting negative

* This article first appeared in *Weltwirtschaftliches Archiv*, **72** (1954) 60-83. Reprinted with the permission of the Institut für Weltwirtschaft an der Universität Kiel.

[1] Kenneth J. Arrow: 1951, "Social Choice and Individual Values," *Cowles Commission for Research in Economics, Monograph* No. 12, New York and London.

result on the possibility of deriving collective preference orderings from individual orderings, which is no doubt relevant for the choice problem of Government economic policy. For the analysis to be exposed here it is, however, preferable to take a rather simple view in this matter. We shall deal with an authority who is in charge of policy-making, and with one or several economists who assist this authority in the following sense: They supply information about the consequences of alternative policy measures, but they do not advise on the desirability of the outcomes. It follows that the preferences that are relevant are those of the responsible authority. We shall not consider the problem of their relation to the individual preferences of the members of the community.

3. INDIRECT REALISATION OF CONFIGURATIONS

A second difficulty is that the configuration chosen as "the best" cannot in general be directly realised. This is immediately clear from the example of Section I.1. The responsible authority may conclude that a gap in the balance of payments of 200 million guilders and 5 per cent unemployment is a configuration which is preferable to all other possibilities, but it is in general not true that the Government can impose this configuration in a straightforward way. The balance of payments is affected by the actions and reactions of importers and exporters; only in the case of a rigorous currency control is it possible for the Government to fix the surplus at a certain definite amount. Similarly, the unemployment percentage is mainly determined by the development of the population and the behaviour of employers.

In principle there are several solutions for a problem like this. For instance, one may consider the set of all possible actions and reactions of the individuals of the community and of groups of individuals as a "game" with many "players" and try to apply von Neumann's and Morgenstern's[2] theory. However, this approach is rather cumbersome for practical applications. In the present phase it seems preferable to use an econometric model. It is then the task of the advising economists to construct such a model and to derive from it a survey of alternative possibilities. We shall illustrate this for the example of section I.1; the model is highly simplified and will be amended in the next sections, but it is useful to illustrate the indirect nature of the realisation of "optimal" configurations.

Suppose that the Government wants to influence the employment percentage by means of the amount of Government expenditure. More specifically, we suppose that next year's employment percentage (E) depends linearly on next year's total production (P):

$$E = \alpha_0 + \alpha P \tag{1.1}$$

and that P depends linearly on the amount of Government expenditure (G):

$$P = \beta_0 + \beta G \tag{1.2}$$

---

[2] John von Neumann, and Oskar Morgenstern: 1947, *Theory of Games and Economic Behavior*, 2nd ed., Princeton.

Similarly, we suppose that the balance of payments (B) depends linearly on P; this may be roughly justified by pointing to the relation between production and imports,

$$B = \gamma_0 + \gamma P \tag{1.3}$$

After eliminating P we find for E and B

$$E = (\alpha_0 + \alpha\, \beta_0) + \alpha\beta G \tag{1.4}$$
$$B = (\gamma_0 + \gamma\, \beta_0) + \gamma\beta G \tag{1.5}$$

The conclusions are as follows. G is a variable that can be directly controlled by the Government. For E and B this is not true. However, E and B can be indirectly controlled via G, for a choice of a G-value determines E and B according to (1.4) and (1.5) respectively. Hence the "optimum" configuration should be realised by adapting G.

Another interesting feature is that not all pairs of values E, B can be realised in this way: After eliminating G from (1.4) and (1.5) we obtain a linear relation between E and B, which is hence a restriction on the possibilities of realisation.

4. INSTRUMENTS AND INDIRECT VARIABLES

Following Tinbergen[3], we shall call variables like G, which can be controlled directly by the Government, its *instruments*. The question whether a certain variable is an instrument or not depends on the social framework of the economy. In a socialistic economy more variables will come under this heading than in a nineteenth-century society. There are some variables, like Government expenditure and tax rates, which are instruments in practically all present-day societies, but this is not true for, say, the industrial wage level, which may or may not be an instrument.

It is the function of the instruments to adapt the other variables, like E and B in the above example, such that the resulting configuration is "optimal." We shall call the latter variables *indirect variables* in view of the way in which they are fixed at certain specified levels. These variables are essential to the problem because the Government is interested in their values. It is important to stress that the same may be true for the instruments: Some or all of the instruments may, in addition to their function of adapting the indirect variables, be valued as such by the Government. For instance, suppose that there is a general wage and price control, so that the wage level is an instrument. Given the prices, this level will affect the welfare of the wage-earning population, and hence we should expect the Government to be interested in this variable, and not merely because it affects other variables in the economy. The situation is different if the model contains a variable the function of which is to take more explicit account of the wage-earners' welfare, e.g. their per capita disposable real income. In such a case the noninstrumental

[3] J. Tinbergen: 1952, "On the Theory of Economic Policy," *Contributions to Economic Analysis*, 1, Amsterdam.

role of the wage level is taken over by the latter variable, so that its function is then merely instrumental. It follows that the question whether a certain instrument has functions of both types (i.e. is "nonneutral") can only be answered by the policy maker if the set of all instruments and indirect variables is specified.

5. A COMPARISON WITH THE THEORY OF CONSUMER'S BEHAVIOUR

When summarising, we are in the following position. The Government is interested in the future values to be assumed by certain variables. Some of them are controlled directly, some indirectly, but it may be in principle that the values assumed by each of them are "valued" in the sense that a higher value is preferred to a lower, *ceteris paribus*, or *vice versa*. We could say — under appropriate conditions — that instruments and indirect variables are the arguments of a *social welfare function*, corresponding to the preferences of the policy maker. This is formally comparable with the utility function of the traditional theory of consumer's behaviour, which is based on the consumer's preferences.

In general it is not true that all sets of values of indirect variables can be realised; in other words, in the space of instruments and indirect variables only certain point sets are available. This is clear for the example of section I.1, for we obtained at the end of section I.3 a linear relation between E and B which had to be obeyed. This too is formally comparable with an aspect of consumer's theory, viz. with the budget plane. A minor difference is that in the present problem there may be several restrictions, which need not be linear.

An important aspect, which deserves here more attention than in consumer's theory, is the question of the adequacy of the model for political decision purposes. Let us suppose, for the sake of convenience, that the relations between instruments and indirect variables are all linear, so that the model may be given as

$$Ax + By = c \tag{1.6}$$

where x is the column vector of instruments, y that of indirect variables, A and B are matrices of parameters and c is a vector of "constant terms." In order that the indirect variables can be controlled *via* the instruments it is necessary that the former variables can each be written as explicit functions of the latter. This is not possible if the rank of B is smaller than the number of indirect variables, e.g. if this number exceeds the number of relations. On the other hand, if B has full rank and the number of relations exceeds that of the indirect variables, the "excess relations" imply certain restrictions on the instruments. Hence, if we impose the following two conditions on (1.6), viz. (*i*) all indirect variables are controlled *via* the instruments, and (*ii*) all instruments can be independently controlled, then B should be square and nonsingular.

6. CHOICE ALTERNATIVES AND PROBABILITY ALTERNATIVES

We should now stress an important point of difference between the traditional theory of consumer's behaviour and the problem considered here. It is that the economic reality cannot be perfectly described by means of a few macroeconomic relations of the type (1.6); and, we might guess, the same will be true for whatever other method. We shall always be faced with errors of several kinds, like those due to variables "neglected" in the model, to effects of aggregation from micro to macrorelations, etc. The most well-known method of dealing with such deviations is to treat them as random drawings from a probability collection with certain specified properties. For instance, we could replace (1.6) by

$$Ax + By = c + u \tag{1.7}$$

where u is a column vector of random deviations.

The acceptance of such deviations has fundamental consequences for our choice problem, which may be illustrated as follows. According to (1.6) it is sufficient for the policy-maker to know which values of the indirect variables result from alternative instrument values. Hence the advising economist should construct a model like (1.6) and derive from it a set of alternative outcomes, "choice alternatives," after which the authority can make up his mind. In vector notation, such a set of choice alternatives may be written as follows:

alternative 1	x^1	y^1
alternative 2	x^2	y^2
alternative 3	x^3	y^3
....		...

However, if the stochastic model (1.7) is accepted, the advising economist should also take account of alternative outcomes of a more probabilistic nature. He should add to each choice alternative a number of "probability alternatives" concerning the deviations u, and add also the probability of their occurrence. In a vector scheme:

		Probability alternatives			
		u^1	u^2	u^3	.....
Choice Alternatives	x^1	y^{11}	y^{12}	y^{13}	.....
	x^2	y^{21}	y^{22}	y^{23}	.....
	x^3	y^{31}	y^{32}	y^{33}	.....
	...	....			

The authority should then choose one of the vectors x^1, x^2, ... such that he prefers this vector together with the resulting set of possible vectors of indirect values (a row in the above scheme), in combination with the probabilities attached to these possibilities, to all other instrument vectors with their resulting probabilities concerning indirect values. For instance, in the simple example of section I.3, the advising economist should add deviations u_1, u_2, u_3 to the right-hand side of (1.1), (1.2), (1.3) respectively, and he should specify their probability distribution in order to draw inferences about E and B, given G.

The *G*-choice of the decision-taking authority should then not be based on one single value of u_1, u_2 and of u_3, but on a whole scala of probability outcomes.

7. THE PROBLEM

The conlusion that both choice and probability alternatives are necessary for an adequate picture of the possible future configurations is natural, but at the same time it is disastrous for practical applications. The number of choice alternatives may already be rather large, which is not always convenient because of the limited time which policy makers usually have at their disposal. When combined with probability alternatives, however, the total number of all alternative outcomes is even considerably larger, so that it is hardly imaginable that policy makers are ready and able to read such intricate memoranda of their advising economists. It is therefore rather tempting to use short-cuts by dropping the probability alternatives altogether and putting the random deviations at, say, their expectations or at their most probable values. As a matter of fact, an approach of this kind is followed by the Central Planning Office of the Netherlands.

The question arises whether this is permissible. It is the purpose of this paper to investigate this more closely. The answer will be that there is an important class of cases where such a short-cut is permissible in the sense that the policy maker, thus informed, is bound to take the *same* decisions concerning instrument values as in the case that he would be fully informed by means of both choice and probability alternatives; but also that in certain specified cases a short-cut of this kind leads the policy maker to decisions which are different from those which he would have taken if he had been more fully informed. In other words, sometimes there will be a "choice bias," but in many cases this will be absent.

8. IRRELEVANT VARIABLES

Before proceeding it is useful to point to a formal relationship with the statistical theory of econometric models, from which models of the type (1.7) are usually derived. The variables of such models are either exogenous or endogenous, and the similarity between exogenous variables and instruments and between endogenous and indirect variables will be evident. Suppose now that a linear econometric model is available, with the following properties: (*i*) it contains all indirect variables relevant for the policy maker, and it contains no "superfluous" endogenous variables, which are considered by the policy maker to be not interesting for his policy purposes; (*ii*) it contains all his instruments, and it does not contain exogenous variables that are noninstrumental. Then this model is simply of the type (1.6) or (1.7), the *x*'s being exogenous variables and instruments at the same time, and the *y*'s endogenous and indirect variables; and the condition that *B* is square (cf. section I.5) implies that the econometric model is a complete one.

Next, let us suppose that some of the endogenous variables of the econometric model and/or some of its exogenous variables are "irrelevant" in the sense that there are no indirect variables and no instruments, respectively. These irrelevant variables should be dropped, in the following way. The irrelevant endogenous variables are eliminated by means of some of the equations. If the original model is complete, the resulting model will be complete as well, for the elimination requires, for each variable, one and only one equation; this conclusion holds of course independently of the linearity of the equations. The noninstrumental exogenous variables are to be replaced by estimated values. For instance, suppose that the import price level of certain commodities is such a variable, and that relevant future indirect values are affected by, say, next year's price level. Then we should replace this level by an estimate and include the possible forecasting error in the vector of deviations u. In other words: Next year's import price level is simply shared between elements of c and of u (cf. (1.7)). Now it will be sometimes possible to estimate this price level statistically in the conventional way, e.g. if it depends on the world price level of raw materials with a sufficient lag. Sometimes, however, this is not possible, and an estimate based on "intuition" and on economic and political "feeling" is then usually the only alternative available. It will be clear that this forces the probability distribution of the vector u to be of a rather subjective nature. Although this is certainly not disastrous — several theories on the foundation of the probability concept are of a "subjective" type — the information available on such distributions will in general be scanty. It is therefore important that the conditions to be imposed on the distribution of u are rather weak, just as it will appear to be true for the conditions concerning the preferences of the policy maker.

9. SOME REFERENCES

The problem of econometric models as a guide to policy is not new; we should mention L.R. Klein[4] as one of the earlier contributors. The first attempts on a larger scale are those of R. Frisch[5] and J. Tinbergen[6]. The present author's indebtedness to Tinbergen's work will be clear from the above. The approach chosen here is different from his as to the rôle attributed to the deviations inherent to the use of econometric models.

II. The Formal Problem

1. THE MODEL

We shall consider m instruments, $x_1, ..., x_m$, and n indirect variables, $y_1, ..., y_n$; we shall often write, in a vector notation x and y. These variables may be either "economic" or "noneconomic"; moreover, the instruments may be quantitative or qualitative, but the indirect variables should all be quantitative. Hence the subsequent analysis is equally valid

---

[4] Lawrence R. Klein: 1947, "The Use of Econometric Models as a Guide to Economic Policy," *Econometrica*, **15**, pp. 111 sqq.

[5] Ragnar Frisch: 1950, "L'emploi des modèles pour l'élaboration d'une politique économique rationnelle," *Revue d'économie politique*, **60**, pp. 474 sqq., 601 sqq., 620 sqq.

[6] Tinbergen, *op. cit.*

for, say, the case in which the Government considers alternative decisions according to which a certain set of schools should be operated by itself or by some religious authority.

As to the relations among the x's and the y's, we shall only need a vector of relations describing each indirect variable as an explicit function of the instruments and of the deviations. Such a vector is obviously related to the well-known reduced form of econometric models. In the case of a linear model like (1.7) the existence of this vector requires that the parameter matrix B of (1.7) should be square and nonsingular; a condition the appropriateness of which has been illustrated at an earlier occasion (section I.5). However, linearity will not be needed here. More specifically, we introduce

Assumption (a) *The indirect variables assume quantitative values only and depend on the instruments according to*

$$y = f(x) + u \tag{2.1}$$

where f *is a vector of* n *single-valued functions and* u *a vector of random deviations with expectation* 0. *The instruments can be independently controlled.*

If some of the instruments are qualitative rather than quantitative, the functions f are not of a conventional type. However, they can easily be split up into functions of this type for each combination of qualitative values assumed by such instruments.

2. THE SOCIAL WELFARE FUNCTION

We shall suppose that the policy maker has a clear idea of the desirability of any set of values assumed by instruments and indirect variables as compared with any other set. This assumption is closely related to the corresponding assumption on consumer's preferences in traditional demand theory. Just as in that field, we shall also suppose that the policy maker's preferences are transitive, so that the set of all fully specified vectors x, y has a complete (social) ordering. In the case of a nonstochastic model ($u \equiv 0$) these assumptions would be sufficient to indicate the policy maker's choice of instrument values: The set of all attainable vectors x, y is then obtained by varying x through its domain and finding the corresponding $y = f(x)$, and the set which is the highest in the ordering will be chosen.[7] This, again, is similar to the analysis of consumer's behaviour.

However, in the case of stochastic models it is not sufficient that the policy maker is able to order all specified vectors x, y. A choice of instrument values will then not determine one single set of indirect values, but only a probability distribution of such sets. Hence, in order to compare alternative measures of policy, he should be able to say whether a probability distribution A is preferable to a distribution B, or *vice versa*, or whether he considers them as equally valuable.

The problem of preferences concerning probability distributions has been extensively investigated by von Neumann and Morgenstern.[8] Their approach may be

[7] Sometimes there will be a multiple solution, but this is not essential.

[8] von Neumann, and Morgenstern, *op. cit.*

roughly described in the following terms. If the set of all attainable vectors x, y has a complete ordering, it is possible to find a function $W(x,y)$, a social welfare function, such that $W(x^1, y^1) > W(x^2, y^2)$ if and only if x^1, y^1 is preferred to x^2, y^2. Just as the utility function in demand theory, it is monotonically invariant; that is, it may be replaced by any function which increases monotonically with W (like W^2 and log W if $W > 0$), and such a function has the same relation to the ordering as the original function W. Hence there is considerable freedom as to the choice of a social welfare function. Von Neumann and Morgenstern make use of this freedom by selecting one type of such functions with convenient properties for the problem of preferences concerning probability distributions: This type is such that the value of a distribution is equal to the mathematical expectation of the values of the underlying stochastic outcomes. In our terms: They choose a function W such that the social welfare of a vector x combined with the corresponding stochastic vector y is equal to

$$EW(x,y)$$

This approach is only possible if the policy maker's preferences obey certain axioms, which are slightly more stringent than that of a complete ordering. It seems reasonable to expect that they are satisfied by the preferences of a responsible policy maker; for a more detailed discussion we must refer to von Neumann and Morgenstern.[9] We therefore introduce:

Asssumption (b) *The policy maker's preferences concerning the set of all specified vectors x, y obey von Neumann and Morgenstern's axioms.*

Under this assumption we may apply the calculus of mathematical expectations. The social welfare function appropriate for these expectations is no longer monotonically invariant; it is only invariant against linear transformations, and hence W is uniquely defined as soon as a zero and a unit of welfare have been fixed.

From now on we shall consider — without mentioning this explicitly — only those social welfare functions W to which the calculus of mathematical expectations is applicable.

---

[9] In rough terms, these axioms imply the following. First, all specified vectors x, y can be ordered according to decreasing preference. Secondly, if x^1, y^1 is preferred to x^2, y^2, then a positive chance p of the former combined with the remaining chance (1-p) of the latter should be preferred as well. Thirdly, if we have three vectors x^i, y^i ($i = 1, 2, 3$), the first being preferred to the second, and the second to the third, then the second is preferred to a stochastic combination of the first and the third, provided the chance of the first is, although positive, sufficiently small. This means that, however preferable the first vector may be, we can make its influence in the stochastic combination arbitrarily weak by making it sufficiently improbable. It may be that the validity of this axiom is somewhat dubious for occasional gamblers, but we should expect it to be obeyed by responsible men. Finally, certain axioms are imposed which render the order of the constituents in stochastic combinations irrelevant.

3. FORMULATION OF THE PROBLEM

Under Assumptions (a) and (b) the optimal policy is the choice of the vector $\hat{x}$ for which social welfare,

$$EW(x,y) = EW(x, f(x) + u) \tag{2.2}$$

is maximal. If nothing is known about the shape of the social welfare function, the appropriate procedure is (cf. section I.6) to prepare a set of choice and probability alternatives. The short-cut mentioned in section I.7 implies that the stochastic vector u is replaced by a nonstochastic vector, after which the probability alternatives are dropped. We shall make this more concrete by supposing that u is replaced by its expectation, 0, so that the (remaining) choice alternatives supply information, not about the stochastic vector y, but about its expectation $Ey = f(x)$. We might therefore say that this short-cut corresponds to *conditional welfare maximization*, the condition being that u equals its expectation. In that case the policy maker has to compare a set of nonstochastic vectors x, Ey. He will then choose the instrument vector $\bar{x}$ which maximizes

$$W(x,Ey) = W(x, f(x)) \tag{2.3}$$

The problem is, under which conditions the maximising vectors $\hat{x}$ and $\bar{x}$ will be equal, and when they will be different. The maximization processes of (2.2) and (2.3) are of course different, but it may be that the actual measures taken ($\hat{x}$ and $\bar{x}$) are the same; and this would be important.

III. On the Shape of the Social Welfare Function

1. GEOMETRICAL REPRESENTATION OF SOCIAL WELFARE

It is useful first to consider certain properties of the social welfare function. The method of indifference loci is convenient here, just as in the analysis of consumer's demand. As the indirect variables alone will prove to be relevant in this respect, we shall consider the n-dimensional y-space, which we think filled up with a family of indifference loci, i.e. hyperplanes of a more or less regular type, the points of which correspond to outcomes which are considered to be equally valuable. Such indifference loci in the y-space are of course subject to the values of those instruments which have noninstrumental functions as well (cf. section I.4).

It should be stressed that indifference loci do not define welfare functions of the von Neumann type uniquely. This is only true for monotonically invariant functions, so that additional information is needed for a specification of the functions in which we are interested here. In spite of this some insight into the general shape of relevant indifference loci, based on a few examples, will prove to be useful for the subsequent analysis.

2. WELFARE COMPARISONS OF INCOMES OF DIFFERENT GROUPS

Let us suppose that the members of the community considered are either wage-earners or capitalists, and that the incomes of both groups, the wage bill and the total profits, are among the policy maker's indirect variables. We shall consider certain alternative types of indifference curves belonging to these variables.

We imagine the wage bill to be constant, whereas the profits increase from $-\infty$ to $+\infty$; this should be considered as a mental experiment, not as a development over time. As long as the profits are excessively negative, it is plausible that the policy maker will attach a positive value to a (small) increase, the wage bill remaining constant. This is illustrated in Diagram 1 by the negative slope of the indifference curves at their

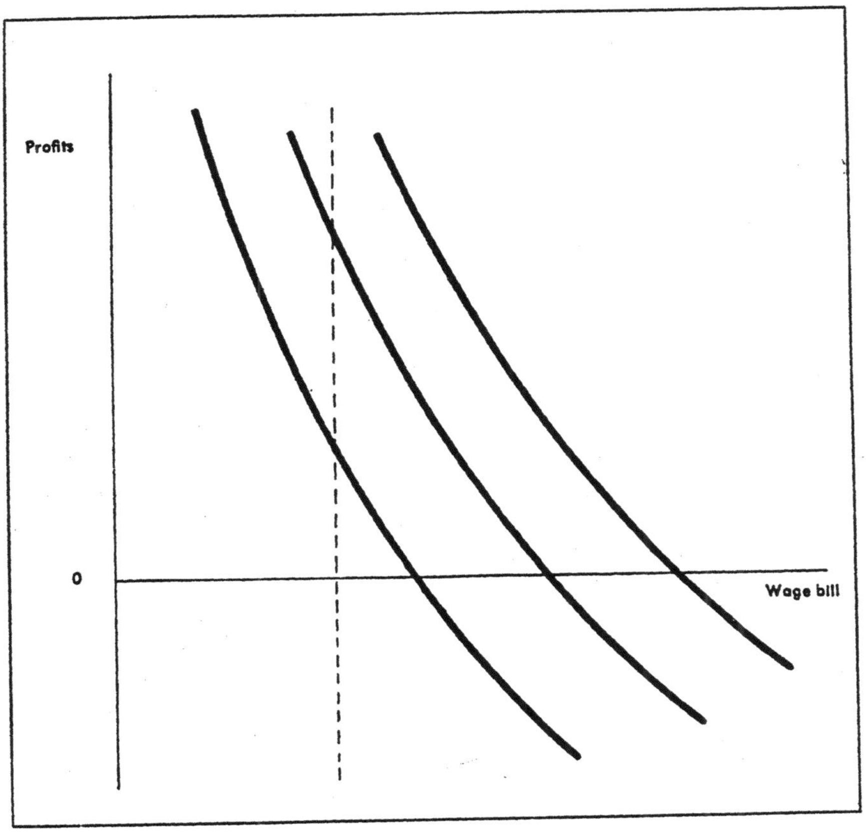

Diagram 1

intersections with the dotted vertical line. It may be that this property holds for all indifference curves cutting the dotted line at any point, however high, like in this diagram. We might say that such a family of indifference curves belongs to a "liberal" policy-maker, because he prefers a higher income of one group to a lower, the income of the second group remaining constant, even if the income of the latter group is negligible as compared with that of the former. But it may also be that the policy maker is of, say, a "Marxist" type, and that he prefers, after profits have reached a certain critical value dependent on the fixed wage bill chosen, a smaller increase of total profits to a larger, given this fixed wage bill (cf. Diagram 2). Finally, it may be that the indifference curves have not only slopes with different signs, but that they are even closed. Suppose e.g. that the policy maker wants to distinguish between the total incomes of capitalists, of industrial wage-earners and of agricultural households. Let us imagine that the income of the third group remains constant, whereas the incomes of the other two groups increase (in an arbitrary, fixed or variable proportion). It is then possible that, if the policy maker is sufficiently agriculturally minded, a point like Q in Diagram 3 is reached where any further increases lead to a lower indifference curve.

We shall not go into the problem whether all these variants should be considered as "reasonable" in some way. Their sole purpose is to supply indifference curves of types that can possibly be relevant.

3. EMPLOYMENT VERSUS BALANCE OF PAYMENTS

We now go back to the example of section I.2 and suppose, in first instance, that the economy is characterized by a serious unemployment. The policy maker will then presumably be inclined to accept a policy of public spending. Such a policy is however unfavourable for the balance of payments, so that the employment advantages have to be compared with the disadvantages as to the balance of payments position. We therefore consider a family of indifference curves for these two variables (cf. Diagram 4). If the deficit on the foreign accounts is serious, the policy maker will presumably consider welfare to be decreased by any additional deficit, unless this is compensated by a sufficiently large increase of the number employed. Hence we should expect the curves to have negative slopes below the horizontal axis. If the balance is sufficiently positive, the policy maker will presumably not attach much value to the payments position, so that large changes in this variable are necessary to compensate given employment changes. We should therefore expect the curves to be almost vertical in this region. If, however, the balance of payments shows such a large surplus that exporters are faced with difficulties because of delays in receiving their revenues, that the policy maker has to consider difficult relations with his colleagues in other countries, etc., then we should expect that additional surpluses will be valued negatively, so that the indifference curves will move upwards to the right.

A new aspect enters here into the picture because employment cannot exceed the full-employment level. Hence the indifference curves break off at the straight vertical line of Diagram 4. "Boundary conditions" of this type will prove important in the subsequent analysis.

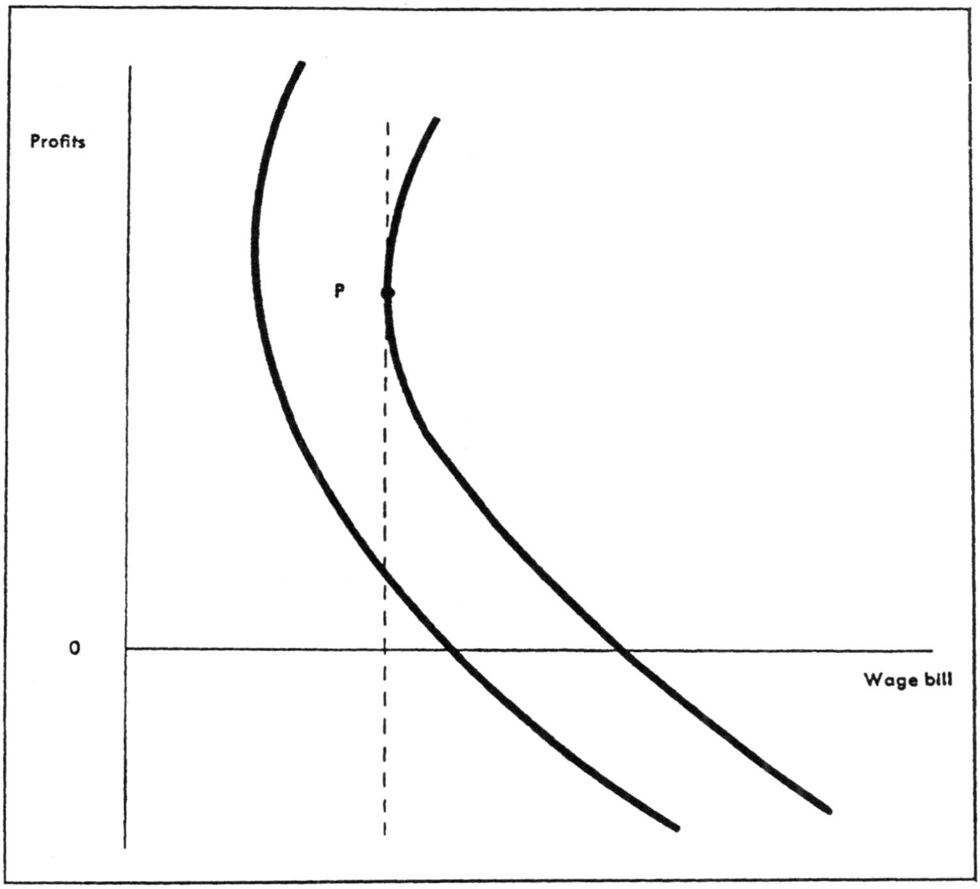

Diagram 2

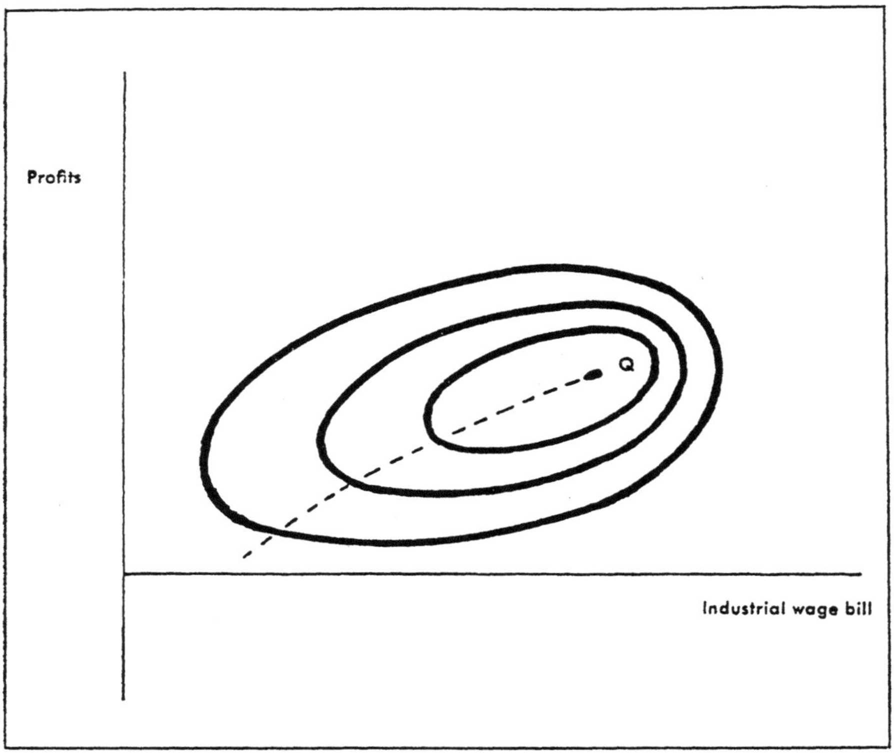

Diagram 3

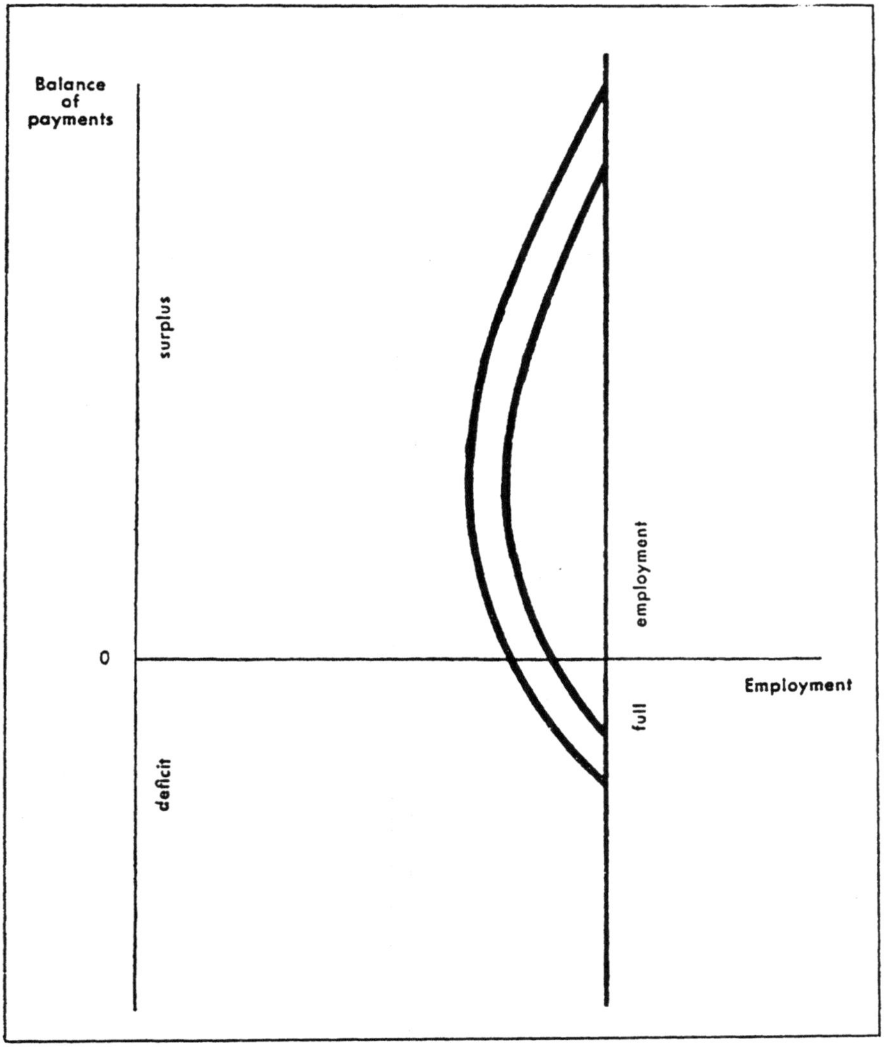
Balance of payments
surplus
0
deficit
employment
full
Employment

Diagram 4

4. QUADRATIC SOCIAL WELFARE FUNCTIONS

It appears from the four diagrams that the indifference curves can presumably be well approximated, for rather wide intervals, by means of quadratic functions. We shall therefore introduce the following social welfare function:

$$W(x,y) = A(x) + \sum_{h=1}^{n} A_h(x)\, y_h + \sum_{h=1}^{n} \sum_{k=1}^{n} A_{hk}\, y_h\, y_k \tag{3.1}$$

More specifically:

Assumption (b.1) *The policy maker's preferences concerning the set of all specified vectors x, y can be described by the social welfare function (3.1), of which A(x) and the $A_h(x)$ are possibly dependent on the instruments, but the A_{hk} are not.*

It should be stressed that this assumption implies more than quadratic contour lines only. For instance, we might replace W of (3.1) by log W (for $W > 0$) without violating the property of quadratic indifference surfaces; but, if W is a welfare function to which the calculus of mathematical expectations can be applied, log W is not, and *vice versa*. However, even (3.1) alone is rather flexible, which may be illustrated by finding the partial derivatives with respect to x's and y's[10],

$$\frac{\delta W}{\delta x_i} = \frac{\delta A}{\delta x_i} + \sum_{h=1}^{n} \frac{\delta A_h}{\delta x_i}\, y_h$$

$$\frac{\delta W}{\delta y_h} = A_h(x) + 2 \sum_{k=1}^{n} A_{hk}\, y_k \tag{3.2}$$

These derivatives (which might be called "marginal welfare," although certain subtle problems are involved here) may evidently depend on all instruments in a fully arbitrary way and linearly on all indirect variables. The coefficients of the y-terms may depend on the x's as far as the derivatives with respect to instruments are concerned and should be constants for the other derivatives. There is hence more flexibility with respect to instruments than with respect to indirect variables. This is important because in economic policy the possible range of variation is usually larger for the instruments than for the indirect variables.

[10] Derivatives with respect to instruments make of course only sense for quantitative instruments.

IV. Choice Bias

1. ABSENCE OF CHOICE BIAS

We now return to the problem as it has been formulated in section II.3. If the policy maker would be fully informed, he would choose the instrument vector $\hat{x}$ which maximizes

$$EW(x,y) = A(x) + \sum_{h=1}^{n} A_h(x) E y_h + \sum_{h=1}^{n} \sum_{k=1}^{n} A_{hk} E(y_h y_k) \tag{4.1}$$

If he would be informed according to the short-cut he would choose the vector $\bar{x}$ which maximizes

$$W(x,Ey) = A(x) + \sum_{h=1}^{n} A_h(x) E y_h + \sum_{h=1}^{n} \sum_{k=1}^{n} A_{hk} E y_h E y_k \tag{4.2}$$

Let us subtract (4.2) from (4.1); then we have, for any values of the x's,

$$\begin{aligned} EW(x,y) - W(x,Ey) &= \sum_{h,k=1}^{n} A_{hk}\{E(y_h y_k) - Ey_h Ey_k\} \\ &= \sum_{h,k=1}^{n} A_{hk} \operatorname{cov}(u_h, u_k) \end{aligned} \tag{4.3}$$

where u_h, u_k are the deviations of (2.1). Hence (4.3) contains the coefficients A_{hk} which are, according to Assumption (b.1), independent of the instruments. We now introduce

Assumption (a.1) *The deviations* u *of* (2.1) *have a finite covariance matrix, which is independent of the instruments.*

This assumption implies that the u's have finite variances, which are the same for all x's (i.e. the u's are homoskedastic); moreover, that the correlations of all pairs u_h, u_k are independent of the x's.

If both Assumptions (a.1) and (b.1) are satisfied, the difference (4.3) is independent of the x's. This means that we can obtain, for any level of instrument values, $EW(x,y)$ from $W(x,Ey)$ by adding a constant. It follows immediately that the vector $\bar{x}$, for which $W(x,Ey)$ is maximal, is the same as the vector $\hat{x}$, for which $EW(x,y)$ is maximal; for the simple case of one (quantitative) instrument this is illustrated in Diagram 5, where d denotes the constant difference between (4.1) and (4.2). It may of course occur that there are two or more vectors for which both functions have the highest value, but this does not lead to any choice bias that can be ascribed to the adoption of the approach (4.2) instead of (4.1). So we have:

Theorem: *Suppose that the Assumptions (a), (a.1), (b), (b.1) are satisfied. Then the conditional welfare maximum, the condition being that the vector of deviations equals its expectation, is reached by the same vector or vectors of instruments as those of the welfare maximum under due regard of the distribution of the deviations.*

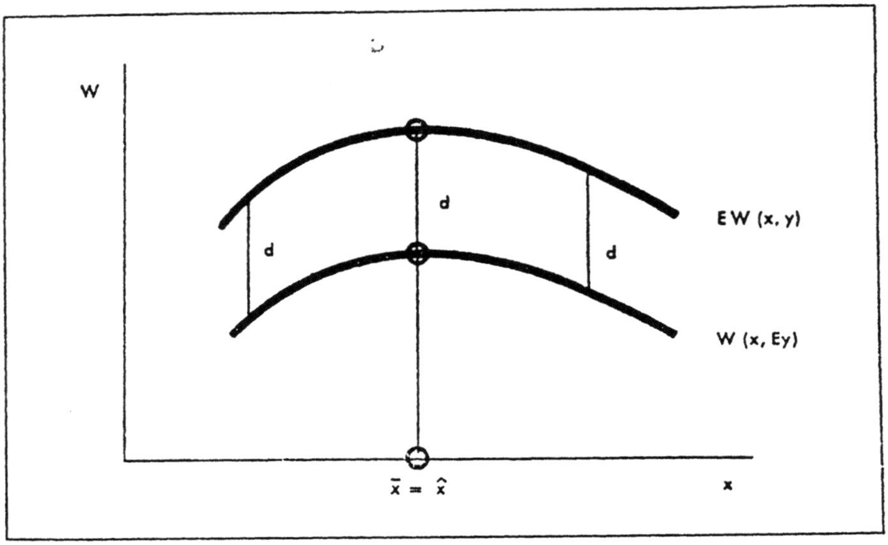

Diagram 5

2. SOCIAL WELFARE FUNCTIONS OF OTHER TYPES

The above result is not at all trivial, for it can easily be shown that it does not hold if the social welfare function is, say, of the third degree in the indirect variables:

$$W(x,y) = A(x) + \sum_{h=1}^{n} A_h(x) y_h + \sum_{h,k=1}^{n} A_{hk} y_h y_k + \sum_{h,k,g=1}^{n} A_{hkg} y_h y_k y_g$$

The difference between *EW(x,y)* and *W(x,Ey)* is then

$$\sum_{h,k=1}^{n} A_{hk} \operatorname{cov}(u_h, u_k) + \sum_{h,k,g=1}^{n} A_{hkg} \{ f_h \operatorname{cov}(u_k, u_g)$$

$$+ f_k \operatorname{cov}(u_h, u_g) + f_g \operatorname{cov}(u_h, u_k) + E(u_h u_k u_g) \}$$

which is dependent on the instruments. If we assume — in addition to the assumptions of the above theorem — that all instruments are quantitative, that the model is linear, and that the third moments $E(u_h u_k u_g)$ and the coefficients A_{hkg} are independent of the instruments, then the difference $EW(x,y) - W(x,Ey)$ is a linear function of the x's. Hence, for those values of x where $W(x,Ey)$ is stationary, $EW(x,y)$ will increase or decrease, at least in some direction. In Diagram 6 the resulting choice bias is illustrated for the case of one instrument.

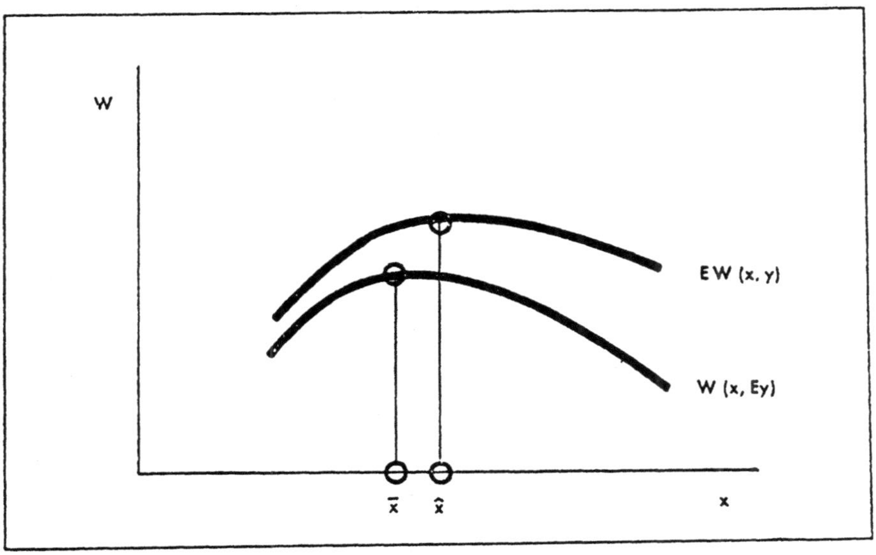

Diagram 6

An example of a more or less intuitive kind may be useful in order to illustrate that such cases may occur. Suppose that the indirect variables are the balance of payments (B, measured in millions of guilders) and employment (U, measured as the percentage of unemployed people). Suppose also that two possibilities can be realised, of which the first is

probability	$\frac{1}{4}$	B	=	0	U	=	5
	$\frac{1}{2}$			-100			5
	$\frac{1}{4}$			-200			5

and the second

probability	$\frac{1}{4}$	B	=	100	U	=	8
	$\frac{1}{2}$			0			8
	$\frac{1}{4}$			-100			8

According to the short-cut the alternatives are $B = -100$; $U = 5$, and $B = 0$; $U = 8$. It may happen that the policy maker, informed according to the short-cut, prefers the former alternative because of the high unemployment percentage of the latter, whereas, if he had been more fully informed, he would have chosen the second policy because of the disastrous implications of a deficit of 200 million guilders on the balance of payments, which he considers much more important than the favourable aspect of a zero deficit, given the probability of occurrence for both of $\frac{1}{4}$. Such a discrepancy cannot be described by means of quadratic welfare functions.

3. NATURAL BOUNDARIES

Boundary conditions, too, will in general lead to a choice bias. Suppose e.g. that we have one indirect variable, viz. employment, and one instrument, viz. Government expenditure. The ceiling of 100 per cent employment will render Assumption (a.1) invalid, which may be illustrated as follows.[11] Consider Diagram 7. The unbroken line gives the expectation of employment, given the level of Government expenditure; the dotted lines give confidence intervals to some specified level of significance. The relation is obviously linear and homoskedastic until the ceiling enters into the picture. Then, when approaching the ceiling, the unbroken line becomes curvilinear, for the probability of exceeding the full employment level is zero. Moreover, both dotted lines also converge to the 100 per cent level. Hence, for sufficiently large values of Government expenditure, the variance of the deviations around their expectations becomes smaller, so that Assumption (a.1) is no longer satisfied.

[11] Full employment is usually not a rigorously defined concept; the subsequent remarks, however, are only affected by this to a minor degree.

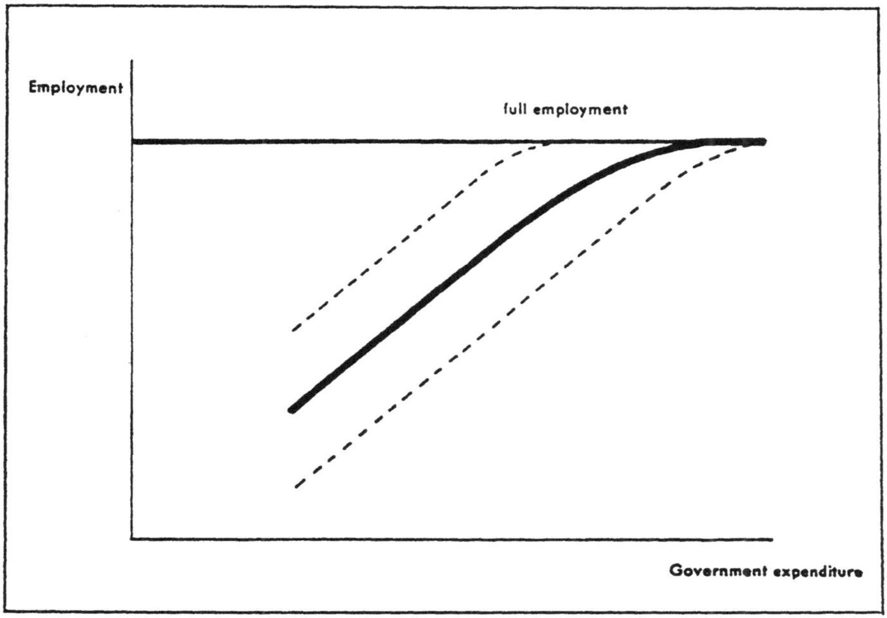

Diagram 7

4. CONCLUSION

The main conclusion is that there is a central class of cases for which the short-cut is permissible: If the covariance matrix of the deviations is independent of the instruments, and if the welfare function of the policy maker is quadratic in the indirect variables, the coefficients of the quadratic terms being independent of the instruments, then the short-cut is bound to lead to the same policy decisions as those taken in the case of full information. The important thing is that this result does not require any additional specifications of the policy maker's preferences.

In other cases the short-cut will usually lead to a choice bias. It is in principle possible to avoid this by replacing the stochastic vector u by a nonstochastic vector different from the expectation, but such a short-cut requires specifications of the welfare function that go much farther than Assumption (b.1).

CHAPTER 63

ON THE THEORY OF ECONOMIC POLICY*

HENRI THEIL
Netherlands School of Economics
(now Erasmus University)
Rotterdam, The Netherlands

1. Introduction

Having been asked to tell something about ideas that are alive among Dutch economists, I do not think that my choice is very difficult. The subject I want to consider, viz., the theory of economic policy, was first analyzed by J. Tinbergen a few years ago (*On the Theory of Economic Policy*, Amsterdam, 1952), and the influence of his work in this field grew so rapidly that at present quite a few economists — and not only econometricians — are thinking in terms of his concepts. Of course, no one can maintain that in our days an analysis of the theory of economic policy can be really the first in an absolute sense; but it is not easy to find an earlier systematic analysis which is so clear and simple and — as I hope to indicate — so well suited to further development as Tinbergen's.

This paper is subdivided as follows. Section 2 gives a brief exposition of Tinbergen's ideas in the light of the circumstances that induced him to work them out. Section 3 is devoted to some of the difficulties connected with the approach, which are illustrated in section 4 by means of an example. Further problems, especially those of model errors, are sketched in the last section.

2. Tinbergen's Theory of Economic Policy

When the second World War was over, the Netherlands as well as several other countries had to face the difficult situation of limited means and many expensive but not unreasonable desires. On the one hand there was the destruction of land and capital equipment due to war and occupation, which called for repair — but this could only partly be done by the Dutch industry itself just because of this destruction. On the other hand, the possibility of buying equipment from other countries was seriously limited, for the ability to pay depends largely on the ability to export, which was only small in those days, again because of the destruction. It is hardly necessary to tell you how important Mr. Marshall's European Recovery Program was in the actual solution of this problem.

---

* This article first appeared in the *American Economic Review*, **46** (1956), 360-366. Reprinted with the permission of the American Economic Association.

In such a situation it is only too easy for politicians to formulate inconsistent desires; e.g., raising the level of consumption, lowering the number of hours worked per week, less dependence on foreign aid, etc. Tinbergen's principal idea was that a clear insight should be given as to this problem of consistency. The means which he proposed in order to achieve this goal is an econometric equation system. I shall not try to sketch in any detail the successive equation systems that have been used for this purpose in the Netherlands in recent years. (One of the systems was published in the Central Economic Plan of 1955.) For my present purposes it is sufficient to say that they are of roughly the same size as Klein's well-known model of the economic system of the United States but that, for obvious reasons, more attention is paid to imports and exports.

The argument is then as follows. The variables of such an equation system are either endogenous or exogenous; e.g., exogenous variables are the volume of government expenditure and the international price level of raw materials and endogenous variables are the level of employment, aggregate consumption, etc. If the system is complete, it has — by definition — as many equations as endogenous variables. Under certain general assumptions it is then possible to express each endogenous variable separately in terms of all exogenous variables; this is the reduced form of the equation system. It describes each of the variables like employment, consumption, balance of payments, etc., as explicit functions of the volume of government expenditure, of the international price level, and so on. Suppose, however, that the number of equations is not only equal to the number of endogenous variables but also to the number of exogenous variables. In the above example this means that the volume of government expenditure is written as dependent on consumption, employment, etc. Clearly, this is just the other way round when compared with the reduced form.

The second variant (we might call it an "inverted reduced form") is the one which Tinbergen needs. It regards the endogenous variables as given and describes the values of exogenous variables as dependent on these. Suppose then that we fix certain values of endogenous variables, to be called "target values," a priori; e.g., we fix the employment level at 95 per cent of full employment, the balance of payments at zero, etc. Then the inverted reduced form shows which set of exogenous values (if any) corresponds to these targets. If such a set exists and if, at the same time, all exogenous variables are controlled by the policy maker, this set describes the measures that should be taken by him in order to reach the targets. If there is more than one set, certain degrees of freedom arise; if there is no such set, the targets are "inconsistent" in the given situation and must be replaced by less ambitious ones.

3. Some Problems Connected with Tinbergen's Approach

It will be clear that this approach is simple and therefore attractive, but at the same time that several difficulties are involved. First, there are in general certain exogenous variables in the system which cannot be controlled by the policy-maker. The weather is a classical example, but several others are more important in this connection, like the international price level of raw materials, the national incomes of other countries, etc. If the system contains such variables and if the policy-maker is concerned with the economic situation of next year (say), then he should make a prediction of the values which these variables will assume in next year. When the remaining number of exogenous variables, which can be controlled by the policy-maker, happens to be equal to the number of equations in the system, the approach of the preceding section can again be applied.

However, the forecasting procedure just mentioned implies the introduction of an element of uncertainty. There are three distinct sources of uncertainty in this connection, of which this is the first. The second is the fact that econometric equations are usually characterized by disturbances, about which only probability information is given. The third is that the "true" parameters of the model are unknown, and that their statistical estimates are merely imperfect substitutes. Therefore, even if noncontrolled exogenous variables are absent and even if there are not disturbances, the statements about the numerical size of the measures to be taken in order to reach certain targets are only approximate. But these provisions are not fulfilled, so that we must expect prediction errors and disturbances to yield errors in addition to those of the approximation.

Finally, the choice criterion of target values is not conventional. It implies that the policy-maker is supposed to be "satisfied" with the "utility level" corresponding to these targets. It does not imply that the policy-maker tries to reach the maximum utility that can be attained under the restrictions imposed upon him by the structure of the economy — except for the special case when the targets coincide with the saturation levels. Hence the choice criterion of target values is not optimal or "best"; it has the character of "good enough." This does not mean that it has to be rejected. On the contrary, there is sufficient reason to believe that the criterion is realistic for many actual policy decisions. (See also H.A. Simon, "A Behavioral Model of Rational Choice," *Quarterly Journal of Economics*, 1955, pages 99-118.) But its suboptimal character is sufficient to justify a further exploration.

4. A Simplified Example

The following (considerably simplified) example may be useful in order to make these problems more transparent. Suppose our policy-maker is a minister of finance or of economic affairs, who is interested in the employment level (E) of his country and in its balance of payments (B). Suppose also that the volume of government expenditure (G) is the policy-maker's instrument; finally, that the interrelationships between the relevant variables (written as deviations from their present values, unless otherwise specified) are the following:

$$P = C + I + X + G , \tag{1}$$

a definition equation which describes the aggregate volume of production (P) in terms of its components: consumption (C), gross investment (I), exports (X) and government expenditure, all measured in constant prices;

$$M = a_1 C + a_2 I + a_3 X + a_4 G \,, \tag{2}$$

an important equation with different "marginal propensities to import" for the separate components of P;

$$C = bP \,, \tag{3}$$

a consumption function;

$$E = cP \,, \tag{4}$$

an equation describing employment as a function of production; and

$$B = p_X X - p_M M \,, \tag{5}$$

an equation describing the balance of payments as the value of exports minus the value of imports, p_X and p_M being price indices of exports and imports, respectively. For simplicity's sake I suppose these price indices (measured with base unity in the present year, say) to be given and constant.

The equations (1) - (5) may be regarded as a complete model in five exogenous variables, P, C, M, E, B and three exogenous variables I, X, G. Under the plausible assumption $b \neq 1$ we can write each endogenous variable as a reduce-form function of the exogenous variables. In particular:

$$E = \frac{c}{1 - b} G + \left[\frac{c}{1 - b} (I + X) \right] \tag{6}$$

$$B = -\left(\frac{a_1 b}{1 - b} + a_4 \right) G - \left[\left(\frac{a_1 b}{1 - b} + a_2 \right) p_M I + \left\{ \left(\frac{a_1 b}{1 - b} + a_3 \right) p_M - p_X \right\} X \right]. \tag{7}$$

The argument is now as follows. Suppose our policy-maker is interested in next year's level of employment and balance of payments. According to (6) and (7), both (unknown) quantities are determined by next year's volume of government expenditure, on one hand, and by next year's investment and export volume, on the other hand. Out of these, the former quantity can be controlled whereas the latter cannot. It is necessary, therefore, to make a prediction of next year's I and X such that, when this forecast is combined with knowledge (or estimates) of the parameters of the system (1) - (5), the terms in square brackets of (6) and (7) are known. They are "known," of course, only in the limited sense that a prediction is available, and this imperfect knowledge implies automatically the possibility of forecasting errors. For the moment, however, I prefer to leave this aspect aside.

After these operations, both E and B have become linear functions of G only, the terms between square brackets being "constant terms." When eliminating G, a linear equation between E and B results. This is the constraint which the policy-maker has to face. This constraint is represented by a straight line in an E, B-diagram, the slope of which is negative under the plausible assumptions, a_1, a_4, $c > 0$ and $0 < b < 1$ [the coefficients of G in (6) and (7) have then opposite signs]. Clearly, the policy-maker can reach any point of this line by a suitable choice of G. When indifference curves of the well-known type for E and B exist, the "best" choice is that of the point where an indifference curve is tangent to the straight line.

However, I am proceeding at present beyond Tinbergen's approach, for the idea of a best choice is that of optimization, not that of accepting target values. Moreover, contrary to Tinbergen's "normal case," we do not have an equality of the numbers of target variables (E and B) and of controlled variables (G). Hence a pair of target variables E, B cannot be imposed by the policy-maker, unless the values happen to satisfy the constraint. But this constraint is not exactly known: we have to predict next year's investment and exports, and this gives rise to forecasting errors; we have to use estimates of the parameters, and this implies sampling errors; and we have disturbances in the equations, which are neglected here. In the behavior equations (2), (3), and (4) no disturbances are introduced, but there is no reason for doing so, except for that of simplicity. If we had introduced disturbances, a linear combination of them would appear in the reduced-form relations (6) and (7).

5. Further Analysis

The above example, especially in its optimization form, suggests a very close formal relationship to the classical theory of consumer's demand: both there and in the example the derivation of the best choice of actions is based upon a linear constraint and its point of tangency with one of the indifference curves or surfaces. Actually, we might expect certain elements of classical consumer's theory to be even more valuable for our present purposes than for consumer analysis itself, for two distinct reasons: first, because the policy-makers we have in mind, like government officials; entrepreneurs, labor union officials, etc., are usually more "rational" than unsophisticated consumers, so that the existence of stable indifference curves seems to be a more realistic assumption for our present case; second, because consumer theory is not very realistic as to the problem of large, indivisible units of some (especially durable) commodities, whereas in the above example — and many others — this problem does not play a significant role in view of the almost perfect divisibility of variables like employment and balance of payments. There are, however, certain differences between the type of analysis we have to perform in this case and classical consumer theory.

First, contrary to the sole budget restriction in consumer's theory, it is not generally true for our present problem that the number of constraints is only one. It was only one in the example, but some minor modifications are sufficient in order to raise this to two. Suppose that our policy-maker does not consider G solely as an instrument by which he can influence E and B, but that he appraises G in its own right because of the immediate welfare implications of changes in the volume of government expenditure (on schools, highways, salaries, etc.). In that case we should replace the indifference curves in the E, B-plane by indifference surfaces in the E, B, G-space. For our present purposes the most important aspect is that the single constraint in the E, B-plane is replaced by the two separate constraints, each being represented by a two-dimensional plane. Another important aspect of this modification of the example is the dual nature which controlled variables may have and generally have: they serve not only as instruments in adapting noncontrolled variables, but are appraised in their own right as well. Sometimes the latter aspect is considered much more important, so that the accompanying changes in noncontrolled variables are merely regarded as (fortunate or unfortunate) by-products. An example is the problem of raising the compulsory minimum school-leaving age. In most cases the proposals of such measures are based on psychological, educational, and social motives, yet economic effect may be quite substantial. An analysis of such effects in the Netherlands was made by W.H. Somermeijer, of the Central Bureau of Statistics, in a paper, "On Economic Consequences of Extending Compulsory Education," read at the Hindsgavl Meeting of the International Association for Research in Income and Wealth in 1955.

A second difference with the traditional theory of consumer demand is the aforementioned fact that the constraints are usually stochastic and not exactly known. A third is that, contrary to the linear budget restriction of consumer's demand theory, the constraints which we have to face are not necessarily linear; and even if they are linear, the multiplicative coefficients of the equations making up the constraints do not necessarily obey the simple sign rule of the consumer's budget restriction. For the coefficients of the latter restriction are simply the prices, which are never negative and usually positive; and compare this with the unequal signs of the G-coefficients in (6) and (7). Similarly, when using a utility function in order to describe the policy-maker the sign is not definite. An example: If employment is among a government policy-maker's (noncontrolled) variables, an increase in this variable will usually be positively valued; hence we might speak of a positive marginal utility. But it is equally well imaginable that unemployment is one of the variables, and the resulting negative marginal utility is proof of the indefiniteness. This example may seem almost trivial; but it is nevertheless conclusive.

A further analysis (see my volume, *Economic Forecasts and Policy*, North Holland, Amsterdam, 1958, second edition, 1961) shows the following:

1. Under certain assumptions, a generalization of the theory of consumer's demand in the policy-maker's direction is possible, and concepts of inferiority, substitution, and complementarity for the policy-maker's variables have a definite meaning and give a useful insight into the choice mechanism.

2. Under certain assumptions, the policy-maker's optimal decisions are not affected if the disturbances are replaced by their mean values. Under alternative assumptions, a "certainty bias" is implied by this replacement, and it appears to be possible to make certain statements about this bias.

3. Under certain assumptions, it is possible to give a numerical expression for the loss of welfare due to errors in the model used. This opens in principle the road to a rational decision as to the amount of effort to be spent on different types of model refinements.

CHAPTER 64

A NOTE ON CERTAINTY EQUIVALENCE IN DYNAMIC PLANNING*

HENRI THEIL
Netherlands School of Economics
(Now Erasmus University)
Rotterdam, The Netherlands

ABSTRACT. According to the static theory of decision-making under uncertainty, the policy maker will take that action that maximizes expected utility. In the dynamic theory several consecutive periods play a role, each of which is characterized by a certain action. The policy maker will then choose a maximizing strategy (i.e., a rule according to which all successive actions are determined by the information which is available at the time when the action has to be taken). This note is confined to the action in the first period of such a strategy. It is shown that, under certain conditions, the first-period action of the strategy which maximizes expected utility is identical with that of the strategy which neglects the uncertainty problem by maximizing utility under the condition that all uncertain elements are equal to their mean values.

1. The Problem

Consider the following situation: A policy maker has at his disposal certain variables, to be called *instruments*, the values of which in the period t are denoted by $x_1(t), ..., x_m(t)$. He is also interested in certain *noncontrolled variables* — denoted by $y_1(t), ..., y_n(t)$ in t — which are subject to a simultaneous probability distribution in which the x's enter parametrically, in a manner to be described below. Suppose that the function the mean value of which he wishes to maximize (his "welfare function") is quadratic in the x's and y's during the period $t = 1, ..., T$:

$$w(x,y) = a'x + b'y + \tfrac{1}{2}(x'Ax + y'By + x'Cy + y'C'x), \tag{1.1}$$

where a, b, A, B, C are vectors and matrices of fixed coefficients (A and B symmetric) and x, y column vectors of mT and nT elements, respectively, which can be partitioned as follows:

* This article first appeared in *Econometrica*, **25** (1957), 346-349. Reprinted with the permission of the Econometric Society.

$$x = \begin{bmatrix} x_1 \\ \cdot \\ \cdot \\ \cdot \\ x_T \end{bmatrix}; \quad x_t = \begin{bmatrix} x_1(t) \\ \cdot \\ \cdot \\ \cdot \\ x_m(t) \end{bmatrix}; \quad y = \begin{bmatrix} y_1 \\ \cdot \\ \cdot \\ \cdot \\ y_T \end{bmatrix}; \quad y_t = \begin{bmatrix} y_1(t) \\ \cdot \\ \cdot \\ \cdot \\ y_n(t) \end{bmatrix}. \tag{1.2}$$

Suppose finally that the distribution of the y's is such that

$$y = Rx + s, \tag{1.3}$$

where R is a matrix of fixed coefficients that can be partitioned according to

$$R = \begin{bmatrix} R_{11} & 0 \cdots & 0 \\ R_{21} & R_{22} \cdots & 0 \\ \cdots & \cdots & \cdots \\ R_{T1} & R_{T2} \cdots & R_{TT} \end{bmatrix}, \tag{1.4}$$

and s is a column vector of nT random elements whose joint distribution is independent of x. The partitioning (1.4) implies that the Rx-part of y_t does not depend on $x_{t'}$ with $t' > t$; and hence, partitioning s in T vectors s_t of n elements each and assuming that R is known to the policy maker, that in period t the subvectors $s_1, ..., s_{t-1}$ are known to him as well.

The maximization of the mean value of (1.1) subject to (1.3) can be carried out if the distribution of s is known. In general, this is not the case; so it would be important if it could be shown that the policy maker's decisions, at least those of the first period, x_1 (which is his immediate concern), are not affected if he acts under the assumption that y equals Rx plus the mean value of s. This is a generalization of Simon's dynamic certainty-equivalence analysis of cost control of production and inventories.[1] His cost corresponds to $-w$, production to our instruments ($m = 1$), inventories to our noncontrolled variables ($n = 1$), and the identity: change in inventories equals production minus sales, to our model (1.3), the sales of the different periods being the elements of our s. We shall follow Simon's line of attack.

[1] H.A. Simon, "Dynamic Programming under Uncertainty with a Quadratic Criterion Function," *Econometrica*, **24** (1956), 74-81.

2. The Solution

Substituting (1.3) into (1.1), we find for the welfare level attained by applying the instrument values x :

$$w_x = w(x, Rx + s) = k_0 + k'x + \tfrac{1}{2}x'Kx , \tag{2.1}$$

where

$$\begin{aligned} k_0 &= b's + \tfrac{1}{2}s'Bs , \\ k &= a + R'b + (C + R'B)s, \\ K &= A + R'BR + CR + R'C', \end{aligned} \tag{2.2}$$

K being symmetric and nonstochastic.

The policy maker's strategy consists in considering, for each period, all possible instrument values, given the information which he has at that time. Supposing that an optimal strategy maximizing εw exists, and denoting it by f, we may partition f according to

$$f = \begin{bmatrix} f_1 \\ f_2(s_1) \\ \cdot \\ \cdot \\ \cdot \\ f_T(s_1, \cdots, s_{T-1}) \end{bmatrix} . \tag{2.3}$$

Any strategy x can then be written as

$$x = f + \varepsilon \upsilon , \tag{2.4}$$

where ε is a scalar and υ a vector to be partitioned as

$$\upsilon = \begin{bmatrix} \upsilon_1 \\ \upsilon_2(s_1) \\ \cdot \\ \cdot \\ \cdot \\ \upsilon_T(s_1, \cdots, s_{T-1}) \end{bmatrix}. \tag{2.5}$$

Substituting (2.4) into (2.1) and taking mean values gives

$$\mathscr{E}w_{f+\varepsilon\upsilon} = \mathscr{E}k_0 + \mathscr{E}(k'f) + \tfrac{1}{2}\mathscr{E}(f'Kf) + \varepsilon\,[\mathscr{E}(k'\upsilon) + \mathscr{E}(f'K\upsilon)] + \tfrac{1}{2}\varepsilon^2\mathscr{E}(\upsilon'K\upsilon)\,. \tag{2.6}$$

The first three terms in the right-hand side are independent of ε, provided it is indeed true that the distribution of s is independent of the instruments. For the first term ($\mathscr{E}k_0$) this requirement follows from the presence of first- and second-order moments of s *via* $b'\mathscr{E}s$ and $\mathscr{E}(s'Bs)$; for the others it follows from the dependence of f on s; *vide* (2.2) and (2.3). This implies in particular that the variances and the covariances of the y's should not depend on the x's. Suppose this is true; then stationarity of $\mathscr{E}w$ in f implies that the fourth term vanishes identically in υ,

$$\mathscr{E}(f'K\upsilon) = -\mathscr{E}(k'\upsilon) \tag{2.7}$$

for any υ; and a sufficient condition for this stationary value to be a maximum is that K be negative-definite (*vide* the last term). Consider then (2.7) and choose υ such that its first element equals 1 and all others zero; after this, such that its second element equals 1 and all others zero; etc. The result is a set of mT equations which can be written as $K\mathscr{E}f = -\mathscr{E}k$, so that

$$\mathscr{E}f = -K^{-1}\mathscr{E}k\,. \tag{2.8}$$

So far we have considered only the optimal strategy. We next consider the certainty case in which it is assumed that s equals its expectation, $\bar{s}$, say. Then (2.1) and (2.2) remain valid, provided we replace s by $\bar{s}$ throughout. This implies that k_0 is changed in a manner which is otherwise irrelevant (since the result is a constant with respect to x), that k is replaced by its expectation $\mathscr{E}k$, and that K remains unchanged. It follows that the x which maximizes in the certainty case is

$$\bar{x} = -K^{-1}\mathscr{E}k\,, \tag{2.9}$$

so that

$$\mathscr{E}f = \bar{x}. \tag{2.10}$$

But the first subvector of f, f_1, is nonstochastic (2.3). Hence it equals its expectation, $\mathscr{E}f_1$, and also, according to (2.10), the first subvector of $\bar{x}$. This establishes the certainty equivalence for the first period.

3. Comments

The above shows that a vector generalization of Simon's result, when conveniently formulated, can be proved in the same way but more simply. It also shows that there is an additional assumption involved, viz., that the variances and covariances of the elements of s are independent of x. In Simon's case this condition is not restrictive, for there is no reason to expect an entrepreneur to be able to affect the variance of his sales by manipulating his production. But in other cases this is not true. Take, e.g., x as the volume of government expenditure and y as employment, the policy maker being a Minister of Finance, say. When employment is near the ceiling, any increment of x will reduce its variance. This example shows also that there is some advantage in distinguishing between (1.1) and (1.3). The policy maker is interested in x and y, so that these vectors are arguments of the welfare function; not, however, in x and the random components of s, at least not directly. An "indirect" welfare function of the type (2.1) is affected by changes in the structure (1.3), and this has little to do with the policy maker's preferences. In view of the possibility of such changes, it seems preferable to make the distinction that was made here.

The result is also, in a sense, a generalization of my own result for the static case.[2] There is a limitation, however, since in that case it is sufficient to assume that w is quadratic in y only; and it is not necessary to assume that the model is linear (as in (1.3)). The reason for the additional restrictions in the dynamic case is that future measures are random within the framework of a strategy; and in that respect they are no different from the noncontrolled variables, for which quadraticity must be assumed anyhow.

---

[2] H. Theil, "Econometric Models and Welfare Maximization," *Weltwirtschaftliches Archiv*, **72** (1954), pp. 60-83. It is also of some interest to note that the maximization analysis considered here can be regarded as a generalization of consumer's theory, where a utility function is maximized subject to one single budget constraint. Just as there, we can distinguish between substitution and complementarity among pairs of variables (i.e., between two instruments, or two noncontrolled variables, or an instrument and a noncontrolled variable). In the present dynamic analysis this should be further specialized according to subperiods; i.e., there may be substitution between $x_1(t)$ and $x_2(t')$, but complementarity between $x_1(t)$ and $x_2(t'')$. It is interesting that the square matrix K of (2.2) is the inverse of the matrix of substitution terms of the instruments of the various subperiods. Cf. my forthcoming *Economic Forecasts and Policy*, North Holland, Amsterdam, 1958, ch. VIII.

CHAPTER 65

MACRODYNAMIC POLICY-MAKING: AN APPLICATION OF STRATEGY AND CERTAINTY EQUIVALENCE CONCEPTS TO THE ECONOMY OF THE UNITED STATES, 1933-1936*

P.J.M. VAN DEN BOGAARD
Netherlands School of Economics
(now Erasmus University)
Rotterdam, The Netherlands

HENRI THEIL
Netherlands School of Economics
(now Erasmus University)
Rotterdam, The Netherlands

1. Introduction

The application of econometric methods and results to policy-making at the government level has been an important aim of econometricians in the last two decades. Tinbergen's work (1939) for the League of Nations, for example, was at least partly originated by the idea that a better knowledge of economic behaviour patterns contributes to the possibilities of macroeconomic engineering. In the last few years several attempts have been made to solve specific and concrete economic problems with such means, especially in Europe, where the names of Frisch and Tinbergen should be mentioned in particular.

Most of these studies are of a static nature. Although several of the models employed are dynamic in the sense that they contain variables of different time periods, no application has ever been made — as far as the present authors are aware — which is "truly dynamic" in the sense that it deals with decision rules for a number of successive periods specifying the appropriate actions at each particular moment, given the information available at that moment. The situation is different with respect to the analysis of policy-making at the level of the firm. In that field several studies have been published which are based on the dynamic strategy concept; an example is that of the control of production and inventories.[1] The appropriate sociological explanation of this lagged evolution in the case of government policy-making is perhaps that the idea of macroeconomic planning is more unpopular in the country where the strategy concept flourishes (the United States) than it is in Europe. Another reason is, no doubt, that the specification of a government preference function is a highly delicate matter.[2]

The present article is to be considered as a modest attempt to deal with the subject of optimal government strategies in an exploratory manner. It is based on Klein's six-equation Model I for the United States, which is briefly summarised in Section 2, and on a preference function which is explained in Sections 3, 4 and 5. The period considered

* This article first appeared in *Metroeconomica* **11** (1959) 149-167. Reprinted with the permission of *Metroeconomica*.

[1] See e.g. H.A. Simon (1956) and the reference quoted there.

[2] An interesting attempt to specify such a function has been made by Frisch (1957).

is that of President Roosevelt's first administration. The relation between the present subject and the theory of certainty equivalence is considered in Sections 6 and 7, after which the numerical evaluation of the results follows in Section 8. Section 9 gives a comparison between the behaviour according to the optimal strategy and certain forecasts of this behaviour. Section 10 contains some concluding remarks.

2. Klein's Small Model of the U.S. Economy

Klein's (1950) well-known Model I consists of six equations, viz., a consumption, an investment and a demand-for-labour equation, as well as three definitions:

$$C = \alpha_0 + \alpha_1\Pi + \alpha_2\Pi_{-1} + \alpha_3(W_1 + W_2) + u_1 , \tag{2.1}$$

$$I = \beta_0 + \beta_1\Pi + \beta_2\Pi_{-1} + \beta_3 K_{-1} + u_2 , \tag{2.2}$$

$$W_1 = \gamma_0 + \gamma_1(Y + T - W_2) + \gamma_2(Y + T - W_2)_{-1} + \gamma_3(t - 1931) + u_3 \tag{2.3}$$

and

$$Y = C + I + G - T , \tag{2.4}$$

$$\Pi = Y - W_1 - W_2 , \tag{2.5}$$

$$K = I + K_{-1} , \tag{2.6}$$

where C stands for consumption, Π is non-wage income (profits), W_1 the private wage bill, W_2 the government wage bill, I net investment, K_{-1} the stock of capital at the beginning of the year, Y net national income, T business taxes, t time, and G government expenditure on goods and services including the surplus on the balance of payments. The α's, β's and γ's are the structural coefficients, the u's random disturbances. All variables are measured in billions of dollars of 1934 purchasing power, except t which is measured in calendar years. The variables C, I, W_1, Y, Π, K are considered endogenous; all others, exogenous.

Several alternative sets of point estimates of the parameters are available (cf. Klein, 1950, pp. 67-76); in what follows we shall use the estimates that have been derived by means of the method of maximum-likelihood under the assumption that the disturbances of the three behavioural equations are uncorrelated.[3] Table 1 contains the reduced-form coefficients which are implied by these estimates.[4] Table 2 specifies the estimated values of the disturbances during the years 1933-1936, which is the period to be considered.[5]

TABLE 1. Estimated Reduced-form Coefficients of Klein's Model I.

	Constant term	Π_{-1}	W_2	$(W_2)_{-1}$	K_{-1}	T	T_{-1}
C	41.816	0.743	0.666	-0.189	-0.098	-0.188	0.189
Π	38.059	0.863	-0.224	0.063	-0.164	-1.281	-0.063
W_1	30.338	0.626	-0.162	-0.237	-0.119	-0.204	0.237
I	26.581	0.746	-0.052	0.015	-0.184	-0.296	-0.015
Y	68.397	1.489	0.614	-0.174	-0.283	-1.484	0.174
K	26.581	0.746	-0.052	0.015	0.816	-0.296	-0.015

	G	Y_{-1}	t-1931	u_1	u_2	u_3
C	0.671	0.189	0.155	1.671	0.671	1.148
Π	1.119	-0.063	-0.052	1.119	1.119	-0.386
W_1	0.831	0.237	0.195	0.831	0.831	1.445
I	0.259	-0.015	-0.012	0.259	1.259	-0.089
Y	1.930	0.174	0.143	1.930	1.930	1.059
K	0.259	-0.015	-0.012	0.259	1.259	-0.089

TABLE 2. Estimated Annual Values of Disturbances of Klein's Model I, 1933-1936.

	u_1	u_2	u_3
1933	0.63	1.04	0.40
1934	-0.13	-0.16	0.30
1935	0.03	0.11	0.04
1936	2.05	1.56	-0.76

[3] For the numerical values of these estimates, see Chernoff and Divinski (1953, pp. 237, 250, 299).

[4] In this and later tables of this article not more than three decimal places have been reproduced. The actual calculations have all been carried out in six decimal places.

[5] These estimates are taken from Klein (1950, p. 69).

It is appropriate to stress that the use of this particular model in the subsequent analysis is restrictive in several respects. In the first place, we assume that the model in its highly aggregative form gives an adequate description of the economic processes in the United States. Also, we assume that the usual conditions which underlie the statistical estimation of such models are satisfied: the variables should be free from observational errors, and the disturbances should have zero mean as well as zero lagged covariances.[6] Finally, it will be necessary to neglect the differences between estimated and "true" values of coefficients and disturbances. There can be no doubt that these approximations — as well as those to be mentioned in the next sections — are serious; the only apology which we can give is that of the exploratory character of the present study.

3. Desired Values of Noncontrolled Variables

As stated in Section 1, we shall consider in particular the period of President Roosevelt's first administration. This period started in the great depression, and it is on this starting point that we shall focus attention in order to formulate certain general targets of economic policy. In broad terms, it will be assumed that the government devises certain measures in order to bring the depression to an end in 1936 (the last year of the administration). More precisely, the government is supposed to aim at the following targets: first, immediate welfare (to be measured by consumption, C); second, future welfare (to be measured by net investment, I); third, a fair distribution of income. In our present case a convenient measure for the last target is the ratio of profits (Π) to the private wage bill (W_1). This ratio has fluctuated around the value 0.5 during the twenties, but it dropped considerably after the beginning of the depression.[7]

Specifying our targets quantitatively, we require that the level of consumption per capita reaches the 1929-value in 1936. Writing the desired level in 1936 as C_{36}^* and the actual level in 1929 as C_{29}, this means

$$C_{36}^* = C_{29}(1 + \alpha)^7 ,$$

α being the annual rate of population growth. Out of these quantities, C_{29} is known at the beginning of 1933, but α is not. However, if we are prepared to work with numerical targets which correspond approximately with our "real" aims, we can replace α by an estimated value, 0.01 say. So

[6] Note, however, that it will not be necessary to assume that the disturbances are homoskedastic, i.e., that they have constant variance.

[7] The numerical data underlying the discussion of this and the next section are all taken from Klein (1950, p. 135).

$$C_{36}^{*} = 57.8 \times 1.01^{7} = 61.97\,.$$

Investment was roughly of the order of 10 per cent of consumption during the twenties. We require this ratio to be restored in 1936, so that $I_{36}^{*} = 0.1,\ C_{36}^{*} = 6.20$. As to the requirement of a fair distribution of income, finally, we suppose that it is deemed desirable to restore the original ratio of profits to the private wage bill. The most convenient way to handle this is to introduce a "distribution variable" $D = W_1 - 2\Pi$, and to put its desired level in 1936 equal to zero: $D_{36}^{*} = 0$.

So far, we confined our attention to the ultimate goals to be reached in 1936. We must also specify desired values in the intermediate years, however. This will be done by linear interpolation between the actual values in 1932 (the last year before President Roosevelt's administration) and the corresponding desired values in 1936:

$$C_{32+i}^{*} = C_{32} + \frac{i}{4}\,(C_{36}^{*} - C_{32}) \qquad (i = 1,\ldots,4)$$

$$I_{32+i}^{*} = I_{32} + \frac{i}{4}\,(I_{36}^{*} - I_{32})$$

$$D_{32+i}^{*} = D_{32} + \frac{i}{4}\,(D_{36}^{*} - D_{32})\,,$$

which leads to the numerical outcomes of Table 3 below. It need hardly be stressed that the derivation of these figures is somewhat arbitrary. This is not essential for the general approach, however, because alternative desired values can be handled in a way which is entirely analogous to the procedure to be described below.

TABLE 3. Desired Values of Noncontrolled Variables, 1933-1936.

	C^{*}	I^{*}	D^{*}
1933	49.69	-3.10	11.25
1934	53.78	0.00	7.50
1935	57.88	3.10	3.75
1936	61.97	6.20	0.00

4. Desired Values of Instruments

The means which will be used in order to achieve (or better: to approximate) the targets formulated in the preceding section are three in number, viz., the government wage bill

(W_2), business taxes (T) and the government expenditure on goods and services (G). These variables will be called the policy-maker's "instruments" or "controlled" variables.

It is appropriate to stress that this adaptation role is not the only purpose for which instruments are used; in general, they have a value of their own to the policy-maker. For example, it seems reasonable to say that in an expanding economy like that of the United States the number of civil servants and their real income should increase gradually, quite apart from the effect which this has on the economy as a whole. Of course, under particular conditions this effect (as measured by the resulting values of the noncontrolled variables) may be considered so unfavourable that the most appropriate course of action is a temporary reduction of the government wage bill; but this is a problem of reconciliation, which is postponed until Section 5. Here, we are interested in the "desirable" values of the variables W_2, T and G, irrespective of the implications of these values for the noncontrolled variables. We shall formulate these desirable values in a very simple manner, viz., by taking the least-squares regressions of W_2, T and G on time during the period 1920-1932:

$$W_2 = 3.531 + 0.215\,(t - 1926),$$
$$T = 5.723 + 0.239\,(t - 1926),$$
$$G = 7.431 + 0.430\,(t - 1926),$$

and by extrapolating these regressions to the period 1933-1936. The results (the desired values W_2^*, T^*, G^*) are shown in Table 4. Again, this derivation is somewhat arbitrary; also, it cannot be denied that the assumption on the controlled character of the variables W_2, T and G (in real terms) is not fully realistic, especially since T represents an amount of taxes collected rather than tax rates,[8] and because G includes the surplus of the balance of payments.

TABLE 4. Desired Values of Instruments, 1933-1936.

	W_2^*	T^*	G^*
1933	5.038	7.396	10.438
1934	5.254	7.635	10.868
1935	5.469	7.874	11.298
1936	5.685	8.113	11.727

[8] An approximate procedure to handle this feature is mentioned in a footnote at the end of Section 8.

5. Minimizing the Deviations from the Desired Values

It is interesting to compare the approach described in the preceding sections with that of Professor Tinbergen in his recent work (1952; 1956) on economic policy. As is well-known, Tinbergen too used desired values or "targets"; however, he applies this concept only to noncontrolled variables (hence the name "target variables"), not to instruments. In broad terms, Tinbergen's approach implies that targets for the noncontrolled variables are specified, after which the model (measuring the relationships between instruments and noncontrolled variables) is used in order to derive the instrument values which are to be applied in order to arrive at these targets.[9] In our case, both instruments and noncontrolled variables have their desired values; and it can only be true in very particular cases that the desired instrument values happen to be identical with the values that lead to the desired noncontrolled values. We must conclude, therefore, that there is in general a certain degree of incompatibility between the various desired values. It will be observed that this imcompatibility is unavoidable as soon as we take account of stochastic elements, because nonstochastic desired values of noncontrolled variables cannot be identical with the stochastic values that follow from the reduced form of an equation system.[10]

Since it is impossible to realise all desired values exactly, our approach will be to minimize the differences between actual and desired values in some appropriate sense. Consider then the sum of squares of these deviations for the noncontrolled variables in each of the four years:

$$Q_i = (C_{32+i} - C^*_{32+i})^2 + (I_{32+i} - I^*_{32+i})^2 + (D_{32+i} - D^*_{32+i})^2 \quad (i = 1,...,4) \tag{5.1}$$

and also the sum of squares of the deviations for the instruments:

$$P_i = \{(W_2)_{32+i} - (W_2^*)_{32+i}\}^2 + (T_{32+i} - T^*_{32+i})^2 + (G_{32+i} - G^*_{32+i})^2 . \tag{5.2}$$

The total sum of squares, $\Sigma(P_i + Q_i)$, is a stochastic quantity; and our aim will be to minimize its expectation:

$$E \sum_{i=1}^{4} (P_i + Q_i) = \text{minimum} . \tag{5.3}$$

---

[9] In general, this procedure leads to unique instrument values only if the number of instruments equals the number of noncontrolled variables. This condition is satisfied in our present case; it is to be stressed, however, that the approach followed here is not characterised by any restriction of this kind.

[10] For this reason, Tinbergen replaces disturbances by their expectations. The theorem to be mentioned in Section 7 can be regarded as a justification of this procedure.

6. A Reformulation in a More General Framework

In the discussion which follows it will prove convenient to introduce column vectors of instrument values (defined as deviations from their desired values), partitioned according to subperiods:

$$x = \begin{bmatrix} x_1 \\ x_2 \\ x_3 \\ x_4 \end{bmatrix}; \quad x_i = \begin{bmatrix} (W_2)_{32+i} - (W_2^*)_{32+i} \\ T_{32+i} - T^*_{32+i} \\ G_{32+i} - G^*_{32+i} \end{bmatrix}, \tag{6.1}$$

and similarly for the noncontrolled variables:

$$y = \begin{bmatrix} y_1 \\ y_2 \\ y_3 \\ y_4 \end{bmatrix}; \quad y_i = \begin{bmatrix} C_{32+i} - C^*_{32+i} \\ I_{32+i} - I^*_{32+i} \\ D_{32+i} - D^*_{32+i} \end{bmatrix}. \tag{6.2}$$

The minimization criterion described in Section 5 can then be considered as the maximization of the mean value of

$$w(x,y) = -\tfrac{1}{2}(x'x + y'y), \tag{6.3}$$

the latter function being a special case of the general quadratic preference function

$$w(x,y) = a'x + b'y + \tfrac{1}{2}(x'Ax + y'By + x'Cy + y'C'x), \tag{6.4}$$

where a, b, A, B, C are column vectors and matrices of appropriate order. The special character of (6.3) compared with (6.4) consists of $A = B = -I$ and $C = O$ (I and O being unit and zero matrices, respectively, of order 12×12 in our case), as well as $a = b = 0$.[11] If we would take A and B as diagonal matrices with negative elements on the diagonals, while C remains a zero matrix, then we would minimize the expectation of a weighted sum of squares of the deviations from the desired values. This alternative and more general specification is useful if we consider a deviation of consumption (say)

[11] Note that we have $a = b = 0$ only because we have defined instrument and noncontrolled values as deviations from their desired levels, the expectation of the sum of squares of which we want to minimize. Note further that x and v in (6.4) are not necessarily defined as deviations from desired values.

from its desirable value more serious than a numerically equal investment deviation; or if we consider 1936-deviations more serious than numerically equal 1935-deviations. A still more general case occurs if A and B are nondiagonal or if C ceases to be a zero matrix; then we consider the extremum of a complete quadratic form. Here, we confine ourselves to the simplest variant (6.3).

The maximization of the preference function (6.3) is carried out subject to the constraint implied by the equation system of Section 2. For our present purpose we should formulate this constraint as follows: we should write the noncontrolled variables of the period 1933-1936 (measured as deviations from their desired values) as linear functions of the exogenous variables and the disturbances of that period. We arrive at these relationships by eliminating the lagged endogenous variables in the reduced form for $C - C^*$, $I - I^*$, $D - D^*$ by successive lagged application of the reduced form; and the result can be written as

$$y = Rx + s, \tag{6.5}$$

R being a nonstochastic matrix and s a stochastic column vector which can be partitioned according to

$$R = \begin{bmatrix} R_{11} & 0 & 0 & 0 \\ R_{21} & R_{22} & 0 & 0 \\ R_{31} & R_{32} & R_{33} & 0 \\ R_{41} & R_{42} & R_{43} & R_{44} \end{bmatrix}; \quad s = \begin{bmatrix} s_1 \\ s_2 \\ s_3 \\ s_4 \end{bmatrix}, \tag{6.6}$$

the submatrices of R being of order 3×3 and those of s of order 3×1. Thus, R_{11} describes the dependence of the 1933-noncontrolled variables on the 1933-instruments, R_{21} describes the dependence of the 1934-noncontrolled variables on the same instruments, etc.; the zero matrices occurring to the right of the diagonal blocks imply that none of the noncontrolled variables depends on later instruments. It will be observed that, in our present case, the diagonal submatrices are equal, and that the same is true for the submatrices parallel to the diagonal blocks; this follows from the fact that the coefficients which describe the dependence of noncontrolled variables on current and lagged instruments are independent of time. So we can write

$$R = \begin{bmatrix} R_1 & 0 & 0 & 0 \\ R_2 & R_1 & 0 & 0 \\ R_3 & R_2 & R_1 & 0 \\ R_4 & R_3 & R_2 & R_1 \end{bmatrix}, \tag{6.7}$$

where R_1 describes the dependence of noncontrolled variables on current instruments, R_2 that on the instruments lagged one year, etc. These submatrices are presented in Table 5.

TABLE 5. The Submatrices R_1, ..., R_4 of the Multiplicative Structure of the Constraints (6.5).

	$W_2 - W_2^*$	$T - T^*$	$G - G^*$
		R_1	
$C - C^*$	0.666	-0.188	0.671
$I - I^*$	-0.052	-0.296	0.259
$D - D^*$	0.285	2.358	-1.427
		R_2	
$C - C^*$	-0.234	-1.014	1.170
$I - I^*$	-0.152	-0.894	0.759
$D - D^*$	0.095	1.172	-0.475
		R_3	
$C - C^*$	-0.172	-1.006	0.859
$I - I^*$	-0.076	-0.518	0.382
$D - D^*$	-0.007	0.186	0.033
		R_4	
$C - C^*$	-0.079	-0.543	0.396
$I - I^*$	-0.005	-0.088	0.024
$D - D^*$	-0.060	-0.285	0.301

The stochastic vector s is a mixture of the following three categories. First, it contains values of variables (endogenous as well as exogenous) belonging to the period before 1933. These can be taken as given, so that their linear combinations in s can be represented by fixed numbers. Second, there are the values taken by the noninstrumental exogenous variables during the period 1933-1936. We recall that (6.5) expresses y as a linear function of all exogenous variables of that period (see the beginning of the preceding paragraph); and hence, since the instrumental exogenous variables fall under Rx, the noninstrumental ones must fall under s. In our case there is only one such variable, viz., time (t); its numerical values during the years 1933-1936, multiplied by appropriate coefficients, are combined with the linear combinations mentioned above. Finally, the vector s contains the disturbances of the equation system during the period 1933-1936, and it does so in the following way: the subvector s_1 (belonging to 1933) depends on the 1933-disturbances, the subvector s_2 depends on both 1933- and 1934-disturbances, etc., and this relationship is linear and independent of time. Hence:

$$s_t = \sigma_t + \sum_{i=1}^{t} S_{t-i+1} u_{32+i} \qquad (t = 1,...,4)\,, \tag{6.8}$$

where σ_1, σ_2, ... are the vectors of order 3 of the numerical values of the first two categories mentioned above, u_{33}, u_{34}, ... the disturbance vectors $\{u_1\ u_2\ u_3\}$ of the equation system during the years 1933, 1934, ..., and S_1, S_2, ... matrices of order 3×3. The σ's and S's are summarised in Table 6.[12]

TABLE 6. The Subvectors σ_1, ..., σ_4 and the Submatrices S_1, ..., S_4 of the Additive Structure of the Constraints (6.5).

	Constant term	u_1	u_2	u_3
	σ_1		S_1	
$C - C^*$	-5.393	1.671	0.671	1.148
$I - I^*$	-3.704	0.259	1.259	-0.089
$D - D^*$	-0.729	-1.427	-1.427	2.217
	σ_2		S_2	
$C - C^*$	-7.554	1.170	1.071	-0.078
$I - I^*$	-4.524	0.759	0.574	-0.287
$D - D^*$	-0.062	-0.475	-0.266	0.792
	σ_3		S_3	
$C - C^*$	-8.034	0.859	0.604	-0.318
$I - I^*$	-5.030	0.382	0.113	-0.213
$D - D^*$	1.998	0.033	0.281	0.213
	σ_4		S_4	
$C - C^*$	-8.228	0.396	0.052	-0.227
$I - I^*$	-5.892	0.024	-0.261	-0.069
$D - D^*$	5.106	0.301	0.508	-0.044

[12] Note that the constant terms (the components of the σ's) are influenced by the fact that all variables in the various years are measured as deviations from their desired values. So, if we would take the variables as deviations from zero instead of deviations from desired values, the resulting σ's would differ from the σ's of Table 6, the differences being linear forms in desired values.

7. Strategies and Certainty Equivalence

The aims described in the preceding pages can simply be considered as the maximization of

$$E\,w(x,y) \tag{7.1}$$

[cf. (6.3) and (6.4)], subject to (6.5)

$$y = Rx + s\,,$$

which is a stochastic and dynamic constraint connecting variables in four successive years. The method to be followed in order to arrive at this maximum is that of the choice of an optimal strategy; that is, of an optimal set of functional relationships connecting the instruments in the various years with relevant information that will have become available before the moment when the decision regarding the instrument value has to be taken. In our present case, this information consists of the realised disturbances u_1, u_2, u_3 of the years which have become history; and hence, since these disturbances are only relevant in the form in which they occur in s, we can write any strategy as

$$\begin{aligned} x_1 &= f_1 \\ x_2 &= f_2(s_1) \\ x_3 &= f_3(s_1,\, s_2). \\ x_4 &= f_4(s_1,\, s_2,\, s_3). \end{aligned} \tag{7.2}$$

Thus, the decision for the values to be taken by the instruments in 1934 (x_1) is made dependent on the 1933-disturbances (which are considered as known in the beginning of 1934), that for the 1935-instruments is made dependent on both the 1933- and the 1934-disturbances, etc. The decision for the first year 1933 can depend only on information belonging to years before the strategy period, so that the set of arguments of its function f_1 is empty.[13]

[13] The dependence of the other x's on s's implies that these x's are stochastic in the present context. It is interesting to compare this with the assumption of the nonstochastic nature of exogenous variables in the statistical estimation of equation systems. It will be noted that because of the stochastic character of the x's, the P's defined in Section 5 are also stochastic (with the sole exception of P_1).

The optimal strategy can be found by varying the f's through the domain of all conceivable functions of the same arguments. This procedure is rather laborious. Fortunately, it is possible to make use of a theorem of one of the authors (Theil, 1957; 1958)[14] which states that the first-year decision x_1 is not affected if we do not maximize (7.1) subject to (6.5), but maximize

$$w(x, E_1 y) \tag{7.3}$$

subject to

$$E_1 y = Rx + E_1 s, \tag{7.4}$$

where E_1 stands for the conditional expectation, given the information available at the beginning of the first year 1933. It follows from (6.8) and from the assumption that the disturbances have zero mean and zero lagged covariances that $E_1 s$ is given by

$$E_1 s = \begin{bmatrix} \sigma_1 \\ \sigma_2 \\ \sigma_3 \\ \sigma_4 \end{bmatrix}. \tag{7.5}$$

This result on "certainty equivalence," which holds for any finite number of periods (not necessarily four as in our case) and for any finite numbers of instruments and of noncontrolled variables (possibly different), implies that we can derive the first-year decision in a straightforward manner, viz., as the first three elements of

$$\bar{x} = -(A + R'BR + CR + R'C')^{-1}[a + R'b + (C + R'B)E_1 s] \tag{7.6}$$

in the case of the general quadratic preference function (6.4).[15] For the special function (6.3) this reduces to

---

[14] Also cf. Simon (1956).

[15] Cf. Theil (1957, pp. 347-348). The most important condition for this result is that the simultaneous distribution of the components of s should be independent of the x's; in particular, the variances should be independent. Heteroskedasticity of disturbances is therefore admissible (cf. the last footnote of Section 2), but the variability of the variances should be determined by other factors than the instruments.

$$\bar{x} = -(I + R'R)^{-1} R'E_1 s \,, \tag{7.7}$$

which will be evaluated in Section 8, where we shall also consider the remaining part of the period. We shall apply the theorem on certainty equivalence year after year, which ensures that we arrive at decisions that are identical with those that would follow from a straightforward application of the optimal strategy.

8. The Optimal Behaviour and its Results, 1933-1936

The numerical behaviour based on the optimal strategy and resulting from the numerical values of relevant information will be termed the policy-maker's *optimal behaviour*. For 1933 this behaviour is derived in a straightforward manner by applying (7.7): if we take for R and $E_1 s$ the values of Tables 5 and 6, using (6.7) and (7.5), we obtain a column vector of order 12, the first three elements of which are

$$\bar{x}_1 = \begin{bmatrix} (W_2)_{33} - (W_2^*)_{33} \\ T_{33} - T_{33}^* \\ G_{33} - G_{33}^* \end{bmatrix} = \begin{bmatrix} 1.10 \\ 1.22 \\ 3.83 \end{bmatrix}. \tag{8.1}$$

Combining this with the desired values of Table 4, we find

$$(W_2)_{33} = 6.13; \quad T_{33} = 8.62; \quad G_{33} = 14.26. \tag{8.2}$$

For the second year 1934 we apply exactly the same procedure. This implies that our new constraints are to be written as

$$\begin{aligned} y_2 &= R_1 x_2 + (R_2 x_1 + s_2) \\ y_3 &= R_2 x_2 + R_1 x_3 + (R_3 x_1 + s_3) \\ y_4 &= R_3 x_2 + R_2 x_3 + R_1 x_4 + (R_4 x_1 + s_4) \,, \end{aligned} \tag{8.3}$$

where x_1 should be interpreted as the numerical vector (8.1). The conditional expectation of the additive structure of the constraints (8.3), given the information available at the beginning of 1934, is then

$$\begin{bmatrix} R_2 x_1 & + \sigma_2 & + S_2 u_{33} \\ R_3 x_1 & + \sigma_3 & + S_3 u_{33} \\ R_4 x_1 & + \sigma_4 & + S_4 u_{33} \end{bmatrix} \tag{8.4}$$

and the multiplicative structure:

$$\begin{bmatrix} R_1 & 0 & 0 \\ R_2 & R_1 & 0 \\ R_3 & R_2 & R_1 \end{bmatrix}. \tag{8.5}$$

Applying (7.7) with R replaced by (8.5) and $E_1 s$ by (8.4), the unit matrix being reduced to the order 9, we obtain a column vector of 9 elements, the first three of which are

$$\bar{\bar{x}}_2 = \begin{bmatrix} (W_2)_{34} & - (W_2^*)_{34} \\ T_{34} & - T_{34}^* \\ G_{34} & - G_{34}^* \end{bmatrix} = \begin{bmatrix} 0.38 \\ 0.70 \\ 2.33 \end{bmatrix}, \tag{8.6}$$

which, when combined with Table 5, gives

$$(W_2)_{34} = 5.64; \quad T_{34} = 8.34; \quad G_{34} = 13.20. \tag{8.7}$$

The optimal behaviour in the last two years are obtained in a similar way. They are summarised in Table 7, together with the noncontrolled values of the period 1933-1936 and the national income figures which result from this behaviour and from the realised disturbances of that period. The table contains also the deviations of these values from the desired values as well as the deviations from the actual values in 1933-1936 that were realised during President Roosevelt's administration;[16] it contains further the realised values of these variables in the last year of President Hoover's administration (1932), which are shown for comparison purposes.

---

[16] For the latter values, cf. Klein (1950, p. 135). The desired values of Y are defined as the values which are obtained by substituting the desired values of C, I, G and T into the definition (2.4).

TABLE 7. The Optimal Behaviour and its Consequences, 1933-1936.

		Instruments			Noncontrolled variables			
		W_2	T	G	C	I	D	Y
Realised values	1932	5.3	8.3	10.2	45.6	-6.2	15.0	41.3
Optimal behaviour & consequences	1933	6.13	8.62	14.26	49.57	-4.80	6.76	50.42
	1934	5.64	8.34	13.20	52.74	-1.81	6.41	55.80
	1935	6.05	7.37	13.83	56.69	0.81	1.83	63.97
	1936	6.28	6.91	13.31	64.43	6.03	-6.76	76.86
Deviations from desired values	1933	1.10	1.22	3.83	-0.12	-1.70	-4.49	0.79
	1934	0.38	0.70	2.33	-1.04	-1.81	-1.09	-1.22
	1935	0.58	-0.51	2.53	-1.19	-2.29	-1.92	-0.43
	1936	0.60	-1.21	1.58	2.46	-0.17	-6.76	5.08
Deviations from realised values	1933	0.53	3.22	4.96	3.07	0.30	0.66	5.12
	1934	-0.36	1.54	3.20	4.04	1.19	0.41	6.90
	1935	-0.05	0.17	3.33	5.39	2.11	-3.37	10.67
	1936	-1.12	-1.39	3.01	6.73	3.93	-8.36	15.06

It is seen that the optimal behaviour leads to a considerable expansion, the 1936-figure of national income being larger than the level that was actually realised in any interwar year except 1941. The deviations from the desired values have mostly signs that are plausible for a depression period: the government expenditure variables (W_2 and G) exceed their desired values in all four years, and consumption and investment are below their desired levels (in all years except C in 1936). As to the policy itself, the table shows that the variable with the largest deviations from its desired values is the government expenditure on goods and services. In that sense the depression policy is an expenditure policy; but it is also a taxation policy, even though the amount of business taxes (T) stays approximately at the 1932-level during the first two years of the strategy, because T as a percentage of national income decreases gradually from 20 in 1932 to less than 10 in 1936.[17] Hence the tax *rates* are reduced.[18] The largest discrepancies from the desired levels are those of the distribution variable D, especially in 1936; we shall come back to this point in Section 9.

[17] This percentage was reduced in the first year of President Roosevelt's administration to 12, after which it remained between this figure and 14 during the three following years. The optimal behaviour according to the criteria considered here implies that it should be reduced to 17 in 1933, 15 in 1934, 12 in 1935, 9 in 1936.

[18] If tax rates are used as instruments instead of amounts of taxes collected, their successive adaptation can be carried out along the lines indicated in the preceding footnote.

9. Forecasts of Future Behaviour and Development

When deriving the optimal behaviour for 1933, we disregarded the last 9 elements of the vector (7.7). As such, this is undoubtedly correct, since these elements refer to the behaviour in 1934 and later years, the optimal behaviour for which is derived (as we saw in Sections 7 and 8) by repeated application of the theorem on certainty equivalence at later stages. However, these elements are not without interest, since they are (conditionally) unbiased point predictions of future optimal behaviour, given the information available at the beginning of 1933 [which is easily seen when it is realised that (7.6) expresses its nine elements as linearly dependent on $E_1 s$ and that, if $E_1 s = s$, the x of (7.6) would maximise $w(x, y)$ subject to $y = Rx + s$, s being as it turns out to be].[19] Thus, the fourth element of the vector (7.7) refers to the W_2 of 1934; and its value (6.26) is a forecast of the W_2 which is to be applied in 1934 and which is derived numerically at the beginning of 1934 (viz., 5.64). Similar forecasts are available for 1935 and 1936 and also for the other instruments T and G. At the beginning of 1934 a nine-element column vector is derived (see the second paragraph of Section 8), the first three elements of which specify the behaviour in 1934, and the last six represent new (revised) forecasts for 1935 and 1936; and so on. In Table 8 these forecasts are arranged in matrix form, the columns referring to the year at the beginning of which the forecasts are made, the rows to the year for which the predictions are made; the table contains also in its main diagonals the figures of the optimal behaviour itself. A closer inspection of these figures reveals that the forecasts are rather accurate: in very few cases the forecast is worse than no-change extrapolation, e.g., the 1933-forecast of the W_2 in 1934 (the prediction error is $6.26 - 5.64 = 0.62$, whereas no-change extrapolation implies an error of $6.13 - 5.64 = 0.49$); in most cases they are substantially better, the median of all 18 prediction errors (disregarding signs) being less than 0.1, whereas the median of the absolute values of the successive differences of the optimal-behaviour figures for all three instruments combined is about five times larger. It is also interesting to note that the 9 forecast revisions [e.g., the revision of the 1933-forecast of T in 1936 (viz., 6.99) to the 1934-forecast (6.87), and the revision of this prediction at the beginning of 1935] make the forecast more acccurate than its predecessor in 5 cases, less accurate in 3, one case being a zero revision in two decimal places.

[19] Note that maximising $w(x, y)$ subject to $y = Rx + s$, s being as it turns out to be (and hence nonstochastic) leads to the absolute maximum which is conceivably attainable. This maximum is not reached by the use of a strategy, because the strategy is based on partial knowledge of s, later disturbances being replaced by conditional expectations. The forecasts of Table 8 are not only unbiased point predictions of the instrument values of the absolute maximum, but also of those of the optimal behaviour according to the strategy, because the latter, too, are unbiased point predictions of the x's of the absolute maximum.

TABLE 8. Forecasts of Future Optimal Behaviour (in billions of 1934 dollars per year).

	1933	1934	1935	1936	1933	1934	1935	1936	1933	1934	1935	1936
		W_2				T				G		
1933	6.13				8.62				14.26			
1934	6.26	5.64			8.45	8.34			13.92	13.20		
1935	6.20	5.96	6.05		7.64	7.43	7.37		13.71	13.66	13.83	
1936	6.36	6.30	6.34	6.28	6.99	6.87	6.92	6.91	13.30	13.36	13.36	13.31

A similar procedure can be applied to the noncontrolled variables, the results of which are summarised in Table 9. At the beginning of 1933 we know the optimal instrument values for that year, but we do not yet know that year's disturbances. So, by using the reduced form and replacing these disturbances by their expectations, we can arrive at unbiased point predictions of the noncontrolled values of 1933. Further, by using the behaviour forecasts for 1934 and later years, we can also find predictions of the noncontrolled variables in these years; the latter forecasts, too, are unbiased point predictions, because they are linearly determined by the behaviour forecasts, which are unbiased themselves. As a whole, therefore, we arrive at 30 forecasts for the three noncontrolled variables combined, which are arranged in the columns of Table 9 according to the year at the beginning of which they are prepared (the *figures* are the values resulting from optimal behaviour and realised disturbances), and in rows according to the year for which they are prepared. It is seen that the errors are in general small, except for 1936. The median of the 30 prediction errors (disregarding signs) for the three noncontrolled variables and the four years is slightly less than 1.5; if 1936 is disregarded, we obtain for the median of the remaining 18 errors a value below 0.3. The median of the first differences (disregarding signs) of the corresponding noncontrolled values which result from the optimal behaviour and the realised disturbances is about 4. The total number of forecast revisions for the three noncontrolled variables is 18; in 11 cases they made the forecast more accurate, in 7 cases less accurate. If we disregard the predictions for 1936 (the revisions of which are all less than 10 per cent of the error of the revised forecast), it becomes 6 against 3. The national income figures of Table 9 show roughly the same picture.

The over-all picture of the forecasts is favourable, with the exception of those of the noncontrolled variables in 1936. To understand why this is the case, it is sufficient to go back to Table 2, which shows that the three 1936-disturbances are all considerably larger in absolute value than any of the corresponding disturbances in the preceding years. This affects all three noncontrolled variables in 1936, but especially the distribution variable D; for the relatively large reduced-form coefficients of the three disturbances in the D-equation have all signs that are opposite to those of the 1936-values of these disturbances, so that their effects re-inforce each other. Of course, these large disturbances do not affect the quality of the instrumental forecasts, because the optimal behaviour in none of the four years takes account of them; but they would surely have affected the forecasts for 1937 if we had considered a five-year strategy ending in 1937.

TABLE 9. Forecasts of Future Development of Noncontrolled Variables and National Income (in billions of 1934 dollars per year).

	1933		1934		1935		1936	
	C							
1933	47.36	*49.57*						
1934	51.77		52.72	*52.74*				
1935	56.37		56.68		56.52	*56.69*		
1936	60.73		60.79		60.75		60.83	*64.43*
	I							
1933	-6.23	*-4.80*						
1934	-2.38		-1.54	*-1.81*				
1935	0.90		0.89		0.67	*0.81*		
1936	3.59		3.38		3.40		3.47	*6.03*
	D							
1933	8.25	*6.76*						
1934	5.02		5.34	*6.41*				
1935	1.91		1.95		1.94	*1.83*		
1936	0.05		0.08		0.06		0.08	*-6.76*
	Y							
1933	46.78	*50.42*						
1934	54.85		56.04	*55.80*				
1935	63.34		63.81		63.66	*63.97*		
1936	70.33		70.66		70.59		70.70	*76.86*

The question arises whether the rather unfavourable picture of the 1936-noncontrolled values must be considered as "normal," or the much more favourable picture of the earlier years. The answer is that, for the model considered here, the "normal" picture lies between these limits. The quality of the forecast depends on the magnitude of the disturbances that will be realised between the formulation of the prediction and the period to which the prediction refers. The nine disturbances during the first three years of the strategy are all smaller in absolute value than their standard deviations; in two years they are even much smaller.[20] In 1936, however, the ratios of the three disturbances to the corresponding standard deviations were 1.8, 1.3 and -1.0. If we add the squares of these figures, the result is slightly below 6; which is just above the 10 per cent significance level of the χ^2-distribution with three degrees of freedom. So, assuming normally and independently distributed disturbances, we should expect that such large or still larger deviations from zero will occur two or three times in twenty years on the average.

10. Concluding Remarks

(i) In reality, of course, one will never have at his disposal an equation system fitted over a period which includes the strategy period. The best one can do is to use a system which is estimated from data which refer to a period just before the strategy period. It seems intuitively obvious that such a model lags behind the events in the case of gradual structural changes, so that the deviations between model predictions and reality should be expected to be larger on the average on that account.

(ii) In general, the model used will contain a larger number of noninstrumental exogenous variables than the one which we had here (time). The theorem on certainty equivalence requires that unbiased point predictions of the values to be taken by these variables in the remainder of the strategy period are used. This is a heavy task, especially when the period to be predicted is far away; but it will be found in most cases that such far-away predictions do not affect present optimal behaviour very much. On the other hand, bad far-away predictions of noninstrumental exogenous variables will reduce the quality of the forecasts of future optimal behaviour.

(iii) To assume that at the beginning of 1933 complete information about 1932 is available is not more than a simplifying assumption. The approach can be generalised to take account of partial lack of information; but it is of course better to speed up the collection of statistical data, because lagged information necessarily leads to less successful adaptation of instruments.

(iv) As stated in Section 1, the specification of the preference function is of great importance. In the first stage of this study some preference functions were used which did not contain all three instruments as arguments. The results suggested that this may easily lead to unrealistic instrument values.

(v) For the numerical specification of a quadratic preference function the use of desired values is quite convenient in order to handle the linear part of this function. The approach is then to maximize the expectation of a negative-definite quadratic form in deviations from desired values. It is to be stressed, however, that the existence of a maximum does not require this form to be definite; it should only be definite under the constraint $y = Rx + s$. This is comparable with the matrix of second-order derivatives of

[20] The (estimated) standard deviations of u_1, u_2, u_3 are 1.14, 1.19 and 0.78, respectively; cf. Klein (1950, p. 69).

the utility function in consumer analysis, which should be definite under the budget constraint.[21]

(vi) The approach considered in (v) can be developed further in an interesting manner. Writing ξ and η for the vectors of desired values of x and y, respectively, we find that the preference function can be written as

$$\begin{aligned} w(x,y) = {} & (a + A\xi + C\eta)'(x - \xi) \\ & + (b + C'\xi + B\eta)'(y-\eta) + \tfrac{1}{2}[(x - \xi)'A(x - \xi) \\ & + (y - \eta)'B(y - \eta) + (x - \xi)'C(y - \eta) + (y - \eta)'C'(x - \xi)], \end{aligned} \tag{10.1}$$

the (irrelevant) constant term being omitted.[22] Hence

$$a + A\xi + C\eta = 0; \quad b + C'\xi + B\eta = 0. \tag{10.2}$$

The x which maximises w subject to $y = Rx + s$, s being as it turns out be be,[23] is [cf. (7.6)]:

$$\hat{x} = -(A + R'BR + CR + R'C')^{-1}[a + R'b + (C + R'B)s]. \tag{10.3}$$

Applying (10.2), we find for the vector in square brackets in the right-hand side of (10.3)

$$a + R'b + (C + R'B)s = -(A + R'C')\xi - (C + R'B)(\eta - s). \tag{10.4}$$

Writing $y_\xi = R\xi + s$ for the y-vector which results from applying the desired instrument values, we have $\eta - s = \eta - y_\xi + R\xi$, so that (10.4) becomes

$$-(A + R'BR + CR + R'C')\xi - (C + R'B)(\eta - y_\xi).$$

Combining this with (10.3), we find

$$\hat{x} - \xi = -(A + R'BR + CR + R'C')^{-1}(C + R'B)(y_\xi - \eta), \tag{10.5}$$

---

[21] Cf. Samuelson (1948, p. 376 n).

[22] Here x and y are evidently not defined in terms of deviations from desired values.

[23] Also cf. the first footnote of Section 9.

which implies that the deviation of the maximizing instrument vector from its desired level is a homogeneous linear function of the deviations of the desired noncontrolled values from those values which would be realised if the desired instrument values were applied (we might term the latter deviations the "inconsistency" of the policy-maker's desires). The matrix of weights of these linear combinations is determined by the multiplicative structure of the constraints (R) and the quadratic part of the preference function (A, B, C).

References

H. Chernoff and N. Divinski: 1953, *The Computation of Maximum-Likelihood Estimates of Linear Structural Equations*, chapter X of *Studies in Econometric Method*, edited by W.C. Hood and T.C. Koopmans, New York-London.

R. Frisch: 1957, *Numerical Determination of a Quadratic Preference Function for Use in Macroeconomic Programming*, memorandum of the University Institute of Economics, Oslo.

L.R. Klein: 1950, *Economic Fluctuations in the United States, 1921-1941*, New York-London.

P.A. Samuelson: 1948, *Foundations of Economic Analysis*, Cambridge, Mass.

H.A. Simon: 1956, "Dynamic Programming under Uncertainty with a Quadratic Criterion Function," *Econometrica* **24**, 74-81.

H. Theil: 1957, "A Note on Certainty Equivalence in Dynamic Planning," *Econometrica* **25**, 346-349.

H. Theil: 1958, *Economic Forecasts and Policy*, Amsterdam.

J. Tinbergen: 1939, *Statistical Testing of Business Cycle Theories*, vol. II: *Business Cycles in the United States of America, 1919-1932*, Geneva.

J. Tinbergen: 1952, *On the Theory of Economic Policy*, Amsterdam.

J. Tinbergen: 1956, *Economic Policy: Principles and Design*, Amsterdam.

SECTION 5.2: FORECASTING

CHAPTER 66

WHO FORECASTS BEST?*

HENRI THEIL
Netherlands School of Economics
(now Erasmus University)
Rotterdam, The Netherlands

Translated from Dutch[1] by L.F. Manneke

1. Introduction

In the *Economic Bulletin for Europe*, July 1953, the Economic Commission for Europe (E.C.E.) examined the reliability of the forecasting experiments of the Netherlands, the United Kingdom and the Scandinavian countries relating to their national incomes and other macro-economic magnitudes.[2] The nature of the analysis is mainly descriptive. In particular no attention is paid to the question of which magnitudes have been forecast with reasonable success and which with considerable errors, nor to the question of what countries have been the most successful.

This article attempts to supplement the analysis. In the first place a measure of the accuracy of forecasts is needed. Section 2 and Section 3 deal with this; in Section 2 the line of thought is expounded intuitively; in Section 3 in more concrete terms. Readers with a limited interest in mathematical-statistical problems may wish to omit Section 3. In Section 4 the question of which magnitudes have been forecast most accurately and which most inaccurately is considered. Section 5 gives a comparison by countries, to which some reservations are added in Section 6.

* This translation of the article (from Dutch) first appeared in *International Economic Papers* **5** (1955) 194-199. Reprinted with the permission of MacMillan Publishing, United Kingdom.

[1] "Wie Voorspelt het Best?," *De Economist*, February 1954. The author, who graduated at the University of Amsterdam in 1950, is now Professor of Econometrics at the Netherlands School of Economics, Rotterdam. He has also been on the staff of the Government Planning Bureau at the Hague, and in 1952 was a visiting teacher at the International Statistical Education Centres in Calcutta and Beirut. In 1954, his *Linear Aggregation of Economic Relations* appeared in the series *Contributions to Economic Analysis*, published by the North Holland Publishing Company.

[2] "National Budgets in Western Europe. Post-War Experiments in National Income Forecasting in the United Kingdom, the Netherlands and Scandinavia" (pp. 63-81). The numerical values given there are the basis of the present calculations. For these calculations the author is indebted to Mr. J.W. Zeilmaker of the Government Planning Bureau at the Hague.

2. A Measure of the Accuracy of Forecasts (I)

For each of the magnitudes to be examined a "forecast" and a "realized" value is known for a number of successive years. The difference between the two is the forecasting error, a time series of which is thus available for every magnitude.

It is clear that there is only one way in which a magnitude can be forecast as well as possible, namely if all forecasts are equal to the corresponding realized values. In that case the series of forecasting errors would consist exclusively of zeros. In general, however, the series will consist of numbers other than zero; some will be positive (too great a value was forecast), some negative. Sometimes all forecasting errors may be either positive or negative; this would suggest the presence of systematic errors.

The distribution of the forecasting errors will then have to give a measure for the accuracy of the forecasts; or at least enter into its determination. The most obvious thing to do is to choose a measure of dispersion such as the classical standard deviation. However, taking the standard deviation of the forecasting errors as a measure of forecasting accuracy has the disadvantage that it only gives the dispersion of the errors round their average value. There is no objection to this if the average is zero, but this is certainly not always the case. A considerable deviation of the average from zero is a sign of systematic errors that can be as important as the deviation of the errors round their average. For this reason a measure has been chosen which comprises both categories equally.

This measure, however, is a preliminary and not the final one, for there are two objections to it. In the first place it depends on the choice of units in which the magnitudes are measured. Since some magnitudes are given in guilders, some in pounds, others as indices, this objection is of importance. In the second place the measure does not take into account how difficult it is to make forecasts. Without entering into a detailed explanation of the problems of economic forecasting, we wish to draw attention to the fact that forecasts are made from year to year so that greater errors can be expected when the differences between the realized values of successive years are greater.[3] So we also need a measure of the distribution of the successive differences of the realized values. It is an obvious course to choose this measure analogously with the measure of forecasting errors discussed above.

If we then divide these two measures by one another, the result obtained is invariant with respect to the units used and also takes into account the problems involved in forecasting. This leads to the forecasting coefficients ψ, defined in Section 3. These

[3] In the extreme case of constant realized values, forecasting is hardly a problem and every forecasting error must be considered serious.

have been calculated for 53 series of forecasts. The result is shown in Table 1.[4] The lower limit of ψ is zero (in the case of perfect forecasts); ψ increases as the forecasts are worse, given the problems of making these forecasts; it reaches the value one if the forecasting errors are as great as the changes in realized values, and it has no finite upper limit, that is to say it can take arbitrarily great values.

TABLE 1. Forecasting Coefficients

		Netherlands	United Kingdom	Norway	Sweden	Denmark	Average
Export:	value	0.16	0.26	0.76	0.62	0.53	0.40
	price level	0.38	-	0.82	0.56	0.40	0.51
	volume	0.42	-	0.72	0.69	0.57	0.59
Import:	value	0.26	0.25	0.73	0.48	0.51	0.41
	price level	0.06	-	0.33	0.29	0.30	0.20
	volume	0.43	-	1.22	0.71	0.69	0.71
Balance invisible items		0.29	0.91	0.97	1.30	0.57	0.72
Balance of payments surplus or deficit		0.48	0.52	0.76	0.71	0.73	0.63
Investment in construction		0.75	-	0.80	0.60	0.65	0.70
Total gross investment in fixed assets		0.78	-	-	0.71	0.56	0.67
National product		0.53	0.63	0.66	0.78	0.56	0.63
Industrial production		0.54	0.51	0.59	0.52	0.81	0.59

3. A Measure of the Accuracy of Forecasts (II)

If we denote the forecast of a certain magnitude in the year t by v_t and the realized value in that year by r_t, then the forecasting error is $(v_t - r_t)$. Let us then consider

$$f_1 = \frac{1}{T} \sum_{t=1}^{T} (v_t - r_t)^2$$

the second moment of the forecasting errors (T is the number of years that has been forecast). This is the preliminary measure discussed in Section 2 above. The second

[4] In some cases the E.C.E. has given the percentage increase from year to year instead of absolute amounts, or indices with a fixed base year. In such cases a recalculation was first made before ψ was calculated. Furthermore, in some cases a range rather than a single value was given (for instance an increase from 2½% to 3%); here the middle value was taken. Finally, some magnitudes have not been taken into the calculations, either because the published realized values are so inaccurate that the resulting forecasting errors would be influenced considerably by the errors of measurement (as is the case in most components of gross investment), or because they were forecast only for a single country and so are of limited significance for purposes of comparison.

moment can be considered as an indicator of the way forecasting errors are dispersed around zero. This measure diverges from the square of the standard deviation because the latter relates to deviations from the average.

In the same way we introduce the second moment of the differences of successive values:

$$f_2 = \frac{1}{T} \sum_{t=1}^{T} (r_t - r_{t-1})^2$$

We consider this quantity to be a measure of the difficulty of forecasting. The ratio between f_1 and f_2 then leads to the forecasting coefficient:

$$\psi = \sqrt{f_1 / f_2}$$

The square root has been taken because f_1 and f_2 are both essentially quadratic quantities.

4. Comparison by Magnitudes Forecast

Besides the separate forecasting indices Table 1 shows, in the last column, the average for all the countries for each of the twelve magnitudes forecast.[5] It is striking that the components of the balance of payments, especially the value and price level of imports and exports, come out better than the other categories. This naturally does not mean that the former quantities have been forecast more exactly than the latter; because we have corrected for the problems related to the forecasting of the various quantities.

The import price level in particular is characterized by a low forecasting coefficient; for each of the participating countries it is the lowest. This is partly due to the fact that this price level follows the world prices of raw materials with a lag. It is noticeable that better results are obtained with regard to the values of imports and exports than to their volumes; the difference is especially striking for imports. The balance of invisible items in the balance of payments obviously offers relatively great difficulties, as does the balance of payments itself. It is always difficult to estimate the difference between two quantities which are both rather uncertain and are of the same order of magnitude.

Both the investment variables also show high coefficients, which is not surprising. It is more noteworthy that the national product and the level of industrial production are characterized by relatively high coefficients. Naturally the successive changes of these variables are not particularly large, so that the absolute errors do not have to be excessive; but taking into account the results for the components of the balance of payments, coefficients of the order of 0.4 could have been expected.

[5] Here, and later, it is a matter of geometrical averages; these are clearly preferable. No weighting has been applied.

5. Comparison by Countries

A comparison by countries is rather less simple because not all countries attempted to forecast the same categories. The U.K., for instance, restricted itself to six, while in Norway total gross investment was not forecast. But for this difficulty, the comparison could simply be made as follows: take the average of the ψ's of all the countries, and the resulting averages arranged in ascending order will show the countries in diminishing order of forecasting "ability." However, since there are some countries for which certain ψ's are lacking, this process of taking averages cannot be used in its simplest form, because the quantities that have not been forecast may be more difficult or easier to forecast than the others. The difficulty could be circumvented easily, merely by taking into account those quantities that have been forecast by all countries; but this would considerably reduce the basis of comparison and this would be undesirable.

Preference is therefore given to a system of bilateral comparisons in the following sense. For some countries, such as the Netherlands and Sweden, all twelve magnitudes have been forcast; it is thus possible to compare the forecasting ability of these countries by taking into account all the quantities. On the other hand only six magnitudes have been forecast in the U.K. This implies that a comparison of the forecasting ability of this country with any other country can be based on only six values. Thus this bilateral method of comparison ensures that the results are always based on a maximum of information. A possible disadvantage is that the relations thus estimated of greater or smaller forecasting ability may not be transitive; for if the Netherlands seems to forecast better than Sweden on the basis of an average of twelve ψ's and the latter better than England on the basis of an average of only six ψ's, it is conceivable that on the basis of these last ψ's England would appear superior to the Netherlands, if the Netherlands owed its superiority over Sweden to the other six ψ's. Fortunately this complication does not arise here.

Table 2 shows the bilateral classification. The numerical values were obtained by taking the average per country[6] for those ψ's of two countries, which are available for both, and then dividing one average by the other. This ratio has been inverted in order to give the country with the highest forecasting ability the highest figure. The result (for instance the ratio 0.75 for the Netherlands-England) should be read as follows: the geometrical averages of the six forecasting coefficients appearing for both the Netherlands and England in Table 1 stand in the ratio of 0.75 to 1 and therefore England is given the number 0.75, given the value 1 for the Netherlands. In the same way the ratio 0.67 for England-Sweden means that the ratio of the English coefficients to the Swedish is, on the average, 0.67: 1. In general: for any pair of countries one first seeks the name of the one country in the left-hand column, and then looks along its row for the number of the other country as listed in the column heads. This number indicates the forecasting ability of the latter country, given a value of unity for the former country.

[6] Geometrical averages. Again no weighting took place.

TABLE 2. Bilateral Classification of Countries

	Netherlands	England	Denmark	Sweden	Norway
1. Netherlands	1	0.75	0.63	0.56	0.45
2. England		1	0.76	0.67	0.63
3. Denmark			1	0.89	0.77
4. Sweden				1	0.85
5. Norway					1

In this comparison the Netherlands comes out very well. Indeed Table 1 shows that the Netherlands takes first place for eight (of which seven are related to items of the balance of payments) out of twelve forecasting categories. The success is smaller in the investment sector, both the Dutch ψ's lying above the average; the Netherlands again takes first place for the national product and does not come out unfavourably in forecasting industrial production. The U.K. is a good second, but here it must be remembered that this country only entered for half of the forecasts.

6. A Reservation

The results of Table 2 being favourable in every respect for the Netherlands, there is good reason for humbleness as long as the dates of publication of the plans remain the same as in the past years. The Dutch plans were published in August (1950) or September (1949 and 1951), the English in February or March (usually the latter), the Norwegian in January or February, the Swedish usually in January and the Danish between March and May! It is obvious that a lag in the date of publication can mean a considerable start in the race registered in Table 2. For instance, when the import price level lags about half a year behind world market prices, one has a considerable chance of success in correctly estimating the average import price level for the whole year in July; on the other hand a forecast in January requires a forecast of the course of the world market price level during the next half year. Indeed the ψ of the import price level for the Netherlands seems to be about 5 times as low as that of the other countries, which can be due, at least partly, to the factor just mentioned.

Furthermore, the results given above are influenced by the economic structure of the various countries. For instance, when the investment of a particular country consists to a considerable extent in remedying a housing shortage, and to this extent is strictly controlled by the government (under a long-term plan), it is conceivable that better investment forecasts can be made than in countries otherwise situated. There is thus very good reason to interpret the results with modesty; one can only note with satisfaction that these results do not speak against the methods applied in the Netherlands.

CHAPTER 67

A STATISTICAL APPRAISAL OF POSTWAR MACRO-ECONOMIC FORECASTS IN THE NETHERLANDS AND SCANDINAVIA*[1]

HENRI THEIL
Netherlands School of Economics
(now Erasmus University), Rotterdam
Central Planning Bureau,
The Hague, The Netherlands

1. Introduction

Since the end of the War, several European countries have published expectations (sometimes in the form of targets) of next year's values of certain macroeconomic variables. It is the purpose of this paper to analyse to what extent these forecasts have been realised for the Netherlands and Scandinavia. The question how these forecasts have been made, will be disregarded; in general, this was a mixture of econometrics, inside information and common sense.

First, some problems of general although simple methodology have to be considered.

In order to analyse the separate variables in a comparable way, all forecasts for year t have been expressed as percentage deviations from the corresponding actual value in t-1, such as these were known at the moment when the forecast was made, whereas all actual outcomes have been expressed as percentage deviations from the corresponding final actual values in the previous year. In formulae:

$$P_t = 100\,\frac{p_t - a'_{t-1}}{a'_{t-1}} \qquad A_t = 100\,\frac{a_t - a_{t-1}}{a_{t-1}},$$

* This article first appeared in the *Bulletin of the International Statistical Institute*, **35**, (1957) 49-64. Reprinted with the permission of the International Statistical Institute 35.

[1] The author is indebted to Mr. L.C. Kuiken, deputy-director of the Central Planning Bureau, The Hague, who did much to clarify the causes of the Dutch forecasting errors, and to Mr. A. Russchen, also of this Bureau, who supplied the large mass of data analysed in this paper. It should be noted that part of these data is provisional, especially for the more recent years, so that the forecasting errors analysed in this paper are not free from errors of observation.

p_t being the value predicted for year t, a_t the actual value and a'_{t-1} the (provisional) actual value for t-1 as it was known when the forecast for year t was made. This procedure implies that the influence of incomplete knowledge of years which are not to be predicted is eliminated.

For the Netherlands 23 different variables have been investigated, of which 3 are prices, 9 quantities and 11 money values. The forecasts refer to four years, viz. 1949-1951 and 1953; 1952 has been excluded, as for this year a set of alternative and no unique forecasts were made. The total number of Dutch forecasts analysed here is hence 92. For Scandinavia this number is 82; it refers to 7 Norwegian, 8 Swedish and 8 Danish variables, and to the four years 1949-1952. For further details we refer to the Appendix.

It will be clear that these large numbers of forecasts are not characterised by statistical independence, and that the same will be true for the forecasting errors. It would, however, only be possible to avoid this cumbersome fact by dropping all variables which are not exogenous, which would however reduce the available observations such that the size of the sample would be another serious obstacle; and it is even to be doubted whether independence can be supposed to exist for variables which are exogenous from one country's point of view. Therefore, all available information has been used, but it should be stressed that statistical tests based on independence assumptions are of limited validity in this field of research.

2. Forecasts Versus Extrapolations

The Diagrams 1 and 2 for the Netherlands and Scandinavia, respectively, give a graphical picture of the forecasting success. If this success had been complete, then all 92 and 82 points would lie on the (unbroken) line $P = A$. This is of course not true, but there is evidently a rather close relationship between the point sets and these straight lines. The broken lines and curves will be discussed in section 3.

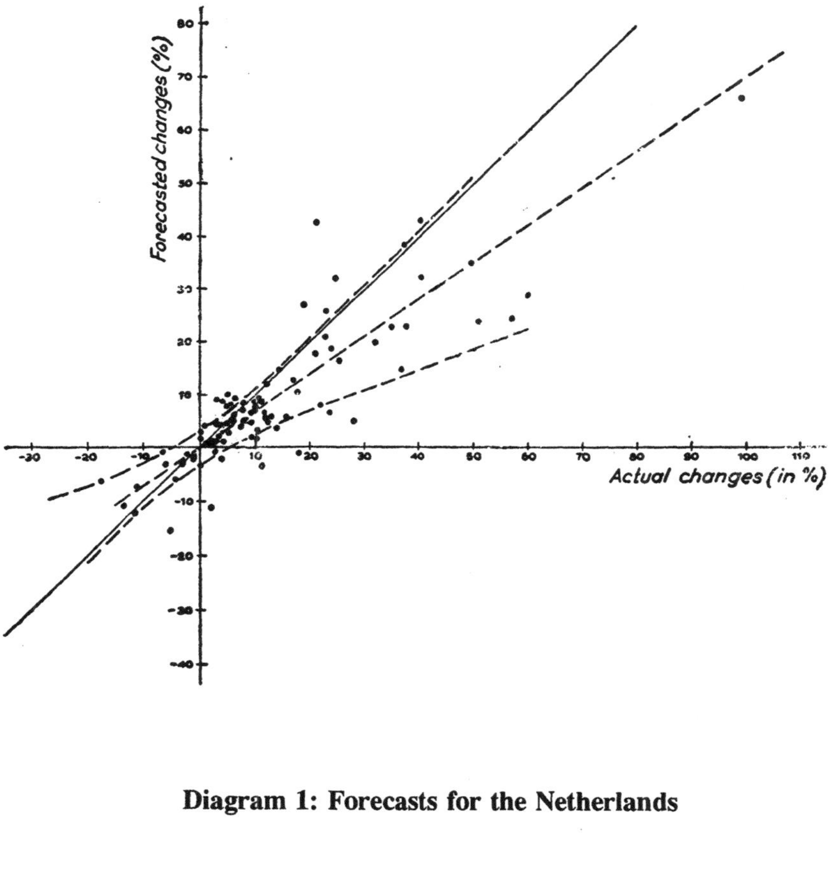

Diagram 1: Forecasts for the Netherlands

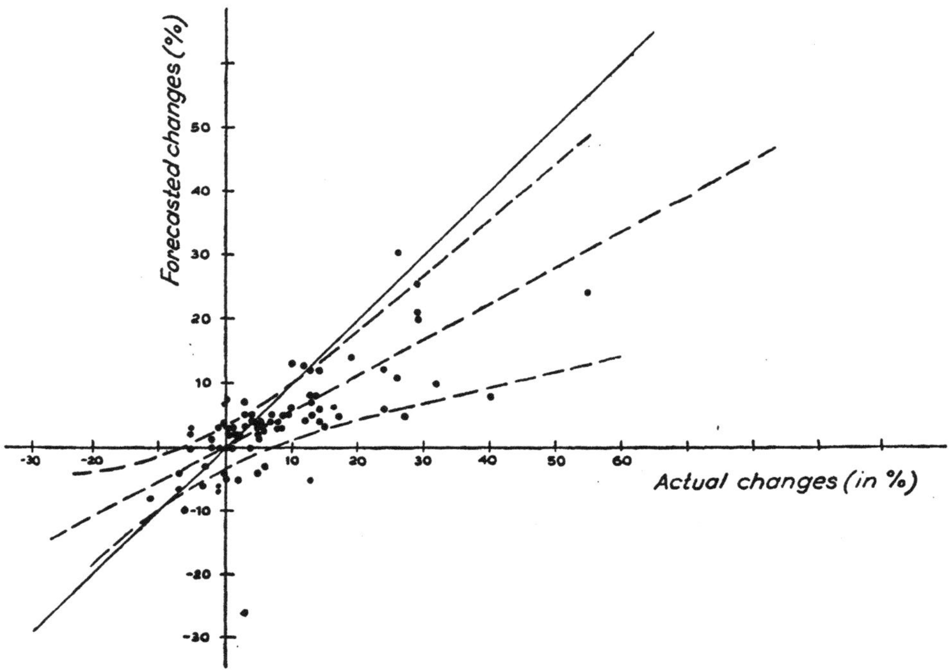

Diagram 2: Forecasts for Scandinavia

The Diagrams 3 and 4 show how the forecasts would have been if they had been based on a simple exponential extrapolation, i.e. $P_t = A_{t-1}$. The result is evidently much worse, both for the Netherlands and for Scandinavia; the percentage of wrongly predicted directions of change ($sgn\ P_t \neq sgn\ A_t$) increases e.g. from 7 to 15 for the Netherlands and from 10 to 23 for Scandinavia. Of course, this extrapolation method is rather crude — although Christ's experiments with Klein's model of the United States suggest that a

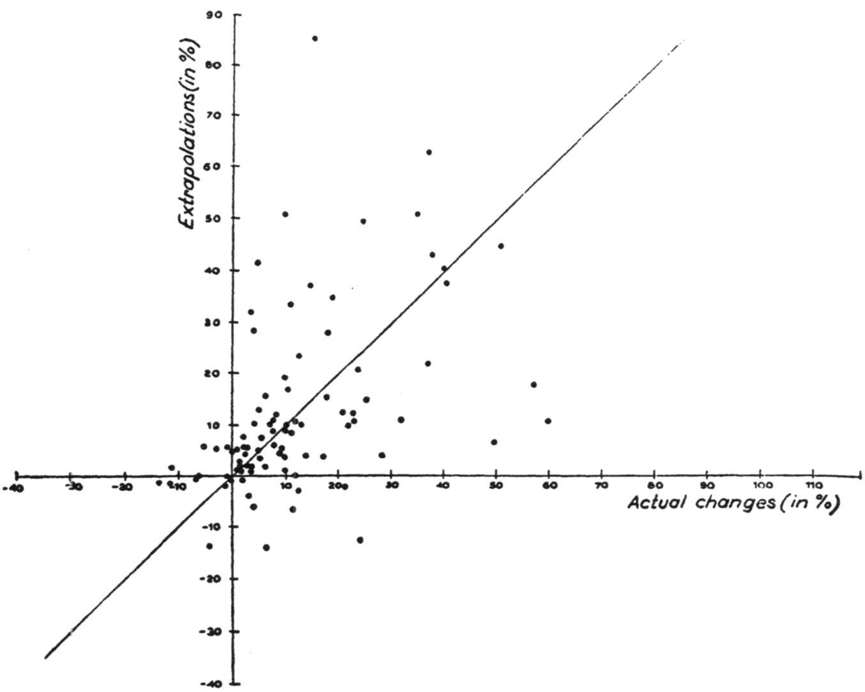

Diagram 3: Extrapolations for the Netherlands

favourable comparison with this extrapolation is by no means trivial[2] —, so that it may seem preferable to extrapolate in a more refined way. As the possibilities in this field are almost unlimited, the best way seems to be to use an extrapolation method which is bound to lead to a maximum of forecasting success in some sense. Therefore, for each variable an "extrapolation factor" k has been determined such that the regression $A_t = kA_{t-1}$ leads to minimum residual variance; these factors, which are of course positive for most variables, are summarised in the Appendix. The Diagrams 5 and 6 show, however, that the forecast kA_{t-1} of A_t leads to results that are still considerably below the level of the

---

[2] C. Christ: 1951, "A Test of an Econometric Model for the United States, 1921-1947," *Conference on Business Cycles*, ed. by the National Bureau of Economic Research, New York, 35-107.

Diagrams 1 and 2. Given the extreme character of the second extrapolation method, the conclusion seems justified that no such method, based on the development of the variables considered since the preceding year, is able to compete with the actual forecasts made.

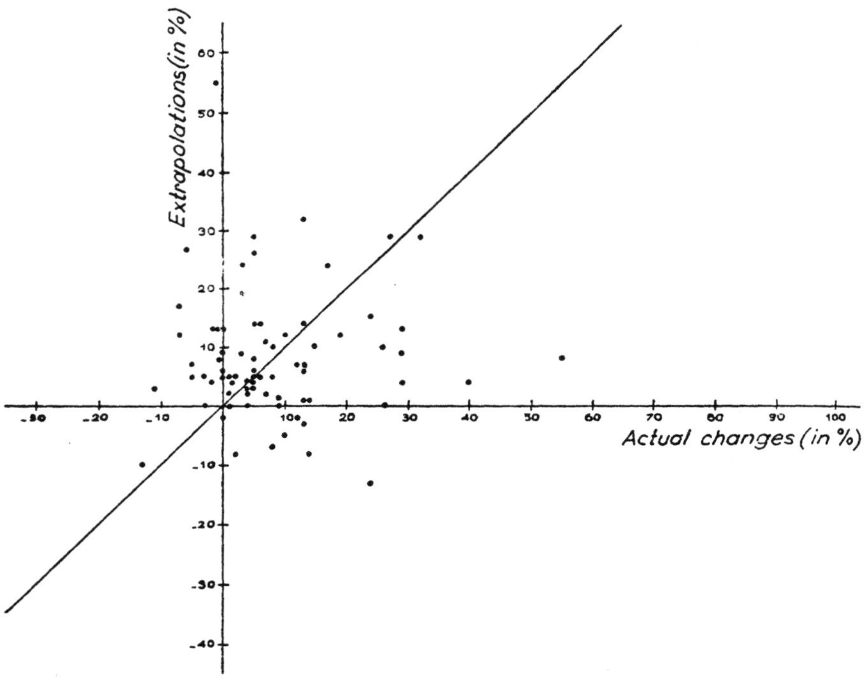

Diagram 4: Extrapolations for Scandinavia

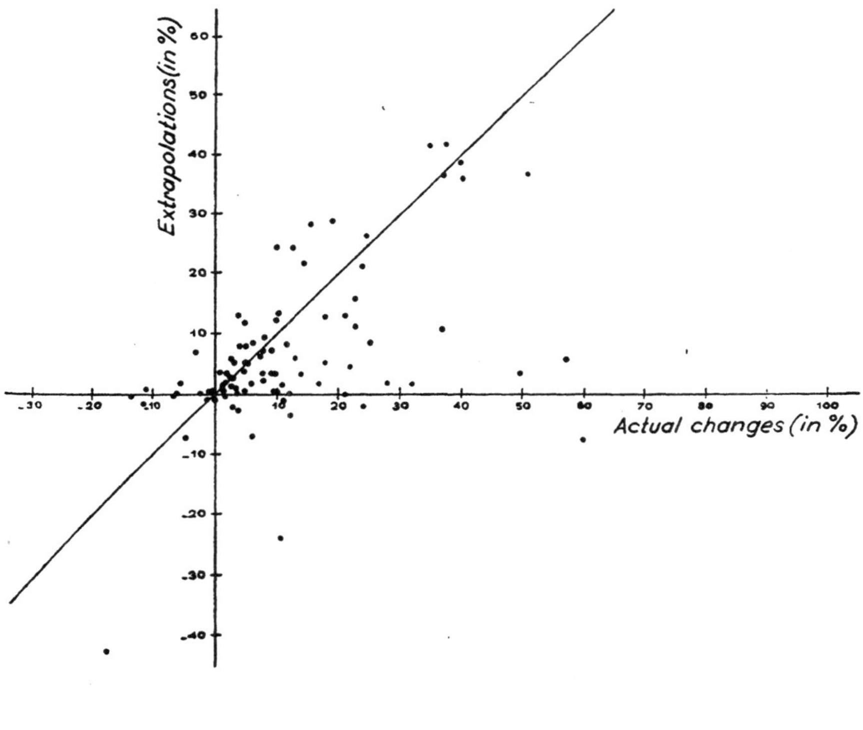

Diagram 5: Adjusted Extrapolations for The Netherlands

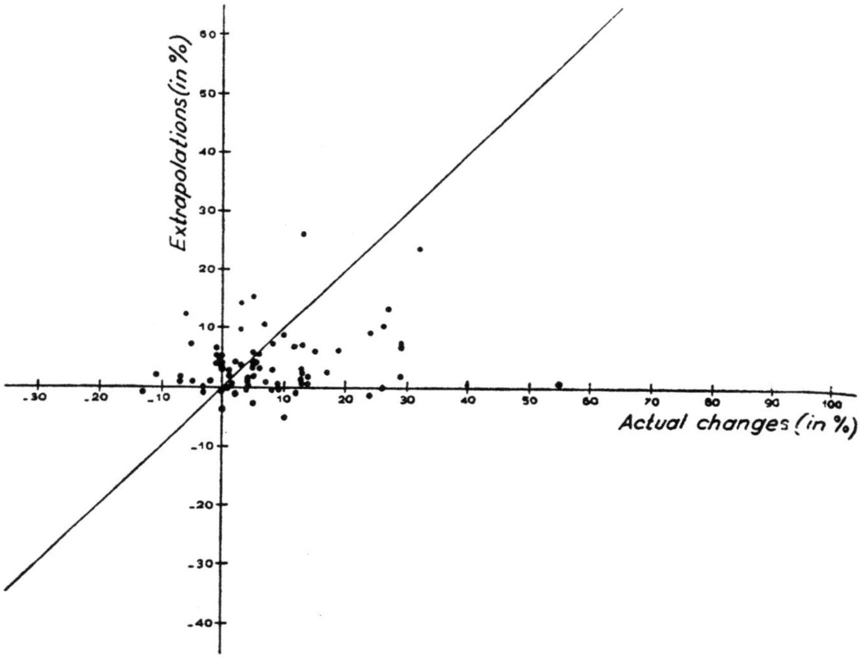

Diagram 6: Adjusted Extrapolations for Scandinavia

The mere fact that the percentage of wrongly predicted directions of change is so much larger for the simple extrapolation method than for the actual forecasts proves that most of the cases where increases were followed by decreases or *vice versa* have been predicted correctly in this respect. An example: in 1948 the volume of consumption in the Netherlands increased by 5.8 per cent, in 1949 it decreased by .9 per cent; the 1949-forecast was a decrease of 2 per cent, which is hence correct as far as signs are concerned. Table 1 gives a survey of all available cases.[3]

Table 1 Survey of Sign Changes (absolute frequencies)

	Actual Change		Forecasted Change		Correctly Forecasted Change	
In symbols →	$sgn\ A_t \neq sgn\ A_{t-1}$		$sgn\ P_t \neq sgn\ A_{t-1}$		both inequalities	
Netherlands total	14		18		13	
1949		2		3		2
1950		3		2		2
1951		1		2		1
1953		8		11		8
Scandinavia total	21		18		15	
Norway		4		6		3
Sweden		9		6		6
Denmark		8		6		6

Another problem which deserves our attention is that of accelerated and retarded developments. In 1949 e.g. the labour productivity in Dutch enterprises increased by 7.4 per cent, in 1950 by 5.2 per cent; there was hence a retardation, which has been predicted correctly, as the 1950-forecast was an increase of 4.7 per cent. A survey is given in Table 2.[4] It appears that about 80 per cent of the accelerations and retardations has been correctly predicted.

[3] Changes of sign which refer to three successive years (because the second year shows an $A_t = 0$) are considered as one change, and the appraisal in Table 1 is not influenced by the sign of the forecast made for this second year. One case (the Danish national product of 1951) has been "half-way" predicted, as the forecast was zero; this case is not represented in the last column of Table 1, because $sgn\ x \neq sgn\ y$ (cf. the second row of this table), has been interpreted as either $x > 0$, $y < 0$, or $x < 0$, $y > 0$.

[4] In this table all cases were excluded for which $A_t = A_{t-1}$. The boundary case $P_t = A_{t-1}$ is represented in the column "incorrectly forecasted."

Table 2 Survey of Accelerated and Retarded Developments (absolute frequencies)

	Correctly Forecasted		Incorrectly Forecasted		Total	
In symbols →	$sgn\ (P_t - A_{t-1}) = sgn\ (A_t - A_{t-1})$		$sgn\ (P_t - A_{t-1}) \neq sgn\ (A_t - A_{t-1})$			
Netherlands total	71		20		91	
1949		19		4		23
1950		15		7		22
1951		20		3		23
1953		17		6		23
Scandinavia total	62		12		74	
1949		15		3		18
1950		14		7		21
1951		20		1		21
1952		13		1		14
Norway		18		4		22
Sweden		25		4		29
Denmark		19		4		23

3. Systematic and Unsystematic Forecasting Errors

The results presented so far suggest that the forecasts, although they are not perfect, have in general yielded a valuable insight into next year's economic development. Nevertheless, they were not perfect. We shall now consider the forecasting errors $(P_t - A_t)$, which will be divided into two main types, viz. systematic and unsystematic errors.

One source of errors of the former type is that of an estimation of the absolute levels of the variables in some year, which is systematically too high or too low. As the variables considered are for the greater part positively associated with general trade cycle fluctuations, this would mean that next year's cyclical position is over or under-estimated, respectively. Now the Diagrams 1 and 2 suggest that there is no reason to suppose the existence of this type of error for the period analysed as a whole; but, when considering separate years, it seems that the cyclical position was overestimated somewhat for the Netherlands in 1951 and for Norway and Sweden in 1952, whereas an under-estimation took place for Sweden in 1949 and for the Netherlands in 1953. But these conclusions are quite tentative, as the number of observations per country per year is rather limited.

A more important source of systematic errors is that of the underestimation of changes. For the Netherlands e.g. about 70 per cent of the points lying to the right of the vertical axis in Diagram 1 are below the line $P = A$. In other words, if we consider the linear regression (through the origin) of predictions on corresponding actual values, $P = mA$, then we shall find $m < 1$. This has been analysed as follows. The point sets of the Diagrams 1 and 2 show a clear heteroskedasticity in the sense that deviations from the regression $P = mA$ have a variance which increases monotonically with $|A|$. Actually, the assumption that this variance is a linear function of A^2 seems to be a reasonable approximation. Therefore, the following iteration procedure has been adopted. First, the medians of the individual ratios P/A were taken as estimates (m_N for the Netherlands, m_S for Scandinavia) of m. Next, the deviations $P - m_i A$ ($i = N,S$) have been squared and correlated with A^2. The graphical result is

$$(P - m_i A)^2 = 10 + 0.1\, A^2. \tag{1}$$

Generalised least-squares leads then to the following estimate of m:

$$\Sigma \frac{PA}{10 + 0.1\, A^2} \Big/ \Sigma \frac{A^2}{10 + 0.1\, A^2}, \tag{2}$$

which turns out to be 0.7 for the Netherlands and 0.55 for Scandinavia, so that the predicted changes were about 70 per cent on the average of the corresponding actual changes in the Netherlands, and about 55% in Scandinavia.[5] In other words: the Dutch forecasts would have to be increased by 40 per cent and the Scandinavian ones by 80 per cent in order that this type of systematic error would be eliminated. These figures are however not fully the same if we consider separate years, although they are consistently below unity; this is shown in Table 3, where outcomes according to (2) per country or group of countries per year are given.

---

[5] No more rounds were made in the iteration, as this would not lead to appreciable refinements, the difference between these estimates and the corresponding first estimates (the medians m_N and m_S) being already small; it will moreover be observed that no account has been taken in (2) of non-zero correlations among the deviations $P - mA$. The graphically derived regression (1) has been based on grouped observations, up to 25 for the largest values of A^2. It is perhaps interesting to note that the functional form of (1) is the same as that of the relationship between the variance of a predicted value of the dependent variable in a two-variables regression problem and the independent variable.

Furthermore, it should be noted that the above analysis has been carried out in the following sense: given the actual outcomes A, how are the forecasts P distributed around these outcomes? This approach is not the same as the one implied by the question: given the forecasts P, how are the actual outcomes A distributed around these P's? The latter approach (the one of the "second regression line") gives a more favourable picture of the degree of underestimation of changes; but nevertheless, even this approach shows a general underestimation.

Table 3 Survey of Means of Forecasts as Fractions of Actual Changes

	Mean fraction			Mean fraction	
Netherlands total	0.7		Scandinavia total	0.55	
1949		0.6	1949		0.6
1950		0.6	1950		0.5
1951		0.9	1951		0.6
1953		0.7	1952		0.5
			Norway		0.4
			Sweden		0.6
			Denmark		0.6

The above algebraic results have been sketched in the Diagrams 1 and 2 by means of broken lines and curves. The straight lines are $P = 0.7\ A$ and $P = 0.55\ A$, respectively, and they give a graphical picture of the average degree of underestimation. The curves are

$$P = 0.7A \pm \sqrt{(10 + 0.1A^2)}$$
$$P = 0.55A \pm \sqrt{(10 + 0.1A^2)},$$

respectively; they give, for each value of A, the standard deviation of P around its mean. About two thirds of the points are situated within the limits of these curves. We may therefore say, in an elementary fashion, that these curves describe the unsystematic errors made.

The most convenient way to describe the systematic error of underestimation is perhaps that of a "conservatism with respect to a zero change." The question arises whether there are more such conservatisms. One of them is perhaps the most interesting, viz. "conservatism with respect to last year's change." This conservatism would be perfect if all forecasts P_t would be identical with A_{t-1}. Needless to say, they are not, for this follows from the difference between the Diagrams 1 and 3, and 2 and 4; but it is nevertheless possible that the forecasters were to some extent influenced by such elementary extrapolation ideas. In order to test this hypothesis, the following equation seems useful:

$$P_t = \alpha_1 A_t + \alpha_2 A_{t-1}. \tag{3}$$

Perfect forecasting requires $\alpha_1 = 1$, $\alpha_2 = 0$ and zero residuals. Conservatism with respect to a zero change without conservatism with respect to last year's change implies $0 < \alpha_1 < 1$, $\alpha_2 = 0$; and if there is some conservatism of the latter type, we should expect $\alpha_2 > 0$.

For each of the 23 Dutch and 23 Scandinavian variables, equation (3) has been estimated by least-squares; as the number of observations per variable is only 4 or less, this method is as good as any other. It appears (see the Appendix) that by far the greater part of the α_1-estimates is positive and smaller than unity, according to expectation. As to the α_2-estimates, they are equally often positive and negative for the Netherlands, whereas there is a two-thirds positive majority in Scandinavia. Hence, if there is some conservatism with respect to last year's change, it is more likely to exist in Scandinavia than in the Netherlands.

4. The Influence of the Time of Publication

The above shows that in general the Dutch forecasts have been better than the Scandinavian ones. Of course, it is impossible to analyse only comparable variables in comparable circumstances, but the following arguments seem nevertheless convincing: (i) the conservatism with respect to zero changes is less in the Netherlands, (ii) conservatism with respect to last year's changes is more likely to exist in Scandinavia, and (iii) there are presumably no appreciable differences between the variances of the unsystematic errors as functions of actual changes, but when the systematic error sub (i) is eliminated by increasing the Dutch forecasts by 40 per cent and the Scandinavian ones by 80 per cent (cf. section 3.3), this would lead to larger unsystematic errors of the latter forecasts.

However, whereas the Scandinavian forecasts were generally published in the beginning of the year to which they refer, the publication data of the Dutch forecasts were often much later, sometimes even in the second half of the year. Although the actual statistical information is often considerably lagging, so that such "forecasts" may nevertheless be valuable, it seems rather plausible that this aspect may have contributed to their quality. This will now be considered.

The simplest way of investigating the influence of time on the success of forecasting is to analyse the successive unpublished versions of the Dutch forecasts. To take an example: there are four versions of the Central Economic Plan of 1949, viz. three preliminary versions (of August 1948, May 1949 and September 1949) and the final version. Two successive versions imply, for each variable, a revision — either a successful or an unsuccessful revision.[6] An example: in August 1948 an increase of 4.2 per cent in Government wages was estimated; in May 1949 this was revised to a decrease of 0.7 per cent; the actual result was a decrease of 6.5 per cent, so that this revision was a successful one.

---

[6] A successful revision is defined as one for which $|P'' - A| < |P' - A|$; for these symbols, cf. inequality (4) below.

As a whole, 97 revisions were available,[7] of which 60 were successful. Table 4 shows that the fraction of success exceeded ½ for each of the years, but that there is an appreciable difference in success between large and small changes. For changes which turned out to be less than 5 per cent, the number of successful revisions is about the same as the number of failures, whereas the former number is considerably larger than the latter when forecasts of actual changes exceeding 15 per cent are considered. Some of these revisions are however quite small; but if all revisions are disregarded which lead to an amelioration or deterioration of less than 10 per cent of the original forecast,

$$\big|\,|P''-A| - |P'-A|\,\big| < 0.1\ |P'| \tag{4}$$

(P' being the original and P'' the revised forecast), then the conclusion — cf. the lower half of Table 4 — remains the same.

Table 4 Survey of Success of Revisions (absolute frequencies)

(a) Per year				
	1949	1950	1951	1953
Success Failure	20 12	20 10	10 8	10 7
(b) According to the magnitude of actual changes				
	$\|A\|$ less than 5%	$\|A\|$ between 5% and 15%	$\|A\|$ more than 15%	Total
Success Failure	13 14	23 17	24 6	60 37
(c) As (a), excluding revisions obeying inequality (4)				
	1949	1950	1951	1953
Success Failure	18 10	15 7	6 4	9 7
(d) As (b), excluding revisions obeying inequality (4)				
	$\|A\|$ less than 5%	$\|A\|$ between 5% and 15%	$\|A\|$ more than 15%	Total
Success Failure	11 12	18 11	19 5	48 28

[7] This number was reduced by the fact that not all variables analysed in this paper were considered in the preliminary versions. A survey of revisions is given in the Appendix; two of them have reference to non-successive versions.

The question arises whether this partial success of revisions must be considered as a corroboration of the assertion that the difference in forecasting achievements between the Netherlands and Scandinavia must be partly or wholly ascribed to unequal dates of publication. The most satisfactory way of answering this question is presumably to analyse the degree of conservatism with respect to zero changes for those preliminary Dutch versions which were made around January of the year to which they refer.[8] This leads to 44 observations, which give, according to formula (2), an estimate of slightly below 0.6 for the mean ratio of (preliminary) forecasts to corresponding actual changes. This is evidently much closer to the Scandinavian figure than to the original Dutch one. Although this outcome is unfavourably influenced by the less-than-proportionate representation of the "good" year 1951, it seems reasonable to conclude that a considerable part of the Netherlands' first place in achievements should be ascribed to its last place in the dates of publication.

5. Remarks on Separate Variables

So far, no attention has been paid to separate variables. All forecasts of all variables have been put together, which is of course a prerequisite in order to obtain a sufficient mass of information. But it is, in two respects, necessary to make a correction on the idea that no differences exist with respect to the forecasting achievements for separate variables.

First, it appears that variables the annual changes of which are less than about 5 per cent on the average have been predicted more accurately than the broken curves of the Diagrams 1 and 2 suggest. This follows from the fact that for these variables the "standardized" forecasting errors (corrected both for the systematic understatement of changes and for the unsystematic variation),

$$\frac{P - mA}{\sqrt{(10 + 0.1A^2)}} \qquad (m = 0.7 \text{ for the Netherlands; } 0.55 \text{ for Scandinavia})$$

have a smaller variance. Hence the margin of error is not only determined by the magnitude of the actual change to be predicted, but also by the average variability of the variable considered. This is perhaps self-evident: an increase of 5 per cent of a normally highly fluctuating variable like net investment will usually be predicted less accurately than the same increase of a relatively rigid variable, e.g. the volume of consumption.

Secondly, there exists a natural difference in forecasting power with respect to certain variables. The Dutch import price level e.g. has been forecasted amazingly well, in spite of its substantial changes; but no variables of this country have been predicted

[8] These versions are: May 1949 for the year 1949, January 1950 for 1950, October 1950 for 1951, and March 1953 for 1953.

in spite of its substantial changes; but no variables of this country have been predicted so badly as the Government wages and the Government material expenditure (in spite of the fact that the forecasts were made by a Government office!) and the imports and exports of services. This outcome clearly reflects the unequal forecasting possibilities: the import price level is mainly determined — with a considerable lag — by the international raw material price level; but the above mentioned Government instruments had to be based on budget estimates, and very little is known of the international service sector. It is perhaps interesting to note that all errors (with only one exception) which have been made in the Netherlands with respect to sign changes — cf. Table 1 — have reference to these variables.

Appendix

Table 5 which follows contains, apart from the extrapolation factors and the estimates of equation (3), the forecast (*P*) and actual outcomes (*A*), which have been derived (a) for the Netherlands: from publications of the Central Bureau of Statistics, sometimes supplemented by computations of the Central Planning Bureau, (b) for Scandinavia: from the Economic Bulletin for Europe of July 1953, published by the Economic Commission for Europe.

Table 6 contains the forecasts according to the preliminary versions of the Dutch Central Economic Plans; they are derived from internal papers of the Central Planning Bureau. It should be noted that the September 1952-version, given below, is an average of four alternative versions prepared in that month, and that the March 1953-version is the "central case" alternative of that month.

Table 5 Survey of Forecasted and Actual Percentage Changes

	1948	1949		1950		1951		1952		1953		Extra-polation factor	ESTIMATES OF	
	A	P	A	P	A	P	A	P	A	P	A		a_1	a_2
Netherlands														
Consumption: price	+4.0	+3	+5.4	+5	+9.2	+9	+10	.	−0.8	−3.1	0	+1.31	+0.89	−0.23
volume	+5.8	−2	−0.9	+2	0	−1	−2.3	.	+1.9	+4.5	+3.7	+0.05	+0.83	−0.31
value	+10.1	+1.3	+4.4	+6.5	+9.1	+7.7	+7.9	.	+1.1	+2.3	+3.6	+0.78	+0.88	−0.12
Net investment (incl. inventories)	+33.8	+9.3	+10.7	+29.0	+60.0	−6.1	−17.5	.	−59.3	+66.9	+99.1	−0.71	+0.62	+0.04
Industrial production	+19.4	+8	+10	+6	+13	+10	+5	.	0	+6	+12	+0.60	+0.21	+0.42
Building activity	+41.7	+8	+5	+8	+5	3	0	.	−2.4	+18	+21	+0.10	+0.88	+0.10
Value added in the business sector	+16.8	+3.1	+10.4	+6.7	+11.9	+8.5	+8.1	.	+4.0	+2.1	+9.8	+0.79	+0.31	+0.15
Labour force	+4.6	+1.1	+2.5	+0.6	+1.5	+1.0	+1.3	.	+1.1	+1.1	+1.4	+0.61	+1.05	−0.32
Labour productivity	+10.1	+4	+7.4	+4.7	+5.2	+4.2	+1.0	.	+2.2	+5.2	+6.2	+0.70	+0.60	+0.14
Employment in business sector	+5.8	+0.6	+2.4	+1.2	+2.9	+1.5	+1.5	.	−0.6	+1.4	+1.8	+0.50	+0.63	−0.09
Employment in public sector	−2.0	−1.8	−1.1	−10.9	−13.5	−5.8	−4.3	.	+6.2	+5.3	+7.9	+0.55	+0.79	+0.19
Wages and salaries paid by Government	−0.8	−0.7	−6.5	−3.2	+11.4	+5.4	+7.9	.	+1.3	+7.3	+9.8	+0.19	+0.08	+0.57
Government purchases of goods and services	+20.5	+6.7	+23.7	+5.0	+12.5	+42.9	+21.0	.	+10.8	+26.1	+22.8	+1.03	+2.14	−1.10
Indirect taxes minus subsidies	+62.9	+38.5	+37.3	+14.9	+14.6	+16.9	+25.4	.	−3.8	+4.6	+3.2	+0.58	+0.65	+0.19
Commodity exports: price	0	−3	−6	+9	+4	+13	+17	.	+1.7	−7	−11	+0.46	+0.75	−0.04
volume	+44.9	+24	+51	+23	+35	+27	+19	.	+4.0	+4	+14	+0.82	−0.12	+0.63
value	+43.5	+23.0	+37.6	+32.5	+40.5	+43.4	+40.2	.	+5.9	−0.6	+2.8	+0.96	+0.95	−0.11
Commodity imports: price	+5.3	−3	−3	+12.4	+12.4	+21.0	+22.9	.	−1.5	−12	−11.5	+1.28	+0.96	−0.14
volume	+8.7	+9	+11	+20	+32	+9	+3	.	−12.6	+19	+24	+0.17	+0.63	+0.21
value	+15.7	+6.4	+6.3	+35.1	+49.6	+32.1	+24.6	.	−13.9	+9.3	+6.2	+0.53	+0.68	+0.28
Exports of services: value	+50.9	+2	+10	+8	+22	+15	+37	.	+7.6	−11	+2	+0.48	+0.50	−0.16
Imports of services: value	+28.7	−2	+4	+5	+28	−1	+18	.	+9.7	−1	+10	+0.45	+0.18	−0.13
Surplus on the balance of services	+85.5	+5.9	+15.5	+10.8	+17.7	+24.5	+57.2	.	+5.9	−15.1	−5.1	+0.33	+0.51	−0.08
Norway														
National products	+4	+3.5	+5	+2	+5	+2	+2	+3	+1			+0.81	+0.28	+0.34
Industrial production	+12	+6	+10	+4	+8	+4	+5	+4	0			+0.72	−0.39	+0.77
Building activity	−8	+4	+14	−4	+5	−6	−3	.	.			−0.20	+0.14	−0.39
Commodity exports: price	.	−5	0	0	4	+8	+40	+3	0			+0.10	+0.19	+0.08
volume	.	+7	0	+11	+26	+3	+5	+3	−5			+0.15	+0.38	+0.08
Commodity imports: price	.	0	−2	+13	+12	+14	+19	+7	+3			+0.51	+0.79	+0.13
volume	.	+6	+14	−3	+6	−5	+13	+7	0			+0.40	−0.65	+0.31
Sweden														
Gross fixed investment	−2	−4	0	+5	+9	+3	+3	+4	+4			+0.41	+0.56	+0.27
National products	+6	+1.5	+5	+2.5	+6	+3	0	+2	+1			+0.62	+0.01	+0.41
Industrial production	.	.	.	+4	+4	+4	+4	+1	−2			+0.25	+0.50	+0.50
Building activity	−8	−5	+2	+5	+4	+2	+1.5	+5	+9			+0.14	+0.48	+0.70
Commodity exports: price	+12	−7	−7	+3	+8	+24	+55	+3	−1			+0.07	+0.44	+0.04
volume	+10	+3	+15	+6	+24	+5	+3	−8	−11			+0.60	+0.27	+0.07
Commodity imports: price	+5	0	+1	+12	+13	+21	+21	+4	+5			+0.52	+0.76	−0.01
volume	−10	−13	−13	+12	+24	+5	+17	−4	−7			+0.09	+0.53	−0.03
Denmark														
Gross fixed investment	+1	+12	+14	+5	+13	−6	−1	.	.			+0.50	+0.86	−0.42
National products	+3	+4	+5	+3	+8	0	−0.5	.	.			+0.52	+0.48	+0.03
Industrial production	+11	+5	+7	+4	+12	.	.	0	−5			+0.95	+0.11	+0.39
Building activity	+2	+4	+7	+7	+13	−7	−1	.	.			+0.41	+0.77	−0.47
Commodity exports: price	+9	0	0	−3	−3	+8	+13	.	.			−0.43	+0.64	+0.01
volume	+9	+20	+29	+10	+32	+8	+13	.	.			+0.82	+0.57	−0.10
Commodity imports: price	+7	+2	−5	+13	+10	+30	+26	.	.			+1.01	+1.04	+0.39
volume	+4	+25	+29	+5	+27	−10	−6	.	.			+0.46	+0.74	−0.36

Table 6 Survey of Provisional Dutch Forecasts

Versions of -	May 1949	Sept. 1949
1949		
Consumption: value	+ 1.6	+ 3.1
Net investment (incl. inventories)	- 7.2	+ 14.7
Value added in the business sector	+ 2.4	+ 3.2
Wages and salaries paid by the Government	- 0.7	- 5.1
Government purchases of goods and services	+ 19.5	+ 2.2
Indirect taxes minus subsidies	+ 38.5	+ 56.5
Commodity exports: value	+ 17.9	+ 19.2
Commodity imports: value	+ 0.8	+ 6.0
Exports of services: value	0	+ 3.4
Imports of services: value	0	+ 2.6
Surplus on the balance of services	0	+ 4.2
Versions of -	**Jan. 1950**	**July 1950**
1950		
Consumption: price	+ 5.1	+ 4.8
volume	+ 1.8	- 0.4
value	+ 7.0	+ 4.4
Net investment (incl. inventories)	+ 5.0	+ 21.2
Industrial production	+ 5.5	+ 6.4
Value added in the business sector	.	+ 7.1
Labour force	+ 1.0	+ 0.6
Labour productivity	+ 4.3	+ 5.7
Employment in the business sector	+ 1.0	+ 1.2
Employment in the public sector	- 6.5	- 10.9
Wages and salaries paid by the Government	0	- 9.2
Government purchases of goods and services	+ 19.6	+ 37.3
Indirect taxes minus subsidies	.	+ 5.8
Commodity exports: volume	.	.
value	+ 30.3	+ 32.5
Commodity imports: volume	.	.
value	+ 21.9	+ 32.3
Surplus on the balance of services	.	+ 10.8

Versions of -	Oct. 1950	July 1951
1951		
Consumption: price	.	+ 9
volume	.	- 1
value	.	+ 7.7
Net investment (incl. inventories)	.	- 6.1
Industrial production	.	+ 9.8
Building activity	.	+ 3.3
Value added in the business sector	.	+ 8.5
Labour force	.	+ 1.1
Labour productivity	+ 4.4	+ 4.0
Employment in the business sector	.	+ 1.5
Employment in the public sector	.	- 5.2
Wages and salaries paid by the Government	.	+ 5.3
Government purchases of goods and services	.	+ 42.9
Indirect taxes minus subsidies	.	+ 16.9
Commodity exports: price	+ 9.2	+ 13
volume	+ 17.5	+ 27
value	+ 29.8	+ 43.7
Commodity imports: price	+ 16.8	+ 21
volume	+ 4.9	+ 9
value	+ 22.1	+ 31.7
Exports of services: value	.	+ 12.6
Imports of services: value	.	- 3
Surplus of the balance of services	.	+ 22.2
Versions of -	**Sept. 1952**	**March 1953**
1953		
Consumption: price	+ 2.9	- 2.6
volume	+ 1.4	+ 3.6
value	+ 4.3	+ 0.9
Net investment (incl. inventories)	.	+ 66.2
Building activity	.	+ 18
Labour productivity	.	+ 6.3
Wages and salaries paid by the Government	.	+ 7.3
Government purchases of goods and services	.	+ 26.1
Indirect taxes minus subsidies	.	+ 3.5
Commodity exports: price	- 1.6	- 4.8
volume	+ 3.3	+ 2.6
value	+ 1.7	- 2.3
Commodity imports: price	- 0.5	- 7.0

CHAPTER 68

SOME OBSERVATIONS ON ADAPTIVE FORECASTING*

H. THEIL
Econometric Institute,
Netherlands School of Economics
(now Erasmus University),
Rotterdam, The Netherlands

S. WAGE
Econometric Institute,
Netherlands School of Economics
(now Erasmus University),
Rotterdam, The Netherlands

1. Introduction

The procedure of "adaptive" or "exponential" forecasting is based on weighted averages of two sources of evidence; one is the latest evidence (the most recent observation), the other the value computed one period before. As such, it is an easy, quick and cheap method; very little information is needed for a forecast; also, the most recent information is used. Reference is made to Brown (1959), Winters (1960a, 1960b) and Muth (1960) for contributions to this method.

This article serves a dual purpose. One is to simplify the forecasting procedure and to clarify its characteristics in the simplest possible manner. This objective is pursued in sections 2-4. The second purpose is to formulate a probabilistic model underlying the prediction procedure and to select weights which minimize the mean-square prediction error. Sections 5 and 6 are devoted to that purpose.

2. The Forecasting Procedure

Many economic time series show a seasonal pattern around a trend movement. The easiest way of handling this is by assuming an additive seasonal pattern and a linear trend. But this assumption is frequently not realistic. One may argue, as Winters did, that a multiplicative seasonal pattern is usually much more realistic, but its combination with a linear trend is mathematically cumbersome. At the same time it is frequently also more realistic to work with an exponential rather than a linear trend; and it is easily seen that a replacement of the values of the original time series by their logarithms transforms the exponential trend into a linear one and simultaneously the multiplicative seasonal pattern into a linear pattern. Therefore, the decomposition of our time series x_t will be as follows:

* Reprinted by permission, "Some Observations on Adaptive Forecasting," H. Theil and S. Wage, *Management Science*, **10**, (Jan. 1964), 198-206, copyright 1964, The Institute of Management Science, 290 Westminster Street, Providence, RI 02903, U.S.A.

$$x_t = \bar{x}_t + s_t + \text{residual} \tag{2.1}$$

$$\bar{x}_t = \bar{x}_{t-1} + e_t, \tag{2.2}$$

where $\bar{x}_t$ is the trend value, e_t the trend change, s_t the seasonal coefficient, and where it is to be understood that all symbols refer to logarithms (if necessary). It should be noted that the procedure of taking logarithms has certain advantages with respect to the mean-square prediction error criterion that will be applied in section 6 below, because it implies that the errors are measured as a fraction of the level to be predicted and not absolutely. The linear formulation (2.1)-(2.2) has also considerable mathematical advantages with respect to adaptive forecasting, which we shall consider now, because this prediction method is essentially linear too.

Let us first consider the trend level and see how it can be computed as a weighted average of new evidence and the value computed one period before (see the first sentence of section 1). At the end of the tth period we have the observation x_t at our disposal and from (2.1) we see that this is equal to $\bar{x}_t$ apart from s_t and the residual. However, no information is available on the residual and on s_t. The residual is replaced by zero and for s_t we take the most recent value, s_{t-L}, as a substitute, where L stands for the length of the seasonal cycle. (For example, $L = 12$ if we have monthly data and an annual period.) We regard $x_t - s_{t-L}$ as the "new evidence" on the trend level. The latest trend value is $\bar{x}_{t-1}$, but this refers to $t - 1$, not to t. We have to add e_t to obtain $\bar{x}_t$, see (2.2), but since e_t is not yet available we take last period's trend change e_{t-1} instead. This leads to the following weighted-average procedure for $\bar{x}_t$:

$$\bar{x}_t = \alpha(x_t - s_{t-L}) + (1 - \alpha)(\bar{x}_{t-1} + e_{t-1}), \tag{2.3}$$

which, given the weights α and $1 - \alpha$, describes $\bar{x}_t$ in terms of the most recent observation (x_t) and previous computed values ($\bar{x}_{t-1}$, e_{t-1}, s_{t-L}).[1]

It will be clear that this computation of $\bar{x}_t$ is by no means perfect, in particular because no account is taken of the residual in (2.1). Therefore, although one might feel justified in using (2.2) for the derivation of e_t, so that this trend change would then be defined as the difference between the $\bar{x}_t$ of (2.3) and the previous $\bar{x}_{t-1}$, it is evidently better not to rely on this difference completely. In fact, the method of adaptive forecasting considers it as new evidence on the trend change and combines it with the old value e_{t-1}:

$$e_t = \beta(\bar{x}_t - \bar{x}_{t-1}) + (1 - \beta)e_{t-1}, \tag{2.4}$$

[1] Equation (2.3) corresponds with equation (11) of Winters (1960a), except that ours is simpler because of the additive seasonal pattern. In the same way our equations (2.4), (2.5) and (2.7) correspond to Winters' equations (12), (13), and (14) respectively.

where β and $1 - \beta$ are the weights of the two sources of evidence. Finally, the same procedure is applied to s_t. The new evidence on the seasonal coefficient is $x_t - \bar{x}_t$, the old value is s_{t-L}. So:

$$s_t = \gamma(x_t - \bar{x}_t) + (1 - \gamma)\, s_{t-L} \,. \tag{2.5}$$

All three pairs of weights will be taken to be positive fractions:

$$0 < \alpha \,, \beta \,, \gamma < 1 \,. \tag{2.6}$$

The determination of their precise numerical values will be considered in sections 5 and 6 below.

Adaptive forecasting is now a relatively simple affair. Suppose that we are at the end of the tth period, so that $\bar{x}_t$, e_t, s_t, s_{t-1}, . . . are at our disposal, see equations (2.3)-(2.5). Suppose also that we wish to predict $x_{t+\tau}$ (τ periods ahead); then we extrapolate the most recent trend change, use the most recent seasonal coefficient for that period and neglect the residual. Specifically, if P_t stands for the prediction operator given the knowledge available at the end of the tth period,

$$P_t\, x_{t+r} = \bar{x}_t + \tau e_t + s_{t-L+\tau}\,, \tag{2.7}$$

provided that $0 < \tau \leq L$. If $L < \tau \leq 2L$ one replaces $s_{t-L+\tau}$ by $s_{t-2L+\tau}$, etc.

3. The Adaptation Equations

We can rewrite equation (2.3) as follows:

$$\begin{aligned} \bar{x}_t - (\bar{x}_{t-1} + e_{t-1}) &= \alpha\,[x_t - (\bar{x}_{t-1} + e_{t-1} + s_{t-L})] \\ &= \alpha\,(x_t - P_{t-1}x_t) = -\alpha f_{t-1,t}, \text{ say,} \end{aligned} \tag{3.1}$$

see (2.7). On the left we have the trend value in t minus the adjusted old value. On the right we have the forecast error ($f_{t-1,t}$) of the prediction for t made at the end to t - 1, multiplied by $-\alpha$. Thus, the procedure (2.3) amounts simply to adapting the old value of the trend value, the adaptation being negatively proportional to the most recent forecast error. When the observation x_t exceeds (is below) the prediction $P_{t-1}x_t$, we raise (lower) the old trend value $\bar{x}_{t-1} + e_{t-1}$.

There are two other adaptation equations. We easily obtain from (2.3)-(2.5):

$$e_t - e_{t-1} = -\alpha\beta f_{t-1,t} \tag{3.2}$$

$$s_t - s_{t-L} = -(1-\alpha)\gamma f_{t-1,t}. \tag{3.3}$$

Thus the adjustments of the trend change and the seasonal coefficients are also negatively proportional to the most recent forecast error, the proportionality factors being $\alpha\beta$ and $(1-\alpha)\gamma$ respectively. From (3.2) and (3.3) we conclude that given β and γ, the seasonal adjustments tend to be larger than the trend adjustments when α is small and *vice versa.* This is the direct consequence of (2.3): when α is small, this means that $\bar{x}_t$ relies much more heavily on the trend-corrected $\bar{x}_{t-1}$ than on the seasonally corrected x_t; it is therefore natural that the seasonal coefficients are subject to larger revisions than the trend changes, since the latter are implicitly considered to be more stable.

4. A Recursive Versus a Simultaneous Approach

The procedure (2.3), (2.4) and (2.5) is "recursive" in the sense that one uses past data on season and trend to find $\bar{x}_t$, after which one uses this $\bar{x}_t$ to obtain new values of season and trend. But it is evident from the second paragraph of section 3 that the use of past data for the computation of $\bar{x}_t$ is only a surrogate; it would be better to use current values. We therefore consider a more "simultaneous" approach, implying that (2.3) is replaced by

$$\bar{x}_t = \alpha(x_t - s_t) + (1-\alpha)(\bar{x}_{t-1} + e_t), \tag{4.1}$$

while (2.4) and (2.5) remain as they are. By substituting these into (4.1) we obtain

$$\begin{aligned}\bar{x}_t &= \alpha[x_t - \gamma(x_t - \bar{x}_t) - (1-\gamma)s_{t-L}] + (1-\alpha)[\bar{x}_{t-1} + \beta(\bar{x}_t - \bar{x}_{t-1}) + (1-\beta)e_{t-1}] \\ &= [\alpha\gamma + (1-\alpha)\beta]\bar{x}_t + \alpha(1-\gamma)(x_t - s_{t-L}) + (1-\alpha)(1-\beta)(\bar{x}_{t-1} + e_{t-1})\end{aligned}$$

and hence

$$\begin{aligned}\bar{x}_t &= \{\alpha(1-\gamma)/(1-\alpha\gamma-(1-\alpha)\beta)\}(x_t - s_{t-L}) \\ &\quad + \{(1-\alpha)(1-\beta)/(1-\alpha\gamma-(1-\alpha)\beta)\}(\bar{x}_{t-1} + e_{t-1}) \\ &= \alpha'(x_t - s_{t-L}) + (1-\alpha')(\bar{x}_{t-1} + e_{t-1})\end{aligned} \tag{4.2}$$

with $0 < \alpha' < 1$, which is of the same general form as (2.3). The results (3.1), (3.2) and (3.3) remain unaffected, except that α should be replaced by α'. Note that $\alpha' = \alpha$ when $\beta = \gamma$.

5. A Stochastic Model

The arguments used in the preceding pages explain precisely how the forecasts are made but they are far from explicit with respect to the justification of the method. In fact, this is the reason why Winters had to be completely empirical when determining the optimal values of the weights α, β, γ. A much more satisfactory procedure is to formulate an explicit stochastic model as a basis for the forecasting method. This will be done here for the simplest case and under the simplest conditions; the former implies that we disregard seasonality and consider only forecasts one period ahead, the latter that we impose zero means and constant variances and zero covariances throughout. Specifically, we write

$$x_t = \xi_t + u_t \tag{5.1}$$

$$\xi_t = \xi_{t-1} + \eta_t , \tag{5.2}$$

where ξ_t is the mean of x_t and η_t the trend change from period t - 1 to period t. These equations are analogous to (2.1)-(2.2) and from now on we shall interpret $\bar{x}_t$ and e_t as estimators of ξ_t and η_t respectively. Note that the parent analogue of s_t is absent here. This is due to the fact that we postulate the absence of seasonality, so that all s's and γ of the preceding equations will be interpreted as zero from now on.

The trend change η_t is postulated to be generated by

$$\eta_t = \eta_{t-1} + v_t , \tag{5.3}$$

where v_t as well as u_t are time series with zero mean, constant variance and zero covariances of all kinds:

$$\begin{aligned}
\mathscr{E}u_t &= \mathscr{E}v_t = 0 \\
\mathscr{E}(u_t u_{t'}) &= \sigma_u^2 \quad \text{if } t = t' \\
&= 0 \quad \text{if } t \neq t' \\
\mathscr{E}(v_t v_{t'}) &= \sigma_v^2 \quad \text{if } t = t' \\
&= 0 \quad \text{if } t \neq t' \\
\mathscr{E}(u_t v_{t'}) &= 0 \quad \text{for all pairs } (t, t') .
\end{aligned} \tag{5.4}$$

Note that these probabilistic conditions can be considered as implicitly underlying the prediction equation (2.7). To make this clear, let us disregard the seasonal coefficient of that equation, so that the forecast of $x_{t+\tau}$ becomes $\bar{x}_t + \tau e_t$, which in turn can be regarded as an estimator of $\xi_t + \tau\eta_t$. The latter expression does not contain $u_t, u_{t-1}, \ldots$, which can be interpreted in the sense that $u_{t+\tau}$ is considered to be uncorrelated with these previous u's. A similar argument can be applied to $v_{t+\tau}$, and $v_t, v_{t-1}, \ldots$.

At the end of the tth period we make a forecast of x_{t+1}, using (2.7). The forecast error is

$$\begin{aligned} f_{t,t+1} &= \bar{x}_t + e_t - x_{t+1} = \bar{x}_t + e_t - (\xi_t + \eta_t + v_{t+1} + u_{t+1}) \\ &= A_t + B_t - u_{t+1} - v_{t+1}, \end{aligned} \tag{5.5}$$

where

$$A_t = \bar{x}_t - \xi_t; \qquad B_t = e_t - \eta_t. \tag{5.6}$$

Hence the forecast error is the sum of three terms: one is the sampling error of the expected value of the series in t; the second is the sampling error of the trend change in t; and the third is a disturbance combination which refers to $t + 1$, not to t.

Using the adaptation equations (3.1)-(3.2), we can eliminate the sampling errors A_t and B_t successively. Let us write (3.1) in the form:

$$\bar{x}_t - \xi_t - (\bar{x}_{t-1} - \xi_{t-1}) - (e_{t-1} - \xi_t + \xi_{t-1}) = -\alpha f_{t-1,t},$$

then some minor further rearrangements are sufficient to show that A_t can be written as follows:

$$A_t = (1 - \alpha)(A_{t-1} + B_{t-1}) + \alpha u_t - (1 - \alpha) v_t. \tag{5.7}$$

In the same way we obtain for B_t:

$$B_t = -\alpha\beta A_{t-1} + (1 - \alpha\beta) B_{t-1} + \alpha\beta u_t - (1 - \alpha\beta) v_t. \tag{5.8}$$

6. Mean-Square Error Minimization

Our objective will be to determine the adaptation parameters α and β such as to minimize the expected square of the forecast error $f_{t,t+1}$, given the assumptions (5.4) and the way in which the error depends on α, β, the u's and v's as shown in (5.5)-(5.8). It will prove useful to write (5.7)-(5.8) in vector form:

$$\begin{bmatrix} A_t \\ B_t \end{bmatrix} = P \begin{bmatrix} A_{t-1} \\ B_{t-1} \end{bmatrix} + Q \begin{bmatrix} u_t \\ v_t \end{bmatrix}, \tag{6.1}$$

where

$$P = \begin{bmatrix} 1-\alpha & 1-\alpha \\ -\varepsilon & 1-\varepsilon \end{bmatrix}, \quad Q = \begin{bmatrix} \alpha & -(1-\alpha) \\ \varepsilon & -(1-\varepsilon) \end{bmatrix}, \quad \varepsilon = \alpha\beta. \tag{6.2}$$

Obviously, the optimal adjustment of α and ε is equivalent to the optimal adjustment of α and β.

By eliminating the vector $\{A_{t-1}\ B_{t-1}\}$ of (6.1) successively we obtain

$$\begin{bmatrix} A_t \\ B_t \end{bmatrix} = P^n \begin{bmatrix} A_{t-n} \\ B_{t-n} \end{bmatrix} + \sum_{k=0}^{n-1} P^k Q \begin{bmatrix} u_{t-k} \\ v_{t-k} \end{bmatrix}.$$

Now the first term on the right converges to zero for $n \to \infty$ when the latent roots of P are within the unit circle, which is indeed the case when α and β (and hence ε) are positive.[2] On combining this with (5.5) we find

$$f_{t,t+1} = [1 \quad 1] \sum_{k=0}^{\infty} P^k Q \begin{bmatrix} u_{t-k} \\ v_{t-k} \end{bmatrix} - u_{t+1} - v_{t+1}. \tag{6.3}$$

On squaring and taking the expectation we obtain[3]

[2] The latent roots are $1 - \eta \pm (\eta^2 - \varepsilon)^{1/2}$ where $\eta = \frac{1}{2}(\alpha + \varepsilon)$. When roots are real, $\varepsilon > 0$ is a sufficient condition in order that they be less than 1 in absolute value. When they are conjugate complex, the square of the absolute value is $1 - \alpha$, which is less than 1 if $\alpha > 0$.

[3] Since the series to be forecast is not stationary, there is no guarantee that the expression on the right of (6.4) converges. However, it is easily seen that the forecast errors are identical with the corresponding errors of the second differences of the original series, and these second differences form a stationary time series under our assumptions. See also the paper by Nerlove and Wage, "On the Optimality of Adaptive Forecasting," *Management Science*, **10**, No. 2 (Jan. 1964), 207-224.

$$\mathscr{E}f_{t,t+1}^2 = [1 \quad 1](QDQ' + PQDQ'P' + P^2QDQ'P'^2 + \ldots)\begin{bmatrix}1\\1\end{bmatrix} + \sigma_u^2 + \sigma_v^2 , \tag{6.4}$$

where

$$D = \begin{bmatrix}\sigma_u^2 & 0\\ 0 & \sigma_v^2\end{bmatrix}. \tag{6.5}$$

Our first problem is to simplify the expression on the right of (6.4). Let us write

$$S = QDQ' + PQDQ'P' + P^2QDQ'P'^2 + \ldots \tag{6.6}$$

and let us subtract

$$PSP' = PQDQ'P' + P^2QDQ'P'^2 + \ldots \quad .$$

The result is

$$S - PSP' = QDQ' , \tag{6.7}$$

which can be regarded as a set of linear equations in the three elements s_{11}, s_{12}, s_{22} of S. (It is obvious from (6.6) and (6.5) that S is symmetric, so that $s_{21} = s_{12}$.) We can write (6.7) in the following explicit form:

$$\begin{bmatrix}s_{11} & s_{12}\\ s_{12} & s_{22}\end{bmatrix} - \begin{bmatrix}1-\alpha & 1-\alpha\\ -\varepsilon & 1-\varepsilon\end{bmatrix}\begin{bmatrix}s_{11} & s_{12}\\ s_{12} & s_{22}\end{bmatrix}\begin{bmatrix}1-\alpha & -\varepsilon\\ 1-\alpha & 1-\varepsilon\end{bmatrix}$$

$$= \begin{bmatrix}\alpha & -(1-\alpha)\\ \varepsilon & -(1-\varepsilon)\end{bmatrix}\begin{bmatrix}\sigma_u^2 & 0\\ 0 & \sigma_v^2\end{bmatrix}\begin{bmatrix}\alpha & \varepsilon\\ -(1-\alpha) & -(1-\varepsilon)\end{bmatrix},$$

which is equivalent to

$$\begin{bmatrix} \alpha(2-\alpha) & -2(1-\alpha)^2 & -(1-\alpha)^2 \\ (1-\alpha)\varepsilon & \alpha+2\varepsilon-2\alpha\varepsilon & -(1-\alpha)(1-\varepsilon) \\ -\varepsilon^2 & 2\varepsilon(1-\varepsilon) & \varepsilon(2-\varepsilon) \end{bmatrix} \begin{bmatrix} s_{11} \\ s_{12} \\ s_{22} \end{bmatrix} = \begin{bmatrix} \alpha^2\sigma_u^2+(1-\alpha)^2\sigma_v^2 \\ \alpha\varepsilon\sigma_u^2+(1-\alpha)(1-\varepsilon)\sigma_v^2 \\ \varepsilon^2\sigma_u^2+(1-\varepsilon)^2\sigma_v^2 \end{bmatrix}.$$

The solution is:

$$\begin{bmatrix} s_{11} \\ s_{12} \\ s_{22} \end{bmatrix} = \frac{1}{\alpha\varepsilon(4-2\alpha-\varepsilon)} \tag{6.8}$$

$$\times \begin{bmatrix} (2-\alpha\varepsilon)\varepsilon & 2(1-\alpha)^2\varepsilon & (1-\alpha)^2(2-\alpha) \\ -(1-\alpha)\varepsilon^2 & (4\alpha-2\alpha^2-\varepsilon)\varepsilon & (1-\alpha)(2\alpha-\alpha^2-\varepsilon) \\ (2-\alpha)\varepsilon^2 & 2(\alpha^2-2\alpha+\varepsilon)\varepsilon & 2\alpha^2-\alpha^3+2\varepsilon-2\alpha\varepsilon) \end{bmatrix} \times \begin{bmatrix} \alpha^2\sigma_u^2+(1-\alpha)^2\sigma_v^2 \\ \alpha\varepsilon\sigma_u^2+(1-\alpha)(1-\varepsilon)\sigma_v^2 \\ \varepsilon^2\sigma_u^2+(1-\varepsilon)^2\sigma_v^2 \end{bmatrix}.$$

Going back to (6.4) we observe that we should premultiply S by [1 1] and post-multiply by the transpose of that vector. Hence we should consider $s_{11} + 2s_{12} + s_{22}$, which means that we have to premultiply the vector (6.8) by [1 2 1]. Now the product of the latter vector and the 3 × 3 matrix in the right-hand side of (6.8) is simply [2ε 2ε $2-\alpha$]; and on combining this with (6.4) we obtain the following mean-square prediction error:

$$\begin{aligned} \mathscr{E}f_{t,t+1}^2 &= s_{11}+2s_{12}+s_{22}+\sigma_u^2+\sigma_v^2 \\ &= \sigma_u^2(4\alpha+2\varepsilon)/\alpha(4-2\alpha-\varepsilon)+\sigma_v^2(2-\alpha)/\alpha\varepsilon(4-2\alpha-\varepsilon) \qquad (6.9) \\ &= \sigma_u^2(g^2(2-\alpha)+4\alpha\varepsilon+2\varepsilon^2)/\alpha\varepsilon(4-2\alpha-\varepsilon), \end{aligned}$$

where

$$g^2 = \sigma_v^2/\sigma_u^2, \tag{6.10}$$

the ratio of the variance of the trend changes to that of the additive error term. Normally, one should expect g to be a small number.

Our task is to minimize the ratio behind the third = sign in (6.9). Its derivative with respect to ε is

$$4\varepsilon^2 - g^2(2-\alpha)(2-\alpha-\varepsilon)/\tfrac{1}{2}\alpha\varepsilon^2(4-2\alpha-\varepsilon)^2 ,$$

which is negative when ε is sufficiently close to zero (and when $\alpha \ll 2$). We therefore reduce the mean-square prediction error by raising ε from zero up to a certain positive level. The minimum is obtained by putting the numerator of the derivative equal to zero, which leads to a quadratic equation in ε. Only the positive root is relevant; it is

$$\varepsilon = h^2(2-\alpha) , \tag{6.11}$$

where

$$h^2 = -\frac{1}{8}g^2 + \frac{1}{2}g\left(1 + \frac{1}{16}g^2\right)^{1/2} . \tag{6.12}$$

The expression (6.11) gives the ε which minimizes the mean-square prediction error, given a certain choice of α. It is seen that this ε is a decreasing linear function of α. For the derivations which follow it will be more convenient to work with h (interpreted as the positive square root of h^2) than with g; it is easily found that the latter parameter can be simply described in the former:

$$g^2 = 4h^4/(1-h^2). \tag{6.13}$$

On substituting the ε-value of (6.11) into (6.9) we obtain:

$$\begin{aligned} \operatorname{Min}_\varepsilon \mathscr{E} f_{t,t+1}^2 &= \sigma_u^2(g^2 + 4h^4 + 2h^2(2-h^2)\alpha)/h^2(2-h^2)\alpha(2-\alpha) \\ &= \sigma_u^2(4h^2/(1-h^2) + 2\alpha)/\alpha(2-\alpha). \end{aligned} \tag{6.14}$$

Differentiating with respect to α and putting the result equal to zero, we obtain a quadratic equation whose relevant root is positive. The following simple results emerge:

$$\begin{aligned} \alpha &= 2h/(1+h) \qquad & 2-\alpha &= 2/(1+h) \\ e &= 2h^2/(1+h) \qquad & \beta &= h, \end{aligned} \tag{6.15}$$

while a substitution into the function to be minimized gives:

$$\mathrm{Min}_{\alpha,\varepsilon}\, \mathcal{E} f_{t,t+1}^2 = \sigma_u^2 (1 + h)/(1 - h). \tag{6.16}$$

These results are tabulated below for a few values of g^2.

	$g^2 = \sigma_v^2/\sigma_u^2$							
	10^{-8}	10^{-7}	10^{-6}	10^{-5}	10^{-4}	10^{-3}	10^{-2}	10^{-1}
h^2	$0.0^{4}500$	$0.0^{3}158$	$0.0^{3}500$	$0.0^{2}158$	$0.0^{2}499$	0.0157	0.0488	0.146
$h = \beta$	$0.0^{2}707$	0.0126	0.0224	0.0397	0.0706	0.125	0.221	0.382
α	0.0140	0.0248	0.0437	0.0765	0.132	0.223	0.362	0.553
ε	$0.0^{4}99$	$0.0^{3}312$	$0.0^{3}978$	$0.0^{2}304$	$0.0^{2}932$	0.0279	0.0799	0.211
MS error*	1.0142	1.0255	1.0457	1.0828	1.1520	1.2864	1.5668	2.2375

*Minimum value of the mean square prediction error (to be multiplied by σ_u^2).

References

Brown, R.G.: 1959, *Statistical Forecasting for Inventory Control*, McGraw Hill, New York.

Muth, J.G.: 1960, "Optimal Properties of Exponentially Weighted Forecasts of Time Series with Permanent and Transitory Components," *Journal of the American Statistical Association* **55**, 299-306.

Winters, P.R.: 1960a, "Forecasting Sales by Exponentially Weighted Moving Averages," *Management Science* **6**, 324-342.

Winters, P.R.: 1960b, Chapter 14 of *Planning Production, Inventories and Work Force*, by C.C. Holt, J.R. Muth, F. Modigliani and H.A. Simon, Prentice-Hall, New York.

CHAPTER 69

FORECAST EVALUATION BASED ON A MULTIPLICATIVE DECOMPOSITION OF MEAN SQUARE ERRORS*

HENRI THEIL
University of Chicago
Chicago, Illinois, U.S.A.

MYRON SCHOLES
University of Chicago
Chicago, Illinois, U.S.A.

1. Introduction

The evaluation of forecasts is frequently hampered by the heterogeneity of the underlying data. Suppose, for example, that three forecasters, X, Y, and Z, all predict the same variable one year ahead in a number of consecutive years. Suppose further that it is agreed to use the mean square error as the criterion of the forecasts. Then an ordinary estimated mean square is frequently an imperfect instrument for the evaluation because different years may correspond to different populations, some years being easy to predict and some very difficult. What is needed is a separation of effects (a "forecaster effect" and a "year effect" in this example), which is not unlike the separation procedure of classical variance analysis.

The objective of this paper is the formulation and the application of such a separation method. The order of discussion is as follows. We start in section 2 with a description of a series of successive forecasts by the Netherlands Central Planning Bureau and the corresponding estimates of recent changes by the Central Bureau of Statistics. They deal with annual changes in several macroeconomic variables. These changes are predicted, the predictions are revised several times, and when the year has passed, the changes are estimated and the estimates are revised several times. Hence there are three effects: that of the particular variable concerned, that of the stage of prediction or estimation, and that of the year during which the change takes place. Section 3 is devoted to the mathematics of the separation procedure and to its application to the data of section 2. In section 4 we try to analyze to what extent the variation of the performance from year to year can be ascribed to the variation of the degree to which the successive years are subject to large or small changes. The underlying idea is that, on the average, large changes will be predicted and estimated with larger error than small changes. Section 5 is a test of the normality of the errors. The remaining sections deal with a similar separation method for input-output prediction errors.

* This article originally appeared in *Econometrica*, **35** (1967), 70-88. Reprinted with the permission of the Econometric Society. The computations were carried out on the IBM 7094 computer at the University of Chicago with funds provided by the Graduate School of Business.

2. Seven Successive Stages in Prediction and Estimation

The Central Planning Bureau's annual Central Economic Plans and the Central Bureau of Statistics' estimates of past realizations can be regarded as successive attempts to reduce today's uncertainty with respect to changes in certain important macroeconomic variables in the near future and the recent past. We shall now describe the forecasts of future changes and the estimates of changes in the past for any fixed year t. There are, as a whole, seven systematic attempts to predict or estimate the changes in t from the level of the preceding year t-1:

1. In September of t-1, the Central Planning Bureau submits a preliminary version of the Central Economic Plan of year t. This is stage 1.
2. In December of t-1, the definitive version of the Central Economic Plan of year t is completed: stage 2.
3. In September of t the preliminary version of the Central Economic Plan of year t+1 is released. This document also contains preliminary data on year t, which form stage 3 in the series of predictions and estimates for that year.
4. In December of t the definitive version of the Central Economic Plan of year t+1 is released. Its figures on year t form stage 4.
5. The task of the Central Planning Bureau has now come to an end and we turn to the Central Bureau of Statistics, which is in charge of the computation of estimates of past realizations. Its first (preliminary) estimates are made available in September of year t+1. This is stage 5.
6. One year later (September of t+2) the Central Bureau of Statistics revises its preliminary estimates.
7. One more year later (September of t+3) the Bureau revises its estimates again. This is stage 7, which will be regarded as the set of "true" values (even though it does occur from time to time that additional revisions are made later on, e.g., when new census data become available).

We shall measure the variables in terms of the log-changes (changes in the natural logarithms).[1] Specifically, x_{iht} stands for the log-change in the ith variable in year t according to stage h. Here i takes the values 1,...,19 (the number of variables to be considered), h the values 1,...,7, and t the values 1,...,10 (for the years 1953 through 1962).

Since we regard x_{i7t} as the true value of the log-change in the ith variable in year t, the prediction or estimation error is of the form $x_{iht} - x_{i7t}$. Our objective is to determine the mean square of such an error. The total number of (i, h, t) combinations is 19 x 6 x 10 = 1140 (disregarding the trivially zero errors for the final stage 7); we should expect that the corresponding mean squares are all different. However, there is (at most) only

[1] The data are taken from H. Theil, *Applied Economic Forecasting*, Vol. 4 of *Studies in Mathematical and Managerial Economics*, North-Holland Publishing Company, Amsterdam, and Rand McNally and Company, Chicago, 1966. For further details see the Appendix.

one observation for each combination, so that it is necessary to impose a certain pattern on the mean squares. The pattern that will be used is of the following multiplicative form:

$$\mathscr{E}(x_{iht} - x_{i7t})^2 = A_i B_h C_t \,. \tag{2.1}$$

The coefficient A_i measures the quality of the forecast with respect to the variable concerned. A large value indicates that the quality is low, a small value that it is high (according to the mean square error criterion). B_h measures the quality of the successive stages. One should obviously expect that successive B's decrease in value, given that each subsequent stage is based on more data than those of its predecessor C_t, measures the quality of the forecasts and estimates for a particular year. Some years may have been predicted and estimated more successfully than other years, in which case the C's will take different values. For example, it may be that year t is quiet in the sense that its changes are moderate, whereas t+1 is wild in the sense that its changes are sizeable, either positive or negative. One may guess that, when corresponding variables and stages are compared for the two years, the errors of t+1 are on the average larger than those of t, which implies $C_t < C_{t+1}$. (We shall come back to such explanations in section 4 below.) Note that the A's, B's, and C's are subject to two multiplicative degrees of freedom. This is due to the fact that we may multiply A_i by $\alpha > 0$ and each B_h by $\beta > 0$ and each C_t by $1/\alpha\beta$ without affecting the pattern (2.1). Hence the total number of coefficients to be adjusted is 19 + 6 + 10 - 2 = 33. This is a sizeable reduction compared with the original number of 1140.

The pattern (2.1) is restrictive in the sense that it does not allow for interaction between the three determining factors. It is conceivable, for example, that the mean square errors for each variable and each stage are constant over time except for some stage k for which the mean squares decrease uniformly over time. In that case it would be appropriate to multiply the right-hand side of (2.1) by a coefficient D_{ht} which measures the stage-time interaction. Although this extension is perfectly feasible, it will not be pursued here because of the very substantial number of additional coefficients involved.

The decomposition idea and also the terminology ("interaction") are very close to the familiar concepts of variance analysis. The main difference is that the present decomposition is multiplicative rather than additive. It is of course possible to proceed in the usual additive manner by replacing the right-hand side of (2.1) by the sum $A_i^* + B_h^* + C_t^*$, but it is to be doubted whether it is good to do so. The reason is that the effect on the mean squares of the successive stages (and the successive years) would be very large for variables with small prediction and estimation errors and very small for variables with large errors. For example, suppose that there is no effect of the successive years ($C_t = 1$ or equivalently $C_t^* = 0$ for each t) and let the mean square error of the ith variable and the first stage be 10^{-4} and that of the jth variable and the same stage 10^{-2}. In the additive specification $A_i^* + B_h^* + C_t^*$, we should add the same number $B_2^* - B_1^*$ to obtain the mean square of stage 2, which obviously has a much more drastic effect for the ith variable than for the jth. The multiplicative pattern (2.1) implies that both 10^{-4} and 10^{-2} are to be multiplied by the same ratio B_2/B_1, which is evidently much more reasonable.

Also, the multiplicative pattern has the advantage that, if we divide the mean square error by another expression which is of similar multiplicative form (as we shall do in section 4), the resulting ratio has the same simple form. The ratio of two linear expressions is less convenient, because it cannot be separated in terms of the three indices, *i, h* and *t* individually. Note finally that the root-mean-square (RMS) error has the same multiplicative form under condition (2.1): $(\sqrt{A_i})\,(\sqrt{B_h})\,(\sqrt{C_t})$.

3. The Adjustment of the Multiplicative Mean-Square-Error Pattern

The following method is a rather obvious adjustment procedure for the right-hand coefficients of (2.1). Let us divide the square of any error $x_{iht} - x_{i7t}$ by B_hC_t; then the expectation of the resulting ratio is simply A_i according to (2.1), and hence independent of *h* and *t*. The average of all such ratios over all *h* and *t* values has therefore the same expectation. Let us therefore estimate A_i by this average and apply the same procedure to B_h and C_t:

$$\frac{1}{n_{i..}} \sum_h \sum_t \frac{(x_{iht} - x_{i7t})^2}{B_h\, C_t} = A_i\,, \tag{3.1}$$

$$\frac{1}{n_{.h.}} \sum_i \sum_t \frac{(x_{iht} - x_{i7t})^2}{A_i\, C_t} = B_h\,, \tag{3.2}$$

$$\frac{1}{n_{..t}} \sum_i \sum_h \frac{(x_{iht} - x_{i7t})^2}{A_i\, B_h} = C_t\,. \tag{3.3}$$

Here $n_{i..}$ stands for the total number of observations for the *i*th variable, and similarly, $n_{.h.}$ and $n_{..t}$ for the total numbers of observations in stage *h* and year *t*, respectively. If there were a complete set of observations [in the sense of one observation for each of the 1140 (*i, h, t*) combinations], these numbers would be $n_{i..} = 60$ for each *i*, $n_{.h.} = 190$ for each *h*, and $n_{..t} = 114$ for each *t*. This is not the case, however, because several observations are missing. The actual values of $n_{i..}$ vary between 34 and 60, those of $n_{.h.}$ between 157 and 190, and those of $n_{..t}$ between 98 and 114. For further details see the last column of Table 5 below.

The adjustment equations (3.1) through (3.3) are nonlinear in the unknowns A_i, B_h, C_t. We shall therefore proceed in the following iterative manner. We start with (3.1) and put $C_t = 1$ for each *t* and $B_h = \frac{1}{6}(7 - h)$. This amounts to assuming, in the first round at least, that there is no heterogeneity of the prediction and estimation picture of the 10 different years and that the mean square errors of the six successive stages decrease linearly. The left-hand side of (3.1) can then be computed, which gives the

TABLE 1. The Coefficients A_i and A_i' of the Nineteen Variables for the Patterns (2.1) and (4.1)

Variable		$100\sqrt{A_i}$			$100\sqrt{A_i'}$		$\sqrt{(A_i/A_i')}$	
	1953 -1962	1953 -1957	1958 -1962	1953 -1962	1953 -1957	1958 -1962	1953 -1962	1953 -1957
1. Consumption	3.63	3.38	3.39*	5.94	5.91	5.56	.611	.573
2. Consumer price level	1.58	1.96	1.15	2.79	3.79	1.93	.565	.517
3. Nonwage income	9.96	9.67	9.09	8.45	9.98	6.87	1.179	.968
4. Private production	3.02	3.48	2.46	5.60	5.85	5.17	.539	.595
5. Private employment	1.34	1.23	1.28*	1.92	1.87	1.81	.701	.659
6. Private investment	11.48	15.68	7.80	14.18	14.81	11.95	.809	1.059
7. Residential construction	11.39	12.46	9.44	8.91	12.84	4.76	1.279	.971
8. Wage rate	4.47	5.45	3.59	7.37	8.85	5.96	.607	.615
9. Investment price level	3.03	4.60	1.47	3.54	5.28	1.70	.857	.871
10. Indirect taxes	5.45	5.90	4.57	9.36	4.65	10.61	.583	1.271
11. Government wage bill	5.11	5.19	4.54	11.16	12.56	9.52	.458	.413
12. Other government consumption	11.64	12.44	9.74	10.99	10.11	10.47	1.059	1.231
13. Government investment	16.29	29.30	6.35	15.78	21.61	11.16	1.032	1.356
14. Imports	3.97	5.55	2.47	11.83	13.27	9.88	.336	.418
15. Exports	4.95	5.80	3.85	9.49	8.88	8.99	.522	.653
16. World trade	6.31	5.32	5.56*	8.46	8.65	7.91	.747	.615
17. Import price level	2.65	3.37	1.93	4.02	5.18	2.85	.659	.651
18. Export price level	2.96	4.30	1.76	2.97	3.95	1.95	.996	1.090
19. Word price level	2.94	2.29	2.69*	2.85	3.21	2.37	1.029	.713

estimate of A_i. Using this estimate and C_t - 1 we then compute the left hand side of (3.2), which implies a new estimate of B_h. These estimates are scaled such that $B_1 = 1$, after which they are substituted, together with the first-round A_i values, in the left-hand side of (3.3) to obtain new estimates of the C's. These are scaled again (such that $C_1, ..., C_{10}$ have unit average) after which the process starts all over again by computing a second estimate of A_i from (3.1), using the new estimates of the B's and C's, and so on.

No formal proof of the convergence is available yet, but the experience obtained from the data handled in this paper indicates that the convergence is rather fast. The results for the A_i are presented in the first three columns of Table 1. The figures shown are $100\sqrt{A_i}$ and hence refer to root-mean-squares rather than to mean squares; the multiplication by 100 implies that RMS is measured in percentages, given that log changes are — approximately — relative changes. The first column deals with the ten-year period 1953-1962, the second and third with the two halves of that period. Since the normalization is such that $B_1 = 1$ and $(1/10)\Sigma C_t = 1$, we may regard the figures as percentage RMS values for the first stage, averaged over the 20 years.[2] It is seen that the outcomes vary widely: from 1.3 per cent for Private employment to 16.3 per cent for Government investment (first column). It is also seen that for most of the variables A_i is less in the second half of the period than it is in the first (second and third column); there are only four exceptions, marked by an asterisk in the third column. We shall come back to this feature in the next section, where the other columns of the table will also be discussed.

The results for the B's are shown in Table 2. The first three columns contain their values (under the normalization $B_1 = 1$) for the ten-year and the two five-year periods. The next three columns contain minus the natural logarithms of the ratios of successive B's, $-\log(B_h/B_{h-1})$, which measure the uncertainty reduction of each stage over its predecessor. [We could also measure the uncertainty reduction by means of the relative B change, $(B_h - B_{h-1})/B_{h-1}$, but the logarithmic measure has the convenient additive property

$$\log \frac{B_{h+1}}{B_{h-1}} = \log \frac{B_{h+1}}{B_h} + \log \frac{B_h}{B_{h-1}}$$

which means that the reduction of uncertainty by stage $h + 1$ over stage $h - 1$ is equal to the sum of the two successive reductions; the relative B change does not have this elegant property.] The last three columns measure the same uncertainty reduction per month. That is, if the stage h forecast or estimate becomes available three months after that of stage $h - 1$ (stage h in December, stage $h - 1$ in September) we divide $-\log(B_h/B_{h-1})$ by 3; if it becomes available nine months after stage h -1 (stage h in September, stage $h - 1$ in December) we divide by 9; and if the time difference is twelve months (h and $h - 1$ both in September) we divide by 12. It is seen that stage 4 is characterized by the largest

[2] For the five-year periods we have $C_1 + ... + C_5 = 5$ and $C_6 + ... + C_{10} = 5$.

uncertainty reduction per month. Stage 2 is next and stage 3 third (except for the second five-year period in which their places are interchanged). The uncertainty reductions of the last two stages, which represent preliminary estimates of changes in the recent past, are very small compared with those of the earlier stages.

TABLE 2. The Stage Coefficients B_h of the Pattern (2.1)

h	B_h			$-\log \frac{B_h}{B_{h-1}}$			$-\frac{1}{N_h} \log \frac{B_h}{B_{h-1}}$		
	1953 -1962	1953 -1957	1958 -1962	1953 -1962	1953 -1957	1958 -1962	1953 -1962	1953 -1957	1958 -1962
1	1	1	1						
2	.676	.598	.736	.392	.514	.306	.131	.171	.102
3	.261	.271	.241	.952	.791	1.119	.106	.089	.124
4	.137	.140	.123	.642	.661	.671	.214	.220	.224
5	.123	.108	.118	.112	.259	.038	.012	.029	.004
6	.092	.094	.077	.291	.143	.424	.024	.012	.035

Note: $N_h = 3$ for $h = 2$ and 4; $N_h = 9$ for $h = 3$ and 5; $N_h = 12$ for $h = 6$.

The two superior stages (2 and 4) are both definitive in the sense that they are based on the official Central Economic Plans. All other stages are preliminary, i.e., either preliminary versions of the Central Economic Plans or preliminary estimates by the Central Bureau of Statistics. This might be an explanation of the difference in uncertainty reduction per month between stages 2 and 4 on the one hand and all other stages on the other hand; for it is conceivable that preliminary versions receive less care than definitive versions do. It remains true, however, that the uncertainty reduction of the last two stages is surprisingly small. This feature can be explained to some extent if we suppose that the definitive data (stage 7) are subject to observational errors which have certain statistical properties. Let us write $x_{i\infty t}$ for the really true value of the log-change in the ith variable during year t, so that any observed error can be written as the difference between the corresponding true error and the observational error of stage 7:

$$x_{iht} - x_{i7t} = (x_{iht} - x_{i\infty t}) - (x_{i7t} - x_{i\infty t}) .$$

On squaring both sides and taking the expectation we find

$$\mathscr{E}(x_{iht} - x_{i7t})^2 = \mathscr{E}(x_{iht} - x_{i\infty t})^2 + \mathscr{E}(x_{i7t} - x_{i\infty t})^2$$
$$-2\mathscr{E}\left[(x_{iht} - x_{i\infty t})(x_{i7t} - x_{i\infty t})\right].$$

The cross-moment on the second line vanishes if the observational error in the definitive data has zero mean and is uncorrelated with true errors of the corresponding earlier stages. Let us assume that this is true; let us also assume that we have the following pattern for the moments of the true errors:

$$\mathscr{E}(x_{iht} - x_{i\infty t})^2 = A_i \bar{B}_h C_t\,. \tag{3.4}$$

On combining these results with (2.1) we find

$$A_i B_h C_t = A_i \bar{B}_h C_t + A_i \bar{B}_7 C_t\,,$$

or equivalently

$$\bar{B}_h = B_h - \bar{B}_7, \quad h = 1,\ldots,6\,. \tag{3.5}$$

We conclude that under the conditions stated the coefficients B_h underestimate the true quality of the first six stages by a constant amount $\bar{B}_7$. Clearly, if we subtract $\bar{B}_7$ from B_h to obtain the true $\bar{B}_h$, the relative effect will be larger for the later stages than for the earlier ones. This is illustrated in Table 3 for the ten-year period in the special case $\bar{B}_7 = .04$. The first column contains $\bar{B}_h = B_h - \bar{B}_7$, $h=1,\ldots,6$, and $\bar{B}_7 = .04$. These figures are scaled in the second column such that the stage 1 value becomes unity; hence that column is to be compared with the first column of Table 2. The last column of Table 3 contains the uncertainty reductions per month. [Note that there is now also such a reduction for stage 7, which is equal to -(1/12) log ($\bar{B}_7/\bar{B}_6$]). It will be clear that it is immaterial whether we compute these reductions from the first or from the second column of the table.

If we compare the figures of the last column of Table 3 with the corresponding figures in column 7 of Table 2, we observe that the picture of stages 5 and 6 is improved, but that it is still not very excellent. Of course, the main weakness of the procedure is that nothing is really known about $\bar{B}_7$. It seems reasonable to impose $0 \leq \bar{B}_7 < \frac{1}{2} B_6$, because $\bar{B}_7 \geq \frac{1}{2} B_6$ would imply $\bar{B}_7 \geq \bar{B}_6$ according to (3.5). However, we know nothing about the location of $\bar{B}_7$ in the interval $(0, \frac{1}{2}B_6)$; and the choice does affect the uncertainty reductions of the later stages rather substantially. We shall therefore not pursue this approach further.

TABLE 3. Adjusted Coefficients $\bar{B}h$

h	$\bar{B}_h$	$\frac{\bar{B}_h}{\bar{B}_1}$	$-\frac{1}{N_h} \log \frac{\bar{B}_h}{\bar{B}_{h-1}}$
1	.960	1	
2	.636	.662	.137
3	.221	.230	.117
4	.097	.101	.274
5	.083	.086	.017
6	.052	.054	.039
7	.040	.042	.022

TABLE 4. The Coefficients C_t AND C_t' of the Ten Years for the Patterns (2.1) and (4.1)

	C_t			C_t'			$\sqrt{(C_t/C_t')}$		
Year	1953 -1962	1953 -1957	1958 -1962	1953 -1962	1953 -1957	1958 -1962	1953 -1962	1953 -1957	1958 -1962
1953	1.894	1.229		2.170	1.470		.934	.914	
1954	2.535	1.746		1.351	1.272		1.370	1.171	
1955	1.144	.885		1.029	.833		1.054	1.031	
1956	.880	.695		1.084	.835		.901	.913	
1957	.685	.444		.920	.590		.863	.868	
1958	.995		1.793	.648		1.240	1.239		1.202
1959	.520		.943	.669		.917	.882		1.014
1960	.481		.822	1.173		1.508	.640		.738
1961	.467		.747	.446		.638	1.024		1.082
1962	.399		.695	.511		.696	.884		.999

Finally, we turn to the C_t, which are the coefficients that measure the degree of inaccuracy of the forecasts and estimates for year t. They are presented in the first three columns of Table 4. The first refers to the complete ten-year period 1953-1962 and reveals a strong declining tendency of the mean square errors in the successive years. The next two columns show that this trend applies to each of the five-year periods separately. The conclusion is, therefore, that the quality of the forecasts and estimates increased systematically on the basis of the mean square error criterion. The last six columns of the table will be discussed in the next section.

4. Prediction Errors in Relation to the Size of the Changes to be Predicted

Table 4 presents clear evidence on the development of the mean square errors in the successive years; we observed the same tendency in Table 1 when we found that A_i is smaller in the second five-year period than in the first for most of the variables. The question arises whether this development is due to an increasing competence of the forecasters or to the possibility that the later years could be predicted more easily than the earlier years. It is not particularly easy to answer this question, but the following approach does seem to have certain merits. Let us assume that sizeable changes are predicted and estimated, on the average, with larger error than small changes.[3] If this is the case, variables which are subject to rather small annual changes and also years that are comparatively quiet should be characterized by relatively small prediction and estimation errors. When formulated in this way, the size of the change in any particular variable in any given year has a two-dimensional nature: this size may be large because the year is one of exceptional development. It will prove useful to formalize this feature by assuming that the log-change x_{i7t} in the ith variable and the tth year is the outcome of a stochastic process which satisfies

$$\mathscr{E} x_{i7t}^2 = A_i' \, C_t' \,, \tag{4.1}$$

where A_i' measures the degree of change of the ith variable and C_t' the degree of change of the tth year. This specification is particularly convenient in relation to the mean-square-error pattern (2.1). We can combine the two as follows:

$$\frac{\mathscr{E}(x_{iht} - x_{i7t})^2}{\mathscr{E} x_{i7t}^2} = \frac{A_i}{A_i'} B_h \frac{C_t}{C_t'} \,, \tag{4.2}$$

which shows that the ratio of the mean square prediction or estimation error to the mean square successive difference of the variable can again be separated in terms of the three indices. In particular, suppose that all years are predicted and estimated equally well and

[3] There are situations in which this is trivially true. Suppose that a change is sizeable because it differs substantially from the expected value, and that the prediction is equal to that expectation. Then it is necessarily true that both the change and the error are simultaneously large.

that they are all characterized by the same degree of change: $C_t = C_t' = 1$ for each t. Then, using the normalization B_1=1, we have

$$\frac{\mathscr{E}(x_{i1t} - x_{i7t})^2}{\mathscr{E}x_{i7t}^2} = \frac{A_i}{A_i'} .$$

Hence the ratio A_i/A_i' is simply the ratio of the mean square stage 1 forecast error to the mean square successive of the variable predicted, which is nothing else than the square of the inequality coefficient.[4] The more general formulation (4.2) takes account of different performance levels in different years (C_t) and of different degrees of change (C_t'). Also, it considers other stages besides stage 1.

The adjustment of A_i' and C_t' is carried out in the manner of (3.1) through (3.3) except that the B's and (3.2) are deleted. The results for A_i' (in the form $100\sqrt{A_i'}$) are shown in columns 4 through 6 of Table 1. The last three columns of that table contain the square roots of the ratios A_i/A_i'. These are (see the previous paragraph) the inequality coefficients of the stage 1 forecasts adjusted for different performance levels in different years. Column 4 shows that the value is less than one for fourteen variables, larger than one for five. No-change extrapolation would have been better for the latter group (because the left-hand side of (4.1) is the mean square error if the log-change x_{i7t} is predicted to vanish). In the first five-year period there are also five values above one, in the second there are three. In particular, Nonwage income, Private investment, Residential construction, Other government consumption, Government investment, the Export price level, and the World price level are variables whose stage 1 forecasts are not substantially better than no-change extrapolations. To compare the stage 2 forecasts with these extrapolations we should multiply the square roots of A_i/A_i' by $\sqrt{B_2}$, which is .821 for the ten-year period. This implies that in that period the stage 2 forecasts of all variables are superior to no-change extrapolation except Residential construction.

On the whole, there is not much evidence that the forecasts and estimates of the second five-year period are superior to those of the first when the criterion consists of a comparison of their mean square errors with the mean square successive differences in the same period. This follows from the last two columns of Table 1, which show that the ratio A_i/A_i' of the second periods exceeds that of the first in the case of 9 variables while the opposite is true in the case of 10 variables. This aspect is pursued in more detail, year by year, in Table 4, which contains the annual coefficients C_t' of the specification (4.1) as well as the ratios C_t/C_t'. (Square roots have been taken to increase their comparability with $\sqrt{(A_i/A_i')}$ of Table 1). We conclude that the prediction achievements when measured relative to the changes to be predicted have been fairly stable. 1954 and 1958 were relatively bad, 1960 relatively good; for the seven other years $\sqrt{(C_t/C_t')}$ varies between .86 and 1.05.

---

[4] Inequality coefficient "new style." See *Applied Economic Forecasting*, section 2.4.

5. Standardized Prediction and Estimation Errors

If we divide the errors $x_{iht} - x_{i7t}$ by the square root of $A_i B_h C_t$, we obtain standardized errors

$$\xi_{iht} = \frac{x_{iht} - x_{i7t}}{\sqrt{(A_i B_h C_t)}}, \tag{5.1}$$

which have a unit second moment for each of the 19 values of i, for each of the 6 values of h, and for each of the 10 values of t. This follows from the adjustment procedure (3.1)-(3.3). The corresponding means are

$$\alpha_i = \frac{1}{n_{i..}} \sum_h \sum_t \xi_{iht},$$

$$\beta_h = \frac{1}{n_{.h.}} \sum_i \sum_t \xi_{iht}, \tag{5.2}$$

$$\gamma_t = \frac{1}{n_{..t}} \sum_i \sum_h \xi_{iht}.$$

The variances are obtained by subtracting the squared mean from the second moment. Hence they are equal to $1 - \alpha_i^2$, $1 - \beta_h^2$, and γ_t^2, respectively.

It is of some interest to see whether these standardized errors can be regarded as being normally distributed. For this purpose we compute the familiar skewness and kurtosis measures:

$$\text{Skewness} = \frac{\frac{1}{n_{i..}} \sum_h \sum_t (\xi_{iht} - \alpha_i)^3}{(1 - \alpha_i^2)^{1\frac{1}{2}}}$$

$$\text{Kurtosis} = \frac{\frac{1}{n_{i..}} \sum_h \sum_t (\xi_{iht} - \alpha_i)^4}{(1 - \alpha_i^2)^2}.$$

These definitions refer to the set of all forecasts and estimates for the ith variable. The definitions for stage h and year t are analogous. The results are shown in Table 5. One striking feature is that the means α_i, β_h, γ_t are almost all negative. This is due to a combination of two circumstances. One is that most of the variables increased in most of the years; the other is that most of the forecasts and estimates were correct as far as the direction of change was concerned and, therefore, indicated an increase most of the time, but the increases predicted were mostly smaller than the observed values according to the definitive data.

TABLE 5. Mean, Skewness and Kurtosis of Standardized Prediction Errors for each Variable, Stage, and Year, 1953-1962

Variable, stage, or year	Mean	Skewness	Kurtosis	# of Observations
1. Consumption	-.554	-.336	2.834	60
2. Consumer price level	-.419	.014	2.620	60
3. Nonwage income	-.335	.597	2.603	60
4. Private production	-.473	.043	2.423	60
5. Private employment	-.294	.642	4.138	60
6. Private investment	-.317	-.055	1.931	52
7. Residential construction	.087	-.676	4.516	52
8. Wage rate	-.390	.143	3.426	60
9. Investment price level	-.338	.067	2.044	60
10. Indirect taxes	-.179	-.407	2.768	60
11. Government wage bill	-.321	.373	2.762	60
12. Other government consumption	-.116	-.164	2.584	52
13. Government investment	-.233	-1.378	5.023	52
14. Imports	-.298	-.346	2.838	60
15. Exports	-.124	-.150	2.724	60
16. World trade	-.615	-.106	2.560	34
17. Import price level	-.068	.306	2.932	60
18. Export price level	-.175	.052	3.318	60
19. World price level	.359	.362	2.140	41
Stage 1	-.238	.431	2.933	188
Stage 2	-.370	.088	2.777	190
Stage 3	-.295	-.000	2.984	187
Stage 4	-.226	-.061	3.031	183
Stage 5	-.212	-.494	3.112	157
Stage 6	-.187	-.053	3.224	158
1953	-.276	.126	3.179	98
1954	-.575	.291	3.299	99
1955	-.648	.635	3.190	102
1956	-.391	.062	2.464	101
1957	-.296	-.576	4.262	108
1958	.122	-.354	3.312	110
1959	-.159	-.006	2.686	109
1960	-.319	-.331	2.720	110
1961	.003	.038	3.396	112
1962	-.124	-.211	2.572	114

The skewness appears to be positive for ten variables, negative for nine; positive for two stages, negative for three, zero (in three decimal places) in one case; positive for five years, negative for five other years. There is, therefore, no evidence of a consistent skewness pattern for the data as a whole. The kurtosis coefficient is less than 3 (the value of the normal distribution) for fourteen variables out of nineteen; the median is 2.76. For the separate stages and years the kurtosis values are more evenly distributed around 3. We conclude that on the whole there is not much evidence against the hypothesis that the prediction and estimation errors are normally distributed around means which are mostly negative. Exact significance tests are difficult to apply owing to the numerous interdependencies of variables, stages, and possibly years as well.

6. Input-Output Forecasts of Intermediate and Primary Demand

We shall now consider another application of the multiplicative mean-square-error pattern, in the field of input-output prediction. Let there be n industries and write x_{ij} for the flow of goods and services from industry i to industry j. Then $a_{ij} = x_{ij}/x_j$ is an industry input coefficient, where x_j is the total output of industry j. Write also

$$z_i = \sum_{j=1}^{n} x_{ij} \quad \text{and} \quad f_i = x_i - z_i$$

for the total intermediate and the total final demand, respectively, for the products of industry i. It is well-known that, given the n-element final demand vector f, and the corresponding industry input coefficient matrix $A = [a_{ij}]^{-1} - I$. Therefore, the conditional forecast of z in year $t+\tau$ based on the industry input coefficient matrix A_t of the earlier year t, given the final demand vector $f_{t+\tau}$ in the prediction year, is

$$[(I - A_t)^{-1} - I]\, f_{t+\tau} = A_t (I - A_t)^{-1} f_{t+\tau} \,. \tag{6.1}$$

For primary demand we proceed in the same way. Let γ_{hj} be the flow of the hth primary input absorbed by industry j and write $b_{hj} = \gamma_{hj}/x_j$ for the corresponding primary input coefficient. The total demand for the hth primary input is then

$$y_h = \sum_{j=1}^{n} y_{hj} = \sum_{j=1}^{n} b_{hj} x_j \,,$$

or in vector form $y = Bx = B(I-A)^{-1}f$. We conclude that the conditional forecast of y in year $t+\tau$ based on the primary input coefficient matrix B_t and the industry input coefficient matrix A_t of some earlier year t, given the prediction year's final demand vector $f_{t+\tau}$, is equal to

$$B_t(I - A_t)^{-1} f_{t+\tau} . \tag{6.2}$$

Forecasts of the type (6.1) and (6.2) have been analyzed on a large scale in *Applied Economic Forecasting*, chapters 6 and 7, for the Dutch input-output tables of the ten years 1948-1957. Consider now the ith component of the prediction vector (6.1), divide it by the ith component of the observed $z_{t+\tau}$, and then take the natural logarithm of this ratio. This is the logarithmic prediction error $e_{it\tau}$ of the total intermediate demand for the products of industry i, the prediction year being $t+\tau$ and the year of the underlying input-output table t. The logarithmic prediction errors of primary demand, based on (6.2), are derived in a fully analogous manner.

The present errors $e_{it\tau}$ depend on three indices, just as the errors $x_{iht} - x_{i7t}$ of section 2. In what follows we shall proceed under the simplifying assumption that the mean square of $e_{it\tau}$ is independent of t; that is, the mean square is supposed to vary from industry to industry and it is also supposed to vary with the time span τ over which prediction takes place, but not with the year t whose input coefficients are used for the prediction. The model is

$$\mathscr{E} e_{it\tau}^2 = D_i E_\tau , \tag{6.3}$$

where D_i measures the degree of inaccuracy corresponding to industry i and E_τ refers to the inaccuracy of predicting τ years ahead. The application of the adjustment procedure of section 3 to this case is in principle straightforward, but since it involves a substantial amount of data we decided to simplify it as follows. For each (i, τ) combination the mean square over t of $e_{it\tau}$ is available (see *Applied Economic Forecasting*, Table 6.3 on page 179). This mean square involves only two indices, i and τ, and this was substituted for the left-hand side of (6.3). When τ is large, the number of $e_{it\tau}$'s for any given (i, τ) combination is rather small, so that some aggregation is desirable. We shall therefore consider six τ values: τ = 1,2,3,4, and τ = 7, ..., τ= 10). This simplification reduces the number of basic data to be handled by more than 90 percent.

The procedure is applied to the 35-industry tables of the Netherlands in the ten-years 1948-1957. Actually, we shall consider the intermediate demand for the products of only twenty-seven industries (listed in Table 6), the intermediate demand of the other eight being insignificant. In addition, there are three primary inputs: Imports, Wages, and Gross profits, the last of which is the sum of depreciation, indirect taxes, subsidies (with a minus sign) and other income such as profits and interest. The results for D_i are shown in the form $100\sqrt{D_i}$ in the first two columns of Table 6. Since the normalization used is $E_i = 1$, $100\sqrt{D_i}$ corresponds to the percentage RMS error or predicting one year ahead. The adjustment of the first column is based on all 30 sectors (industries plus primary inputs) simultaneously. The outcomes for the industries vary from an RMS error of three and one-half per cent (Metal products and machinery) to almost seventeen per cent (Coal mining); they are on the low side for the primary inputs, particularly for Gross profits. The second column shows the difference which is obtained if one adjusts

TABLE 6. The Sector Coefficients D_i, D_i' and D_i^*, of the Patterns (6.3), (6.4) and (7.1)

Industries and primary inputs	$100\sqrt{D_i}$		$100\sqrt{D_i}$	$\sqrt{(D_i/D_i'}$	$100\sqrt{D_i^*}$		$\sqrt{(D_i^*/D_i)}$
	(1)	(2)	(3)	(4)	(5)	(6)	(7)
1. Agriculture, forestry and fishing	5.23	5.19	16.50	.317	5.78	5.35	1.022
2. Coal mining	16.71	16.58	23.28	.718	19.38	17.89	1.071
3. Crude petroleum, salt mining, etc.	5.84	5.80	21.44	.272	7.65	7.05	1.208
4. Food manufacturing (animal products)	5.59	8.55	8.94	.960	9.38	8.66	1.008
5. Food manufacturing (other products)	4.37	4.34	7.68	.569	4.62	4.26	.976
6. Beverages and tobacco manufacturers	8.23	8.14	13.65	.603	9.00	8.31	1.010
7. Textiles	4.76	4.74	6.75	.706	5.48	5.10	1.071
8. Footwear and other wearing apparel	12.03	11.97	12.25	.982	11.68	10.80	.898
9. Wood and furniture	9.57	9.49	8.23	1.164	5.69	5.31	.555
10. Paper and paper products	8.26	8.24	14.15	.584	7.32	6.82	.825
11. Printing, publishing, etc.	6.84	6.79	8.56	.799	5.62	5.18	.758
12. Leather and rubber products (excl. footwear)	9.28	9.18	14.15	.656	10.18	9.40	1.013
13. Chemicals and petroleum refineries	4.97	4.94	18.88	.263	3.89	3.62	.729
14. Earthenware, glass, lime, etc.	6.24	6.19	31.50	.198	6.70	6.19	.992
15. Basic metal industries	14.80	14.66	18.49	.801	16.89	15.60	1.054
16. Metal products and machinery	3.44	3.42	5.83	.590	4.34	3.99	1.161
17. Electrical machinery and apparatus	8.66	8.63	9.18	.943	11.26	10.38	1.199
18. Transport equipment	9.43	9.39	17.55	.538	10.93	10.08	1.068
19. Other metal products and diamond industry	8.25	8.20	9.80	.841	7.60	7.03	.852
20. Construction	9.16	9.09	8.72	1.050	10.53	9.72	1.061
21. Electricity, gas and water	13.76	13.63	13.11	1.049	9.93	9.17	.667
22. Wholesale trade	6.59	6.55	11.59	.568	7.90	7.30	1.108
23. Banks and other financial institutions	10.97	10.88	19.38	.566	10.03	9.21	.840
24. Insurance	4.02	4.01	4.63	.870	4.79	4.42	1.098
25. Transport (excl. ocean and air transport)	7.81	7.77	5.77	1.353	4.27	3.99	.511
26. Communication	5.87	5.85	9.72	.604	6.33	5.84	.994
27. Business services	10.52	10.43	7.73	1.360	10.73	9.89	.941
28. Imports	4.75	4.97	6.70	.710	3.56	3.33	.702
29. Wages	4.31	4.57	5.08	.849	4.00	3.70	.859
30. Gross profits	2.35	2.48	2.91	.809	2.90	2.68	1.139

where D_i^* measures the degree of inaccuracy with respect to the ith industry (or primary input), E_τ^* the degree of inaccuracy if one predicts τ years ahead from the year of the correction day, and F_q^* the degree of inaccuracy due to the fact that the input-output table is q years older than the correction data. The adjustment is similar to that of the previous section, the normalization being $E_1^* = F_1^* = 1$; for details see the Appendix. All adjustments are based on the thirty sectors, industries and primary inputs combined.

The D_i^* (in the form $100\sqrt{D_i^*}$) are presented in the fifth column of Table 6. The E_τ^* take the following values:

τ	1	1½	2	2½	3	3½	4	4½	5	6	7
E_τ^*	1	1.080	1.857	2.136	2.111	2.407	2.403	2.726	3.925	4.037	4.375.

They increase rather regularly with τ, thus indicating that the mean square errors become larger when the year to be predicted is farther away from the year of the correction data. [The halves of the τ values are due to the combination of "five years ahead" and "six years ahead". For example, when we take $q+\tau = 5½$ and $q = 4$ in (7.1), we have $\tau = 1½$; if $q+\tau = 8$ and $q = 5½$ or $q+\tau = 5½$ and $q = 3$, then $\tau = 2½$, etc.]

The results for F_q^* are as follows:

q	1	2	3	4	5½
F_q^*	1	.853	.720	.860	.701.

This outcome is surprising, for it suggests that the corrected forecasts tend to become more accurate when the input-output table is more outdated compared with the correction data (the time distance between t and $t+q$ becoming larger). Since this is very implausible, we decided to re-estimate D_i^* and E_τ^* of (7.1) under the additional restriction $F_q^*=1$ for each q, which means that the time distance between the input-output table and the correction data is assumed to have no effect on the mean square error. The new D_i^* results are shown in the sixth column of Table 6, and the corresponding ratios $\sqrt{(D_i^*/D_i)}$ in the seventh. It turns out that fifteen ratios are larger than one, fifteen smaller than 1. The correction procedure is therefore medianwide about as successful (according to the mean square error criterion) as ordinary input-output forecasting from the table of the correction year $t+q$.[5] The new E_τ^* estimates are as follows:

τ	1	1½	2	2½	3	3½	4	4½	5	6	7
E_τ^*	1	1.087	2.012	1.778	2.464	2.402	2.420	3.185	3.310	4.030	5.108.

[5] This remarkable result is considered in detail in *Applied Economic Forecasting*, where it is ascribed to observational errors in input coefficient matrices.

On comparing these figures with the E_τ values of the first column of Table 7 we conclude t an increasing time span of prediction has roughly the same effect for the correction proced as it has for ordinary input-output forecasting. It will be noticed, of course, that τ of E^*_τ refers the distance in time between the prediction year and the year of the correction data, wherea of E_τ refers to the time distance between the prediction year and the year of the input-out table.

TABLE 8. Supplementary Data on Stage 6 and 7 Estimates

Variable	1961 Stage 7	1962 Stage 6	1962 Stage 7	Stage 7 estimates of No. 16	Stage 7 estimates of No. 19	Yea
1. Consumption	560	477	634	276	-502	195
2. Consumer price level	187	240	221	843	-284	195
3. Nonwage income	-191	75	393	1098	149	195
4. Private production	339	328	408	935	363	195
5. Private employment	131	197	227	611	237	195
6. Private investment	783	373	520	40	-315	195
7. Residential construction	-111	-546	-243	843	-233	195
8. Wage rate	690	727	553	1328	149	196
9. Investment price level	150	210	149	488	-284	196
10. Indirect taxes	939	790	818	751	- 20	196
11. Government wage bill	961	1119	1223			
12. Other government consumption	845	1410	1018			
13. Government investment	1067	1267	1057			
14. Imports	658	558	554			
15. Exports	227	676	649			
16. World trade	488	594	751			
17. Import price level	-141	-111	-111			
18. Export price level	-151	- 60	- 40			
19. World price level	-284	49	- 20			

Note: All figures are log-changes multiplied by 10^4.

SECTION 6.1: MANAGEMENT SCIENCE

CHAPTER 70

MANAGEMENT SCIENCE IN EUROPE*

HENRI THEIL
Director, International Center for Management Sciences,
Rotterdam, The Netherlands
TIMS Council Member 1963-1964

It is a great pleasure for me to be here in this group and to be able to tell you something about recent activities in management science in Europe. Unfortunately, I shall have to confine myself to certain aspects of this area; I shall run the risk of being told by several Europeans, after my return, that I did not mention this or that subject. That is the fate of anyone in my present position, which is my meagre justification of my modest selection.

As to the history of the subject, there is an important difference between Britain and Continental Europe. England was on the free side in the War and it mobilized science to win the war. Its contributions to the start of operations research are too familiar to be recapitulated here. But it would in my view be wrong to attribute its contributions to the war situation alone. Another, at least equally important cause of its success is the practical, common-sense attitude prevailing in that country, which is also one of the main reasons why an applied field of mathematics like statistics has flourished there since so many decades. When we compare this with, for example, Germany, we find great differences. The difference is not only that Germany had cut off itself from the rest of the world as early as 1933, but also that its mathematicians were, generally speaking, so much more inclined to pure mathematics than to applied mathematics, while moreover its economists and business-economists are not very mathematically inclined. This situation is surely changing, but even now it is apparent from the participation in the various European and world meetings that the country is still lagging behind.

There are still many subjects of management science to which Europeans contributed in an important way. Well known are the English Vajda and Beale in the field of mathematical programming. There is a textbook by Jean Simonnard on linear programming in French, one by Künzi and Krelle on nonlinear programming in German. My compatriots Zoutendijk, Boot and Van de Panne also contributed to nonlinear programming, in particular quadratic programming. Marcel Boiteux, who heads an important group of research workers in the *Electricité de France*, contributed to marginal cost analysis. His compatriot Claude Berge is the author of a well known book on graph theory. At the more fundamental level I should mention Italy's Bruno de Finetti for his early contributions to subjective utility theory.

* This article first appeared in *Bulletin of The Institute of Management Science*, 11, (1964), 1-4. Reprinted with the permission of the Institute of Management Sciences. This is the text of a talk delivered at TIMS 11th International Meeting in Pittsburgh in March 1964.

This is just a small sample, probably not even a random sample. Rather than trying to make it bigger I should like to consider in more detail a subject which I feel is somewhat farther developed analytically in Europe than it is in the United States, viz., the management of the economy as a whole. In this management problem the government acts as the decision maker. The existence of this problem is denied when we would adopt a complete *laissez-faire* attitude, but few would do so nowadays, given that in most countries the government itself is the largest single spending unit. In particular, in many underdeveloped countries one mainly relies on the government measures, not on the natural accumulation process which removed poverty in Western countries. Norway's Ragnar Frisch is one of the main exponents in proposing sophisticated mathematical methods as an aid to development policy. But there are also some countries in Europe which use relatively sophisticated methods for policy purposes. I would like to consider two countries, The Netherlands and France, which use different methods.

The Dutch approach is based on an econometric system. Such a system, as it is formulated by the Central Planning Bureau, contains a consumption function, which describes the consumers' decisions on how much they spend as a function of income, liquid assets, and other determining factors; it contains an investment function which describes the entrepreneurs' decisions on how much they spend for investment purposes as a function of profits, liquid assets, available capital stock, and so on. There are about a dozen equations, which deal with such variables on employment, imports, and prices. There are also numerous definitional equations, partly derived from national accounts relationships. Now this system is built in such a way that it contains both the important decision variables and the most important variables which are not government controlled. Among the latter I should mention the level of employment, the surplus on the balance of payments, the price level of consumer goods, the level of investment, and the share of wages in national income. The most obvious decision variables are government expenditure and various tax rates. By solving the equation system one can estimate the effect of alternative measures of economic policy on the noncontrolled variables. For example, when it is decided to raise government expenditure by 1 billion the result is that the surplus on the balance of payments changes by so-and-so, possibly after a certain lag, that the price level goes up by a certain percentage, and so on. Needless to say, such effects cannot be given with complete precision; they are only estimated. But it is, I think, an interesting example of a mathematical technique which is used as a guide to policy.

The Central Planning Bureau's efforts are largely confined to a description of the economy in terms of relationships between its various components. No attempt is made to formulate a social objective function which is maximized subject to the constraints implied by the model. This would be the natural second step; use the econometric equation system to describe the operation of the economy as it reacts to government measures and outside forces, and use an objective function to describe social preferences. It can be done, as I have tried to show in *Optional Decision Rules for Government and Industry*, at least under certain conditions. When we use a quadratic objective function and linear constraints, and when we maximize over time, the result is a set of linear decision rules which describe the appropriate actions to be taken by the government in successive periods. Such rules are mathematically equivalent to the decision rules which were developed independently by Holt, Modigliani, Muth and Simon for the purpose of cost minimization in a Pittsburgh factory. Of course, much research remains to be done for adequate formulations of social functions. But in my view the method is promising, not only for policy-making but also for decisions at the research level. For one can compute the loss which is associated with an erroneous specification of the constraints. You can be assured that the art of making econometric models has not yet reached the stage of perfection, so that such erroneous specifications belong to the normal things of daily life. In such a case, when it is possible to compute how serious such an error is, we have an important guide for the decision as to the allocation of research resources.

Let me now turn to the French system as it has been developed by the *Commissariat Général du Plan* under the leadership of Jean Monnet and, more recently, Pierre Massé. It differs from the Dutch approach in several respects. For one thing, it deals with medium-term planning; the period covered by each Plan is four years, that of the Dutch system only one year. For another, its method of obtaining the final Plan figures is somewhat less sophisticated but much more labour-intensive. The initial step amounts to the formulation of a number of preliminary estimates of some of the more important macroeconomic variables by the *Commissariat Général*. These estimates are derived from a simple model and are based on the maximum growth of the economy which is compatible with a number of equilibrium conditions formulated beforehand. Input-output analysis is then applied to obtain figures for about 20 sectors; these are the starting point for the next round.

This second round consists of human iteration. The figures just mentioned are presented to 25 committees, each consisting of 30 or 40 members—government officials, entrepreneurs, representatives of trade unions and employers' organizations, and independent experts. These committees create sub-committees containing outside experts as well. It is estimated that as a whole more than 3000 people worked in this way for the Fourth French Plan. The committees proceed in a very detailed manner and distinguish, for example, between different kinds of investment goods when discussing the investment plans of individual firms in the iron and steel industry. They consider the demand for raw materials, semi-finished products and labour for separate parts of the industry, not only for the industry as a whole. Naturally, the figures thus obtained will imply certain discrepancies with the original estimates. Thus, when a committee has obtained its first results it sends them to the *Commissariat Général*, which will observe that these results have a number of implications for other committees. They have to be informed and will apply a number of revisions. This process continues, round after round, and until the final product is available a huge human machinery is continuously active during a period of several years.

What can be said about the merits of this procedure, in particular the merits relative to those of the Dutch procedure? I would hesitate to make such a comparison, especially because there is such a large difference between the investments made for the Plans themselves. But it is of great interest to know that the French planners believe that the work for their Plan has important psychological implications. They think that the participation of such a large number of prominent representatives of the country's business community implies more than an increased accuracy of the estimates obtained.

In particular, they believe that this participation leads to a social harmony, to a co-ordination of decisions planned and made by individual entrepreneurs and the government. I cannot claim to be an expert in psychology; but if we interpret management science broadly, as TIMS does, then this aspect too has to be taken into our consideration. There are other aspects as well, such as the danger of cartelization which may result from the government's efforts to bring business leaders together; this is undoubtedly a subject which needs further investigation.

I have given you a rather one-sided picture of management science in Europe. The real picture is not so one-sided, as you will see when you attend the meetings in Europe. TIMS had its first European international meeting in 1959, followed by a second one at Brussels in 1961, and there will be a third European international meeting in 1965, in Vienna. The European Section of TIMS had its first meeting in Dublin in 1962; the second will be in Zurich in September this year. We Europeans owe a great debt to TIMS and in particular to its Council members of these ten years, who took the initiative of organizing management science on a European scale. I hope very much that many of you will attend some of the European meetings, which have an old-world atmosphere which you will surely like. I also hope that some of you will have the opportunity to spend a longer period in the International Center for Management Science in Rotterdam. I have the honour to be the Director of this TIMS sponsored institution, which I hope many of you will know from its publications which are regularly announced in TIMS BULLETIN. Its research varies from programming and queuing and simulation and gaming to inspection and replacement policies and thus exhibits a new-world atmosphere, which is in social harmony with the old-world atmosphere of our part of the world.

Computer Sharing Exchange and Service Center Established

A Computer Sharing Exchange and a Computer Service Center have recently been established at the National Bureau of Standards (U.S. Department of Commerce) on an experimental basis. The new facilities were created in response to a request of the Bureau of the Budget, which has found that great savings in both time and money can be realized through computer sharing.

The Sharing Exchange will coordinate requests of Federal Government agencies in the Washington, D.C. metropolitan area for help in locating appropriate computer time and services for their essential work. The Exchange will maintain records of the availability for sharing purposes of the electronic computer facilities of these agencies.

A similar experimental sharing exchange has been operating in Philadelphia, Penna., under Bureau of the Budget sponsorship. Up to now, the presence of the Philadelphia exchange has substantially increased the incidence and value of sharing among Government agencies there.

CHAPTER 71

ECONOMETRICS AND MANAGEMENT SCIENCE: THEIR OVERLAP AND INTERACTION*

HENRI THIEL
International Center for Management Science
Rotterdam, The Netherlands

ABSTRACT. This is an expository article on the relationship of econometrics and management science. After some general observations it considers a number of applications, such as prediction on the basis of input-output models and of econometric macromodels and decision-making based on linear decision rules. These rules are applied to cost minimization in a factory and welfare maximization for a country as a whole. In the last part of the paper some attention is paid to uncertainty problems with respect to the constraints subject to which maximization or minimization takes place.

1. Introduction

Econometrics is a fairly young field in the discipline of economics. Management science in its modern form is a very novel approach in the area of business administration and related disciplines. One observes that research workers in these two fields organize joint meetings, both in Europe and in the United States. The idea of joint meetings is not at all new in the United States. It is fairly common to have December meetings in that country in which the American Statistical Association, the Econometric Society, the American Economic Association, and the American Farm Economic Association all participate at the same time. But in Europe such common meetings are a recent development in our scientific area. So the question arises: What is the virtue of combining econometrics and management science?

To answer this question it is, I think, important to compare the objects of analysis of the two fields. In econometrics the object is mainly (not exclusively) the economy of a country as a whole and the structure of large sectors of the economy. In management science the object of analysis is mainly (not exclusively) the decision process in smaller organizations, in particular the business firm. This distinction is in my view largely

* Reprinted by permission, "Econometrics and Management Science: Their Overlap and Interaction", H. Theil, *Management Science*, **11**, (1965,) Series B, B200-B212. Copyright 1965, The Institute of Management Sciences, 290 Westminster Street, Providence, RI 02903. Received October 1964. Invited address to the Joint Meeting of TIMS and the Econometric Society at Zurich, Switzerland on September 9, 1964. Sponsored by The Institute of Management Sciences and affiliated with the Econometric Institute of the Netherlands School of Economics.

responsible for the considerable differences in the mental attitude of the workers in the two areas. In macroeconomics one is concerned with millions and even billions. There is hardly anybody who carries personal responsibility for amounts of that order of magnitude. Clearly, this stimulates the imagination, which has its virtues but also its defects. In the worst possible case the economic theorist lives on a little island and stares into the sky but he does not see the movements of the economic ocean around him. But even if he carries a considerable degree of responsibility for his country's economic well-being (as for example a Minister of Finance), there is the difficulty that his observations on what actually happens do not enable him to test his ideas about the economic process easily; the reason being that the economic process is complicated and the observations imperfect.

In the business firm one concentrates on pennies and cents rather than billions. I do not want to be misunderstood; I do not mean to say that the problems of business firms are little problems. On the contrary, those who are in charge carry important responsibilities to their workers, to their Board of Directors, to their customers and suppliers, and to the communities in which their plants are located. The important thing is, however, that they see many of these people eye-to-eye. Staring into the sky and speculative theorizing do not lead to any profits, neither in the form of financial revenues for the firm itself nor in the form of improved relations with other persons and organizations. This means that on the average theories in this field tend to be down-to-earth, which is good if the term means "sound" but not so good if it means unimaginative. However, many of these theories do have one special feature compared with traditional economics: They try to prescribe what one should do, i.e., they are *normative*. They try to supply answers to questions that occur in actual practice rather than to present grandiose schemes.

Econometrics in its traditional form is not very normative. The oldest field of applied econometrics is that of the Engel curves, which describe the relationships between the amounts spent on various commodity groups and available income. Such an attempt to specify existing relations in quantitative terms is not normative; it certainly does not give an answer to the question of how one *should* spend his income. A similar statement can be made with respect to other areas of applied econometrics, such as input-output analysis, the estimation of production functions, and the construction of econometric models for an economy as a whole.

One qualification should be made. Input-output analysis enables us in principle to give approximate answers to questions of the following kind: If we require that the final bill of goods be so-and-so, how large should the output of each individual sector be? In the same way we can use econometric macromodels to answer the following question: If the government is interested in certain target values for the endogenous variables of the model, what values should the government-controlled variables have in order that these targets be reached? Certainly, these approaches are normative; they are normative in a conditional sense ("If you want this and this, then do that and that"). But the important point is that their normative character is of a very simple kind. They use fixed targets. However, if it turns out that it requires considerable sacrifices to reach these targets, wouldn't it be advisable to change the targets a little? This is surely done in practice; we should expect that in many cases an iterative procedure of this kind leads to an acceptable solution. If this is the real situation, however, isn't it better to take it into account immediately? When we say that reaching certain targets requires considerable sacrifices, this means that the decision maker's preferences do not involve these targets only but also the measures to be taken to reach them. The fixed-target approach must then be replaced by a more sophisticated approach; e.g., that of a preference function whose arguments are all factors which enter into the decision maker's evaluation. Also, I should mention that the fixed-target approach faces considerable problems when there is uncertainty. Even if it is true that the decision maker's preferences depend on these target values and nothing else, even then he may miss his goal due to the fact that his optimal actions are computed on the basis of a model which describes the real world only imperfectly. This will not be very serious in practice when the discrepancies are small; but it would be wrong to hope that this will always be the case.

What econometrics can learn from management science is the problem-solving attitude. What management science can learn from econometrics is in particular its accumulated experience in the area of economic relationships as well as the imagination displayed in deriving them. Needless to say, these are broad statements which need appropriate qualifications. For example, when I advocate the preference approach in the econometric field I ought to add that the basic tool of this approach — the utility function — has a long standing in consumer demand analysis. But apart from such qualifications, which to some extent deal with priorities and are therefore not really important, the main thing is simply that they can learn from each other, the main reason being that they have so much in common. Essentially, they have two common features. One is the object of investigation, which is usually a problem in economics — either microeconomics or macroeconomics. The other is the tool of analysis, which is mathematical to a large extent and includes probability theory to handle problems of uncertainty.

I shall now try to illustrate these general ideas with two examples. The first is completely macroeconomic in character, but it has direct connections with similar problems in microeconomics. The second is completely dual with respect to both areas.

2. The Accuracy of Macroeconomic Predictions

One of the advantages of a mathematical approach is that it forces the research worker to be precise, so that his successes and his failures can be seen in a clear light. This means that when somebody pretends that he has found a method which enables him to make forecasts, it should be possible to find out to what extent his claim is justified simply by applying the method which he advocates.

An example is input-output prediction. Let us divide a country's business sector into n sectors (agriculture, metal industry, etc.) and let us write x_{ij} for the flow of commodities and services from the selling sector i to the buying sector j in a certain base year. The heroic assumption made by input-output analysis in its classical form is that each sector j needs a constant input of goods and services to be supplied by sector i for every dollar of total production. This means

$$x_{ij} = a_{ij}P_j \tag{2.1}$$

where P_j is the total output of the jth sector and a_{ij} is the constant input coefficient. But P_j consists of the commodities sold by the jth sector to all sectors, Σx_{jk} (sum over k), plus what is sold to the non-business sector such as consumers, the government, and foreign countries. This non-business component is called the final demand for the products of the jth sector (written f_j), whereas the business components (x_{jk}) are called intermediate demand. Hence (2.1) can be written as

$$x_{ij} = a_{ij}(\text{—} \textstyle\sum_{k=1}^{n} x_{jk} + f_j) \, . \tag{2.2}$$

We now introduce total intermediate demand for the products of each sector:

$$x_j = \textstyle\sum_{k=1}^{n} x_{jk} \qquad (j = 1, ..., n) \tag{2.3}$$

then we obtain after summation of equation (2.2) over j :

$$x_i = \textstyle\sum_{j=1}^{n} a_{ij}(x_j + f_j) \tag{2.4}$$

There are n such equations, one for each x_i. Remember that a_{ij} is assumed to be constant over time. Evidently, if we have a complete set of values a_{ij} for some given year; and if we would specify a complete set of values $f_1, ..., f_n$ for some future year, we would be able to use the n equations (2.4) to obtain forecasts for each sector's total intermediate demand ($x_1, ..., x_n$) in that future year. Such forecasts are conditional predictions, because they are conditional on the final-demand values $f_1, ..., f_n$ which are specified for the future year.

How well does the procedure work? Nobody will expect that this simple procedure will yield perfect predictions. But the proof of the pudding is in the eating. We have an analysis, carried out by G. Rey and C.B. Tilanus (1963), which deals with the Dutch input-output tables in the ten consecutive years 1948 through 1957. These tables contain 35 sectors. It is, in principle, possible to use each year as base year and to predict total intermediate demand for every sector in every year, given the observed final demand values in that year. For example, one can take 1948 as a base and predict 1949, in which case one predicts one year ahead; or one can take the same base but predict 1950, in which case the forecast is two years ahead; and so on. It seems intuitively obvious that forecasts referring to a farther future are worse than those which refer to the near future; this turns out to be actually the case, at least on the average. Let us take relative prediction errors (percentage errors) and let us evaluate them by means of their root-mean-square:

$$\text{RMS} = \sqrt{\frac{1}{n}\sum_i e_i^{\,2}} \tag{2.5}$$

where e_i is the error of the ith prediction and n the number of predictions. The RMS-values will be different for different sectors and will also vary according to the time span to be predicted. If we take the median value over all sectors the picture of the RMS prediction errors is as follows:

1 year ahead	7.5 per cent
2 years ahead	11.3 per cent
3 years ahead	11.9 per cent
4 years ahead	11.1 per cent
5 or 6 years ahead	13.4 per cent
7-10 years ahead	15.0 per cent

One observes that there is indeed a tendency of the RMS values to increase with the number of years over which prediction takes place, but the increase is evidently less than proportional.

Another tool of economic prediction is an econometric macromodel. The Netherlands Central Planning Bureau has used such models for many years; it is therefore interesting to pay some attention to its experience. Such models contain a number of "structural" equations, each of which describes a certain part of the economy. For example, there is a consumption function which deals with the decisions made by consumers as to their expenditures, given a certain number of factors which determine these decisions. So consumer expenditure is described by the consumption equation as a function of wage income, of non-wage income, of the available liquid assets, and so on. In the same way there is an investment equation which describes entrepreneurial decisions as to their investment outlays as a function of their sales, liquid assets, capital stock at the beginning of the year, and so on.

The model as a whole consists of a number of such structural equations plus a certain number of definitional equations, which are so called because they follow directly from the definitions of their variables. For example, capital stock at the end of the year equals capital stock at the beginning of the year plus the addition during the year in the form of net investment. As to the variables of the model, their number exceeds that of the equations. So it is impossible to use the model to solve for all variables. However, some of the variables are regarded as exogenous; that is, the values which they take are supposed to be determined by the outside, i.e., by factors which operate independently of the economy described by the model. An example is the import price level, which is mainly determined by conditions abroad. The variables which are not exogenous are called endogenous; if their number equals the number of equations the model is said to be complete. It is then under certain general conditions possible to use such a model to obtain conditional forecasts of the endogenous values in some future year, given certain specified values taken by the exogenous variables. This is entirely comparable with the input-output predictions, which are conditional on the final demand values. In fact, the final demand for the products of each sector is an exogenous variable in the simple input-output model.

The Central Planning Bureau has applied this procedure for many years. I should add that, although their forecasts as published in the Central Planning Bureau are based on such a model, the procedure followed is not as simple as one might infer from the preceding observations. For one thing, the model was changed frequently — as frequently as one considered it desirable to make a change. I shall consider the ten-year period 1953-1962, but there is no single model that was used for each of these years. For another, the model results were not always accepted in a mechanical way. Sometimes the results were considered to be unbelievable in the light of other evidence; they were then changed to the level at which one was willing to believe them. Also, there are the errors in predicting the exogenous values. Econometric models supply conditional forecasts of the endogenous values given the values taken by the exogenous variables. But in practice these values are usually not given. It is then necessary to predict them by other means, which implies necessarily that we have exogenous prediction errors besides the conditional forecast errors of the model itself. The combination of the two will generally lead to worse results than either of them separately. However, this is to some extent compensated for by the fact that the model was not applied in a mechanical manner, provided of course that it is true that such deliberate deviations from the model outcomes are justified in a sufficient majority of all cases.

How good or how bad are the results of this highly mixed procedure? Table 1 presents an answer for 21 variables in the period 1953-1962. For each variable and each year we have a relative change from the level of the preceding year, both a predicted and a realized change. Their difference is the forecast error. The first column of Table 1 contains the RMS prediction error divided by the RMS value that would have been realized if the forecasters had abstained from any sophistication by predicting a zero change for every year. The figures show that these ratios are less than 1 with only one exception. Their median is 0.56, which means that medianwise the Central Planning Bureau's results are about twice as good (on the basis of the RMS criterion) as the nochange extrapolation method.

Before creating the illusion that we can be very satisfied, I should add that the standard of comparison is very modest. The postwar economic development was characterized by changes in production, prices, etc., which were certainly not zero on the average. The second column of Table 1 tries to meet this objection. It measures the RMS prediction error of each variable, not as a fraction of the zero change RMS value, but as a fraction of the RMS value that would have been realized if the forecasters had

TABLE 1. The RMS Criterion Applied to the Forecasts of Some Dutch Macroeconomic Variables.

1953-1962

	U	U'
1. Consumption	.36	.77
2. Consumer price level	.46	.80
3. Nonwage income	.82	1.19
4. Taxes on wage income	.54	1.37
5. Taxes on nonwage income	1.28	2.12
6. Total production	.45	.91
7. Private employment	.32	.63
8. Private investment	.76	1.00
9. Residential construction	.65	.75
10. Wage rate	.27	.76
11. Investment price level	.88	1.11
12. Indirect taxes	.46	.61
13. Government wage bill	.25	.71
14. Other government consumption	.65	.80
15. Government investment	.72	.95
16. Imports	.40	.64
17. Exports	.56	1.42
18. World trade	.62	1.35
19. Import price level	.56	.60
20. Export price level	.53	.56
21. World price level	.66	.76
Median	.56	.80

$$U = -\sqrt{\frac{1}{10}\sum_{t=1}^{10} (P_t - A_t)^2} \Big/ \sqrt{\frac{1}{10}\sum_{t=1}^{10} A_t^2}$$

where P_t = predicted change

A_t = observed change

$$U' = \sqrt{\frac{1}{10}\sum_{t=1}^{10} (P_t - A_t)^2} \Bigg/ \sqrt{\frac{1}{10}\sum_{t=1}^{10} (\bar{A} - A_t)^2} \quad \text{where } \bar{A} = \frac{1}{10}\sum_{t=1}^{10} A_t$$

used the average annual realized change during the ten-year period as a prediction in every year. This comparison is not completely fair, of course, since the competing prediction method requires that we know in 1954, say, what the average annual change from 1953 through 1962 will be. But it is at least useful to the extent that it enables us to see whether the forecasters were able to predict the variation around the average change. The figures of the second column show that the test is positive ($U' < 1$) in a two-thirds majority, and that medianwise this constant-change procedure was about 25 percent worse than the actual achievements.

I think it is of great importance that we obtain detailed numerical insight into the achievements of economic prediction methods. Most of the published results are in the macroeconomic area up till now. It would, in my view, be very worthwhile if business firms were willing to cooperate with research workers to analyze the merits of their forecasts in the marketing field and other areas. Chances are better in the United States than in Europe, where there is a considerable tendency of being afraid that the competitors will see too much; but my guess is that in the long run all parties will benefit.

3. Linear Decision Rules

Many economic problems have the character of minimization or maximization. We have classical textbook examples of cost curves which serve to describe the amount of cost incurred as a function of output; and producing at minimum average cost is evidently an interesting possibility. But in reality the amount of cost incurred depends frequently on many more factors than just output. In a highly stimulating study dealing with a paint factory in Pittsburgh, Holt, Modigliani, Muth, and Simon (1960) considered four different kinds of costs. One category deals with normal payroll costs:

$$k_1 Q_t \tag{3.1}$$

where k_1 is a constant (depending on the wage rate) and Q_t is the size of the labor force in month t. The second cost category deals with hiring and layoff. These costs are assumed to be proportional to the square of the change in the labor force:

$$k_2 (Q_t - Q_{t-1})^2 \tag{3.2}$$

Third, we have overtime and idle-time costs. We write P_t for production in month t and k_4 for the maximum output of an average worker. Then overtime costs are incurred when the difference P_t - k_4Q_t is positive and idle time costs when it is negative. This cost category is approximated by the square of this difference:

$$k_3\,(P_t - k_4Q_t)^2 + k_5P_t - k_6Q_t \tag{3.3}$$

where it is to be understood that the terms k_5P_t and -k_6Q_t are added to improve the quality of the approximation. Finally, we have the group of inventory, back order, and machine setup costs. We define net inventory as physical inventory less backlog; then the optimal net inventory level is approximated by a linear function of sales (k_8 + k_9S_t , where S_t is the rate of orders in month t) and the cost of deviating from this optimum is approximated by a quadratic expression:

$$k_7\left[I_t - (k_8 + k_9S_t)\right]^2 \tag{3.4}$$

where I_t is the net inventory level in month t.

The objective is now to minimize the sum of these four cost functions, (3.1) through (3.4), over a horizon consisting of T months:

$$\begin{aligned}
\textstyle\sum_{t=1}^{T}\ [\,k_1Q_t & \qquad \text{normal payroll costs}\\
+\, k_2(Q_t - Q_{t-1})^2 & \qquad \text{hiring and layoff}\\
+\, k_3(P_t - k_4Q_t)^2 + k_5P_t - k_6Q_t & \qquad \text{overtime and idle time}\\
+\, k_7\{I_t - (k_8 + k_9S_t)^2\}\,] & \qquad \text{inventory connected costs}
\end{aligned} \tag{3.5}$$

This minimization procedure is of the conditional variety, since it is subject to the constraint that in each month the change in inventories equals the excess of production over shipments:

$$I_t - I_{t-1} = P_t - S_t \qquad (t = 1, ..., T) \tag{3.6}$$

It is obvious that this conditional minimization problem is characterized by uncertainty, since the factory manager does not know his future shipments in advance. So we change our criterion to that of minimizing *expected* total costs, future shipments being regarded as random variables. Given that the problem is dynamic in nature (there are decisions to be made in successive time periods) our task is then to formulate a strategy or decision rule, which specifies for each month the appropriate decision to be made given the information which is available at the moment. We have here the special case of a quadratic objective function and linear constraints. It can be shown that in this special case the optimal decision rule is linear in the expected values of future shipments and in the initial work force and inventory level. For the numerical cost data obtained by Holt *et alii* and the special case of an infinite horizon ($T = \infty$) the weights of the decision rules for production and work force are given in Table 2.[1]

TABLE 2. Decision Rules for Production and Work Force

	Production	Work Force
Initial work force	1.01	.742
Expected shipments:		
1 month ahead	.46	.0100
2 months ahead	.24	.0087
3 months ahead	.11	.0070
4 months ahead	.05	.0054
5 months ahead	.01	.0041
6 months ahead	.00	.0030

The results show that the factory manager should formulate his sales expectations in the successive future months. He is supposed to produce 46 percent of the expectation of the month to come, 23 percent of the expectation of the month thereafter, and so on, the weights declining regularly. Note that this gradual weight pattern implies that sudden changes in expected sales are "smoothed out" by production. This effect is even more pronounced in the decision rule for the work force, since its expected-sales coefficients decrease much more slowly. Note also that the initial work force has a positive effect on both variables. This is due to the cost structure. When the initial work force is large there is an incentive to keep it large, because layoff is expensive; and when the work force is large there is an incentive to produce at a high rate, because idle time is expensive.

This procedure of linear decision rules, which solves the problem of maximizing or minimizing a quadratic objective function subject to linear constraints over time under conditions of uncertainty, can be applied to a variety of cases, including problems of macroeconomics. I shall illustrate this with a simple example, which is based on a small econometric model constructed by L.R. Klein (1950) for the U.S. economy in the period between the two World Wars. This model consists of three structural equations, one of which is a consumption function:

[1] The coefficients of the initial inventory levels are the same as those of expected shipments 1 month ahead, apart from sign. The expected shipments farther ahead than 6 months have nonzero coefficients too (because the horizon is infinite), but these are very small. The constant terms of the decision rules are not presented here, since they are not particularly interesting.

$$C = \alpha_0 + \alpha_1 \Pi + \alpha_2 \Pi_{-1} + \alpha_3 (W_1 + W_2) \tag{3.7}$$

Here C is consumption, Π profits, Π_{-1} profits earned in the preceding year, W_1 the wage bill paid by private industry, W_2 the government wage bill (hence $W_1 + W_2$ equals the total wage bill), and the α's the coefficients of that function. The second structural equation is an investment function:

$$I = \beta_0 + \beta_1 \Pi + \beta_2 \Pi_{-1} + \beta_3 K_{-1} \tag{3.8}$$

where I is net investment, K_{-1} capital stock at the beginning of the year, and the β's the coefficients of the equation. The third is a demand-for-labor equation:

$$W_1 = \gamma_0 + \gamma_1 (Y + \bar{T} - W_2) + \gamma_2 (Y + \bar{T} - W_2)_{-1} + \gamma_3 (t - 1931) \tag{3.9}$$

The left-hand variable is the wage bill paid by private industry; it is written here as a linear function of national income (Y) plus business taxes ($\bar{T}$) minus the government wage bill (W_2), of the same variable lagged one year, and of time (t, measured in calendar years). Finally, there are three definitional equations:

$$\begin{aligned} Y + \bar{T} &= C + I + G \\ Y &= \Pi + W_1 + W_2 \\ K &= I + K_{-1} \end{aligned} \tag{3.10}$$

the first of which states that national income plus indirect taxes equals consumption plus investment plus government expenditure on goods and services, the second that national income equals profits plus the total wage bill, and the third that the change in capital stock equals net investment.

This simple model was used by P.J.M. van den Bogaard and H. Theil (1959) in a pilot study which serves to illustrate the decision rule method for macroeconomic policy problems.[2] The period considered is 1933-1937 which is President Roosevelt's first administration. The macroeconomic decision maker is supposed to be interested in three variables which he does not control, viz., consumption (C), investment (I), and the ratio of profits to the private wage bill (Π/W_1). He is supposed to influence the operation of the economy by means of certain variables which he does control, for which we take the government wage bill (W_2), indirect taxes ($\bar{T}$), and government expenditure on goods and services (G). A quadratic social preference function is postulated in all 6 variables and all 4 years (hence it has 24 arguments as a whole), which is to be maximized in the same

[2] See also Theil (1964) for a discussion of the methods used.

way as the manager of the paint factory is supposed to minimize his quadratic cost function. As in the paint factory case we are not looking for an unconstrained extremum. The social preference function is to be maximized subject to the constraints under which the economy operates. When we specify these constraints in accordance with the linear model (3.7) through (3.10) we are back at the situation with which we started in the paint factory case: that of a quadratic objective function whose extremum we have to find subject to linear constraints.

There is uncertainty, too, as in the factory case. The structural equations do not hold exactly but are subject to random error terms. Also, there are usually exogenous variables in the model which are not government-controlled, such as, for example, the price level of imported commodities. The decision maker must predict the values to be taken by such variables in the prediction period, which will lead to forecast errors in the same way as the factory manager can predict his future shipments only imperfectly. The result is, therefore, of precisely the same type as in the microeconomic case: a decision rule for each of the government-controlled variables specifying what to do at the relevant moment, given the available information.

The analogy of the two applications in this respect is so straightforward that it is unnecessary to go into detail. Instead, I prefer to consider an extension of the topic. It was assumed until now that the coefficients of the structural equations (the α's, β's, and γ's) are fixed and given. But that is not true in general. Such coefficients have to be estimated from statistical data and the results are point estimates which are characterized by sampling errors. For the consumption function (3.7) these point estimates are

$$\begin{aligned} \hat{\alpha}_0 &= 16.786 \\ \hat{\alpha}_1 &= .020 \\ \hat{\alpha}_2 &= .225 \\ \hat{\alpha}_3 &= .800 \end{aligned} \tag{3.11}$$

These point estimates are asymptotically unbiased and have the following asymptotic covariance matrix:

$$V = \begin{bmatrix} (\hat{\alpha}_0) & (\hat{\alpha}_1) & (\hat{\alpha}_2) & (\hat{\alpha}_3) \\ 1.6454 & -.0085 & -.0146 & -.0292 \\ -.0085 & .0099 & -.0061 & -.0014 \\ -.0146 & -.0061 & .0083 & -.0004 \\ -.0292 & -.0014 & -.0004 & .0014 \end{bmatrix} \begin{matrix} (\hat{\alpha}_0) \\ (\hat{\alpha}_1) \\ (\hat{\alpha}_2) \\ (\hat{\alpha}_3) \end{matrix} \tag{3.12}$$

The square roots of the diagonal elements are the asymptotic standard errors. We observe that the standard errors of $\hat{\alpha}_1$ and $\hat{\alpha}_2$ are rather large (both almost .1) but that of $\hat{\alpha}_3$ much smaller (less than .04).

Suppose now that the decision maker proceeds as if the coefficients are equal to their estimated values. They are not, so the decision maker commits a specification error with respect to the constraints. This induces him to make a decision which deviates from the optimum. It can be shown that such a decision error is approximately a homogeneous linear combination of the sampling errors which are the cause of the decision error. A decision error leads to a loss of utility, i.e., it depresses the preference level attained below the maximum level that would be attained when the optimal decision had been made. This loss is under quadratic preference and linear constraint conditions a quadratic function of the decision error. Given that this error is linear in the sampling errors the loss is thus a quadratic function of these sampling errors. Taking the expectation, so that we obtain the expected loss, we conclude that this is a linear function of all variances and covariances of the sampling errors; in short, the expected loss is linear in the sampling variances and covariances of the coefficients estimates:

$$\varepsilon\,(\text{loss}) = \sum_{i=0}^{3} \sum_{j=0}^{3} k_{ij} \operatorname{cov}(\hat{\alpha}_i, \hat{\alpha}_j) \tag{3.13}$$

It is instructive to consider the various components of this expected loss: k_{ii} var $\hat{\alpha}_i$ for a variance and $(k_{ij} + k_{ji})$ cov $(\hat{\alpha}_i, \hat{\alpha}_j)$ for a covariance. This breakdown is presented in Table 3, which contains each component normalized in such a fashion that the largest variance contribution is 1. That figure is the contribution of the sampling variance of $\hat{\alpha}_3$ to the expected loss, which thus turns out to be larger than those of the sampling variances of $\hat{\alpha}_1$ and $\hat{\alpha}_2$ in spite of the fact that the standard errors of the latter estimates are so much larger than that of $\hat{\alpha}_3$ (see (3.12) and the discussion immediately following that equation). It thus turns out that the impact of the sampling variability of coefficient estimates, when used for policy purposes, may differ substantially from the image created by the standard errors.

Needless to say, these numerical outcomes depend on the preference function which is used. So when it is replaced by a different function the figures of Table 3 would become different, too. Since the construction of a social preference function is no trivial matter, this implies that the evaluation of the sampling variability for decision purposes is usually subject to a certain degree of arbitrariness. But it is easily conceivable that a fairly wide degree of variation in the preference functions adopted leads to a fairly consistent evaluation of the sampling variances and covariances. This would be important, since it provides us with a key for the allocation of our research resources. Thus we found that at the level of standard errors the best thing to do seemed to be to work on $\hat{\alpha}_1$ and $\hat{\alpha}_2$; but given the preference function chosen, $\hat{\alpha}_3$ proved to be much more important from a decision point of view. In fact, I think that at the present level of our knowledge this evaluation of sampling variability for different preference functions is the most important practical application of the decision rule method, at least for social decisions. But for decisions within the firm, similar applications can also be made. An example is the evaluation of prediction errors of future sales. Another is that of specification errors in coefficients of a cost function. In all such cases we are in principle able to compute the loss or expected loss which they cause and thus obtain a really relevant measure of their seriousness, in a way which is completely comparable with similar macroeconomic applications.

Table 3. Breakdown of the Expected Loss (3.13) According to Sampling Variances and Covariances of the Consumption Function Coefficients

	$\hat{\alpha}_0$	$\hat{\alpha}_1$	$\hat{\alpha}_2$	$\hat{\alpha}_3$
$\hat{\alpha}_1$	.84	-.10	-.11	-1.10
$\hat{\alpha}_2$		.63	-.50	-.59
$\hat{\alpha}_2$			.22	-.12
$\hat{\alpha}_3$				1

References

Boggard, P.J.M. van den, and H. Theil: 1959, "Macrodynamic Policy-Making: An Application of Strategy and Certainty Equivalence Concepts to the Economy of the United States," *Metroeconomica* **11**, 149-167.

Holt, C.C., F. Modigliani, J.F. Muth and H.A. Simon: 1960, *Planning Production, Inventories, and Work Force*, Prentice-Hall, Inc., Englewood Cliffs, N.J.

Klein, L. R.: 1950, *Economic Fluctuations in the United States, 1921-1941*, John Wiley and Sons, Inc., New York.

Rey, G., and C.B. Tilanus: 1963, "Input-Output Forecasts for the Netherlands, 1949-1958, *Econometrica* **31**, 454-463.

Theil, H.: 1964, *Optimal Decision Rules for Government and Industry*, North-Holland Publishing Company, Amsterdam, and Rand McNally & Company, Chicago, Ill.

SECTION 6.2: OPERATIONS RESEARCH

CHAPTER 72

QUADRATIC PROGRAMMING AS AN EXTENSION OF CLASSICAL QUADRATIC MAXIMIZATION*

HENRI THEIL[1]
Netherlands School of Economics
(now Erasmus University),
Rotterdam, The Netherlands

C. VAN DE PANNE
Netherlands School of Economics
(now Erasmus University),
Rotterdam, The Netherlands

ABSTRACT. The article describes a procedure to maximize a strictly concave quadratic function subject to linear constraints in the form of inequalities. First the unconstrained maximum is considered; when certain constraints are violated, maximization takes place subject to each of these in equational (rather than inequality) form. The constraints which are then violated are added in a similar way to the constraints already imposed. It is shown that under certain general conditions this procedure leads to the required optimum in a finite number of steps. The procedure is illustrated by an example while also a directory of computations is given.

1. Introduction

The problem of quadratic programming consists of maximizing a quadratic function of a vector x,

$$Q(x) = a'x - \tfrac{1}{2}x'Bx \ , \tag{1.1}$$

subject to the condition that none of the components of x be negative:

$$x \geq 0 \ , \tag{1.2}$$

and possibly also subject to certain additional linear constraints:

$$C^{*\prime} x \leq d^{*} \ . \tag{1.3}$$

* Reprinted by permission, "Quadratic Programming as an Extension of Classical Quadratic Maximization," H. Theil and C. Van de Panne, *Management Science*, **7**, (1960), 1-20. Copyright 1960, The Institute of Management Sciences, 290 Westminstter Street, Providence, RI 02903, U.S.A.
[1] The authors are indebted to Mr. P.J.M. van den Bogaard of the Econometric Institute for his detailed comments on an earlier version of this paper.

It is assumed that the matrices, a, B, C^* and d^* are given and that B is a positive-definite $n \times n$ matrix. Further, it will prove convenient to combine the constraints (1.2) and (1.3) such that they are written as

$$C'x \leq d \ , \tag{1.4}$$

which implies $C = [-I \quad C^*]$, $d' = [0 \quad d^{*\prime}]$. Here C' is an $N \times n$ matrix with $N \geq n$.[2]

Usually, a quadratic programming problem is solved by starting with some x which satisfies the constraints but which does not necessarily maximize Q, after which this x is replaced by a series of other x's—all of which satisfy the constraints—until the required solution is found.[3] Quite a different procedure is that of maximizing Q without taking account of the constraints, to see whether the resulting solution does or does not satisfy the constraints, and to use this information as a basis for further computations. This approach will be followed here; it was inspired by the work done by one of the authors (Theil, 1958) on quadratic criterion functions in economics, and it is based on the consideration that maximizing a quadratic function subject to linear equations is so much simpler than maximizing subject to linear inequalities. An outline of the procedure is given in Section 2, a more rigorous analysis in Section 3. Section 4 contains an example, Section 5 some concluding remarks.

2. Outline of the Procedure

2.1 INFORMATION SUPPLIED BY THE UNCONSTRAINED MAXIMUM

The vector which maximizes Q without regarding the constraints is

$$x^0 = B^{-1}a \ , \tag{2.1}$$

as is easily verified by straightforward differentiation. Clearly, if x^0 satisfies the constraints (i.e., if $C'x^0 \leq d$), then x^0 is the required solution because a constrained maximum can never exceed the unconstrained maximum. The interesting possibility is therefore the one in which x^0 violates one or more constraints. Consider then Fig. 1 which deals with the simple case $n = 2$ in which the only constraints are the nonnegativity constraints.

[2] The procedure to be proposed is also applicable when none or only some of the nonnegativity constraints (1.2) are imposed. In that case we may have $N < n$.

[3] For other contributions to the problem of quadratic programming, see the list of references at the end of this paper.

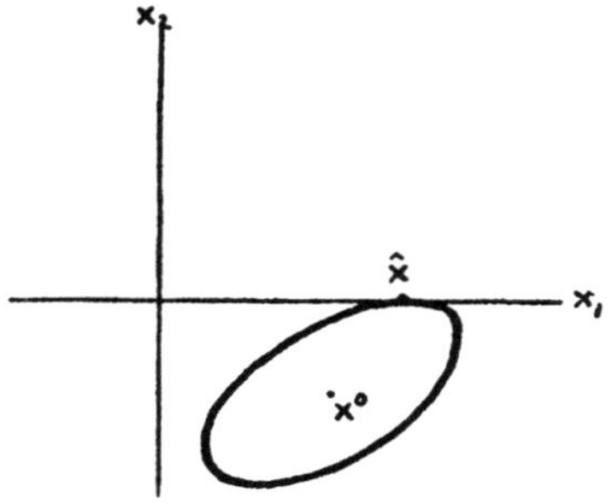

FIGURE 1

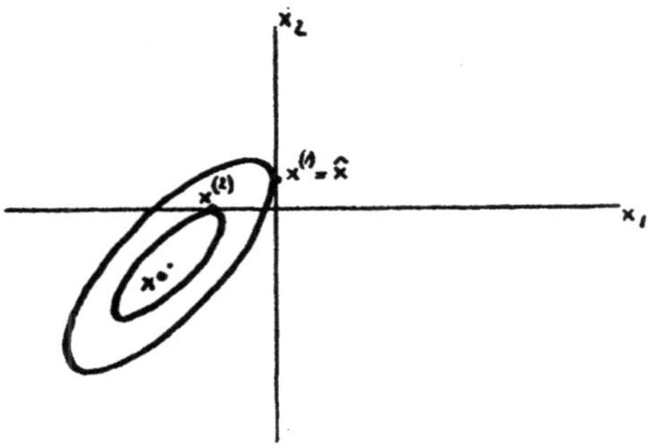

FIGURE 2

The condition $x_2 \geq 0$ is violated by x^0; so we have to be satisfied with a lower Q-value than $Q(x^0)$. Now given the fact that B is positive-definite, the locus of constant Q-values is a family of concentric ellipses (ellipsoids if $n \geq 3$) around x^0. The optimal solution will then be such that it lies in the admissible region (the positive quadrant) and on the ellipse which is nearest to x^0. Clearly, this is the point where an ellipse touches the horizontal axis; in algebraic terms, it is the vector which is obtained by maximizing Q subject to $x_2 = 0$, i.e, subject to the second nonnegativity constraint written in the form of an equation instead of an inequality. We shall say in such a case that this constraint is *satisfied exactly* by the vector considered, or that it is *satisfied in equational form.* Since the vector considered is the optimal vector (to be written as $\hat{x}$ from now on), the result of the example of Fig. 1 can simply be described as follows: The vector of the unconstrained maximum violates one of the constraints, and the constrained maximum (the optimal vector) satisfies the same constraint in equational form.

Next, consider Fig. 2 in which x^0 violates both nonnegativity constraints. Given our experience with the case of Fig. 1, the obvious approach seems to be to impose the two constraints in equational form one after the other. Thus, when imposing $x_2 = 0$ we obtain a vector $x^{(2)}$ which violates the constraint $x_1 \geq 0$;[4] and if we impose $x_1 = 0$ we obtain $x^{(1)}$ which violates no constraint and which is obviously—as graphical inspection shows—the optimal vector $\hat{x}$. This result suggests that the rule mentioned at the end of the preceding paragraph should be extended as follows: If the vector of the unconstrained maximum violates one or more constraints, one of these is satisfied exactly by the optimal vector.

Further investigations show that the expression "one of these" is to be replaced by "at least one of these." For example, if we consider Fig. 3 and note that x^0 violates the constraint $x_2 \geq 0$, then the obvious approach is to impose $x_2 = 0$. But the resulting vector $x^{(2)}$ violates $x_1 \geq 0$, and it is easily seen that the optimal vector is the origin, $x^{(1,2)}$, which satisfies both constraints exactly. The situation is precisely the same when we have additional constraints besides the nonnegativity constraints. This case is illustrated in Fig. 4 for two nonnegativity constraints (indicated by 1 and 2) and two additional constraints (3 and 4). The shaded area is the admissible region. It is seen that x^0 violates constraints 3 and 4, that maximizing subject to 3 or to 4 in equational form does not lead to $\hat{x}$ [because both $x^{(3)}$ and $x^{(4)}$ violate one constraint, viz., 4 and 3 respectively], and that $\hat{x}$ satisfies both 3 and 4 exactly. Here, therefore, all constraints violated by x^0 are satisfied exactly by $\hat{x}$. All these cases discussed so far are covered by the following Rule, the proof of which will be given in Section 3:

RULE 1: *If x^0 (the vector of the unconstrained maximum) violates certain constraints, then $\hat{x}$ (the optimal vector) satisfies at least one of these exactly.*

2.2 MAXIMIZATION SUBJECT TO SUBSETS OF CONSTRAINTS IN EQUATIONAL FORM

The preceding discussion shows that $\hat{x}$ is found by maximizing Q subject to a certain subset S of the N constraints $C'x \leq d$ written in equational form ($C'x = d$).[5] Of course,

---

4 We shall introduce the notation $x^{(2)}$ for the vector which is obtained by maximizing Q subject to constraint 2 in equational form, $x^{(2,4)}$ for the vector obtained by maximization subject to constraints 2 and 4 in equational form, etc.

5 This subset may be the empty set, viz., when the vector of the unconstrained maximum does not violate any of the constraints ($x^0 = \hat{x}$). Note also that in some cases the process of maximization subject to S in equational form is trivial, viz., when S is such that only one x satisfies S in equational form. This is the case in Figs. 3 and 4.

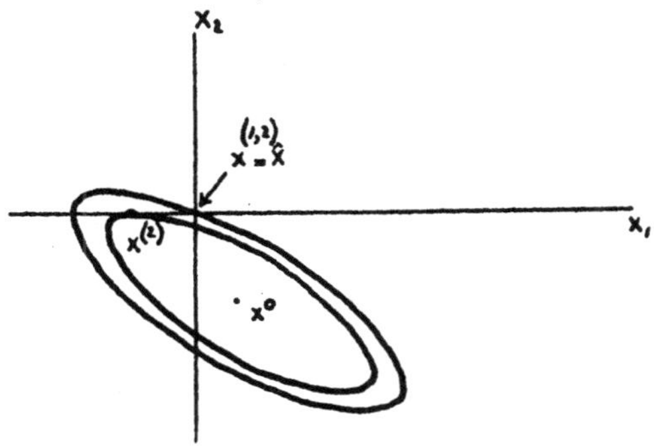

FIGURE 3

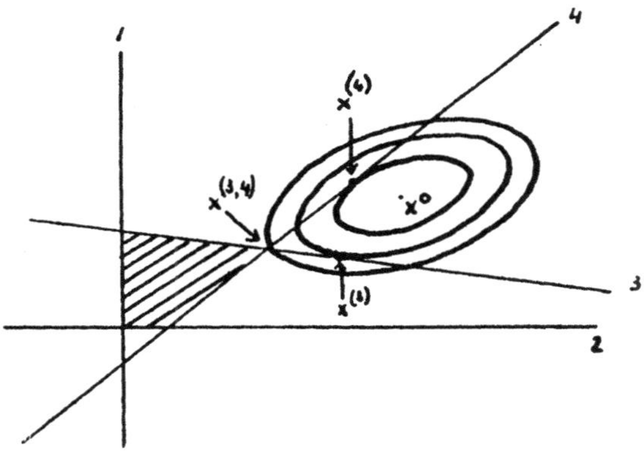

FIGURE 4

in general we do not know this particular S and, in fact, our main task will be to find it. Even so, it is important to observe at this stage that we can easily derive for any S the vector x^S which maximizes Q subject to S in equational form. Let us therefore arrange the N constraints such that those of S are the first ones, and let us denote by T the set of constraints not in S. Then the coefficient matrices of (1.4) can be partitioned according to

$$C = [C_S \quad C_T] \; ; \qquad d = \begin{bmatrix} d_S \\ d_T \end{bmatrix}. \tag{2.2}$$

Consider then the well-known Lagrangean expression

$$a'x - \tfrac{1}{2}x'Bx - \lambda_S'(C_S'x - d_S) , \tag{2.3}$$

where λ_S is a vector of Lagrange multipliers and $C'_S x - d_S = 0$ are the constraints in S written in equational form. Differentiating (2.3) with respect to x, we obtain

$$x^S = x^0 - B^{-1}C_S\lambda_S . \tag{2.4}$$

Premultiplying (2.4) by C_S' gives

$$C_S'B^{-1}C_S\lambda_S = C_S'x^0 - d_S , \tag{2.5}$$

because $C_S'x^S = d_S$. If we now define

$$E = C'B^{-1}C = \begin{bmatrix} C_S'B^{-1}C_S & C_S'B^{-1}C_T \\ C_T'B^{-1}C_S & C_T'B^{-1}C_T \end{bmatrix} = \begin{bmatrix} E_S & F' \\ F & E_T \end{bmatrix}, \text{ say;} \tag{2.6}$$

$$e = C'x^0 - d = \begin{bmatrix} C_S'x^0 - d_S \\ C_T'x^0 - d_T \end{bmatrix} = \begin{bmatrix} e_S \\ e_T \end{bmatrix}, \text{ say,} \tag{2.7}$$

it is easily seen that (2.5) implies

$$\lambda_S = E_S^{-1}e_S , \tag{2.8}$$

which expresses λ_S in known quantities; the existence of E_S^{-1} is ensured if the rank of C_S equals the number of constraints in S. Furthermore, by premultiplying (2.4) by C_T' we find

$$C_T'x^S = C_T'x^0 - C_T'B^{-1}C_S\lambda_S , \tag{2.9}$$

and the right-hand side should be $\leq d_T$ in order that x^S satisfies the constraints in T. Applying (2.6), (2.7) and (2.8), we find that this condition can be written in the simple form

$$FE_S^{-1}e_S - e_T \geq 0 \ . \tag{2.10}$$

As will appear below, the left-hand side of (2.10) is the only thing that needs to be computed for the relevant subsets S of the constraints. It is also easily verified that the corresponding Q-value is

$$Q(x^S) = \frac{1}{2}x^{0\prime}Bx^0 - \frac{1}{2}e_S' E_S^{-1}e_S = \frac{1}{2}a'B^{-1}a - \frac{1}{2}e_S' E_S^{-1}e_S \ , \tag{2.11}$$

because $Q(x^S) = \frac{1}{2}x^{0\prime}Bx^0 - \frac{1}{2}(x^S - x^0)'B(x^S - x^0)$ follows from (1.1) and (2.1), and $(x^S - x^0)'B(x^S - x^0) = e_S'E_S^{-1}e_S$ from (2.4).

2.3 FURTHER STEPS OF THE COMPUTATION

The above shows that we can in principle derive $\hat{x}$ by considering x^S for all subsets of the N constraints (1.4), viz., by verifying whether they satisfy the constraints and by computing their Q-values, see (2.10) and (2.11). However, this is far from efficient for several reasons. Firstly, it follows from Rule 1 that we can confine our attention to those sets S that contain at least one constraint violated by x^0. Secondly, it obviously makes no sense to consider a set S of which the constraints are contradictory when written in equational form. For example if two of the N constraints are

$$x_1 + x_2 \geq 1 \qquad \text{and} \qquad x_1 + x_2 \leq 5 \ ,$$

then no x^S exists for any S containing these two constraints. Thirdly, we can extend Rule 1 in a manner which may be described as follows. Suppose x^0 violates constraints 1, 2, and 3. It seems obvious to compute in the next round x^S for those sets S which consist of one constraint. We can then confine ourselves to $x^{(1)}, x^{(2)}, x^{(3)}$ [corresponding to S = (1), (2), (3) respectively], because $x^{(i)} = \hat{x}$ for $i \geq 4$ is impossible in view of Rule 1. Suppose then that none of the three vectors $x^{(1)}, x^{(2)}, x^{(3)}$ satisfies all constraints; more precisely, that $x^{(1)}$ violates constraints 3 and 5, that $x^{(2)}$ violates 3, and that $x^{(3)}$ violates 1 and 2. The question arises what to do next. The answer is supplied by

RULE 2. *Suppose that two or more constraints are satisfied exactly by $\hat{x}$ and partition the set of these constraints into two subsets, S and S′, containing at least one constraint each. Then x^S (the vector which maximizes Q subject to S in equational form) violates at least one constraint which is an element of S′.*[6]

[6] For an exception to this Rule, see the last paragraph of Section 2.3.

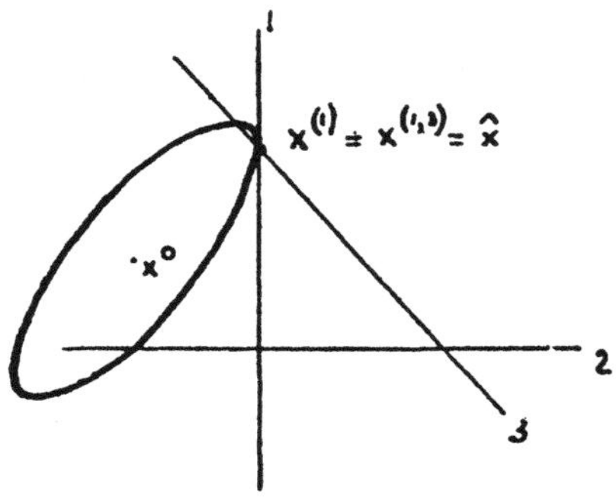

FIGURE 5

Applying this Rule to our example, we observe first that it is indeed applicable because $\hat{x}$ has to satisfy at least two constraints exactly: both x^0 and $x^{(1)}$, $x^{(2)}$, $x^{(3)}$ violate at least some constraint, so Rule 1 does not admit the possibility of an $\hat{x}$ which satisfies less than two constraints in equational form. Suppose now for a moment that constraint 1 is one of the constraints which is satisfied exactly by $\hat{x}$. Then Rule 2 states that $x^{(1)}$ violates some constraint which is satisfied exactly by $\hat{x}$, which means that $\hat{x}$ must satisfy exactly, not only constraint 1, but also 3 or 5, and so in the next round, when considering all relevant x^S's for two-element constraint sets S, we should take S = (1, 3) and (1, 5). However, this argument is based on the assumption that constraint 1 is one of the constraints satisfied exactly by $\hat{x}$; and we cannot be sure that this is true. The only thing we can be sure about is that $\hat{x}$ satisfies either 1 or 2 or 3 in equational form, because these are the constraints violated by x^0. Hence we must repeat the same argument under the alternative assumptions that $\hat{x}$ satisfies 2 or 3 exactly. Assuming then that constraint 2 is one of the constraints satisfied by $\hat{x}$, we find that S = (2, 3) is the two-element constraint set to be considered in the next round, since $x^{(2)}$ violates constraint 3. Similarly, assuming that 3 is one of the constraints satisfied by $\hat{x}$ in equational form, we find that S = (3, 1) and (3, 2) are to be considered. As a whole, therefore, five two-element constraint sets appear: (1, 3), (1, 5), (2, 3), (3, 1), (3, 2), from which however the last two can be deleted since they are identical with the first and the third respectively. For each of the remaining three we have to verify whether their x^S does or does not violate certain constraints. If none of these x^S's satisfies all constraints, we have to proceed to three-element constraint sets. This does not lead to any novel features, as will be seen in Section 4; Rule 2 is then applicable just as it was here, its vector x^S being interpreted as corresponding to a two-element rather than a one-element set S.

It is to be noted that there is one exception to Rule 2. It may happen that x^S coincides with $\hat{x}$ even though x^S is imposed to satisfy fewer constraints than $\hat{x}$ does. This is a degenerate case in which x^S happens to satisfy in equational form one or more constraints which do not fall under S. An example is given in Fig. 5: maximizing Q subject to constraint 1 in equational form leads to a vector $x^{(1)}$ which happens to satisfy constraint 3 exactly. Hence $x^{(1)} = x^{(1,3)}$ ($= \hat{x}$) in this case. In this article it will be assumed that there are no such problems of degeneracy.[7]

2.4 COMPLETING THE COMPUTATION: VERIFICATION OF THE SOLUTION

The procedure described above amounts to considering first the vector of the unconstrained maximum, then the vectors which maximize Q subject to certain one-element subsets of constraints in equational form, then vectors corresponding to two-element subsets, and so on. At a certain point we shall arrive at a vector x^S which violates no constraint, and the question then arises whether this is the vector $\hat{x}$ which we look for. It would be convenient if this would always be true, but unfortunately this is not the case as can be shown by means of the example illustrated in Fig. 6. There x^0 violates 3 and 4, so that in the next round we consider $x^{(3)}$ and $x^{(4)}$. Doing so, we find that $x^{(3)}$ violates 4 [implying that $x^{(3,4)}$ is to be considered next] while $x^{(4)}$ violates 2 [so that $x^{(2,4)}$ is to be considered. Now, $x^{(3,4)}$ violates no constraints, so that it might be the optimal vector; but $x^{(2,4)}$ does not violate any constraint either and hence it is clear that a special rule is necessary in order to find out whether or not such an x^S equals $\hat{x}$. This is provided by

RULE 3. *Suppose that for some subset S of the constraints, x^S exists and violates none of the constraints; then $x^S = \hat{x}$ if and only if every x^{S^h} violates the h-th constraint where S^h is the set of all constraints satisfied exactly by x^S excluding the h-th.*

The application of this Rule to our example runs as follows. Considering $x^{(3,4)}$ we observe that (3,4) is the set of constraints that are satisfied in equational form, so the sets S^h to be analyzed are the one-element set (3)—obtained by excluding constraint h = 4—and the one-element set (4), obtained by excluding h = 3. Hence we have to verify whether it is true that $x^{(3)}$ violates constraint 4 and that $x^{(4)}$ violates constraint 3. An inspection of Fig. 6 shows that this is the case as far as $x^{(3)}$ is concerned, but not for $x^{(4)}$; this vector violates constraint 2, not 3. Next, consider $x^{(2,4)}$; it satisfies constraints 2 and 4 exactly, so we have to consider $x^{(4)}$ and $x^{(2)}$ and to verify whether $x^{(4)}$ violates constraint 2 and $x^{(2)}$ violates constraint 4. The answer is positive as Fig. 6 shows and we can therefore conclude that $x^{(2,4)} = \hat{x}$. Of course, this result is immediately obvious by graphical inspection, but a graphical device works only when the number of variables is very small. When we deal with more than a few variables, an algebraic device like that of Rule 3 cannot be avoided.

[7] Some partial results on the problem of degeneracy have been obtained, but they are not reported here. We expect to come back to it in a later publication.

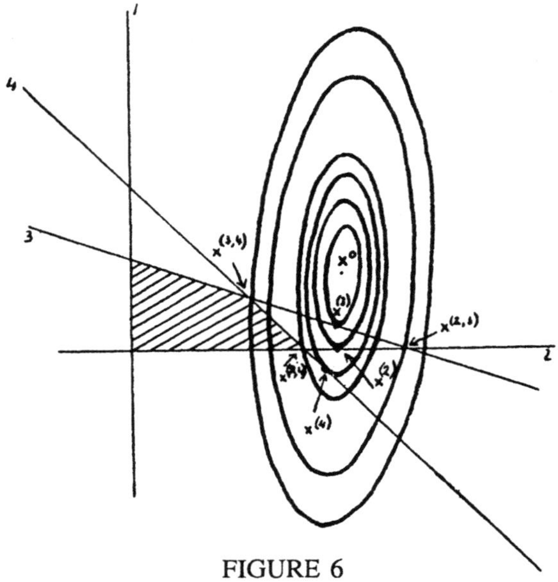

FIGURE 6

3. Analysis of the Procedure

PROBLEM. *Maximize* (1.1) *subject to* (1.4), *where all vectors and matrices are real-valued, the vectors x, a, d containing n, n, N elements respectively, the matrix B being of order n × n and C of order n × N. The vectors and matrices a, B, C, d are known.*

It will prove very convenient to apply the language of set theory to the sets of N constraints $C'x \leq d$. In particular, we shall consider subsets consisting of constraints that are satisfied exactly by some x ($c'_h x = d_h$ for some $h = 1, \ldots, N$) as well as subsets of constraints that are violated by x ($c'_h x > d_h$). Further, we shall write 0 for the empty set,[8] $S = S'$ if the sets S and S' are identical, $S \neq S'$ if they are not, $S \subset S'$ if all elements of S are also elements of S', $h \in S$ if h is an element of S, SS' for the set of elements both in S and in S', $S + S'$ for the set of elements either in S or in S' (with the understanding that there are no elements both in S and in S', i.e., $SS' = 0$), and $S - S'$ for the set of elements in S but not in S'.

DEFINITION 1. *For each vector x of n elements, U(x) is the subset of the N constraints C'x ≤ d that are satisfied exactly by x (in equational form), and V(x) is the subset of the N constraints violated by x.*

[8] As a general rule, the symbol 0 will occur in this section only as the empty set. There is only one exception to this rule; it also occurs in the expressions like $0 < \theta < 1$ to indicate that θ is a positive number smaller than 1. No confusion is likely to arise.

DEFINITION 2. *Subject to conditions of existence and uniqueness, $\hat{x}$ is the vector which maximizes* (1.1) *subject to* (1.4) *and x^S is the vector which maximizes* (1.1) *subject to some subset S of the N constraints $C'x \leq d$ in equational form.*

We shall make three assumptions, the first of which is made in order to ensure that a solution exists (which requires that there is at least one x satisfying the constraints) and that there is maximization in a nontrivial sense (which requires that at least two different x's satisfy the constraints). The second assumption ensures that the solution is unique, the third that there are no problems of degeneracy. The last assumption implies that maximizing Q subject to any subset S of the constraints in equational form leads to a vector x^S which satisfies only the constraints of S exactly.

ASSUMPTION 1. *There exist at least two vectors x and x^* of n elements each such that $x \neq x^*$ and $V(x) = V(x^*) = 0$.*

ASSUMPTION 2. *The matrix B is positive-definite.*

ASSUMPTION 3. *For each subset S of the N constraints $C'x \leq d$ for which x^S exists and is unique, $U(x^S) = S$.*

We shall first prove two lemmas and then proceed to the main theorems.

LEMMA 1. *For any two vectors x and x^* of n elements each,*

$$Q(y) > \text{Min}\,[Q(x), Q(x^*)] \qquad \text{where } y = \theta x + (1-\theta)x^* , \tag{3.1}$$

provided that $x \neq x^*$ and $0 < \theta < 1$.

Proof. The quadratic function Q is strictly concave in every n-dimensional interval of its arguments (Assumption 2), hence

$$\begin{aligned} Q\{\theta x + (1-\theta)x^*\} &> \theta Q(x) + (1-\theta)Q(x^*) \\ &= Q(x) + (1-\theta)\{Q(x^*) - Q(x)\} \\ &= Q(x^*) + \theta\{Q(x) - Q(x^*)\} \end{aligned}$$

where $x \neq x^*$ and $0 < \theta < 1$. The inequality (3.1) follows immediately.

LEMMA 2. *For any vector x of n elements,*

$$U(x)\,V(x) = 0 . \tag{3.2}$$

For any two vectors x and x^* of n elements each, if $y = \theta x + (1-\theta)x^*$, then

$$U(x)\,U(x^*) \subset U(y) \text{ for any } \theta ; \tag{3.3}$$

$$V(y) = 0 \text{ if } V(x) = V(x^*) = 0 \text{ and } 0 \leq \theta \leq 1 ; \tag{3.4}$$

$$V(y) = 0 \text{ for some } \theta\ (0 < \theta < 1) \text{ if } V(x) = U(x)\,V(x^*) = 0 . \tag{3.5}$$

Proof. (3.2): $c'_h x = d_h$ and $c'_h x > d_h$ contradict each other.

(3.3): If $h \in U(x)U(x^*)$, then $c'_h x = c_h' x^* = d_h$ and hence

$$c'_h y = \theta c'_h x + (1 - \theta)\, c'_h x^* = \theta d_h + (1 - \theta)\, d_h = d_h \ .$$

(3.4): $V(x) = V(x^*) = 0$ implies $c'_h x \le d_h$, $c'_h x^* \le d_h$ for all h. Hence $c'_h y = \theta c'_h x + (1 - \theta) c'_h x^* \le d_h$ for all h provided that $0 \le \theta \le 1$.

(3.5): If $V(x^*) = 0$, then it is given that $V(x) = V(x^*) = 0$ and hence $V(y) = 0$ for *all* θ in (0,1) according to (3.4). Assume next $V(x^*) \ne 0$; this implies $x \ne x^*$, for $x = x^*$ is contradicted by $V(x) = 0 \ne V(x^*)$. If $h \in V(x^*)$, then $c'_h x^* > d_h$ and $c'_h x < d_h$ because $c'_h x > d_h$ is excluded by $V(x) = 0$ and $c_h' x = d_h$ is excluded by $U(x)V(x^*) = 0$. But $c'_h x < d_h$, $c'_h x^* > d_h$ implies that there exists a θ_h such that $\theta_h c'_h x + (1 - \theta_h) c'_h x^* = d_h$ and $0 < \theta_h < 1$. For all $h \in V(x^*)$, write $\theta' = \text{Max}_h\ \theta_h$; then $V(y) = 0$ if $\theta' \le \theta \le 1$.

THEOREM 1 (existence and uniqueness). *There is exactly one vector $\hat{x}$ satisfying Definition 2, and for each subset S of the N constraints $C'x \le d$ there is either exactly one vector x^S satisfying Definition 2 or none at all.*

Proof. Assumptions 1 and 2 ensure that there exists at least one vector which maximizes Q. Suppose that there are two different vectors $\hat{x}$ and $\hat{x}^*$ which both maximize Q subject to the constraints. Then for any $y = \theta\hat{x} + (1 - \theta)\hat{x}^*$ with $0 < \theta < 1$, $Q(y) > Q(\hat{x}) = Q(\hat{x}^*)$ because of Lemma 1 and $V(y) = 0$ because $V(\hat{x}) = V(\hat{x}^*) = 0$ [Lemma 2, (3.4)]. This contradicts the assumption that both $\hat{x}$ and $\hat{x}^*$ maximize Q subject to the constraints.

Suppose similarly that both x^S and $y^S \ne x^S$ maximize Q subject to S in equational form. Then for any $y = \theta x^S + (1 - \theta) y^S$ such that $0 < \theta < 1$, we have $Q(y) > Q(x^S) = Q(y^S)$ because of Lemma 1 and $S = U(x^S)U(y^S) \subset U(y)$ because of Lemma 2, (3.3), which contradicts again the assumption made. Note that we cannot exclude the possibility that no x^S exists because S may be contradictory in equational form.

COROLLARY 1. *For any vector x of n elements,*

$$V(x) = 0 \ \textit{implies either}\ x = \hat{x}\ \textit{or}\ Q(x) < Q(\hat{x}) \ . \tag{3.6}$$

For any x and any subset S of the N constraints $C'x \le d$ such that x^S exists,

$$S \subset U(x)\ \textit{implies either}\ x = x^S\ \textit{or}\ Q(x) < Q(x^S) \ . \tag{3.7}$$

Proof. Trivial, given the existence and uniqueness of $\hat{x}$ and the uniqueness of x^S if it exists.

THEOREM 2 (exploring the attainable summit). *For any subset S of the N constraints $C'x \le d$ such that x^S exists, exactly one of the following possibilities applies:*

I. (approaching the summit). $U(x^S) \subset U(\hat{x}) \neq U(x^S)$ *implying* $U(\hat{x})\, V(x^S) \neq 0$.

II. (reaching the summit). $U(x^S) = U(\hat{x})$ *implying* $x^S = \hat{x}$.

III. (leaving the summit). $U(\hat{x}) \subset U(x^S) \neq U(\hat{x})$ *implying* $Q(x^S) < Q(\hat{x})$.

IV. (missing the summit). $U(\hat{x}) \neq U(\hat{x})U(x^S) \neq U(x^S)$ *implying either* $V(x^S) \neq 0$, *or* $V(x^S) = 0$ *and* $U(x^S)V(x^{S^h}) = 0$ *for some* $S^h = U(x^S) - (h)$ *where* (h) *is a one-element subset of the constraints satisfying*

$$h \in U(x^S) - U(\hat{x})\, U(x^S) \ .$$

Proof. The possibilities listed are the only ones, because the intersection $U(\hat{x})U(x^S)$ is either identical with both sets (II), or identical with one of them and a proper subset of the other (I, III), or a proper subset of both (IV).

I. We have $\hat{x} \neq x^S$, because $\hat{x} = x^S$ would imply $U(\hat{x}) = U(x^S)$. Then $S = U(x^S) \subset U(\hat{x})$ implies $Q(\hat{x}) < Q(x^S)$ according to Corollary 1, (3.7); and this implies $V(x^S) \neq 0$ according to (3,6). Assume $U(\hat{x})V(x^S) = 0$. Then some θ exists such that $0 < \theta < 1$ and $V(y) = 0$ where $y = \theta\hat{x} + (1 - \theta)x^S$ [Lemma 2, (3.5)] and $Q(y) > \text{Min}\ [Q(\hat{x}), Q(x^S)] = Q(\hat{x})$ (Lemma 1). This is a contradiction; hence $U(\hat{x})V(x^S) \neq 0$.

II. We have $S = U(x^S) = U(\hat{x})$, so either $\hat{x} = x^S$ or $Q(\hat{x}) < Q(x^S)$ in view of (3.7). Assume $\hat{x} \neq x^S$, in which case $V(x^S) \neq 0$ [because if $\hat{x} \neq x^S$ and $V(x^S) = 0$, then $Q(x^S) < Q(\hat{x})$ according to (3.6); and this is impossible in view of our previous conclusion: either $\hat{x} = x^S$ or $Q(\hat{x}) < Q(x^S)$]. Now $U(\hat{x})V(x^S) = U(x^S)V(x^S) = 0$ [Lemma 2, (3.2)]; and hence, noting that $V(\hat{x}) = 0$ by definition and applying Lemma 2, (3.5), we conclude that some θ exists such that $0 < \theta < 1$ and $V(y) = 0$ where $y = \theta\hat{x} + (1 - \theta)x^S$. But also $Q(y) > \text{Min}\ [Q(\hat{x}),Q(x^S)] = Q(\hat{x})$ according to Lemma 1. So the assumption $\hat{x} \neq x^S$ leads to a contradiction, hence $\hat{x} = x^S$.

III. Here $x^S \neq \hat{x}$ because $x^S = \hat{x}$ would imply $U(x^S) = U(\hat{x})$. Also

$$U(\hat{x})\, V(x^S) \subset U(x^S)\, V(x^S) = 0$$

in view of Lemma 2, (3.2). Then, for some θ such that $0 < \theta < 1$, $V(y) = 0$ and $Q(y) > \text{Min}\ [Q(\hat{x}), Q(x^S)]$ where $y = \theta\hat{x} + (1 - \theta)x^S$; see Lemma 2, (3.5), and Lemma 1. Hence necessarily $Q(x^S) < Q(\hat{x})$.

IV. We have either $V(x^S) \neq 0$ or $V(x^S) = 0$. Since the statement specifies nothing with respect to the first possibility,[9] we consider $V(x^S) = 0$. Further, we take $V(x^{S^h}) \neq 0$ for all $S^h = U(x^S) - (h) = S - (h)$ [where

$$h \in U(x^S) - U(\hat{x})\, U(x^S)]$$

[9] This possibility is a real one, see Fig. 7. There we have $S = U(x^S) = (1)$, $U(\hat{x}) = (2)$, $V(x^S) = (2)$.

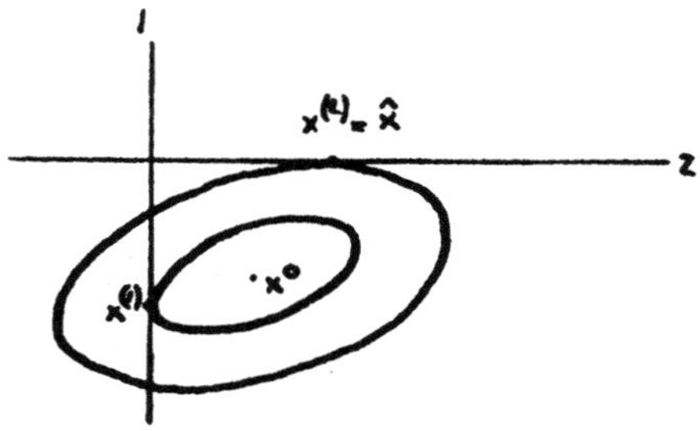

FIGURE 7

because the assertion $U(x^S)\ V(x^{S^h}) = 0$ for some S^h is trivially true if

$$V(x^{S^h}) = 0$$

for some S^h. Then $\hat{x} \neq x^S$ [because $\hat{x} = x^S$ would imply $U(\hat{x}) = U(x^S) = U(\hat{x})U(x^S)$] and $x^{S^h} \neq \hat{x}$, $x^{S^h} \neq x^S$ for all S^h because

$$V(x^{S^h}) \neq V(\hat{x}) = V(x^S) = 0\ .$$

Assume $U(x^S)V(x^{S^h}) \neq 0$ for all S^h and consider $y = \theta\hat{x} + (1 - \theta)\Sigma\theta_h x^{S^h}$ where $0 < \theta$, $\theta_h < 1$ and $\Sigma\theta_h = 1$.[10] Write also $c'_k\hat{x} = d_k - \delta_k$ and

$$c'_k x^{S^h} = d_k + \varepsilon_{kh}$$

for $k \in U(x^S) - U(\hat{x})U(x^S)$. Then $\delta_k > 0$ [because $\delta_k < 0$ is excluded by $V(\hat{x}) = 0$, and $\delta_k = 0$ by $(k)U(\hat{x}) = 0$], $\varepsilon_{kh} = 0$ if $k \neq h$ [because $(k)U(x^{S^h}) = (k)U(x^S) - (k)(h) = (k)U(x^S) = (k)$ if $k \neq h$], and $\varepsilon_{kh} > 0$ if $k = h$ [because $\varepsilon_{kh} = 0$ if $k \neq h$, $\varepsilon_{kh} \leq 0$ if $k = h$ for all k and fixed h would contradict $U(x^S)V(x^{S^h}) \neq 0$]. Applying this δ, ε-notation, we have

[10] In the special case when S is a one-element constraint set, h takes only one value and θ_h must be taken as 1. The case $S = 0$ is excluded in Possibility IV, because $S = 0$ implies $U(x^S) = U(\hat{x})U(x^S)$ (= 0).

$$c_k'y = \theta(d_k - \delta_k) + (1-\theta)\sum_h \theta_k(d_k + \varepsilon_{kh}) \\ = d_k - \theta\delta_k + (1-\theta)\theta_k\varepsilon_{kk}$$

for any $k \in U(x^S) - U(\hat{x})U(x^S)$. Now if we choose θ, θ_k such that

$$\theta\delta_k = (1-\theta)\theta_k\varepsilon_{kk} ,$$

this means $U(x^S) - U(\hat{x})U(x^S) \subset U(y)$.[11] But also $U(\hat{x})U(x^S) \subset U(y)$, as follows from repeated application of Lemma 2, (3.3);[12] and hence $U(x^S) \subset U(y)$. However, $Q(y) >$ $\text{Min}_h\ [Q(\hat{x}),\ Q(x^{sh})]$, as follows from repeated application of Lemma 1;[13] and $Q(\hat{x}) >$ $Q(x^S)$ because $V(x^S) = 0$ and $\hat{x} \neq x^S$ [see (3.6)] and $Q(x^{sh}) > Q(x^S)$ because $S^h \subset U(x^S)$ and $x^{sh} \neq x^S$ [see (3.7)]. Hence

$$Q(y) > Q(x^S) .$$

But we just derived $S = U(x^S) \subset U(y)$, which implies either $y = x^S$ or

---

11 When S is a one-element constraint set, we take $\theta_k = 1$ and $\theta = \varepsilon_{kk}/(\delta_k + \varepsilon_{kk})$; see footnote 10. In the general case, when the index k takes p values (say), the θ_k are to be specified such that

$$\frac{\theta_1\varepsilon_{11}}{\delta_1} = \cdots = \frac{\theta_p\varepsilon_{pp}}{\delta_p}$$

and such that $\Sigma\theta_k = 1$. Given the positive signs of the δ's and ε's involved, this leads to unique positive values of the θ_k. Finally, $\theta = \theta_k\varepsilon_{kk}/(\delta_k + \theta_k\varepsilon_{kk})$ for any k.

12 We have $U(\hat{x})U(x^S) \subset U(\hat{x})$ and $U(\hat{x})U(x^S) \subset U(x^{sh})$ for all S^h such that $h \in U(x^S) - U(\hat{x})U(x^S)$. Hence $U(\hat{x})U(x^S)$ is a subset of the intersection of $U(\hat{x})$ and all relevant $U(x^{sh})$; and the statement made in the text is proved when it is shown that all constraints of this intersection are satisfied exactly by any linear combination y of $\hat{x}$ and the x^{sh}. This can either be proved directly [by means of a trivial extension of the proof of (3.3)] or by repeated application of (3.3), as follows. Write the vectors $\hat{x}$, x^{sh} as z_1, z_2, ··· and $y = \Sigma\varepsilon_i z_i$ with $\Sigma\varepsilon_i = 1$. Supposing that i takes 3 values, we can write

$$y = \varepsilon_1 z_1 + (1-\varepsilon_1)\frac{\varepsilon_2 z_2 + \varepsilon_3 z_3}{\varepsilon_2 + \varepsilon_3} ,$$

so that $U(z_1)U(z^*) \subset u(y)$ according to (3,3), where $z^* = (\varepsilon_2 z_2 + \varepsilon_3 z_3)/(\varepsilon_2 + \varepsilon_3)$. But $U(z_2)U(z^*) \subset U(z^*)$, hence $U(z_1)U(z_2)U(z_3) \subset U(y)$. This is easily extended to the case in which i takes more values.

13 In the notation used at the end of footnote 12, we have to prove $Q(y) > \text{Min}\ [Q(z_1), Q(z_2), Q(z_3)]$. Now $Q(y) \geq \text{Min}\ [Q(z_1), Q(z^*)]$ and $Q(z^*) \geq \text{Min}\ [Q(z_2), Q(z_3)]$, where the equality sign holds if and only if the two vectors between square brackets (z_1, z^* and z_2, z_3) are equal. Hence the statement made holds except when the vectors z_1, z_2, z_3 are all equal. This exception does not occur here, since $\hat{x}$ differs from the x^{sh} as follows from $V(\hat{x}) = 0 \neq V(x^{sh})$. The extension to the case of a larger number of vectors is equally simple.

$$Q(y) < Q(x^S) ,$$

both of which contradict $Q(y) > Q(x^S)$. Hence $U(x^S)V(x^{S^h}) = 0$ for some S^h such that $h \in U(x^S) - U(\hat{x})U(x^S)$.

COROLLARY 2. *$\hat{x} = x^S$ for some subset S of the N constraints $C'x \leq d$.*

Proof. Write $\hat{S} = U(\hat{x})$ and consider $x^{\hat{S}}$. We have $U(\hat{x}) = \hat{S} = U(x^{\hat{S}})$ which implies that we are in Possibility II; hence $\hat{x} = x^{\hat{S}}$.

COROLLARY 3. *$\hat{x} = x^0$ if any only if $V(x^0) = 0$.*

Proof. The necessity of the condition $V(x^0) = 0$ is obvious, so we confine ourselves to the sufficiency. Applying (3.6), we find that $V(x^0) = 0$ implies either $x^0 = \hat{x}$ or $Q(x^0) < Q(\hat{x})$; applying (3.7), we find that $0 \subset U(\hat{x})$ implies either $\hat{x} = x^0$ or $Q(\hat{x}) < Q(x^0)$. Hence $\hat{x} = x^0$ (which means that we are in Possibility II of Theorem 2 for $S = 0$).

COROLLARY 4 (Rules 1 and 2).[14] *If $S + S' = U(\hat{x})$ and $S' \neq 0$, then x^S exists and $S'V(x^S) \neq 0$.*

Proof. The existence of x^S follows from the fact that the constraints of S are not contradictory in equational form; for if they were contradictory, so would those of $S + S' = U(\hat{x})$ be, implying the non-existence of $\hat{x}$ (which is ruled out by Theorem 1). Considering Possibility I of Theorem 2, we find that it implies $U(\hat{x})V(x^S) = (S + S')V(x^S) = S'V(x^S) \neq 0$ because

$$SV(x^S) = U(x^S)\, V(x^S) = 0$$

in view of Lemma 2, (3.2). The other possibilities of Theorem 2 are all excluded, because $U(x^S) = S \subset S + S' = U(\hat{x}) \neq U(x^S)$ leads to Possibility I only.

COROLLARY 5 (Rule 3). *Suppose that for some subset S of the N constraints $C'x \leq d$, x^S exists and $V(x^S) = 0$. Then $x^S = \hat{x}$ if and only if*

$$U(x^S)\, V(x^{S^h}) \neq 0$$

for all $S^h = S - (h)$ where (h) is a one-element subset of the constraints such that $h \in S$.

Proof. (a) *Necessity:* We have to prove for any x^{S^h} that if $x^S = \hat{x}$ [in which case it is necessarily true that $V(x^S) = 0$], $U(x^S)V(x^{S^h}) \neq 0$. Suppose

$$U(x^S)\, V(x^{S^h}) = U(\hat{x})\, V(x^{S^h}) = 0$$

for some x^{S^h}. Consider then $y = \theta\hat{x} + (1 - \theta)x^{S^h}$ for $0 < \theta < 1$; since

[14] Rule 1 deals with the case $S = 0$, Rule 2 with $S \neq 0$.

$$U(x^{S^h}) = S^h \neq S = U(x^S) = U(\hat{x})$$

we have $\hat{x} \neq x^{S^h}$ and hence $Q(y) > \text{Min}\,[Q(\hat{x}), Q(x^{S^h})]$ in view of (3.1); also $Q(\hat{x}) < Q(x^{S^h})$ because $S^h \subset U(x^S) = U(\hat{x})$ and $x^{S^h} \neq \hat{x}$, see (3.7). Hence $Q(y) > Q(\hat{x})$. However, $V(y) = 0$ for some θ such that $0 < \theta < 1$, as follows from $U(\hat{x})V(x^{S^h}) = 0$. This involves a contradiction, hence $U(x^S)V(x^{S^h}) \neq 0$ for each x^{S^h}.

(b) *Sufficiency*: We have to prove that if $V(x^S) = 0$ and if $U(x^S)V(x^{S^h}) \neq 0$ for each x^{S^h}, then $x^S = \hat{x}$. Considering Possibility I first, we observe that it must be ruled out because its implication $U(\hat{x})V(x^S) \neq 0$ is contradicted by $V(x^S) = 0$ which is given. The same applies to Possibility IV, because it implies $U(x^S)V(x^{S^h}) = 0$ for some x^{S^h} if $V(x^S) = 0$, which is contradicted by $U(x^S)V(x^{S^h}) \neq 0$ for each x^{S^h}. As to Possibility III, consider

$$y = \theta\hat{x} + (1 - \theta)\sum \theta_h x^{S^h}$$

where $0 < \theta, \theta_h < 1$ and $\Sigma\theta_h = 1$,[15] the constraints h over which summation take place satisfying $h \in U(x^S) - U(\hat{x})$. We have $Q(y) > \text{Min}_h\,[Q(\hat{x}), Q(x^{S^h})]$ as follows from repeated application of Lemma 1;[16] also $Q(\hat{x}) > Q(x^S)$ because this is the implication of Possibility III; and $Q(x^{S^h}) > Q(x^S)$ for all x^{S^h} (all $h \in S$) because of (3.7) [the possibility $x^{S^h} = x^S$ being excluded because

$$U(x^{S^h}) = S^h \neq S = U(x^S)] \ .$$

Hence $Q(y) > Q(x^S)$. Further, we have $U(\hat{x}) \subset U(x^{S^h})$ for all x^{S^h} considered here [because $U(\hat{x}) \subset U(x^S)$ and $h \in U(x^S) - U(\hat{x})$], so $U(\hat{x}) \subset U(y)$.[17] But in addition to this, we can choose θ, θ_h such that $U(x^S) - U(\hat{x}) \subset U(y)$,[18] in which case $U(x^S) \subset U(y)$. This, however, contradicts $Q(y) > Q(x^S)$ according to (3.7). Hence Possibility III is also ruled out. So only Possibility II remains implying $x^S = \hat{x}$.

---

[15] Except that one must take $\theta_h = 1$ if S is a one-element constraint set (in which case $\hat{x} = x^0$, given that Possibility III is assumed to apply to S here).

[16] See footnote 13. We have $V(\hat{x}) = 0 \neq V(x^{S^h})$, hence $\hat{x} \neq x^{S^h}$; so the exception mentioned in that footnote occurs neither here nor there.

[17] The proof is entirely similar to that of footnote 12.

[18] The proof is entirely similar to that of footnote 11 and the accompanying text of the proof of Possibility IV of Theorem 2.

4. An Example; Directory of Computations

The computational procedure will be illustrated by means of an example used by Houthakker (Dantzig, 1959) for the illustration of his capacity method. He considers a monopolist who faces four linear demand functions for his four products:

$$\begin{cases} x_1 = 18.239 - 2.086p_1 + 0.255p_2 + 1.033p_3 - 0.374p_4 \\ x_2 = 1.898 + 0.255p_1 - 0.499p_2 - 0.129p_3 + 0.217p_4 \\ x_3 = -4.916 + 1.033p_1 - 0.129p_2 - 0.759p_3 + 0.254p_4 \\ x_4 = 7.923 - 0.374p_1 + 0.217p_2 + 0.254p_3 - 0.512p_4 \end{cases} \tag{4.1}$$

where the x's are the quantities produced and sold and the p's prices. The problem is to maximize the total gross revenue subject to certain constraints. Total gross revenue is of the form $\Sigma p_i x_i$, which is a quadratic form in the prices given that the x's are linear in the prices, see (4.1). But we may also express the programming problem in quantities instead of prices by solving the system (4.1) for the p's, which leads to four "inverted demand equations" which are linear in the x's; and this, in turn, makes $\Sigma p_i x_i$ quadratic in the x's. As long as there is no problem of uncertainty about the numerical values of the coefficients of the problem, it does not matter whether we work with p's or x's. Following Houthakker, we shall use the x-approach, which leads to the objective function

$$\begin{aligned} Q(x) = \sum_1^4 p_i x_i = 18x_1 + 16x_2 + 22x_3 + 20x_4 \\ -\tfrac{1}{2}\left\{6x_1^2 + 2x_1x_2 + 16x_1x_3 + 10x_2^2 + 2x_2x_3 + 8x_2x_4 + 17x_3^2 + 6x_3x_4 + 11x_4^2\right\}, \end{aligned} \tag{4.2}$$

or in the matrix notation of (1.1):

$$a = \begin{bmatrix} 18 \\ 16 \\ 22 \\ 20 \end{bmatrix}; \qquad B = \begin{bmatrix} 6 & 1 & 8 & 0 \\ 1 & 10 & 1 & 4 \\ 8 & 1 & 17 & 3 \\ 0 & 4 & 3 & 11 \end{bmatrix}. \tag{4.3}$$

There are two types of constraint subject to which maximization takes place. First, there is the requirement that none of the quantities be negative:

1. $x_1 \geq 0$
2. $x_2 \geq 0$
3. $x_3 \geq 0$
4. $x_4 \geq 0$.

Second, there are constraints due to the limited availability of certain factors of production. Thus, the production of each unit of x_1, x_2, x_3 or x_4 requires 1 unit of a factor A of which the supply is limited to $1^{2/3}$ units; and there is a factor B which is used for x_1 and x_3, and a factor C which is used for x_2 and x_4, both of which are in limited supply. So we have three additional constraints which are specified as

$$\begin{array}{ll} 5. & x_1 + x_2 + x_3 + x_4 \leq 1\tfrac{2}{3} \\ 6. & 5x_1 + 10x_3 \leq 2 \\ 7. & 4x_2 + 5x_4 \leq 3. \end{array}$$

Combining these seven constraints, we arrive at the general form $C'x \leq d$ when we specify

$$C' = \begin{bmatrix} -1 & 0 & 0 & 0 \\ 0 & -1 & 0 & 0 \\ 0 & 0 & -1 & 0 \\ 0 & 0 & 0 & -1 \\ 1 & 1 & 1 & 1 \\ 5 & 0 & 10 & 0 \\ 0 & 4 & 0 & 5 \end{bmatrix}; \quad d = \begin{bmatrix} 0 \\ 0 \\ 0 \\ 0 \\ 1\tfrac{2}{3} \\ 2 \\ 3 \end{bmatrix}. \tag{4.4}$$

The computational procedure can then be described conveniently in terms of the following three steps:

Initial Step. Compute the vector e defined in (2.7), i.e.,

$$e = C'x^0 - d = C'B^{-1}a - d \ .$$

If all elements of e are nonpositive, then the unconstrained maximum $x^0 = B^{-1}a$ satisfies all constraints and no further computations are necessary. If one or more elements of e are positive, compute E defined in (2.6), i.e. $E = C'B^{-1}C$; proceed then to the Intermediate Steps.

In our example, we have for $-e$:[19]

$$-e = \{4.560 \quad 0.475 \quad -1.229 \quad 1.981 \quad -4.119 \quad -8.508 \quad -8.802\},$$

which shows that x^0 violates constraints 3, 5, 6, 7. So we have to compute E, which is the symmetric matrix

$$\begin{bmatrix} 1.043 & -0.128 & -0.516 & 0.187 & -0.586 & -0.051 & -0.426 \\ -0.128 & 0.250 & 0.064 & -0.108 & -0.078 & -0.007 & -0.457 \\ -0.516 & 0.064 & 0.379 & -0.127 & 0.200 & -1.211 & 0.377 \\ 0.187 & -0.108 & -0.127 & 0.256 & -0.208 & 0.333 & -0.846 \\ -0.586 & -0.078 & 0.200 & -0.208 & 0.673 & 0.936 & 1.352 \\ -0.051 & -0.007 & -1.211 & 0.333 & 0.936 & 12.363 & -1.636 \\ -0.426 & -0.457 & 0.377 & -0.846 & 1.352 & -1.636 & 6.056 \end{bmatrix}.$$

Intermediate Steps, No. 1. Set up a "sign table of quadratic programming" which is a rectangular array of signs (plus, minus, or zero) the rows of which correspond to the N constraints, the columns to vectors x^S obtained by maximizing Q subject to a subset of S of these constraints in equational form; these signs are for any x^S the signs of the successive elements of $FE_S^{-1}e_S - e_T$, which should be nonnegative in order that x^S satisfies the constraints, see (2.10). Indicate then the signs of $-e$ for x^0 in the first column (we have $-e = FE_S^{-1}e_S - e_T$ if $S = 0$) and write the constraint numbers corresponding to negative signs in the headings of the next columns. After this, compute $FE_S^{-1}e_S - e_T$ for all constraint sets S which consist of the single elements in the headings just-mentioned (in accordance with Rule 1); indicate the signs of the successive elements of $FE_S^{-1}e_S - e_T$ in the relevant place of their column, a dot being used for those signs which are imposed to be zero. As soon as a column emerges which has no minus signs, the further parts of this step are to be omitted and one should proceed to the Final Step immediately; when all columns have at least one minus sign, one has to proceed to Intermediate Step No. 2.

The signs of the first column are supplied immediately by the Initial Step, and so we write 3, 5, 6, 7 in the headings of the next columns (see the Sign Table below). We then have to consider $FE_S^{-1}e_S - e_T$ for S = (3), (5), (6), (7). For S = (3) e.g. this is

[19] The computations have been made in five decimal places; but they are reported here in three only.

$$\begin{bmatrix} -0.516 \\ 0.064 \\ -0.127 \\ 0.200 \\ -1.211 \\ 0.377 \end{bmatrix} [0.379]^{-1}(1.229) - \begin{bmatrix} -4.560 \\ -0.475 \\ -1.981 \\ 4.119 \\ 8.508 \\ 8.802 \end{bmatrix} = \begin{bmatrix} 2.886 \\ 0.684 \\ 1.570 \\ -3.473 \\ -12.430 \\ -7.582 \end{bmatrix},$$

and the six resulting signs are specified in the second column of the Sign Table; the dot in the third row indicates that the third constraint is imposed in equational form. It is seen that each of the four vectors $x^{(3)}, x^{(5)}, x^{(6)}, x^{(7)}$ violates at least three constraints, so we have to proceed to Intermediate Step No. 2.

SIGN TABLE OF QUADRATIC PROGRAMMING:
HOUTHAKKER'S MONOPOLIST

Con-straint	*	One-element constraint sets				Two-element constraint sets								Three-element constraint sets								
		3	5	6	7	3, 5	3, 6	3, 7	5, 2	5, 6	5, 7	6, 7	7, 2	3, 5, 2	3, 5, 6	3, 5, 7	3, 6, 7	3, 7, 2	5, 2, 6	5, 2, 7	5, 6, 7	6, 7, 2
1	+	+	+	+	+	+	+	+	+	+	+	+	+	+	+	+	+	+	+	+	+	+
2	+	+	—	+	—	—	+	—	.	+	—	—	.	.	+	—	+	.	.	.	—	.
3	—	.	—	—	—	.	.	.	—	—	—	—	—	.	.	.	.	.	—	+	—	—
4	+	+	+	+	+	+	+	+	+	+	+	+	+	+	+	+	+	+	+	+	+	+
5	—	—	.	—	—	.	—	—	.	.	.	—	—	.	.	.	+	—	.	.	.	—
6	—	—	—	.	—	—	.	—	—	.	—	.	—	—	.	—	.	—	.	—	.	.
7	—	—	—	—	.	—	—	.	—	—	.	.	.	—	—	.	.	.	—	.	.	.

*No constraint imposed in equational form.

Intermediate Steps, No. 2. Indicate in the headings of the open columns next to the columns of the one-element constraint sets which were prepared in Intermediate Step No. 1, the two-element sets which are to be considered next; do so in accordance with Rule 2, viz., by combining the constraint which is imposed in equational form with each of the violated constraints. Compute then

$$FE_S^{-1}e_S - e_T$$

for each of the resulting (two-element) sets S. As soon as a column emerges without minus signs, the further parts of this step should be omitted and one should proceed to the Final Step immediately; otherwise one has to proceed to Intermediate Step No. 3.

In our case we have to consider 8 two-element sets; we note that six additional sets, viz., (5, 3), (6, 3), (6, 5), (7, 3), (7, 5), (7, 6), need not be analyzed separately because they occur in reverse order also [like (3, 5), (3, 6), etc.]. We then compute $FE_S^{-1}e_S - e_T$ for each of these eight S's. For example, taking $S = (3, 5)$, we have,

$$\begin{bmatrix} -0.516 & -0.580 \\ 0.064 & -0.078 \\ -0.127 & -0.208 \\ -1.211 & 0.936 \\ 0.377 & 1.352 \end{bmatrix} \begin{bmatrix} 0.379 & 0.200 \\ 0.200 & 0.673 \end{bmatrix}^{-1} \begin{bmatrix} 1.229 \\ 4.119 \end{bmatrix} - \begin{bmatrix} -4.560 \\ -0.475 \\ -1.981 \\ 8.508 \\ 8.802 \end{bmatrix} = \begin{bmatrix} 0.962 \\ -0.002 \\ 0.707 \\ -2.809 \\ -0.527 \end{bmatrix},$$

and the resulting signs (with dots inserted in the third and the fifth place) are specified in the column under (3, 5). It is seen that in each of the eight columns there are at least two negative entries, so we proceed to Intermediate Step No. 3.

Intermediate Steps, No. 3. In accordance with Rule 2, indicate in the headings of the open columns next to the columns of the two-element constraint sets which were prepared in Intermediate Step No. 2, the three-element sets S which are to be considered next. Compute for each of these $FE_S^{-1}e_S - e_T$ but proceed to the Final Step immediately as soon as such a vector contains nonnegative elements only; otherwise proceed to Intermediate Step No. 4 which deals with four-element constraint sets in the same way.

Our example requires the consideration of 9 three-element sets. Considering in particular the fourth, (3, 6, 7), we find for $FE_S^{-1}e_S - e_T$

$$\begin{bmatrix} -0.516 & -0.051 & -0.426 \\ 0.064 & -0.007 & -0.457 \\ -0.127 & 0.333 & -0.846 \\ 0.200 & 0.936 & 1.352 \end{bmatrix} \begin{bmatrix} 0.379 & -1.211 & 0.377 \\ -1.211 & 12.363 & -1.636 \\ 0.377 & -1.636 & 6.056 \end{bmatrix}^{-1} \cdot \begin{bmatrix} 1.229 \\ 8.508 \\ 8.802 \end{bmatrix} - \begin{bmatrix} -4.560 \\ -0.475 \\ -1.981 \\ 4.119 \end{bmatrix} = \begin{bmatrix} 0.400 \\ 0.233 \\ 0.414 \\ 0.620 \end{bmatrix}.$$

All elements of this vector are positive, so we proceed to the Final Step. For completeness' sake, the columns of the five remaining vectors $[x^{(3,7,2)}, \ldots, x^{(6,7,2)}]$ are also specified; but this is not required since we can proceed to the Final Step immediately after the fourth vector.

Final Step. As soon as an Intermediate Step has led to an x^S which violates none of the constraints, verify the hypothesis $x^S = \hat{x}$ by considering all vectors x^{Sh}. If each x^{Sh} violates constraint h, then the hypothesis is correct. If some x^{Sh} does not violate constraint h, the hypothesis is not correct. In that case, one has to take up the Intermediate Steps again and to proceed until a new x^S is found which violates none of the constraints, after which the Final Step is applied to this x^S; and so on.

In our case there are three sets S^h to be considered, viz., (3, 6), (3, 7), and (6, 7). It happens that the corresponding vectors have all been considered in Intermediate Step No. 2: $x^{(3,6)}$ violates constraint 7 (and also 5), $x^{(3,7)}$ violates 6 (and also 2 and 5), and $x^{(6,7)}$ violates 3 (and also 2 and 5). The conclusion is $x^{(3,6,7)} = \hat{x}$; the numerical value of this vector is

$$\hat{x} = \{0.400 \quad 0.233 \quad 0 \quad 0.414\} ,$$

as follows from the numerical specification given in Intermediate Step No. 3.[20] The corresponding Q-value is [see (2.11)]:

$$Q(\hat{x}) = \tfrac{1}{2}[18 \quad 16 \quad 22 \quad 20]\begin{bmatrix} 6 & 1 & 8 & 0 \\ 1 & 10 & 1 & 4 \\ 8 & 1 & 17 & 3 \\ 0 & 4 & 3 & 11 \end{bmatrix}^{-1}\begin{bmatrix} 18 \\ 16 \\ 22 \\ 20 \end{bmatrix}$$

$$-\tfrac{1}{2}[1.229 \quad 8.508 \quad 8.802]\begin{bmatrix} 0.379 & -1.211 & 0.377 \\ -1.211 & 12.363 & -1.636 \\ 0.377 & -1.636 & 6.056 \end{bmatrix}^{-1}\begin{bmatrix} 1.229 \\ 8.508 \\ 8.802 \end{bmatrix} = 17.037 .$$

5. Concluding Remarks

Whether the present method is or is not computationally efficient compared with other methods of quadratic programming is a question that does not admit a unique answer applicable to all cases.[21] To take an extreme example, Houthakker's capacity method works in the simplest conceivable way when $\hat{x} = 0$ (because this method "starts in the origin") but it is much worse off when the optimal vector is that of the unconstrained maximum. On the other hand, the present method is simplest when the latter alternative

---

[20] When nonnegativity constraints are imposed on each of the elements of x, the vector $FE_S^{-1}e_S - e_T$ (completed with zeros at appropriate places) gives x^S immediately. If this is not the case, x^S is to be found from

$$x^S = x^0 - B^{-1}C_S E_S^{-1} e_S = B^{-1}(a - C_S E_S^{-1} e_S) ,$$

where C_S is the submatrix of C corresponding to the constraints of S. This result follows directly from (2.4) and (2.8).

[21] There is a computational advantage of the present method which seems worth-while, viz., that there is no problem of accumulation of rounding errors in the successive intermediate steps. The reason is that at every step we turn back to the basic matrix E and vector e.

applies, while it is much poorer when $\hat{x} = 0$ because this implies that as many as n constraints are satisfied in equational form. Generally, the method is simple as long as the constrained maximum satisfies few constraints exactly. This follows directly from the fact that the successive intermediate steps require the inversion of matrices the order of which increases successively.

There is one important situation in which the method seems to be very advantageous. Suppose that a quadratic programming problem has been solved (by one method or another) and that one is interested in the sensitivity of the solution for changes in the constraints or in the coefficients of the objective function. As long as such changes are small, there is a good chance that the set S of constraints which the new optimum satisfies in equational form is the same as the similar set of the old optimum. This hypothesis can be tested in a straightforward fashion by means of Rule 3, which means that the initial step and all intermediate steps can be deleted if the test turns out to be positive; and the final step which is carried out gives then the new optimum immediately.

References

Arrow, K.J., L. Hurwicz and H. Uzawa: 1958, *Studies in Linear and Nonlinear Programming*, Stanford University Press, Stanford, California.

Beale, E.M.L.: 1955, "On Minimizing a Convex Function Subject to Linear Inequalities," *Journal of the Royal Statistical Society* (B) **17**, 173-184.

Beale, E.M.L.: 1959, "On Quadratic Programming," *Naval Research Logistics Quarterly* **6**, pp. 227-243.

Dantzig, G.B.: 1959, "General Convex Objective Forms," RAND Corporation Report P 1664.

Frank, M. and P. Wolfe: 1956, "An Algorithm for Quadratic Programming," *Naval Research Logistics Quarterly* **3**, 95-110.

Hildreth, C: 1957, "A Quadratic Programming Procedure," *Naval Research Logistics Quarterly* **4**, 79-85.

Houthakker, H.S.: 1959, "The Capacity Method of Quadratic Programming," Technical Report No. 71, Department of Economics, Stanford University.

Markowitz, H.: 1956, "The Optimization of a Quadratic Function Subject to Linear Constraints," *Naval Research Logistics Quarterly* **3**, 111-133.

Theil, H: 1958, *Economic Forecasts and Policy*, North-Holland Publishing Co., Amsterdam.

Wolfe, P.: 1959, "The Simplex Method for Quadratic Programming," *Econometrica* **27**, 382-398.

Zoutendijk, G.: 1959, "Maximizing a Function in a Convex Region," *Journal of the Royal Statistical Society* (B) **21**, pp. 338-355.

Zoutendijk, G.: 1960, *Methods of Feasible Directions, a Study in Linear and Non-Linear Programming*, Thesis, Amsterdam.

CHAPTER 73

THE EFFECT OF FORECASTING ERRORS ON OPTIMAL PROGRAMMING*

HENRI THEIL
Netherlands School of Economics
(now Erasmus University)
Rotterdam, The Netherlands

E. KAPTEIN
Netherlands School of Economics
(now Erasmus University)
Rotterdam, The Netherlands

ABSTRACT. A programming method proposed by one of the authors is applied to a problem of anti-depression policy. The method is applicable whenever the problem of a policy-maker can be formulated as that of maximizing a quadratic welfare or objective function subject to linear restrictions. A distinction is made between instrument variables which are controlled by the policy-maker and noncontrolled variables which form the subject of the policy-maker's preferences and can be influenced indirectly by means of the instruments.

Attention is paid to the problem of uncertainty arising from the fact that the constraints of the problem are only known imperfectly by the time the policy-maker has to take his decisions, and so have to be predicted. The "welfare" effect of errors in forecasting is studied in detail for the case of a government policy-maker whose restrictions are derived from an econometric model of his economy. The economy chosen for the application is that of the United States in the period 1933-1936. The object of the policy is supposed to be to end the depression. The uncertainty is thought of as restricted to the disturbances of the structural equations of the model.

1. Introductory

In this article we shall be concerned with a policy-maker who faces certain constraints and whose goals are measured in terms of a preference function. The policy-maker may be anybody who has to take certain decisions on the basis of incomplete information, but we impose the following mathematical restrictions: the constraints should be linear, and the preference function quadratic. In spite of this, however, the approach is applicable to a large range of problems; here we shall give an application to a relatively simple problem of anti-depression policy. The approach to be described is dynamic in the sense that the decisions taken are based on some strategy; we shall be concerned in particular with the effect of forecasting errors, the presence of which is due to the absence of complete information. For a detailed description of the general theoretical background of these ideas reference is made to a recent monograph of one of the authors (Theil, 1958).

The organization of this paper is as follows. In Section 2 the general problem will be formulated, first for the abstract mathematical case and then for the application.

* This article first appeared in C.W. Churchman and M. Verhulst, eds., *Management Sciences, Models and Techniques*, 1 (1960), Pergamon Press PLC, Oxford, U.K., 295-322. Reprinted with the permission of Pergamon Press PLC.

Section 3 deals with the problem of the maximizing strategy and in particular with the first-period behaviour of this strategy, which is derived by means of a theorem on certainty equivalence. In Section 4 we deal with the consequences of suboptimal first-period decisions, with their effect on later decisions and with the loss which they cause, while in Section 5 we shall consider the case in which these suboptimal decisions are due to errors of forecasting. Section 6 contains some concluding remarks.

2. Formulation of the Problem

2.1. THE GENERAL CASE

Suppose that our policy-maker has certain variables which he controls. We call these variables *instruments* and write them as $x_{(1)}, \ldots, x_{(m)}$ (or x as a column vector). Suppose also that the policy-maker is interested in certain variables $y_{(1)}, \ldots, y_{(n)}$ (or y in vector notation) which he does not control, but which he may try to influence indirectly, viz., by means of his instruments. These variables will be called *noncontrolled variables*. The policy-maker's preferences are measured in terms of a preference function, which is supposed to be quadratic in the instruments and the noncontrolled variables:

$$w(x, y) = a'x + b'y + \tfrac{1}{2}(x'Ax + y'By + x'Cy + y'C'x), \tag{2.1}$$

where a and b are column vectors (and a', b' their transpose) and A, B and C matrices, all of appropriate order. These vectors and matrices are taken as fixed and known.

The problem is to maximize (2.1) subject to certain constraints, which are assumed to describe each of the noncontrolled variables linearly in terms of the instruments:

$$y = Rx + s, \tag{2.2}$$

R being an $n \times m$ matrix and s a column vector of n components. R is considered as a fixed and known matrix, but s will be assumed to be a random vector. Hence the constraints subject to which the maximization of (2.1) takes place are stochastic, which means that our policy-maker has to take decisions under uncertainty. This will be elaborated in Section 3.

The situation described above is essentially static, since all variables are assumed to refer to one period of time. We proceed to generalize this as follows. Suppose that the policy-maker has a horizon of T periods; and write $x_h(t)$ for the h-th instrument in the t-th period, and similarly $y_i(t)$. We write the instruments and noncontrolled variables as column vectors of mT and nT components, respectively, and group them according to time in subvectors as follows:

$$x = \begin{bmatrix} x_1 \\ \cdot \\ \cdot \\ \cdot \\ x_T \end{bmatrix}; \quad x_t = \begin{bmatrix} x_1(t) \\ \cdot \\ \cdot \\ \cdot \\ x_m(t) \end{bmatrix};$$
$$y = \begin{bmatrix} y_1 \\ \cdot \\ \cdot \\ \cdot \\ y_T \end{bmatrix}; \quad y_t = \begin{bmatrix} y_1(t) \\ \cdot \\ \cdot \\ \cdot \\ y_n(t) \end{bmatrix}. \tag{2.3}$$

As in the static case, we assume that the preference function is quadratic. Hence the form (2.1) is applicable here too, except that a and b are now column vectors of mT and nT components respectively, and that A, B and C are likewise enlarged.

Again, the problem is to maximize the preference function subject to linear constraints. These constraints will be written in the form (2.2), x and y now being interpreted according to (2.3). Also, R is again interpreted as a matrix of fixed and known coefficients, and s as a random vector; but we assume in addition that R can be partitioned into T^2 submatrices (all of order $n \times m$) as follows:

$$R = \begin{bmatrix} R_{11} & 0 & \dots & 0 \\ R_{21} & R_{22} & \dots & 0 \\ \dots & \dots & \dots & \dots \\ R_{T1} & R_{T2} & \dots & R_{TT} \end{bmatrix} \tag{2.4}$$

This assumption implies a restriction only as far as the zero submatrices above the diagonal blocks are concerned; it implies that no noncontrolled variable depends on instruments of later periods:

$$y_t = \sum_{\tau=1}^{t} R_{t\tau} x_\tau + s_t , \tag{2.5}$$

s_t being a subvector of s (in the same way as y_t is a subvector of y). It will be evident that the assumption that no $y_i(t)$ depends on later x's is a reasonable one.

2.2. OPTIMAL MACRODYNAMIC POLICY-MAKING[1]

In our example a government policy-maker is interested in bringing the depression of the United States in the period 1933-1936 (which is the period of President Roosevelt's first administration) to an end. We start with the constraints which this policy-maker has to face, and we shall specify them by means of a very simple econometric model constructed by Klein[2]. This model runs as follows. First, there is a consumption function which describes aggregate consumption in year t (C_t) in terms of non-wage income (profits, Π_t), non-wage income lagged one year (Π_{t-1}) and total wage income ($W_{1t} + W_{2t}$):[3,4]

$$C_t = 16.78 + .020\Pi_t + .225\Pi_{t-1} + .800(W_{1t} + W_{2t}) + u_{Ct}, \tag{2.6}$$

u_{Ct} being a random disturbance; the separate symbols W_{1t} and W_{2t} refer to the private wage bill and the government wage bill respectively. Second, there is an investment function describing net investment (I_t) in terms of non-wage income, non-wage income lagged one year, and the stock of capital goods at the beginning of the year (K_{t-1}):

$$I_t = 17.79 + .231\Pi_t + .546\Pi_{t-1} - .146K_{t-1} + u_{It}. \tag{2.7}$$

Third, there is a demand-for-labour equation which describes the private wage bill in terms of national income (Y) including business taxes (T) but excluding the government wage bill, of the same variable lagged one year $[(Y + T - W_2)_{t-1}]$, and of time (t):

$$W_{1t} = 1.60 + .420(Y + T - W_2)_t + .164(Y + T - W_2)_{t-1} + \\ + .135(t - 1931) + u_{Wt}. \tag{2.8}$$

---

[1] The general set-up of this example has been taken from Van den Bogaard and Theil (1958), to which we refer for further details.

[2] Model I, described in Klein (1950, pp. 58-80).

[3] The numerical values of the coefficients in the following three equations are full-information maximum-likelihood estimates derived under the assumption that the disturbances of the three equations are uncorrelated; they are taken from Chernoff and Divinski (1953, pp. 237, 250, 299). The numerical values given in this paper are in general specified up to three decimal places, but the actual computations have all been carried out in six decimal places.

[4] All variables of this model are measured in billions (10^9) of dollars of 1934 purchasing power (except t which is measured in calendar years).

Finally, there are three identities:

$$\left.\begin{aligned} Y_t &= C_t + I_t + G_t - T_t \\ \Pi_t &= Y_t - W_{1t} - W_{2t} \\ K_t &= I_t + K_{t-1}, \end{aligned}\right\} \tag{2.9}$$

G_t being the government expenditure on goods and services in year t.

The purpose of this six-equation system is to describe six endogenous variables, viz., C, I, W_1, Y, Π and K, in terms of the four exogenous variables W_2, T, G and t. Among the endogenous variables, C (total consumption) is particularly interesting because it is a direct measure for the level of well-being of the population. In fact, C will be one of the noncontrolled variables, which can be explained conveniently as follows. Suppose that our policy-maker stands at the beginning of 1933 and that he considers a "desired value" of consumption in 1936 (the last year of the four-year period) that value which implies a per capita consumption level equal to the 1929 level. Assuming a 1 per cent annual increase of the population,[5] this implies $C_{36}^* = 61.97$ (in billions of 1934 dollars), where C_{36}^* stands for the desired value of total consumption in 1936.[6] Another interesting endogenous variable is I (net investment) because it is concerned with the future well-being of the population. Now during the twenties, investment was about 10 per cent of the amount of consumption; let us then specify the desired value of investment in 1936 as 10 per cent of C_{36}^*, i.e., $I_{36}^* = 6.20$. Still another important feature is the income distribution. In the twenties, the ratio of profits to the private wage bill (Π/W_1) had fluctuated around ½, but it dropped considerably in the early thirties. We shall handle this by introducing a "distribution variable" $D = W_1 - 2\Pi$ and putting its desired value in 1936 equal to zero, $D_{36}^* = 0$. The desired values of the three variables C, I and D in the first three years (1933-1935) are obtained by linear interpolation between the realized value in 1932 and the desired value for 1936; they are shown in the last three columns of Table 1.

[5] The actual increase of the population is now known, of course, but what matters in this connection is the policy-maker's knowledge at the beginning of 1933.

[6] The numerical data underlying the discussion of this and the next paragraph are all taken from Klein (1950, p. 135).

TABLE 1. Desired Value of Instruments and Noncontrolled Variables, 1933-1936 (in Billions of 1934 Dollars per Year)

	W_2^*	T^*	G^*	C^*	I^*	D^*
1933	5.04	7.40	10.44	49.69	-3.10	11.25
1934	5.25	7.63	10.87	53.78	.00	7.50
1935	5.47	7.87	11.30	57.88	3.10	3.75
1936	5.68	8.11	11.73	61.97	6.20	.00

Before applying the general framework of Section 2.1 to our present set-up we want to handle first our instruments in a similar manner. As government instruments we shall take three of the four exogenous variables, viz., W_2 (government wage bill), T (business taxes) and G (government expenditure on goods and services). These variables showed an increasing trend over the period 1920-1932, which should be regarded as a natural development for an expanding economy like that of the United States. Accordingly, we shall introduce as "desired values" of these instruments the extrapolated values of their least-squares regressions on time fitted to the period 1920-1932; the resulting numerical values are given in the first three columns of Table 1.

It is, of course, easily possible to make objections to the desired values of the two preceding paragraphs and to formulate alternative values which are at least equally reasonable; but this is not essential for the method as such, and it is in fact quite simple to handle a series of alternative values.[7] Also, it will be clear that it is in general impossible to attain all desired results simultaneously. But it is exactly here that the general framework of Section 2.1 becomes of importance. To see this, let us write both instruments (W_2, T, G) and noncontrolled variables (C, I, D) as deviations from their desired values; thus, going back to (2.3), we have

$$x = \begin{bmatrix} x_{33} \\ x_{34} \\ x_{35} \\ x_{36} \end{bmatrix}; \quad x_{32+t} = \begin{bmatrix} (W_2)_{32+t} - (W_2^*)_{32+t} \\ T_{32+t} - T_{32+t}^* \\ G_{32+t} - G_{32+t}^* \end{bmatrix};$$
$$y = \begin{bmatrix} y_{33} \\ y_{34} \\ y_{35} \\ y_{36} \end{bmatrix}; \quad y_{32+t} = \begin{bmatrix} C_{32+t} - C_{32+t}^* \\ I_{32+t} - I_{32+t}^* \\ D_{32+t} - D_{32+t}^* \end{bmatrix}. \tag{2.10}$$

[7] This is because the optimal behaviour is linear in the desired values; cf. footnote 14 below.

Furthermore, let our goal be, not the attainment of all desired values (which is in general not feasible), but the minimization of the sum of squares of the deviations between realized and desired values. Hence our preference function is

$$w(x, y) = -(x'x + y'y), \tag{2.11}$$

which is easily seen to be a special case of (2.1) with

$$a = b = 0; \; -\tfrac{1}{2}A = -\tfrac{1}{2}B = I; \; C = 0\,, \tag{2.12}$$

I being the unit matrix of order 12.[8]

Our problem has now been reduced to the maximization of the simple quadratic form (2.11) subject to the constraints implied by the model (2.6)-(2.9). This model is, however, not yet in the form required by (2.2) and (2.5), because its equations contain endogenous variables in their right-hand sides. We must therefore write the model in reduced form, which implies that each of the endogenous variables is written explicitly as a linear function of current and lagged exogenous variables, lagged endogenous variables, and disturbances.[9] But this is still not yet the required form, because the occurrence of lagged endogenous variables is admissible only insofar as they refer to years before 1933 (in which case the values taken by these variables are supposed to be known numerically). Insofar as these lagged endogenous variables refer to 1933 or later, they have to be eliminated by means of their reduced-form equation.[10] The result is an equation system of the type (2.2) and (2.5) in which the x and y-variables are as specified in (2.10). The matrix R can be partitioned as in (2.4), but it has the further interesting property that the diagonal blocks, as well as the submatrices parallel to these blocks, are equal.

This simple form of partitioning holds because of the fact that the coefficients of the equation system are independent of time. Thus, the submatrix R_I describes the dependence of the noncontrolled variables on

[8] Note that we have $a = b = 0$ only because we have defined instruments and noncontrolled variables as deviations from the desired values, the sum of squares of which is to be minimized.

[9] This reduced form exists for a linear model of the type (2.6)-(2.9) provided that (i) the model is complete in the sense that it contains as many equations as endogenous variables, and (ii) the coefficient matrix of the endogenous variables in this model [which is square because of (i)] is nonsingular.

[10] For example, the reduced-form equation for C_{34} contains K_{33} in its right-hand side. Then we eliminate the latter variable by applying the reduced-form equation for K_{33}, which does not contain endogenous variables of 1933 in its right-hand side. This procedure must be applied twice for C_{35} (because its reduced-form equation contains K_{34}, and this variable has a reduced-form equation containing endogenous variables of 1933, which must in turn be eliminated); it has to be applied three times for C_{36}.

$$R = \begin{bmatrix} R_1 & 0 & 0 & 0 \\ R_2 & R_1 & 0 & 0 \\ R_3 & R_2 & R_1 & 0 \\ R_4 & R_3 & R_2 & R_1 \end{bmatrix} \tag{2.13}$$

current instruments, R_2 describes the dependence of these variables on the instruments lagged one year, etc. These matrices are given in the first three columns of Table 2.

TABLE 2. Parameters of the Constraints in the Macrodynamic Problem

	$W_2 - W_2^*$	$T - T^*$	$G - G^*$	u_C	u_I	u_W	Constant term
		R_1			S_1		σ_{33}
$C - C^*$	.666	-.188	.671	1.671	.671	1.148	-5.393
$I - I^*$	-.052	-.296	.259	.259	1.259	-.089	-3.704
$D - D^*$	.285	2.358	-1.427	-1.427	-1.427	2.217	-.729
		R_2			S_2		σ_{34}
$C - C^*$	-.234	-1.044	1.170	1.170	1.071	-.078	-7.554
$I - I^*$	-.152	-.894	.759	.759	.574	-.287	-4.524
$D - D^*$	.095	1.172	-.475	-.475	-.266	.792	-.062
		R_3			S_3		σ_{35}
$C - C^*$	-.172	-1.006	.859	.859	.604	-.318	-8.034
$I - I^*$	-.076	-.518	.382	.382	.113	-.213	-5.030
$D - D^*$	-.007	.186	.033	.033	.281	.213	1.998
		R_4			S_4		σ_{36}
$C - C^*$	-.079	-.543	.396	.396	.052	-.227	-8.228
$I - I^*$	-.005	-.088	.024	.024	-.261	-.069	-5.892
$D - D^*$	-.060	-.285	.301	.301	.508	-.044	5.106

As to the additive structure (s) of the constraints this consists of several components. First, it contains values of variables (endogenous as well as exogenous) of years before 1933; these values are known numerically, so that their linear combinations in s are simply represented by fixed numbers. Second, there are the values taken by the noninstrumental exogenous variable t (time) during the four-year period 1933-1936. These values are of course known too at the beginning of 1933, so that they can be combined with the fixed numbers mentioned above. Together, both categories lead to a column vector σ of 12 components, which can be partitioned in four subvectors of three components each, σ_{33}, ..., σ_{36}, according to the year to which they refer; this vector is specified numerically in the last column of Table 2. Further, there are the disturbances of the model. The relevant disturbance vector u can be partitioned in four subvectors, u_{33}, ..., u_{36} (according to the year to which they refer), and each of them consists of three components, viz., the disturbance of the consumption, of the investment, and of the demand-for-labour function. Now it is easy to see that the first subvector s_{33} of the additive structure of the constraints depends only on 1933-disturbances (i.e., on u_{33}), that the second subvector s_{34} depends on u_{33} and u_{34}, etc.; also, that s_{33} depends linearly on u_{33} in a way which is identical with that in which s_{34} depends on u_{34}, simply because the equation system (2.6)-(2.9) is linear with constant coefficients. Hence the additive structure of the constraints has the form

$$s = \sigma + Su, \tag{2.14}$$

where S is a square matrix of order 12 which can be partitioned in submatrices of order 3×3 as follows:

$$S = \begin{bmatrix} S_1 & 0 & 0 & 0 \\ S_2 & S_1 & 0 & 0 \\ S_3 & S_2 & S_1 & 0 \\ S_4 & S_3 & S_2 & S_1 \end{bmatrix} \tag{2.15}$$

in which S_1 is the matrix which describes the dependence of a subvector of s corresponding to any year on the disturbances of the same year, similarly S_2 for the dependence on the disturbances of the preceding year, etc. The matrices S_1, ..., S_4 are given in Table 2.

3. Strategies and Certainty Equivalence

3.1. THE MAXIMIZING STRATEGY IN THE GENERAL CASE

In the preceding discussion the problem of uncertainty was not discussed except in a casual way. It will form the main problem in the present section.

Let us go back to the simple static case of Section 2.1 and consider the level of the preference function which is attained by applying some vector of instruments x. This level is obtained by substituting (2.2) into (2.1):

$$w_x = w(x, Rx + s) = k_0 + k'x + \frac{1}{2}x'Kx, \tag{3.1}$$

where k_0 is a scalar, k a column vector, and K a square matrix:

$$k_0 = b's + \frac{1}{2}s'Bs \tag{3.2}$$

$$k = a + R'b + (C + R'B)s \tag{3.3}$$

$$K = A + R'BR + CR + R'C'. \tag{3.4}$$

It is then easily seen that the vector which maximizes the preference function is

$$x^0 = -K^{-1}k, \tag{3.5}$$

the existence condition of the maximum being that K be negative-definite.

Suppose now, however, that the additive structure of the constraints (s) is random, the other vectors and matrices (a, b, A, B, C, R) being fixed and known. In that case maximization of the preference function is not feasible (for the arguments of this function are partly random); we shall suppose that the policy-maker is then satisfied with maximizing the expectation of the preference function. This expectation is

$$Ew_x = Ew(x, Rx + s) = Ek_0 + (Ek)'x + \frac{1}{2}x'Kx, \tag{3.6}$$

where use is made of the fact that K is nonstochastic [cf. (3.4)]. It follows that the x-vector which maximizes Ew_x is

$$\hat{x} = -K^{-1}Ek. \tag{3.7}$$

But suppose now that, instead of taking the expectation of the preference function, we replace the stochastic arguments of this function by their expectations:

$$\begin{aligned} w(x, Ey) &= b'Es + \frac{1}{2}(Es)'BEs \\ &+ [a + R'b + (C + R'B)Es]' \\ &+ \frac{1}{2}x'(A + R'BR + CR + R'C')x \\ &= b'Es + \frac{1}{2}(Es)'BEs + (Ek)'x + \frac{1}{2}x'Kx. \end{aligned} \tag{3.8}$$

Evidently, the function (3.8) differs from the expected preference function (3.6) only as to the constant term, which means that $\hat{x}$ according to (3.7) maximizes not only (3.6) but also (3.8).[11] In other words: if one is interested in maximizing the expectation of the quadratic preference function (2.1) subject to the constraints $y = Rx + s$ with s stochastic, then there is no objection to replacing this maximization problem by the simpler problem of maximizing (2.1) subject to $y = Rx + Es$, since the two procedures are bound to lead to the same decision $\hat{x}$. This is indicated by saying that the expectation of s is a *certainty equivalent* in decision-making.

The situation with respect to the dynamic case is slightly more complicated. It remains true that w_x as given by (3.1) measures the level of the preference function attained by applying some vector x (which is now to be specified for the whole period 1, ..., T), provided that k_0, k and K are interpreted in the appropriate dynamic way (implying that k has mT elements and that K is square of that order. It remains also true that (3.5) specifies then correctly the vector which maximizes the preference function subject to the constraints; but there is a difference as soon as we proceed to problems of uncertainty. In the dynamic case we must then formulate a *strategy*, i.e., a rule according to which the decisions of the successive periods are made dependent on the information that will be available at the time when the decision has to be taken. In our present case, this information consists of the knowledge of previous subvectors of s;[12] hence any strategy can be written as:

[11] It is to be assumed, of course, that the elements of s have finite second moments; furthermore that the first and second moments are independent of x, for otherwise Ek_0 and the constant term of (3.8) are not constants with respect to x. In fact, the theorem mentioned here can be generalized rather considerably; cf. Theil (1954), and (1958, pp. 421-425).

[12] Applying (2.5), we find that the subvector s_t is equal to $y_t - R_{t1}x_1 - \dots - R_{tt}x_t$. Hence, at the beginning of period t, when the values taken by all variables before t are known, the subvectors $s_1, \dots, s_{t-1}$ are known (the R-matrix being assumed to be known).

$$x = \begin{bmatrix} x_1 \\ x_2(s_1) \\ \cdot \\ \cdot \\ \cdot \\ x_T(s_1, \ldots, s_{T-1}) \end{bmatrix}. \tag{3.9}$$

Let us suppose that the policy-maker chooses the strategy which maximizes the expectation of the preference function; we shall call it the *maximizing strategy*. It is then easily seen that there can be no certainty equivalence in the sense that this strategy is identical with the x-vector which maximizes (2.1) subject to $y = Rx + Es$, because the latter vector is determined numerically by the expectation of s while the strategy is a function of s [cf. (3.9)]. However, the latter statement does not apply to the subvector of the maximizing strategy which refers to the first period [again cf. (3.9)]; and it can in fact be shown under appropriate conditions[13] that this first subvector is identical with the first subvector of the decision $\hat{x}$ that is taken when s is replaced by its expectation. In other words, the subvector x_1 of the maximizing strategy equals the first m elements of the vector $-K^{-1}Ek$ [cf. (3.7)].[14] This means that there is no complete certainty equivalence as in the static case, but only a *first-period certainty equivalence*; the decisions according to the maximizing strategy for the later periods (2, ..., T) can be derived by repeated application of this procedure, but this is beyond the scope of this paper.[15] We only note that the last $m(T-1)$ components of the vector $-K^{-1}Ek$ can be regarded as forecasts of these later decisions; these predictions are unbiased, as is easily verified by taking the expectation of (3.5) and comparing the results with (3.7).

3.2. ON THE MAXIMIZING STRATEGY IN THE MACRODYNAMIC CASE

In the macrodynamic case we compute the first-year decision of the maximizing strategy as the first three elements of [cf. (3.7), (3.3)-(3.4) and (2.12)]:

[13] Cf. Theil (1957) and (1958, pp. 514-519) and Simon (1956). The most important condition is that the joint distribution of the elements of s should be independent of x.

[14] It follows that the first-period decision of the maximizing strategy is linear in the expectation of s and also in the parameter vectors a and b of the constraints. If one formulates the preference function in terms of desired values (as we did in Section 2.2), and if these desired values are changed (e.g. because one is interested in deriving the consequences of the use of alternative preference functions), then a and b are linearly affected by this change while A, B and C remain as they are; and hence, since the first-period decision of the maximizing strategy depends linearly on a and b, it depends also linearly on the desired values. Cf. footnote 7 above.

[15] Cf. Van den Bogaard and Theil (1959) for a more complete numerical analysis of a strategy and its consequences in successive periods.

$$-K^{-1}Ek = -(I + R'R)^{-1}R'Es = -(I + R'R)^{-1}R'\sigma, \tag{3.10}$$

where σ (= Es) is the column vector of 12 components which is given in the last column of Table 2.[16] The results are shown in Table 3; the first column contains the first subvector x_1 of the maximizing strategy, the other columns give forecasts of the subvectors x_2, x_3, x_4 of this strategy. The table specifies the instruments as deviations from their desired values as given in Table 1; Table 4 specifies the absolute levels, together with the values that were actually attained under President Roosevelt's administration.

TABLE 3. The First-year Decision and Forecasts of Later-period Decisions According to the Maximizing Strategy in the Macrodynamic Case (in Billions of 1934 Dollars per Year)

	Decision	Forecasts of decisions		
	1933	1934	1935	1936
$W_2 - W_2^*$	1.10	1.01	.73	.68
$T - T^*$	1.22	.82	-.23	-1.12
$G - G^*$	3.83	3.05	2.41	1.57

TABLE 4. Same as Table III, But in Absolute Amounts; and Actual Values Realized in 1933-1936 (in Billions of 1934 Dollars per Year)

	Decision	Forecasts of decisions			Actual			
	1933	1934	1935	1936	1933	1934	1935	1936
W_2	6.13	6.26	6.20	6.36	5.6	6.0	6.1	7.4
T	8.62	8.45	7.64	6.99	5.4	6.8	7.2	8.3
G	14.26	13.92	13.71	13.30	9.3	10.0	10.5	10.3

[16] The expectation of s equals σ because the disturbances of the model are considered as random with zero mean and zero lag correlations. It is to be noted that, if the disturbances have zero mean but nonzero lag correlations, the expectation of s is not equal to σ but to σ plus some linear combination of the 1932-disturbances (and possibly earlier disturbances as well). The reason is that we have to take the conditional expectation of s, given the information available at the beginning of 1933.

Table 3 shows that the deviations between the desired instrument values and the values according to the maximizing strategy [as predicted with (3.10)] tend to decrease in the successive years. The two categories of government expenditure (W_2 and G) are above their desired values, which is as one could expect for an anti-depression policy. The difference T - T^* has, surprisingly enough, the expected negative sign only in the last two years. Table 4 shows that the predicted behaviour corresponding with the maximizing strategy differs from the actual 1933-1936 values in several respects: the realized government expenditures on goods and services are considerably below the strategy values in all four years, and the realized tax receipts increase from 5.4 to 8.3 billions while the strategy values decrease from 8.6 to 7.0 billions.[17]

When computing $Rx + Es$ (x being interpreted according to the numerical values of Table 3), we obtain forecasts of the development of the noncontrolled variables in the four successive years. They are given as deviations from the desired values in Table 5, in absolute amounts in Table 6 (together with the realized values). Table 5 shows a picture similar to that of Table 3: the deviations for C and I are negative (which is natural for a depression period), and for all of the three variables the deviations tend to diminish in the course of time. Table 6 reveals that the development of consumption and investment over time is more favourable according to the strategy values than according to the values that were actually realized, at least according to the preference function which is chosen here.

TABLE 5. Forecasts of Values Taken by the Noncontrolled Variables Corresponding with the Maximizing Strategy in the Macrodynamic Case (in Billions of 1934 Dollars per Year)

	1933	1934	1935	1936
C	-2.33	-2.01	-1.51	-1.24
I	-3.13	-2.38	-2.20	-2.61
D	-3.00	-2.48	-1.84	.05

[17] It is of some interest to note that the tax receipts as a percentage of national income decrease regularly from 17 in 1933 to 9 in 1936 if we take the strategy values, and that it is approximately constant (between 12 and 14) according to the realized data.

TABLE 6. Same as Table 5, But in Absolute Amounts; and Actual Values Realized in 1933-1936 (in Billions of 1934 Dollars per Year)

	Forecasts of decisions				Actual			
	1933	1934	1935	1936	1933	1934	1935	1936
C	47.36	51.77	56.37	60.73	46.5	48.7	51.3	57.7
I	-6.23	-2.38	.90	3.59	-5.1	-3.0	-1.3	2.1
D	8.25	5.02	1.91	.05	6.1	6.0	5.2	1.6

4. Suboptimal Decisions and Optimal Revisions of Future Decisions

4.1. THE GENERAL CASE

It was mentioned at the end of Section 3.1 that the last $m(T\text{-}1)$ components of $-K^{-1}Ek$ are unbiased forecasts of the corresponding decisions of the maximizing strategy. Of course, in spite of this unbiased character it remains true that these forecasts do not predict the strategy values perfectly. But in fact, even the maximizing strategy itself cannot be said to be completely perfect, because it is based on incomplete information. The only decision which is really *optimal* is x^0 as given by (3.5), k and hence s being as they are actually (even though the policy-maker has no complete information about them at the time when relevant decisions have to be taken). Any other decision x leads to a *loss* $L(x)$, which is the difference between the value of the preference function attained by applying x^0 and the value attained by applying x:

$$L(x) = k_0 + k'x^0 + \tfrac{1}{2}x^{0\prime}Kx^0 - (k_0 + k'x + \tfrac{1}{2}x'Kx) = -\tfrac{1}{2}(x - x^0)'K(x - x^0), \tag{4.1}$$

from which it follows that the loss is a positive-definite quadratic form in the "decision error" $x - x^0$, the matrix of this form being $-\frac{1}{2}K$. This result can be used in order to analyze the consequences of instrument deviations from their optimal values; this will be done in Section 4.2.

In the dynamic strategy case this result is also applicable as soon as we specify the decision x for the whole period 1, ..., T. But in addition to this, there is the interesting problem of the loss associated with a first-period decision error. We define this loss, $L_1(x_1)$, as the difference between the preference maximum that was attainable before this error was made and the (conditional) maximum which is still attainable, given the first-period decision x_1. Let us indicate the given first-period decision by x_1^* and derive the conditional maximum by means of a vector μ of Lagrange multipliers:

$$k_0 + k'x + \tfrac{1}{2}x'Kx - \mu'(x_1 - x_1^*) .$$

Differentiation with respect to x gives:

$$k + Kx^1 - \begin{bmatrix} \mu \\ 0 \end{bmatrix} = 0 ,$$

x^1 being the instrument vector of the conditional maximum. Hence:

$$x^1 = -K^{-1}k + K^{-1}\begin{bmatrix} \mu \\ 0 \end{bmatrix} = x^0 + H\begin{bmatrix} \mu \\ 0 \end{bmatrix} = x^0 + \begin{bmatrix} H_{11} \\ \cdot \\ \cdot \\ \cdot \\ H_{T1} \end{bmatrix}\mu , \tag{4.2}$$

where

$$H = K^{-1} \tag{4.3}$$

and H_{11}, H_{21}, ... are submatrices of order $m \times m$ of H (H_{11} corresponding to first-period instruments only, H_{21} to second and first-period instruments, etc.). For the first period (4.2) implies $x_1^1 = x_1^0 + H_{11}\mu$. But it is given that $x_1^1 = x_1^*$. Hence $\mu = H_{11}^{-1}(x_1^* - x_1^0)$, so that

$$x^1 - x^0 = \begin{bmatrix} H_{11} \\ \cdot \\ \cdot \\ \cdot \\ H_{T1} \end{bmatrix} H_{11}^{-1}(x_1^* - x_1^0) . \tag{4.4}$$

The difference between the preference maximum that was attainable before x_1^* was applied and the conditional maximum given x_1^* is then found by specifying the vector $x - x^0$ of (4.1) as $x^1 - x^0$ of (4.4):

$$L_1(x_1^*) = -\tfrac{1}{2}(x_1^* - x_1^0)' H_{11}^{-1} \left[H_{11} .. H_{1T}\right] H^{-1} \begin{bmatrix} H_{11} \\ \cdot \\ \cdot \\ \cdot \\ H_{T1} \end{bmatrix} H_{11}^{-1} (x_1^* - x_1^0) \qquad (4.5)$$

$$= -\tfrac{1}{2} (x_1^* - x_1^0)' H_{11}^{-1} (x_1^* - x_1^0) ,$$

a result which can be applied in a manner similar to that of (4.1).

It is of considerable interest to note that the last $m(T\text{-}1)$ components of (4.4) are to be interpreted as optimal revisions of the decision x^0, which itself has lost its optimality due to the application of x_1^*. This result, too, will be applied in Section 4.2.

4.2. OPTIMALITY AND SUBOPTIMALITY IN THE MACRODYNAMIC CASE

For the problem of the anti-depression policy we need the matrix [cf. (3.4) and (2.12)]

$$-\tfrac{1}{2} K = I + R'R , \qquad (4.6)$$

which is given in Table 7. The exposition is simplified if we start with the first-period loss, for which we need the matrix $-\frac{1}{2}H_{11}^{-1}$. This is found by inverting the matrix of Table 7 and then taking the inverse of the leading 3 × 3 submatrix; it is equal to

$$-\tfrac{1}{2} H_{11}^{-1} = \begin{bmatrix} 1.58 & .79 & -.23 \\ .79 & 7.84 & -4.73 \\ -.23 & -4.73 & 4.83 \end{bmatrix} . \qquad (4.7)$$

Applying (4.5), we find that the first-period loss is here equal to the sum of three quadratic terms,[18]

$$1.58\,(W_2 - W_2^0)^2 + 7.84\,(T - T^0)^2 + 4.83\,(G - G^0)^2 , \qquad (4.8)$$

plus the sum of three cross-terms:

[18] The superscripts 0 refer, as in Section 4.1 to the optimal value. It will be evident that the variables of (4.8) and (4.9) all refer to the year 1933, which is the reason why no time subscript has been added.

$$2[.79(W_2 - W_2^0)(T - T^0) - .23(W_2 - W_2^0)(G - G^0) - 4.73(T - T^0)(G - G^0)]. \tag{4.9}$$

The result (4.8) suggests that, as far as the quadratic terms are concerned, a correct value of T is much more important than that of W_2 or G. This statement is slightly misleading, however, because the dollar levels of these variables are not the same. An inspection of Table 4 shows that G is about two thirds larger than T in 1933. Thus, assuming a 1 per cent deviation for each of the three instruments, we find that the loss caused by the T-deviation is of the order of ten times larger than the loss caused by the W_2-deviation, and that the loss due to the G-deviation exceeds the loss due to the T-deviation by more than 50 per cent. So much for the quadratic terms (4.8); as to the cross-terms (4.9), we observe that their coefficients are rather small relative to the coefficients of the corresponding squares in (4.8) except for the T, G-term. The coefficient of this term is negative and rather large; it implies that T and G-deviations of the same sign compensate each other partly, which is a natural feature of an anti-depression policy.

Next, we consider the optimal revisions for 1934, 1935 and 1936, given certain deviations in 1933. For this purpose we need the matrix

$$\begin{bmatrix} H_{21} \\ H_{31} \\ H_{41} \end{bmatrix} H_{11}^{-1} = \begin{bmatrix} .071 & .251 & -.357 \\ -.003 & -.231 & .013 \\ .105 & .532 & -.525 \\ \cdots & \cdots & \cdots \\ .029 & .114 & -.144 \\ .022 & .113 & -.110 \\ .013 & .013 & -.066 \\ \cdots & \cdots & \cdots \\ .009 & .028 & -.043 \\ .011 & .052 & -.055 \\ -.002 & -.021 & .010 \end{bmatrix} \tag{4.10}$$

The three columns of this matrix refer to the 1933 decision errors of W_2, T and G; the horizontal partitioning refers to the three later years, and the rows within each submatrix are concerned with the revision of W_2, T or G of the corresponding year. For example, the first row specifies the optimal revision of W_2 in 1934:

TABLE 7. The Matrix -½ K of the Loss of Welfare Due to Suboptimal Decisions in the Macrodynamic Problem*

		1933			1934			1935			1936		
		W_2	T	G	W_2	T	G	W_2	T	G	W_2	T	G
1933	W_2	1.66	1.32	-.63	-.06	.62	-.66	-.10	.05	-.19	-.07	-.13	.03
	T		11.58	-7.35	.14	5.46	-4.75	-.48	1.08	-1.64	-.44	-.54	.02
	G			6.85	.28	-3.09	3.30	.49	-.27	.97	.35	.63	-.16
1934	W_2				1.65	1.26	-.58	-.07	.55	-.59	-.11	.04	-.13
	T					11.20	-7.04	.04	4.92	-4.24	-.59	.78	-1.07
	G						6.61	.35	-2.74	2.94	.56	-.20	.63
1935	W_2							1.61	1.05	-.41	-.12	.31	-.33
	T								9.88	-5.99	-.29	3.22	-2.58
	G									5.72	.60	-1.56	1.66
1936	W_2										1.53	.56	.03
	T											6.68	-3.57
	G												3.55

* The elements below the main diagonal are obtained by transposition.

$$(W_2^1)_{34} - (W_2^0)_{34} = .071\left\{(W_2)_{33} - (W_2^0)_{33}\right\} + .251\,(T_{33} - T_{33}^0) - .357\,(G_{33} - G_{33}^0)\,. \tag{4.11}$$

It is seen that W_2-deviations in 1933 do not give rise to important revisions, the elements of the first column of (4.10) being at most of the order of .1; this is in accordance with the relatively small first-period loss caused by such deviations. For the other two variables, however, the revisions are much larger. For example, if in 1933 T exceeds its optimal value, then the 1934 optimal value of T is reduced by about one quarter of this excess, and those of W_2 and G are raised by one quarter and one half, respectively, of the same excess; similarly, if in 1933 G exceeds its optimal value, then its optimal value in 1934 is reduced by one half of this excess, that of W_2 by about one third, while that of T remains practically the same. These results are in qualitative accordance with conventional ideas about anti-depression policy, but they are much more specific.

Finally, we turn to the loss which is due to the application of an instrumental vector which is specified for the whole four-year period. According to (4.1) this loss is a quadratic form with $-\frac{1}{2}K$ as specified in Table 7 as matrix. A quick glance at this table shows that the figures tend to decrease when we move from North-West to South-East.[19] Another survey is presented in Tables 8 and 9. Table 8 contains the diagonal elements of $-\frac{1}{2}K$, which are the coefficients of the squares (i.e., the coefficients of the squares of $W_2 - W_2^0$ in the four years 1933-1936, and similarly for T and G); it contains also the other elements of the diagonal submatrices of $-\frac{1}{2}K$, which are the coefficients of the cross-terms containing variables of the same year [i.e., the coefficients of the product terms $(W_2 - W_2^0)(T - T^0)$ for each of the years 1933-1936, and similarly for the W_2, G and the T, G-combinations]. It is seen that the consequences of given T or G-deviations at the beginning of the four-year period are much more serious than at the end, but that this effect is much less pronounced for W_2. Roughly speaking, the picture of Table 8 is not very much different from that of the coefficients of the first-period loss. Table 9 specifies the coefficients of some of the product terms which contain variables in two successive years, like $(T_{33} - T_{33}^0)(T_{34} - T_{34}^0)$ (which is 5.46). These are unimportant for W_2, but much larger in the case of T and G, for which they are generally positive. This means that T-errors of opposite sign in successive years compensate each other partly, and similarly for G-errors. The opposite is true, however, if we consider the combined effect of a T and a G-error in two successive years; they cause an additional loss if

[19] This is necessarily true for the diagonal elements, since the South-Eastern diagonal submatrix is $I + R_1'R_1$, the one next to it $I + R_1'R_1 + R_2'R_2$, etc.; hence, when going from Sout-East to North-West, we find that each diagonal submatrix is obtained from its predecessor by adding a positive-definite (or at least semi-definite) matrix.

they have opposite signs, which is larger if the T-error precedes the G-error in time than in the other case.

TABLE 8. Coefficients of the Loss of Welfare for the Macrodynamic Problem Corresponding to Variables in the Same Year

	Squares			Product terms		
	W_2	T	G	W_2,T	W_2,G	T,G
1933	1.66	11.58	6.85	1.32	-.63	-7.35
1934	1.65	11.20	6.61	1.26	-.58	-7.04
1935	1.61	9.88	5.72	1.05	-.41	-5.99
1936	1.53	6.68	3.55	.56	.03	-3.57

TABLE 9. Coefficients of the Loss of Welfare for the Macrodynamic Problem Corresponding to Variables in Successive Years

	W_2	T	G	T,G^*	G,T^{**}
1933/34	-.06	5.46	3.30	-4.75	-3.09
1934/35	-.07	4.92	2.94	-4.24	-2.74
1935/36	-.12	-1.56	1.66	-2.58	-1.56

* T in the first, G in the next year.
** G in the first, T in the next year.

5. Suboptimal Decisions Due to Forecasting Errors

5.1. FORECASTING ERRORS IN THE ADDITIVE STRUCTURE OF THE CONSTRAINTS: THE GENERAL CASE

The uncertainty problem, which was the main subject of Section 3, did not play an important rôle in Section 4. In fact, the decision errors which we considered there were considered as such and no attention was paid to their cause. But suppose now that they are due to forecasting errors of the additive structure of the constraints. More precisely, suppose (as before) that the coefficients of the preference function and the multiplicative structure are known, but that the policy-maker bases his decision on an estimate s_e of the additive structure in the sense that he decides on that instrument vector that would lead to a preference maximum if the additive structure were indeed

s_e. For example, we may have $s_e = Es$, which is the certainty-equivalent procedure of Section 3. It is easily seen [cf. (3.3)-(3.5)] that this instrument vector is

$$x = -K^{-1}[a + R'b + (C + R'B)s_e], \tag{5.1}$$

whence it follows that the decision error which is due to this prediction error is

$$x - x^0 = -K^{-1}(C + R'B)(s_e - s). \tag{5.2}$$

Combining (5.2) and (4.1), we find the loss which is caused by the prediction error $s_e - s$:[20]

$$\begin{aligned} \bar{L}(s_e) &= -\tfrac{1}{2}(s_e - s)'(C + R'B)'K^{-1}KK^{-1}(C + R'B)(s_e - s) \\ &= -\tfrac{1}{2}(s_e - s)'(C + R'B)'H(C + R'B)(s_e - s), \end{aligned} \tag{5.3}$$

which shows that this loss is a quadratic form in the forecasting error with matrix $-\frac{1}{2}(C + R'B)'H(C + R'B)$.[21] In particular, if we consider the mathematical expectation of this loss and assume that the certainty-equivalence procedure $s_e = Es$ is applied, then we obtain a linear combination of variances and covariances of forecasting errors.

The preceding paragraph deals with the static case. For the dynamic variant we will assume that the policy-maker bases his first-period decision on an estimate s_e of s which now refers to the whole series of T periods. This is in accordance with the certainty-equivalence procedure if $s_e = Es$, but we do not want to exclude the possibility that our policy-maker is imperfect in the art of unbiased forecasting. It is then easily seen that in this dynamic case (5.1) is still applicable, but that it must be interpreted as a vector of mT components of which the first m form the relevant first-period decision:

$$x_1 = -[H_{11} \,..\, H_{1T}][a + R'b + (C + R'B)s_e], \tag{5.4}$$

so that the first-period decision error is

$$x_1 - x_1^0 = -[H_{11} \,..\, H_{1T}](C + R'B)(s_e - s). \tag{5.5}$$

[20] In order to avoid confusion, we shall write L for loss if the predicted additive structure is its argument.

[21] Note that this matrix may be positive semi-definite instead of positive-definite. In particular, it is necessarily semi-definite if the number of instruments is below the number of components of the additive structure ($m < n$). This implies that there exist certain nonzero prediction errors which lead to a zero decision error and hence to a zero loss.

Combining this with (4.5), we obtain

$$\bar{L}_1(s_e) = -\tfrac{1}{2}(s_e - s)'(C + R'B)' \begin{bmatrix} H_{11} \\ \cdot \\ \cdot \\ \cdot \\ H_{T1} \end{bmatrix} H_{11}^{-1}\left[H_{11} \,..\, H_{1T}\right] \times (C + R'B)(s_e - s)\,; \tag{5.6}$$

which is the dynamic generalization of (5.3).[22]

5.2. THE EFFECT OF DISTURBANCES IN THE MACRODYNAMIC CASE

For the problem of the anti-depression policy we shall confine ourselves to the expected loss of the certainty-equivalence procedure, which leads — as we will show — to an evaluation of the disturbances of the structural equations.

It is easily seen [cf. (5.5), (2.12) and (2.14)] that the first-period decision error of this procedure is

$$\hat{x}_1 - x_1^0 = 2[H_{11}..H_{14}]R'(Es - s) = -2[H_{11}..H_{14}]R'Su\,, \tag{5.7}$$

where u is the twelve-element vector of disturbances of the three behavioural equations (consumption, investment, and demand for labour) in the four years 1933-1936. Comparing (5.7) with (5.5) and (5.6), we find that the expected first-period loss of the certainty-equivalence procedure is

$$E[\bar{L}_1(u)] = E(u'Mu)\,, \tag{5.8}$$

where M is the matrix

$$M = -2S'R \begin{bmatrix} H_{11} \\ \cdot \\ \cdot \\ \cdot \\ H_{41} \end{bmatrix} H_{11}^{-1}[H_{11}..H_{14}]R'S \tag{5.9}$$

[22] Note that the matrix of this quadratic form is semi-definite as soon as $m < nT$; cf. footnote 21.

which is specified numerically in Table 10. Now suppose that the twelve random disturbances are all uncorrelated, and that they are homoscedastic for each of the three behavioural equations. The former assumption implies that the matrix M is relevant only as far as its diagonal elements are concerned; the latter that the expected loss (5.8) is simply reduced to

$$\begin{aligned}&(m_1 + m_4 + m_7 + m_{10})\ var\ u_C \\ &+ (m_2 + m_5 + m_8 + m_{11})\ var\ u_I \\ &+ (m_3 + m_6 + m_9 + m_{12})\ var\ u_W ,\end{aligned}$$

where m_i is the i-th diagonal element of M, and var u_C, var u_I, var u_W the variance of the disturbances of the three equations. Hence the total expected loss consists of three components which can be directly ascribed to the random nature of each of these equations. Applying Klein's estimates of the variances[23], we obtain for the relative share of the equations in the expected first-period loss

$$.44 \quad .37 \quad .19, \tag{5.10}$$

which implies that the disturbed character of the consumption function is most serious while that of the demand-for-labour function is not very serious. It is quite interesting to compare this appraisal of the merits of the various equations with the conventional method of appraisal in econometrics. A well-known criterion is that of the ratio of the variance of the disturbances to the variance of the left-hand variable. From this point of view the consumption function is much better than the investment function. Another criterion is the variance of the disturbances measured in (squared) dollars per year; then the consumption function is still better, though not very much. The present appraisal shows, however, that the investment equation is better for decision purposes, at least under the preference criterion which we adopted here.

Two additional remarks are in order. First, an inspection of Table 10 shows that the diagonal elements outside the leading submatrix of M (m_4, m_5, ...) contribute very little to the expected loss; hence the result (5.10) is not very sensitive for deviations from homoscedasticity. Second, it is of some interest to find out how (5.10) is affected if correlations between disturbances of the same year are considered. Applying Klein's estimates of these correlations,[24] we find that the shares (5.10) are to be replaced by

$$.34 \quad .29 \quad .15, \tag{5.11}$$

---

[23] These are (in the order u_C, u_I, u_W): 1.30, 1.42, .61; cf. Klein (1950, p. 69).

[24] These correlations are: .32 for u_C and u_I, -.51 for u_C and u_W, .30 for u_I and u_W; cf. Klein (1950, p. 71). It is to be noted that the parameter estimates of the model which have been used here have been derived under the assumption that these correlations vanish; cf. footnote 4.

TABLE 10. The Matrix M of the Loss of Welfare Due to Suboptimal Decisions in the Macrodynamic Problem*

		1933			1934			1935			1936		
		u_C	u_I	u_W	u_C	u_I	u_W	u_C	u_I	u_W	u_C	u_I	u_W
	u_C	4.650	3.870	-2.405	.917	1.016	.807	.200	.080	.297	.027	-.072	.084
1933	u_I		3.506	-2.882	.845	.960	.708	.176	.063	.267	.022	-.070	.074
	u_W			4.186	-.600	-.797	-.324	-.086	.008	-.156	-.001	.071	-.041
	u_C				.278	.280	.289	.070	.037	.098	.012	-.017	.028
1934	u_I					.297	.266	.065	.030	.094	.010	-.020	.027
	u_W						.336	.081	.050	.109	.015	-.013	.032
	u_C							.020	.012	.026	.004	-.003	.008
1935	u_I								.008	.015	.002	-.001	.005
	u_W									.036	.005	-.005	.011
	u_C										.001	-.000	.001
1936	u_I											.002	-.001
	u_W												.003

* The elements below the main diagonal are obtained by transposition.

which does not add up to unity because of the presence of covariance terms. These terms are: .19 for the covariance of u_C and u_I, .10 for that of u_C and u_W, and -.08 for that of u_I and u_W. Hence the covariation of disturbances of the investment and the demand-for-labour equation is a "gain."

6. Concluding Remarks

Although the method of analysis given in the preceding pages is very promising in our view, it is nevertheless evident that several objections can be raised. We consider the following ones:

(i) As to the example of the anti-depression policy, it is of course true that in practice we never have a model which is fitted over a period that includes the strategy period. Also, it may be doubted whether a small model of the kind which we used gives a satisfactory picture of the working of a whole economy. Reference is made to Van den Bogaard and Barten (1959), who carried out a similar analysis for the Dutch economy based on a much larger model and included 1959 in the strategy period. Still another problem is the fact that the estimated coefficients of the model have been accepted as the "true" parameters. We refer to Theil and Kloek (1959), who considered the loss of welfare caused by the use of wrong coefficients.

(ii) It has been noted that the development over time of the non-instrumental exogenous variables has to be predicted at the beginning of the strategy period. In our macrodynamic example this refers only to the variable t (time), for which predictions are trivial; but in general they are not. Also, we assumed that values taken by variables in earlier periods are known;[25] in practice they are known only with a certain delay and generally imperfectly, which gives rise to a problem of observational errors.

(iii) A delicate question for macrodynamic problems is the choice of a social preference function. Reference is made to Frisch (1957), who constructed a preference function based on the convictions of a Norwegian politician.

(iv) It should be remarked again, as we did in the Introduction, that the programming method outlined here and applied to a case of government policy making, is not restricted to government planning, but can be applied every time when a policy-maker having a quadratic preference function, or a preference function which can be reasonably approximated by a quadratic one, faces linear constraints. For an example in the field of production planning, cf. in particular Holt et al. (1956) and Holt et al. (1955) and also a more extensive version of the present paper (Theil and Kaptein, 1959).

(v) Further work should be done in several directions. We mention here only the problem of inequalities and nonnegativity conditions, the general bias towards underestimation of changes (cf. Theil [1958, chap. V]) which acts as an impediment

[25] Cf. footnote 12.

with respect to the application of the certainty-equivalence procedure, and the economic interpretation of the various mathematical results. As to the third problem, it is interesting to note that the matrix K^{-1} of Section 3.1 can be interpreted as a substitution matrix (cf. Theil [1958, chap. VIII]).

References

Bogaard, P.J.M. van den, and A.P. Barten: 1959, "Optimal Macroeconomic Decision Rules for the Netherlands, 1957-1959," Report 5915, Econometric Institute, Netherlands School of Economics.

Bogaard, P.J.M. van den, and H. Theil: 1959, "Macrodynamic Policy-Making: An Application of Strategy and Certainty Equivalence Concepts to the Economy of the United States, 1933-1936," *Metroeconomica* **11**, 149-167.

Chernoff, H., and N. Divinski: 1953, "The Computation of Maximum-Likelihood Estimates of Linear Structural Equations," chapter X of *Studies in Econometric Method*, edited by W.C. Hood and T.C. Koopmans, New York-London.

Frisch, R.: 1957, "Numerical Determination of a Quadratic Preference Function for Use in Macroeconomic Programming," Memorandum of the University Institute of Economics, Oslo.

Holt, C.C., F. Modigliani, and J.F. Muth: 1956, "Derivation of a Linear Decision Rule for Production and Employment Scheduling," *Management Science* **2**, pp. 159-177.

Holt, C.C., F. Modigliani, and H.A. Simon: 1955, "A Linear Decision Rule for Production and Employment Scheduling," *Management Science* **2**, 1-30.

Klein, L.R.: 1950, *Economic Fluctuations in the United States, 1921-1941*, New York-London.

Simon, H.A.: 1956, "Dynamic Programming under Uncertainty with a Quadratic Criterion Function," *Econometrica* **24**, 74-81.

Theil, H.: 1954, "Econometric Models and Welfare Maximisation," *Weltwirtschaftliches Archiv* **72**, 60-83.

Theil, H.: 1957, "A Note on Certainty Equivalence in Dynamic Planning," *Econometrica* **25**, 346-349.

Theil, H.: 1958, *Economic Forecasts and Policy*, Amsterdam.

Theil, H., and E. Kaptein: 1959, "The Effect of Forecasting Errors on Optimal Programming of Production-Inventory and Anti-Depression Policies," Report 5906 of the Econometric Institute of the Netherlands School of Economics.

Theil, H., and T. Kloek: 1959, "The Operational Implications of Imperfect Models," Report 5911 of the Econometric Institute of the Netherlands School of Economics.

CHAPTER 74

SOME REFLECTIONS ON STATIC PROGRAMMING UNDER UNCERTAINTY*

HENRI THEIL
Netherlands School of Economics
(Now Erasmus University)
Rotterdam, The Netherlands

I. Introduction

The not-so-simple character of programming under uncertainty is well illustrated by the fact that a full session of the 1957 Stockholm conference of the International Statistical Institute was devoted to this subject while only one of the papers presented there[1] had a direct bearing on the uncertainty aspect. There are, of course, several contributions to this problem by now; but almost all focus on particular applications and do not attempt to present a general theory of programming under uncertainty. The present paper is to be regarded as a modest attempt in this direction, the adjective "modest" being in particular applicable due to the fact that the analysis will be confined to static decision-making, i.e., to the process of formulating optimal decisions for a given period at the beginning of that period. Thus, dynamic decision-making based on strategies or decision rules will not be considered here. The specific points which will be raised in this paper are: the need for a careful distinction between variables which are controlled and those which are not; the way in which the preference function and the constraints are to be handled when the transition from certainty to uncertainty is made; and the method of certainty equivalence as a convenient tool for reducing programming under uncertainty to programming under certainty. The paper is therefore largely methodological; it does not consider in any detail the numerical aspects of actually solving the programming problem. Also, the attention will be confined to the case in which all variables are real-valued and in which the uncertainty is of the probabilistic type; even more specifically, to the case in which the uncertainty problem can be handled (at least partially) by maximizing the expectation of

---

* This article first appeared in *Weltwirtschaftliches Archiv* **87** (1961) 124-138. Reprinted with the permission of the Institut für Weltwirtschaft an der Universität Kiel.

Remark: I am indebted to Dr. J.H. Drèze of the University of Louvain and Messrs. P.J.M. van den Bogaard and J.C.G. Boot for their comments on this paper.

[1] Stefan Vajda, "Inequalities in Stochastic Linear Programming," *Bulletin de l'Institut International de Statistique*, T.XXXVI, 3e Livraison, Stockholm, 1958, pp. 357 sqq.

the preference function. Generalizations are possible in some cases and will be mentioned at appropriate places.

The organization and terminology of this paper can be understood more easily if we consider programming under uncertainty at the "farthest" vertex of the "parallelogram" defined by the following vertices:

(i) "Classical maximizing" either without constraints or with constraints which however take the form of equations only; and no uncertainty being present. A simple example in economics is that of the classical theory of consumer's demand. Such a consumer is supposed to maximize a utility function which depends on the quantities $q_1, \ldots, q_n$ of the commodities which he may buy:

$$u = u(q_1, \ldots, q_n) \tag{1.1}$$

subject to the constraint that the available income be exactly spent. Denoting income by M and the various prices by $p_1, \ldots, p_n$, we can write this budget constraint as:

$$\sum_{i=1}^{n} p_i q_i = M \tag{1.2}$$

If we suppose that the p_i and M are given, then — under some appropriate further assumptions — certain unique values $q_1^0, \ldots, q_n^0$ result which maximize (1.1) subject to (1.2).

(ii) "Classical" programming, i.e., maximization subject to constraints which take at least partly the form of inequalities, and no uncertainty being present. The above example can be easily re-formulated such that it falls under this category, viz., when the requirement that the available income be exactly spent is replaced by the requirement that total expenses be at most equal to income. In that case (1.2) is replaced by

$$\sum_{i=1}^{n} p_i q_i \leqq M \tag{1.3}$$

and the problem becomes to maximize (1.1) subject to the inequality (1.3). Other well-known inequality constraints are the nonnegativity restrictions ($q_1 \geqq 0$, $q_2 \geqq 0$, ... in the present case).

(iii) Maximizing under uncertainty, the constraints if any being all of the equation type as under (i). Such a case will occur e.g. when our consumer plans his expenditure for the next month, say, and when he does not know that month's income (which he is supposed to spend exactly). In that case, (1.2) is again applicable, but there is the difficulty that its right-hand side is uncertain.

(iv) Programming under uncertainty, part of the constraints being of the inequality type as under (ii). Such a case will arise when the example under (iii) is applied to (1.3) instead of (1.2).

This paper deals with the "vertices" (iii) and (iv), in particular with the latter. I shall follow the convention of reserving the term "programming" when inequalities enter into the picture, and "maximizing" when this is not the case.[2] It will further be assumed throughout that the constraints with which we deal are neither contradictory nor dependent.

The order of discussion is as follows. Sections II-IV deal with maximizing, the first with the case of no constraints, the second with that of nonstochastic constraints, the third with the case of stochastic constraints. In all cases there is uncertainty, which is of course necessarily at the level of the preference function if there are no stochastic constraints. Sections V-VII deal with programming, the first for the case of nonstochastic constraints, the last two for that of stochastic constraints.

II. Maximizing Without Constraints

At the risk of seeming pedantic, I shall try to make a careful distinction between the variables which are controlled by the policy-maker (let us call him that way) and those which are not; I hope to be able to show below - in Sections IV and V - that this is indeed a useful thing to do. "Controlled" is to be understood here in the sense that the policy-maker is in a position to manipulate such variables independently of each other. We shall call them *controlled variables* or, following Tinbergen,[3] *instruments* and denote them by $x_1, ..., x_m$ or x as a vector. All other variables are by definition *noncontrolled variables* and written $y_1, ..., y_n$ or y as a vector.

The policy-maker's preference function is then written in the form

$$w = w(x, y) \tag{2.1}$$

and this is the function to be maximized in the sense that a higher w-value is always preferred to a lower w-value. For example, let the x's be quantities of various commodities produced by a manufacturer and the y's their net prices (unit gross revenue minus unit cost). Assuming that the quantities are controlled but the net prices not, and assuming that it is the manufacturer's goal to maximize his net returns, his preference function takes the simple bilinear form $w = \Sigma x_h y_h$; and this is to be maximized.

There is, however, the difficulty that only part of the arguments of the preference function are under the policy-maker's control. Specifically the y's are not, which means

---

[2] This terminology is unfortunately not completely in accordance with the one used recently by Herbert A. Simon: 1956, "Dynamic Programming Under Uncertainty With a Quadratic Criterion Function," *Econometrica*, **XXIV**, 74 sqq., and myself (H. Theil: 1951, "A Note on Certainty Equivalence in Dynamic Planning," *ibid.*, **XXV**, 346 sqq.), but it seems appropriate for the present purposes.

[3] J. Tinbergen: 1952, *On the Theory of Economic Policy*, Contributions to Economic Analysis, I, Amsterdam. J. Tinbergen: 1956, *Economic Policy: Principles and Design*, Contributions to Economic Analysis, Amsterdam.

in general that they are either controlled by other persons or by "nature." From the policy-maker's point of view, therefore, there is uncertainty as to the numerical values to be taken by the y's. Assuming that this uncertainty is of the probabilistic type, we have to deal with a distribution function $F(y)$ in n dimensions. It is then impossible for the policy-maker to maximize the preference function (2.1) as it stands; instead, it has become customary[4] to replace this maximization problem by another one, viz., that of maximizing expected utility.[5] More precisely, we "weigh" the values (2.1) by the probabilities of the relevant y's and maximize

$$\int w(x,y)\, dF(y) \tag{2.2}$$

the integration being extended over the domain of the y's. Hence the problem has been shifted: orginally it was that of determining the x-vector (or set of x-vectors) which maximizes (2.1), but this problem admits of no solution because such a maximizing vector becomes different when the probability mechanism produces different y-values, and so we are now satisfied with the vector which maximizes the expectation (2.2). More precisely, we choose that x-vector (or possibly that set of x-vectors) which depends on the preference function w and the distribution function F and which maximizes (2.2) in the class of all x-vectors which are determined by w and F. Note that this formulation implies that our x-vectors are taken as nonstochastic and hence can be treated as parameters in any expression of which we want to take the expectation.[6] This follows from the fact that they depend on the distribution function of the noncontrolled variables, not on these variables themselves.

For an important class of cases, the process of maximizing the expectation (2.2) can be simplified considerably. Let us go back to the example given at the end of the second

---

[4] There are exceptions, though; e.g., Harry M. Markowitz: 1959, *Portfolio Selection, Efficient Diversification of Investments*, Cowles Foundation for Research in Economics at Yale University, Monograph 16, New York, which is based on minimizing the variance of returns for any given values of the expectation.

[5] Specifically, under appropriate conditions there is a class of functions w of x and y such that the policy-maker behaves as if he maximizes the expectation of w; see John von Neumann and Oskar Morgenstern: 1947, *Theory of Games and Economic Behavior*, 2nd ed., Princeton; also Jacob Marschak: 1950, "Rational Behavior, Uncertain Prospects, and Measurable Utility," *Econometrica*, **XVIII**, 111 sqq., and Leonard J. Savage: 1954, *The Foundations of Statistics*, Wiley Publications in Statistics, New York and London. This class is unique up to a linear transformation; for maximization problems not characterized by uncertainty (like the classical theory of consumer's demand) a wider class of functions w can be used, viz., one which is unique up to a monotonic transformation. The Neumann-Morgenstern result is frequently used somewhat too easily by assuming that the w-function which is at hand belongs to the smaller class.

[6] Note also that in the case of dynamic programming, the optimal x-vector is in general stochastic, at least from the second period onwards. The reason for this is that the choice of a strategy impies that the decision for any period is made dependent on the information that will become available before the moment when this decision has to be taken; and at the beginning of the strategy period, such information refers to the future and is therefore uncertain.

paragraph of this section; and let us assume that the distribution of the y's is independent of the x's and that the expectations of the y's are finite, to be written Ey. Then the expectation (2.2) takes the simple form $\Sigma x_h \, Ey_h$, which means that maximizing this expectation is equivalent to maximizing the original preference function $w = \Sigma x_h y_h$, after the random arguments (the y_h) are replaced by their expectations. In other words: if instead of choosing the x which maximizes (2.2) we choose the x which maximizes (2.1) with y replaced by Ey, then in this particular case at least we find that these two x-vectors are the same. In such a case it is said that Ey is a *certainty equivalent* of the true y.[7]

The example of the preceding paragraph is thus solved in a very simple manner - provided that it has a solution. In fact, it is easily seen that it has not, because the function to be maximized ($\Sigma x_h \, Ey_h$) is linear in the x's and hence unbounded, the Ey_h being constant with respect to x because the distribution of the y's is independent of x. As soon as appropriate inequalities are added, a solution emerges; this will be considered in Section V. Here, we shall consider a more interesting extension within the field of maximizing proper, which can be described as follows. Suppose that the expectation of the net price y_h is not a constant but a function of the vector x: $Ey_h = F_h(x)$, the F_h being single-valued but otherwise perfectly arbitrary. Suppose further that the variances and covariances of the y_h are all independent of x. Suppose finally that the preference function (2.1) is quadratic in y:

$$w(x,y) = A(x) + \sum_i A_i(x)y_i + \tfrac{1}{2}\sum_i \sum_j A_{ij}y_iy_j \tag{2.3}$$

the coefficients of the quadratic terms (A_{ij}) being independent of x. Then the expectation (2.2) becomes

$$A(x) + \sum_i A_i(x)F_i(x) + \tfrac{1}{2} \sum_i \sum_j A_{ij}\{F_i(x)F_j(x) + \operatorname{cov}(y_i, y_j)\} \tag{2.4}$$

while replacing y by its own expectation in (2.3) yields

$$A(x) + \sum_i A_i(x)F_i(x) + \tfrac{1}{2} \sum_i \sum_j A_{ij}F_i(x)F_j(x) \tag{2.5}$$

Evidently, the expressions (2.4) and (2.5) differ only by a constant, viz. $\frac{1}{2}\Sigma\Sigma A_{ij}$ cov (y_i, y_j), so that the x-vector which maximizes the expectation (2.4) — if such a vector

---

[7] See Simon, *op. cit.*, and Theil, *op. cit. Idem*: 1954, "Econometric Models and Welfare Maximisation," *Weltwirtschaftliches Archiv*, **LXXII**, I, 60 sqq. *Idem*: 1961, *Economic Forecasts and Policy*, Assisted by J.S. Cramer, H. Moerman, A. Russchen, 2nd, rev. ed., *Contributions to Economic Analysis*, 15, Amsterdam.

exists — must necessarily maximize (2.5) at the same time.[8] Hence here again, Ey is a certainty equivalent. It is worthwhile to note that in the present case such a solution can exist; e.g., when $A(x)$, $A_i(x)$ and $F_i(x)$ are all linear functions of x, and when the resulting quadratic function (2.5) is negative-definite.

III. Maximizing Under Nonstochastic Constraints

We proceed to the case in which the preference function (2.1) is applicable in its orginal form, but where maximization should take place subject to one or more constraints. In order not to leave the realm of classical maximizing, we shall deal here with constraints in equational form only. Also, we shall assume here that the constraints are nonstochastic and known. They can then be divided into three groups, depending on whether they put restrictions on instruments only, on noncontrolled variables only, or on both. It is easily seen that the second group is not particularly interesting, since its members imply only restrictions on the distribution function of the noncontrolled variables. Hence we should consider the following constraint types:

$$g_1(x) = 0 \tag{3.1}$$

$$g_2(x, y) = 0 \tag{3.2}$$

The first possibility, (3.1), must be discarded as being a logical impossibility. For we have defined our instruments as variables which can be manipulated independently, and this excludes the possibility of a functional relationship which specifies some of the x's as being determined by other x's. To see more clearly this implication of our definition, let us go back to the consumer's demand example of Section I. There, the constraint as formulated under (i) was $\Sigma p_i q_i = M$, which means that not all of the q's are instruments in the present sense. One of them (savings, say) must then belong to the "noncontrolled" category. The term noncontrolled is used here in a degenerate sense, of course; and indeed, the distinction between the two groups of variables has a greater practical meaning when there is uncertainty. Without uncertainty, there are well-known mathematical advantages in treating the q's symmetrically; see e.g. Hicks.[9]

The situation with respect to (3.2) is slightly more subtle. Let us consider first the case in which (3.2) consists of the following two linear relations:

$$b_{11}x_1 + b_{12}x_2 + b_{13}y_1 = 0$$

---

[8] This result can be generalized for the case in which the x's are not real-valued and are possibly even "qualitative" rather than quantitative variables; see Theil, "Econometric Models and Welfare Maximisation," *op. cit.* - *Idem, Economic Forecasts and Policy, op. cit.*

[9] J.R. Hicks: 1946, *Value and Capital, An Inquiry Into Some Fundamental Principles of Economic Theory*, 2nd ed., Oxford.

$$b_{21}x_1 + b_{22}x_2 + b_{23}y_1 = 0$$

Assuming $b_{13} \neq 0$, we can use the first relation to express y_1 in the x's; and substituting this into the second relation, we find that a linear relation in x_1 and x_2 results which is of the type (3.1). Hence, in this particular case at least, possibility (3.2) is to be discarded. This is not true for all cases, however. If instead of two linear relations we had only one, this could be used to express y_1 in x_1 and x_2, and no logical difficulty arises because this affects only the distribution of the y's. More generally, if (3.2) can be re-written such that some or all of the noncontrolled variables become explicit functions of the instruments (i.e., $y = g_2^*(x)$ when this applies to all y-variables), then there is no contradiction because no relation among the x's is implied. But if such a re-writing is not possible, then there must be a relation among the x's and such a case is to be discarded.

IV. Maximizing Under Stochastic Constraints

Suppose now that the constraints are random. Again, they may either involve instruments only, or noncontrolled variables only, or both; except of course that there are now random elements in addition to these variables. The second case need not be considered because it affects only the distribution function of the noncontrolled variables. So the interesting possibilities are

$$g_3(x; u_3) = 0 \tag{4.1}$$

$$g_4(x, y; u_4) = 0 \tag{4.2}$$

where u_3 and u_4 are vectors of random elements. Again, the first possibility is to be discarded, for it implies that some of the x's are determined by other x's and by the outcome of a chance mechanism. The policy-maker is then not free in the manipulation of his instruments, contrary to their definition. The consumer's case is again convenient as an example. Suppose that $\Sigma p_i q_i = M$ is his constraint and that he knows the p's but not M. Then we can make several alternative assumptions; e.g., the consumer decides on the values $q_1, ..., q_{n-1}$ such that he can certainly pay for these expenses, after which he adjusts q_n (savings, say) according to the income level M as it turns out to be. Clearly, there are n ways in which this procedure can be carried out (depending on which q_i is taken as noncontrolled), and it does make a difference in general which variant is chosen. There are even more possibilities. For example, the consumer may decide on n-2 of the q's (such that he is certainly able to pay for these q's), after which he will decide on the amounts to be spent on each of the two remaining goods by the time when he knows his income. There is then a decision in two stages; and if our consumer is "rational", he will specify a decision rule for the expenditure on the two commodities just-mentioned for any level of income. But this topic, being inside the dynamic area, is beyond the scope of this paper; the example is sufficient to show that stochastic equality constraints on instruments are not acceptable in static maximizing.

The second possibility, (4.2), is as acceptable and as unacceptable as its nonstochastic analogue (3.2). If (4.2) can be written in the form $y = g_4^*(x; u_4)$, there are only implications for the distribution of y; otherwise stochastic relations among the x's are involved which fall under (4.1).

V. Programming Under Nonstochastic Constraints

We proceed to the programming case in which (2.1) is to be maximized subject to constraints in the form of inequalities and possibly also equations. Supposing that these are all nonstochastic, the equations take the form (3.1)-(3.2) while the inequalities can be written as

$$g_5(x) \leq 0 \tag{5.1}$$

$$g_6(x, y) \leq 0 \tag{5.2}$$

inequalities involving y only being disregarded because they affect the distribution of y only.

The equations (3.1)-(3.2) need not be discussed here, since we can refer to Section III. As to the inequalities, (5.1) does restrict the policy-maker's liberty as to the manipulation of his instruments. However, this restriction does not go as far as making some of the instruments functionally dependent (as in Section III) or stochastically dependent (as in Section IV) on the others. Thus, a certain range of free manipulation remains available and I feel inclined to accept this as a sufficient basis for still talking about instruments which can be manipulated freely.[10,11]. This, at the same time, makes the situation with respect to (5.2) less restrictive than that with respect to (3.2). Whether (5.2) implies an

[10] If the inequalities are $x_1 \geq 0$, $x_2 \geq 0$, $x_1 + x_2 \leq 1$, then $x_1 = 1$ necessarily implies $x_2 = 0$ (and similarly $x_2 = 1$ necessarily implies $x_1 = 0$). In such a case the policy-maker's liberty as to x_2 is completely vanished by such a choice of x_1. However, this applies only to a finite number of choices out of the infinity which is available to the policy-maker, and so I feel inclined not to worry about this point. On the other hand, if two inequality constraints are $x_1 + x_2 \leq 1$ and $x_1 + x_2 \geq 1$, then the policy-maker's freedom is restricted much more seriously; but of course, such a pair of inequality constraints is really an equation.

[11] We could also say that the inequalities do not reduce the number of degrees of freedom.

inequality of the type $y \leqq g_6^*(x)$ only,[12] or whether it implies an inequality among the x's as well, in both cases (5.2) is an acceptable constraint in our sense.

The explicit distinction between variables which are controlled and those which are not shows its value in the following application which was discussed by Tintner.[13] Consider a farmer who has the choice of seeding corn or flax; and let us write q_1 for the quantity of corn harvested, and q_2 for the quantity of flax. Let p_1 and p_2 be the corresponding net prices; both are taken as fixed and known. The farmer's preference function is then

$$w = p_1 q_1 + p_2 q_2 \tag{5.3}$$

The constraint is supplied by the available land, which is A acres. One acre yields b_1 bushels of corn or b_2 bushels of flax; these quantities are not fixed but normally distributed with given means and variances.[14]
Hence, if we would apply the constraint

$$\frac{q_1}{b_1} + \frac{q_2}{b_2} \leqq A \tag{5.4}$$

the problem is to choose the values q_1 and q_2 which maximize (5.3) subject to the stochastic constraint (5.4) and to the nonnegativity constraints $q_1, q_2 \geqq 0$.

When posed in this way, the problem does not fall under the category of the present section, for we deal here with nonstochastic constraints only. However, I doubt whether the problem is really posed satisfactorily in this way. The quantities q_1 and q_2 are not instruments in the sense of being fully controlled by the farmer; they are at least partly determined by such factors as weather conditions. The farmer does control the number

---

12 The notation $y \leqq g_6^*(x)$ suggests the existence of upper bounds only, whereas in fact there may be lower bounds as well. This does not lead to any fundamental problems; so the $\leqq$ will be continued to be used in the sequel for reasons of convenience.

13 G. Tintner: 1955, "Stochastic Linear Programming With Applications to Agricultural Economics," in: National Bureau of Standards, U.S. Department of Commerce, Directorate of Management Analysis, *Proceedings of the Second Symposium in Linear Programming*, Washington, D.C., January 27-29, I, 197 sqq.

14 Usually, such means and variances have to be estimated, so that they are known only up to a sampling error. There are then two kinds of randomness, one of which is concerned with the "inherent" stochastic variability of the noncontrolled variables, the other with the random errors of estimates of the parameters of their distribution. This subject was considered recently in detail by J. Durbin: 1959, "The Effect of Forecasting Errors in Dynamic Programming With a Quadratic Cost Function," mimeographed and unpublished; and P.J.M. van den Bogaard: 1960, "On the Static Theory of Certainty Equivalence," Report 6010 of the Econometric Institute of the Netherlands School of Economics.

of acres devoted to corn and flax. Let us denote these by x_1 and x_2 respectively; then (5.4) becomes

$$x_1 + x_2 \leq A \tag{5.5}$$

which is a nonstochastic constraint. The preference function becomes now

$$w = p_1 b_1 x_1 + p_2 b_2 x_2 \tag{5.6}$$

and this contains two noncontrolled variables, viz., $p_1 b_1 = y_1$ and $p_2 b_2 = y_2$, which are the net money yields of an acre devoted to corn and flax respectively. Hence the preference function takes the form $\Sigma x_h y_h$, which was discussed in Section II. It is easily seen that if the farmer's goal is to choose that pattern x_1, x_2 which maximizes his expected profit, all he has to do is to solve the simple linear programming problem of maximizing $\Sigma x_h Ey_h$ (where $Ey_h = p_h Eb_h$) subject to (5.5) and to the nonnegativity constraints $x_1, x_2 \geq 0$. Here, therefore, we have certainty equivalence in linear programming.

A similar result of certainty equivalence in the field of programming can be obtained for the quadratic case considered at the end of Section II. Under the assumptions stated there, it remains true that the expectation of the preference function, (2.4), differs from the certainty value of that function (the value obtained by replacing the y by its expectation) only by a constant; this holds for all values of the instruments and *eo ipso* for the values which satisfy the inequalities (5.1)-(5.2). One should, however, be careful with respect to the following problem. If there are inequalities of the type (5.2), at least part of them can be written in the form $y \leq g_6^*(x)$, which implies an upper bound on the random variation of the y-components. If x is given such a value that this upper bound becomes relevant, we should expect the variances of the y's to become smaller. It is then no longer true that the variance-covariance matrix of the noncontrolled variables is independent of the instruments, so that the difference between (2.4) and (2.5) ceases to be a constant.[15] Such a case may occur when e.g. a manufacturer thinks of charging such a high price for a commodity that the nonnegativity constraint on demand becomes relevant.

VI. Programming Under Stochastic Constraints (1)

In the preceding pages we found that the uncertainty aspect may compel us to reformulate the problem such that maximizing the preference function itself is replaced by maximizing its expectation. Now when we deal with programming under stochastic constraints, another re-formulation may be necessary. To show this, we consider first the simple case in which no noncontrolled variables are present. The preference function takes then the form $w = w(x)$, and this is to be maximized subject to

[15] For a further analysis, see Theil, *Economic Forecasts and Policy, op. cit.*

$$g_7(x;\ u_7) \leq 0 \tag{6.1}$$

where u_7 is a vector of random elements. Now the left-hand side of (6.1) is stochastic, whereas the right-hand side is not. Hence, whether (6.1) is true for any given x-vector or not, is a question which in general can be answered only in probability terms. It is then hardly reasonable to require that such an inequality holds with certainty; instead, it is much more reasonable to require that it holds with a sufficiently large probability:

$$P[\ g_7(x;\ u_7) \leq 0] \geq 1 - \varepsilon \qquad (6.1)'$$

where ε is a small positive number chosen before. Evidently, (6.1)' is a nonstochastic inequality constraint.

The following example, due to van de Panne,[16] may serve to illustrate this procedure.[17] Let our objective be to produce a cattle feed from m raw materials, and to do so as cheaply as possible subject to the constraint that the resulting mixture contains a sufficient percentage of proteins. Writing $x_1, .., x_m$ for the quantities in pounds of raw materials used per pound of feed, and $p_1, .., p_m$ for their prices per pound (which are taken as fixed and given), we have $w = -\Sigma p_h x_h$ as preference function. Further, supposing that the hth raw material contains a fraction b_h of proteins, the constraint is

$$\Sigma b_h\ x_h \geq B$$

where B is the minimum required. Suppose now that the protein content of the raw materials is not stable but differs in successive shipments; more specifically, suppose that the b_h are independently and normally distributed with mean β_h and variance σ_h^2. Then for any given values of the x_h, the left-hand side of our inequality is also normally distributed, its mean being $\Sigma\beta_h x_h$ and its variance $\Sigma\sigma_h^2 x_h^2$. Hence, if we require this inequality to be satisfied with 0.95 probability, say, our new constraint becomes

$$\Sigma\beta_h x_h\ -\ 1.645\sqrt{\Sigma\sigma_h^2 x_h^2}\ \geq B$$

which shows that our original stochastic linear constraint has thus been replaced by a nonstochastic nonlinear constraint.

---

[16] C. van de Panne, "Minimum-Cost Cattle Feed Under Probabilistic Protein Constraints," Forthcoming Report of the International Center for Management Science.

[17] A similar procedure was considered recently by A. Charnes and W.W. Cooper: 1959, "Chance Constrained Programs With Normal Deviates and Linear Decision Rules," O.N.R. Research Memorandum No. 28 of The Technological Institute, Northwestern University; their case is however a dynamic one, so I must refrain from discussing it here. Charnes and Cooper applied different probabilities ε_i to the separate (scalar) inequalities of $g_7(x;\ u) \leq 0$. This is of course also possible.

Two points should be added. Firstly, this procedure is easily extended to the case in which the right-hand side (B in the present example) is also stochastic. If we suppose B to be normally distributed (independently of the b_h) with mean $\bar{B}$ and variance σ_B^2, and if we write the stochastic inequality in the form $\Sigma b_h x_h - B \geq 0$, then its left-hand side is normally distributed with mean $\Sigma\beta_h x_h - \bar{B}$ and variance $\Sigma\sigma_h^2 x_h^2 + \sigma_B^2$; and hence we get

$$\Sigma\beta_h x_h - 1.645\sqrt{\Sigma\sigma_h^2 x_h^2 + \sigma_B^2} \geq \bar{B}$$

if we require the stochastic inequality to be fulfilled with 0.95 probability. In the present example B is unlikely to be stochastic, but this may easily be true in other cases; e.g., when B stands for a demand to be met and when this demand is uncertain. The second point is that this kind of procedure can in principle also be used for the case when the stochastic constraints are nonlinear and when the random variation is not normal; but in most cases this will be more complicated, both algebraically and numerically.

Finally, as to the more general case in which the preference function contains uncontrolled variables besides instruments, the further constraint to be considered is

$$g_8(x, y; u_8) \leq 0 \tag{6.2}$$

The problem is then to maximize expected utility, (2.2), subject to (6.2) and possibly to other stochastic and nonstochastic inequality and equational constraints. Referring to the preceding pages for the latter constraints, we observe that (6.2) implies only certain restrictions on the distribution of the noncontrolled variables if it can be written in the form $y = g_8^*(x; u_8)$; otherwise stochastic inequalities among the instruments are involved which can be handled along the lines of the preceding paragraphs.

VII. Programming Under Stochastic Constraints (2)

It is I think perfectly true that it is preferable to replace stochastic inequalities among the instruments by the requirement that such inequalities should hold with a preassigned probability. Nevertheless, one might say that the task of specifying such a probability, if it is not supplied by analysis, shifts part of the burden of analysis on the policy-maker. It seems therefore appropriate to try to find ways by which such a probability is selected rationally.

Let us go back to the production of cattle feed (the example of Section VI) and suppose that the manufacturer guarantees the protein content of his product to the effect that, whenever the content is below B, he pays an indemnification fee of K cents per pound. Then, if an insufficient protein content occurs in a fraction ε of all cases, the expectation of the preference function takes the form

$$-\Sigma p_h x_h - K\varepsilon \tag{7.1}$$

and this is to be maximized subject to the constraint that it is indeed true that an insufficient protein content occurs with probability ε only:

$$\Sigma\beta_h x_h - t_\varepsilon \sqrt{\Sigma\sigma_h^2 x_h^2} \geq B \tag{7.2}$$

the relation between ε and t_ε in the case of normality being given by

$$\varepsilon = \frac{1}{\sqrt{2\pi}} \int_{t_\varepsilon}^{\infty} e^{-\frac{1}{2}x^2}\, dx.$$

The procedure of the preceding paragraph implies a "constant" penalty for violating the stochastic constraint, independent of the extent to which it is violated. An alternative assumption is that of a penalty $K(B - \Sigma b_h x_h)$ which is an increasing function of the degree to which the constraint $\Sigma b_h x_h \geq B$ is violated. We evidently have $K(z) = 0$ when $z \leq 0$; and we should normally expect $dK/dz \geq 0$ when $z > 0$, the case $dK/dz = 0$ having already been considered in the preceding paragraph. The preference function takes then the form

$$w = -\Sigma p_h x_h - K(B - \Sigma b_h x_h) \tag{7.3}$$

and since part of its arguments (the b_h) are now random, we should maximize its expectation. There is now no longer the protein constraint which we should take account of, since it has been absorbed completely by the preference function itself. For the case in which K is a polynomial in z whenever $z > 0$, this can be handled by using the moments of a truncated normal distribution.

In concluding, it is interesting to observe, both for (7.1) and for the more general case (7.3), that the introduction of uncertainty at the level of the constraints affects the form of the preference function. As we saw, uncertainty at the level of the preference function does not affect the constraints if one is satisfied with maximizing expected utility; nor does uncertainty at the level of inequality constraints affect the nature of the preference function, provided that one is satisfied with a fulfillment of such inequalities with probabilities that are chosen before. But if one wants to eliminate the *a priori* character of such probabilities, the nature of the preference function is changed in a fundamental manner and possibly even such that it absorbs the stochastic constraint entirely. This result has, of course, been derived for a special case only; but its extension to the general static case is so straightforward that it need not be formulated explicitly.

CHAPTER 75

A PROCEDURE FOR INTEGER MAXIMIZATION OF A DEFINITE QUADRATIC FUNCTION*

J.C.G. BOOT
Netherlands School of Economics
(Now Erasmus University)
Rotterdam, The Netherlands

HENRI THEIL
Netherlands School of Economics
(Now Erasmus University)
and International Center for
Management Science
Rotterdam, The Netherlands

1. Introduction

This article deals with the problem of maximizing a definite quadratic objective function in case some or all of the variables are constrained to be integers. The problem is an intriguing one, because the vector which maximizes the objective function under this condition may deviate considerably from the vector of the unconditional maximum. In fact, it is always possible to find a quadratic objective function for which the components of these two vectors differ pairwise by more than any pre-assigned quantity.

A simple approach, which is considered to be efficient in case the number of variables is not too large, is described in Section 2. It is generalized in Section 3 for the case in which only part of the variables are constrained to take integer values. Section 4 contains a numerical example as well as a directory of computations. No attempt is made to impose inequality constraints.

2. Description of the Procedure

2.1. DISCRETE AND CONTINUOUS MAXIMUM

We shall write the objective function in the form

$$Q(x) = a'x - \frac{1}{2}x'Bx, \tag{2.1}$$

where x is an m-element decision vector and a and B are known matrices of appropriate order, the latter being symmetric and positive-definite. The elements of x can take only integer values. This means that admissible values of x take the form

$$x = \sum_{h=1}^{m} n_h e_h, \tag{2.2}$$

where n_h is a scalar integer (positive, zero, or negative) and e_h the hth unit vector of order m:

$$e_1 = \begin{bmatrix} 1 \\ 0 \\ 0 \\ \cdot \\ \cdot \\ 0 \\ 0 \end{bmatrix}; \quad e_2 = \begin{bmatrix} 0 \\ 1 \\ 0 \\ \cdot \\ \cdot \\ 0 \\ 0 \end{bmatrix}; \quad \ldots; \quad e_m = \begin{bmatrix} 0 \\ 0 \\ 0 \\ \cdot \\ \cdot \\ 0 \\ 1 \end{bmatrix}. \tag{2.3}$$

If the condition on integer values would not be imposed, the solution vector which maximizes Q would be $B^{-1}a$. But this vector will generally not consist of integer elements, hence it will be called the vector of the *continuous maximum*. For the discussion which follows it will prove convenient to re-define the x-vector such that all elements of the vector of the continuous maximum are between -½ and ½. (This will generally require an adjustment of the linear part of the objective function as will be illustrated in Section 4.) In that case this vector becomes

$$\theta = B^{-1}a \text{ such that } -\tfrac{1}{2} \leq \theta_h < \tfrac{1}{2} \text{ for } h = 1, \ldots, m. \tag{2.4}$$

If θ would consist of integer elements [which would imply $\theta_h = 0$ for all h in view of (2.4)], the problem would be trivial since the continuous maximum would then coincide with the *discrete maximum*, i.e., the maximum of Q for integer x-components. We shall therefore suppose that at least some of the θ-components are not integers. Figures 1 and 2 illustrate what happens in that case for $m = 2$. The ellipses are contour lines of the objective function (concentric ellipses in view of the positive-definite character of B); obviously, the discrete maximum is below the continuous maximum and its vector is the lattice point lying on the inner-most ellipse. It is also clear that this lattice point may be rather far away from θ; this is illustrated in Figure 2. In particular, it is not true that the lattice point which is closest to θ [which is $x = 0$ according to (2.4)] is always the point of the discrete maximum. Nevertheless, this point is of some importance in the discussion which follows, because it supplies a lower bound to the value of the discrete maximum. If we substitute $x = 0$ in (2.1), we obtain $Q(0) = 0$; and hence, any other lattice point is of interest only if it has a positive Q-value. We could of course compute the Q-values of a large number of lattice points, but the trouble is that by doing so we can never be sure that any finite set of such Q-values will contain the value of the discrete maximum. This statement is not correct if we would be able to set limits to the

x_h-values of the discrete maximum; in fact, this is precisely the procedure that will be proposed here. We can then compute the Q-values of all lattice points satisfying these limits and pick out the largest.

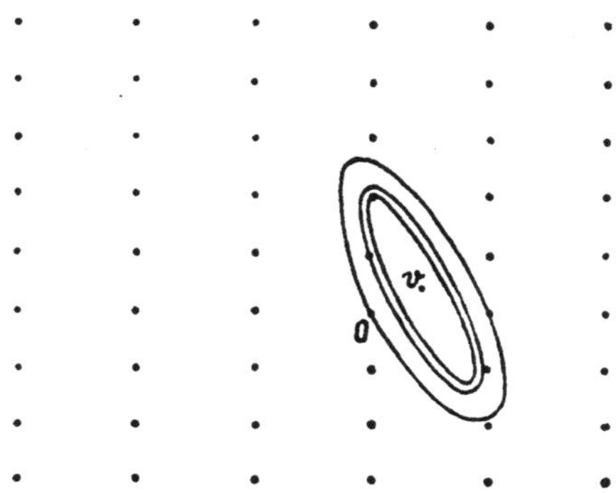

Figure 1

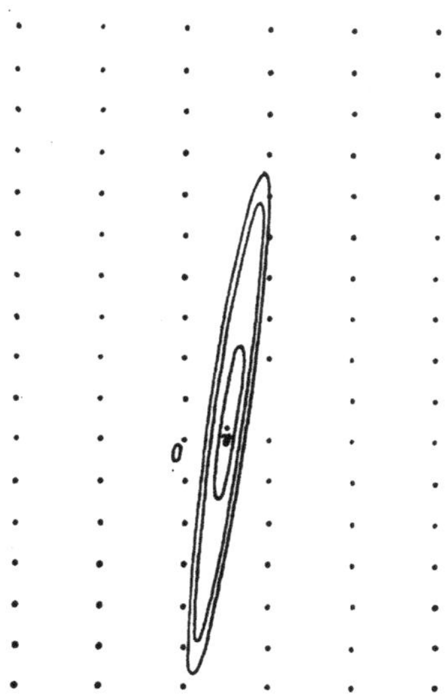

Figure 2

2.2. THE MAXIMUM-DISTANCE APPROACH

Since B is positive-definitive, we can always find a nonsingular linear transformation of our variables such that B is replaced by the unit matrix. Maximizing Q is then equivalent to minimizing a sum of squares, or, in geometric terms, to finding that lattice point which has minimum distance to the point of the continuous maximum. This is not necessarily the $x = 0$ solution of Section 2.1, because the linear transformation implies that another lattice point may have become closer to the point of the continuous maximum. Consider then any hyperplane parallel to the axes of the coordinate system on which lattice points are located; in our original variables, $e_h'x = n_h$ for some integer n_h. Obviously, if the distance from the point of the continuous maximum to such a hyperplane is larger than the distance to the $x = 0$ solution, we can disregard all lattice points lying on that hyperplane.

More specifically, we start by observing that Q can be written in the form

$$Q(x) = \frac{1}{2}\theta' B\theta - \frac{1}{2}(x-\theta)' B(x-\theta). \tag{2.5}$$

Since B and B^{-1} are both symmetric and positive-definite, there exist two $m \times m$ matrices F and G, both of full rank, such that

$$F'F = B; \quad G'G = B^{-1}; \quad F^{-1} = G'. \tag{2.6}$$

Let us introduce

$$y = Fx; \quad \eta = F\theta, \tag{2.7}$$

then the objective function takes the form

$$Q^*(y) = \frac{1}{2}\eta'\eta - \frac{1}{2}(y-\eta)'(y-\eta), \tag{2.8}$$

in other words: we should find that y for which the distance to $\eta = F\theta$ is minimal. There are of course constraints on y. The integer constraints on the original variables are of the form $e_h'x = n_h$. Since $x = F^{-1}y = G'y$, these constraints in the new variables are then $e_h'G'y = n_h$ or

$$g_h'y = n_h, \tag{2.9}$$

where

$$g_h = Ge_h = \begin{bmatrix} g_{11} & \cdots & g_{1m} \\ \cdot & & \cdot \\ \cdot & & \cdot \\ \cdot & & \cdot \\ g_{m1} & \cdots & g_{mm} \end{bmatrix} \begin{bmatrix} 0 \\ \cdot \\ \cdot \\ 1 \\ \cdot \\ \cdot \\ 0 \end{bmatrix} = \begin{bmatrix} g_{1h} \\ \cdot \\ \cdot \\ \cdot \\ g_{mh} \end{bmatrix}, \tag{2.10}$$

i.e., g_h is the hth column of G.

Consider then the distance of η to the hyperplane $g_h'y = n_h$. This distance is

$$D(n_h) = \frac{|g_h'\eta - n_h|}{(g_h'g_h)^{\frac{1}{2}}} \tag{2.11}$$

according to a well-known result in analytic geometry. But $g_h'g_h$ is the $(h,h)^{th}$ element of $G'G = B^{-1}$, hence the right-hand denominator of (2.11) can be written as the positive square root of b^{hh}. In the same way, we have

$$g_h'\eta = g_h'F\theta = (G^{-1}g_h)'\theta = e_h'\theta = \theta_h.$$

Hence (2.11) is simplified to

$$D(n_h) = |\theta_h - n_h| \,/\, \sqrt{b^{hh}}. \tag{2.12}$$

It is easily seen from (2.8) that any point on the hyperplane $g_h'y = n_h$ has a Q^*-value which is at most equal to $\frac{1}{2}\theta'B\theta = \frac{1}{2}\eta'\eta$ minus $\frac{1}{2}$ times the square of $D(n_h)$. Since $Q(0) = Q^*(0) = 0$ it is therefore sufficient to take account, for each h, of those integers n_h which satisfy

$$|n_h - \theta_h| \leqq \sqrt{b^{hh}\theta'B\theta}, \tag{2.13}$$

by which device our problem is reduced to a finite combinatorial problem.

2.3. RAISING THE LOWER BOUND

Even though we have been able to reduce the problem to a finite one, it may nevertheless be one of large size, particularly if m is not small and if given h several integers n_h satisfy (2.13). It is therefore of considerable interest to find out whether simplifications are possible.

One procedure is to raise the lower bound from zero [i.e., from $Q(0) = 0$] to a positive level, which can be done as follows. Suppose we put all components of x equal to zero except x_h, so that we obtain

$$Q(0,\ldots,0,x_h,0,\ldots,0) = a_h x_h - \tfrac{1}{2} b_{hh} x_h^2$$

$$= \tfrac{1}{2} b_{hh} \left(\frac{a_h}{b_{hh}} \right)^2 - \tfrac{1}{2} b_{hh} \left(x_h - \frac{a_h}{b_{hh}} \right)^2 .$$

Given the $m - 1$ zero components of x, the x_h which maximizes Q is the integer ξ_h which is closest to a_h/b_{hh}:

$$\frac{a_h}{b_{hh}} = \xi_h + \delta_h \text{ where } -\tfrac{1}{2} \leqq \delta_h < \tfrac{1}{2}, \tag{2.14}$$

so that the corresponding maximal Q is

$$\tfrac{1}{2} b_{hh}(\xi_h + \delta_h)^2 - \tfrac{1}{2} b_{hh} \delta_h^2 = \tfrac{1}{2} b_{hh} \xi_h (\xi_h + 2\delta_h).$$

This is never negative, because $\xi_h = 0$ belongs to the set of integers from which we choose. On pursuing the line of thought expounded at the end of Section 2.2, we conclude that we can confine ourselves to those integers n_h which satisfy

$$|n_h - \theta_h| \leqq \sqrt{b^{hh}[\theta' B \theta - \max_h b_{hh} \xi_h (\xi_h + 2\delta_h)]}. \tag{2.15}$$

Regarding the maximum of $b_{hh}\xi_h(\xi_h + 2\delta_h)$, it will be evident that we can confine ourselves to those h for which $|a_h| \geq ½ \, b_{hh}$, for $\xi_h = 0$ in all other cases.

2.4. CUTTING THE MARGINS OF THE PROMISING REGION

Let us write

$$\gamma = \sqrt{\theta' B \theta - \max_h b_{hh}\xi_h(\xi_h + 2\delta_h)}, \tag{2.16}$$

then the integers n_h which satisfy (2.15) are all integers of the interval $n_h^L \leqq n_h \leqq n_h^U$ where

$$\begin{aligned} n_h^U &= \text{largest integer} \leqq \theta_h + \gamma\sqrt{b^{hh}} \\ n_h^L &= \text{(algebraically) smallest integer} \geqq \theta_h - \gamma\sqrt{b^{hh}} \end{aligned} \tag{2.17}$$

Obviously, the bounds n_h^U and $-n_h^L$ are both nonnegative integers which are either equal or differ by 1.

The straightforward procedure is then to consider all integer solutions of the 'promising region', i.e., all vectors $(n_1, ..., n_m)$ for which $n_h^L \leqq n_h \leqq n_h^U$, to compute the corresponding Q-values and to pick out the one(s) with the highest Q-value. This is not too much work because the a's and b's of Q have to be multiplied by simple integers, except of course when the promising region contains a very large number of candidate solutions. In that case it is important to find out whether the promising region can be reduced in size. Consider then

$$\begin{aligned} Q(n_1^U, n_2, ..., n_m) = a_1 n_1^U + \sum_{h=2}^{m} a_h n_h - \tfrac{1}{2} b_{11}(n_1^U)^2 \\ - n_1^U \sum_{h=2}^{m} b_{1h} n_h - \tfrac{1}{2} \sum_{h,\,k=2}^{m} b_{hk} n_h n_k, \end{aligned}$$

where $n_2, ..., n_m$ are any integers such that $n_h^L \leqq n_h \leqq n_h^U$. Now if this Q would be smaller than the Q-value which is obtained by replacing n_1^U by $n_1^U - 1$, all other n's remaining unchanged, then the solution $(n_1^U, n_2, ..., n_m)$ can be deleted from the promising region. The condition for this to be true is that

$$b_{11}n_1^U + \sum_{h=2}^{m} b_{1h}n_h > a_1 + \tfrac{1}{2}b_{11}.$$

It would evidently be more interesting if we could reject the whole hyperplane $x_1 = n_1^U$ rather than the single solution $(n_1^U, n_2, ..., n_m)$, because this would enable us to reduce the upper bound n_1^U to $n_1^U - 1$. The condition for this is

$$b_{11}n_1^U + \sum_{h=2}^{m} \min(b_{1h}n_h) > a_1 + \tfrac{1}{2}b_{11}, \tag{2.18}$$

where

$$\begin{aligned} \min(b_{1h}n_h) &= b_{1h}n_h^L \text{ if } b_{1h} \geqq 0 \\ &= b_{1h}n_h^U \text{ if } b_{1h} \leqq 0. \end{aligned} \tag{2.19}$$

To illustrate this procedure, we take the example $m = 3$, $b_{11} = 1$, $b_{12} = \frac{1}{2}$, $b_{13} = -\frac{1}{2}$, $a_1 = -0.6$, $n_1^U = 3$, $n_2^L = -2$, $n_3^U = 4$. Then the left-hand side of (2.18) becomes

$$1 \times 3 - \tfrac{1}{2} \times 2 - \tfrac{1}{2} \times 4 = 0 \tag{2.20}$$

and the right-hand side is -0.1; hence the inequality is satisfied. The conclusion is that we can proceed as if n_1^U is 2 rather than 3. But suppose now that a_1 is -0.1 instead of -0.6, so that the right-hand side of (2.18) becomes 0.4. The inequality is then violated, which implies that we are not in a position to disregard the hyperplane $x_1 = n_1^U$. But we can nevertheless do something. A closer inspection of (2.20) reveals that if we raise n_2 from n_2^L = -2 to -1, the left-hand side of (2.18) would become ½, which exceeds 0.4. The same thing happens if we decide to lower n_3 from $n_3^U = 4$ to 3. The conclusion is that we can delete the hyperplane $x_1 = n_1^U$ from the promising region except for the point $(n_1^U, n_2^L, n_3^U) = (3, -2, 4)$, which has a higher Q-value than (2, -2, 4) has. For such 'exceptional' points one has to compute the Q-values, which are then to be compared with those of the remaining promising region.

Up till now we confined ourselves to the hyperplane $x_1 = n_1^U$. The procedure can be repeated for the other components of x, which implies that we have to calculate the two vectors

$$\begin{bmatrix} b_{11}n_1^U + \sum_{k\neq 1} \min(b_{1k}n_k) \\ \cdot \\ \cdot \\ \cdot \\ b_{mm}n_m^U + \sum_{k\neq m} \min(b_{mk}n_k) \end{bmatrix} ; \begin{bmatrix} a_1 + \frac{1}{2}b_{11} \\ \cdot \\ \cdot \\ \cdot \\ a_m + \frac{1}{2}b_{mm} \end{bmatrix} \tag{2.21}$$

and to make pairwise comparisons of the components. The minimum values of the left-hand vector are defined by

$$\begin{aligned} \min(b_{hk}n_k) &= b_{hk}n_k^L \text{ if } b_{hk} \geqq 0 \\ &= b_{hk}n_k^U \text{ if } b_{hk} \leqq 0. \end{aligned} \tag{2.22}$$

It will be noted that if at some stage n_h^U is reduced to n_h^U - 1, this affects all components of the left-hand vector in (2.21). This will be illustrated in Section 4.

For the lower bounds n_h^L one can proceed in an analogous manner. Such a bound can be raised to $n_1^L + 1$ if the hth component of the following left-hand vector is *smaller* than the corresponding component of the right-hand vector:

$$\begin{bmatrix} b_{11}n_1^L + \sum_{k\neq 1} \max(b_{1k}n_k) \\ \cdot \\ \cdot \\ \cdot \\ b_{mm}n_m^L + \sum_{k\neq m} \max(b_{mk}n_k) \end{bmatrix} ; \begin{bmatrix} a_1 - \frac{1}{2}b_{11} \\ \cdot \\ \cdot \\ \cdot \\ a_m - \frac{1}{2}b_{mm} \end{bmatrix} \tag{2.23}$$

where

$$\max(b_{hk}n_k) = b_{hk}n_k^U \text{ if } b_{hk} \geqq 0$$
$$= b_{hk}n_k^L \text{ if } b_{hk} \leqq 0. \qquad (2.24)$$

3. The Mixed Discrete-Continuous Case

We proceed to consider the case in which some but not all of the variables are constrained to take integer values. Let us write x for the variables to which these constraints apply and z for the other variables (the 'continuous variables'). The quadratic objective function can then be written in the form

$$Q_z(x,z) = a_z'x + b_z'z - \tfrac{1}{2}(x'B_zx + z'C_zz + x'D_zz + z'D_z'x), \qquad (3.1)$$

where it will be assumed that the matrix

$$\begin{bmatrix} B_z & D_z \\ D_z' & C_z \end{bmatrix}$$

is symmetric and positive-definite. If there are no bilinear terms in discrete and continuous variables, i.e., if $D_z = 0$, the objective function can be separated in two quadratic functions, one in discrete and one in continuous variables. The discrete problem is then handled along the lines of Section 2 and the continuous solution is $z = C_z^{-1}b_z$. But the alternative case $D_z \neq 0$ is not difficult either. We note that

$$\max_{x,z} Q_z(x,z) = \max_x\{\max_z Q_z(x,z)\} \qquad (3.2)$$

and that the maximum in curled brackets is a simple continuous maximum problem. Given x, the maximizing z is

$$z = C_z^{-1}b_z - C_z^{-1}D_z'x \qquad (3.3)$$

and on substituting this into (3.1) we obtain a quadratic objective function of the form (2.1) with

$$a^{*} = a_z - D_z C_z^{-1} b_z; \quad B = B_z - D_z C_z^{-1} D_z'. \tag{3.4}$$

(The asterisk is added to a to indicate that it is not yet the a for which the components of $B^{-1}a$ lie between -½ and ½.)

4. An Example; Directory of Computations

There are four discrete and one continuous variables in our example and the coefficient matrices of (3.1) are taken as follows:

$$a_z = \begin{bmatrix} 18 \\ 16 \\ 22 \\ 20 \end{bmatrix}; \; b_z = 14; \; B_z = \begin{bmatrix} 6 & 1 & 8 & 0 \\ 1 & 10 & 1 & 4 \\ 8 & 1 & 17 & 3 \\ 0 & 4 & 3 & 11 \end{bmatrix}; \; D_z = \begin{bmatrix} 4 \\ 7 \\ 6 \\ 4 \end{bmatrix}; \; C_z = 7. \tag{4.1}$$

This example is such that the matrix

$$\begin{bmatrix} B_z & D_z \\ D_z' & C_z \end{bmatrix}$$

is positive-definite but with a small determinant. The same will then be true of the matrix $B = B_z - D_z C_z^{-1} D_z'$ of (3.4), which guarantees that the difference between n_h^U and n_h^L will be rather large, for some h at least.

Preliminary Step (applicable only if the problem is of the mixed discrete-continuous type)
Apply (3.4) *to reduce the mixed problem to the purely discrete problem.*

We have in our example:

$$a^* = a_z - D_z C_z^{-1} b_z = \begin{bmatrix} 18 \\ 16 \\ 22 \\ 20 \end{bmatrix} - \frac{1}{7} \times 14 \times \begin{bmatrix} 4 \\ 7 \\ 6 \\ 4 \end{bmatrix} = \begin{bmatrix} 10 \\ 2 \\ 10 \\ 12 \end{bmatrix}; \tag{4.2}$$

$$\begin{aligned} B = B_z - D_z C_z^{-1} D_z' &= \begin{bmatrix} 6 & 1 & 8 & 0 \\ 1 & 10 & 1 & 4 \\ 8 & 1 & 7 & 3 \\ 0 & 4 & 3 & 11 \end{bmatrix} - \frac{1}{7} \begin{bmatrix} 16 & 28 & 24 & 16 \\ 28 & 49 & 42 & 28 \\ 24 & 42 & 36 & 24 \\ 16 & 28 & 24 & 16 \end{bmatrix} \\ &= \frac{1}{7} \begin{bmatrix} 26 & -21 & 32 & -16 \\ -21 & 21 & -35 & 0 \\ 32 & -35 & 83 & -3 \\ -16 & 0 & -3 & 61 \end{bmatrix}. \end{aligned} \tag{4.3}$$

The problem is now to maximize $a^{*\prime}x$ - ½x′Bx subject to the condition that the x-vector should have integer elements.

First Step (Continuous maximum and transformation of the linear part of the objective function)

Determine B^{-1} and the vector of the continuous maximum, $B^{-1}a^*$, and write x for the m-element column vector of integers nearest to the corresponding components of $B^{-1}a^*$. Then determine

$$a = a^* - B\bar{x} \tag{4.4}$$

and write $\theta = B^{-1}a^* - \bar{x} = B^{-1}a$ *in accordance with* (2.4).

In the example:

$$B^{-1} = \frac{1}{980}\begin{bmatrix} 31409 & 39494 & 4851 & 8477 \\ 39494 & 50764 & 6566 & 10682 \\ 4851 & 6566 & 1029 & 1323 \\ 8477 & 10682 & 1323 & 2401 \end{bmatrix}; \; B^{-1}a^{*} = \begin{bmatrix} 554.4 \\ 704.4 \\ 89.6 \\ 151.2 \end{bmatrix} \tag{4.5}$$

and also

$$\bar{x} = \begin{bmatrix} 554 \\ 704 \\ 90 \\ 151 \end{bmatrix}; \quad \theta = \begin{bmatrix} 0.4 \\ 0.4 \\ -0.4 \\ 0.2 \end{bmatrix}; \quad a = \begin{bmatrix} -2 \\ 2 \\ -5 \\ 1 \end{bmatrix}. \tag{4.6}$$

The problem is thus transformed to that of maximizing $a'x - \frac{1}{2}x'Bx$ with a as the last of the three vectors in (4.6).

Second Step (Determination of the promising region)
Determine for each h for which $|a_h| \geqq \frac{1}{2}b_{hh}$, ξ_h *and* δ_h *from* (2.14). *Then find* γ *and* n_h^U, n_h^L *for each h from* (2.16) and (2.17).

In the example we have $a_1/b_{11} = -14/26$, hence $\xi_1 = -1$ and $\delta_1 = 12/26$. In the same way we find $\xi_2 = 1$, $\xi_3 = \xi_4 = 0$ and $\delta_2 = -\frac{1}{3}$, δ_3 and δ_4 being irrelevant. Hence

$$\begin{aligned} \gamma &= \sqrt{\theta' B\theta - \max_h b_{hh}\xi_h(\xi_h + 2\delta_h)} \\ &= \sqrt{2.2 - b_{22}\xi_2(\xi_2 + 2\delta_2)} = \sqrt{2.2 - 1} = 1.095. \end{aligned} \tag{4.7}$$

We multiply γ by

$$\sqrt{b^{11}} = 5.66; \quad \sqrt{b^{22}} = 7.15; \quad \sqrt{b^{33}} = 1.02; \quad \sqrt{b^{44}} = 1.57,$$

which gives the following values for $\gamma\sqrt{b^{hh}}$ (in the order $h = 1, ..., 4$):

$$6.20;\ 7.83;\ 1.12;\ 1.72. \tag{4.8}$$

These are the upper limits to $|n_h - \theta_h|$. Thus we obtain $|n_1 - 0.4| \leq 6.20$ so that $-5 < n_1 < 6$. Continuing in this way we obtain:

$$\begin{array}{ll} n_1^L = -5 & n_1^U = 6 \\ n_2^L = -7 & n_2^U = 8 \\ n_3^L = -1 & n_3^U = 0 \\ n_4^L = -1 & n_4^U = 1 \end{array} \tag{4.9}$$

The total number of lattice points in the promising region is

$$12 \times 16 \times 2 \times 3 = 1{,}152.$$

This is certainly not very small, and we therefore continue with the next step.

Third Step (Reduction of the promising region; to be omitted if this region is considered to be sufficiently small)
Determine the four vectors (2.21) *and* (2.23). *Find out whether any of the left-hand elements of* (2.21) *are larger than the corresponding right-hand element and, if so, reduce the appropriate* n_h^U *by* 1. *Find out whether any of the left-hand elements of* (2.23) *are smaller than the corresponding right-hand elements and, if so, raise the appropriate* n_h^L *by 1. Then adjust the left-hand vectors in* (2.21) *and* (2.23) *with the* n_h^U *and* n_h^L *thus modified and repeat the procedure, and so on. Apply the procedure of the exceptional points as described below in the Reduction Rule.*[1]

In our case the vectors (2.21) take the following values:

[1] This step is of course not to be applied for those indices h for which $n_h^U = n_h^L = 0$. The corresponding components of the vectors (2.21) and (2.23) can be deleted.

$$\begin{bmatrix} 26 \times 6 & - 21 \times 8 & - 32 \times 1 & - 16 \times 1 \\ -21 \times 6 & + 21 \times 8 & - 35 \times 0_* & \\ -32 \times 5 & - 35 \times 8 & + 83 \times 0 & - 3 \times 1 \\ -16 \times 6_* & & - 3 \times 0 & + 61 \times 1 \end{bmatrix} = \begin{bmatrix} -60 \\ 42 \\ -443 \\ -35 \end{bmatrix} ; \begin{bmatrix} -1 \\ 24\frac{1}{2} \\ 6\frac{1}{2} \\ 37\frac{1}{2} \end{bmatrix}, \quad (4.10)$$

where the subscript stars indicate that the value is a lower limit. In the same way we have for the vectors (2.23):

$$\begin{bmatrix} -26 \times 5 & + 21 \times 7 & + 32 \times 0^* & + 16 \times 1 \\ 21 \times 5 & - 21 \times 7 & + 35 \times 1 & \\ 32 \times 6^* & + 35 \times 7 & - 83 \times 1 & + 3 \times 1 \\ 16 \times 5 & & + 3 \times 1 & - 61 \times 1 \end{bmatrix} = \begin{bmatrix} 33 \\ -7 \\ 357 \\ 22 \end{bmatrix} ; \begin{bmatrix} -27 \\ 3\frac{1}{2} \\ -76\frac{1}{2} \\ -23\frac{1}{2} \end{bmatrix}, \quad (4.11)$$

the superscript stars indicating that the value is an upper limit.

On comparing the left-hand vector of (4.10) with the right-hand vector we observe that the second element of the former exceeds the corresponding element of the latter. This implies that n_2^U can be diminished from 8 to 7. When this has been done the value of this element becomes 21, which is smaller than 24½. Hence n_2^U cannot be decreased any further. The left-hand side of (4.10) must now be adjusted to the new situation with $n_2^U = 7$. This is done in (4.12) below, which will be discussed in the next paragraph. Note that this adjustment leads to larger elements of the left-hand vector, so that some of them may now be larger than the corresponding right-hand element, which would enable us to reduce n_h^U for other h-values. In our example this is not the case. In precisely the same way we find for (4.11) that the second left-hand element is smaller than the corresponding right-hand element, so that n_2^L can be raised from -7 to -6. No further reductions of the promising region are possible, at least not without the 'exceptional point' procedure. The region contains now 12 × 14 × 2 × 3 = 1,008 points and it is therefore of great importance to determine such exceptional points in a systematic manner.

We thereto write (4.10) as a matrix product of which only the diagonal elements are of interest. Using the knowledge that $n_2^U = 7$ we obtain:

$a_h + \frac{1}{2}b_{hh}$ Difference

$$\begin{bmatrix} 26 & -21 & -32 & \underline{-16} \\ \underline{-21} & 21 & -35 & 0 \\ -32 & -35 & 83 & \underline{-3} \\ -16 & 0 & \underline{-3} & 61 \end{bmatrix} \begin{bmatrix} 6 & 6 & 5_{*} & 6 \\ 7 & 7 & 7 & - \\ 1_{*} & 0 & 0 & 0 \\ 1 & - & 1 & 1 \end{bmatrix} \overset{D}{=} \begin{bmatrix} -39 \\ 21 \\ -408 \\ -35 \end{bmatrix}; \quad \begin{bmatrix} -1 \\ 24\frac{1}{2} \\ 6\frac{1}{2} \\ 37\frac{1}{2} \end{bmatrix}; \begin{bmatrix} 38 \\ 3\frac{1}{2} \\ 414\frac{1}{2} \\ 72\frac{1}{2} \end{bmatrix}. \tag{4.12}$$

Here D indicates that the left-hand expression is a square matrix and the right-hand expression is the diagonal of that matrix, written in the form of a column vector. This is followed by the column $[a_h + \frac{1}{2} b_{hh}]$, which will remain the same throughout the computations of this step; the last vector is equal to this column minus the diagonal just-mentioned. It will be noted that the first 4 × 4 matrix in (4.12) is identical with B except that all off-diagonal elements have been given the minus sign. This matrix, too, will remain the same throughout the computations. In each row the negative element with the smallest absolute value has been underlined.

Reduction Rule

(1) *Write the left-hand vector of* (2.21) *as the diagonal vector of a matrix product, see* (4.12), *and determine the difference between the right-hand vector of* (2.21) *and that diagonal vector. If some element of this difference is negative, the upper limit* n_h^U *of the corresponding variable can be reduced by at least 1; otherwise proceed to:* (2) *Determine the ratios of the elements of the difference to the absolute value of the underlined element in the same row of the premultiplying matrix in* (4.12) *and check the upper bound of the variable associated with the smallest ratio thus obtained.*

In this case the ratios are

$$\frac{38}{16}, \quad \frac{3\frac{1}{2}}{21}, \quad \frac{414\frac{1}{2}}{3}, \quad \frac{72\frac{1}{2}}{3},$$

respectively, and we clearly have to scrutinize $n_2^U = 7$ according to Part (2) of the Reduction Rule. Hence we must ask which vectors in the promising region have an inner product with the vector (-21 22 -35 0) which is less than 24½. Obviously, these are only the vectors

$$(6 \;\; 7 \;\; 0 \;\; -1), (6 \;\; 7 \;\; 0 \;\; 0), (6 \;\; 7 \;\; 0 \;\; 1). \tag{4.13}$$

For we cannot increase n_1 or n_3 [lest we leave the promising region, see (4.9)]; nor is it possible to decrease them, for the inner product mentioned above would then exceed 24½ as is easily verified from (4.12). Since the coefficient of n_4 happens to be zero [see the

$(2, 4)^{th}$ element of the premultiplying matrix in (4.12)], we have to consider its full range, $-1 \leq n_4 \leq 1$, see (4.9). No other vectors with $n_2 = 7$ have to be considered and we can therefore decrease n_2^U from 7 to 6, the 'price' to be paid being that we have to compute Q-values of the three vectors (4.13). That there are only three such vectors is due to the fact that we checked n_2^U corresponding with the smallest ratio of Part (2) of the Reduction Rule. In fact, this Rule has been formulated in this way for precisely this reason. If we had checked for n_1^U instead of n_2^U, the number would have been 6 instead of 3; for n_3^U several hundreds of points would have to be considered, and for n_4^U there would be 70 of such exceptional points.

Given that n_2^U is now 6 we get the following new scheme:

$$\begin{bmatrix} 26 & -21 & -32 & \underline{-16} \\ \underline{-21} & 21 & -35 & 0 \\ -32 & -35 & 83 & \underline{-3} \\ -16 & 0 & \underline{-3} & 61 \end{bmatrix} \begin{bmatrix} 6 & 6 & 5_* & 6 \\ 6 & 6 & 6 & - \\ 1_* & 0 & 0 & 0 \\ 1 & - & 1 & 1 \end{bmatrix} \overset{D}{=} \begin{bmatrix} -18 \\ 0 \\ -373 \\ -35 \end{bmatrix}; \quad \overset{a_h + \frac{1}{2}b_{hh}}{\begin{bmatrix} -1 \\ 24\frac{1}{2} \\ 6\frac{1}{2} \\ 37\frac{1}{2} \end{bmatrix}}; \quad \overset{\text{Difference}}{\begin{bmatrix} 17 \\ 24\frac{1}{2} \\ 379\frac{1}{2} \\ 72\frac{1}{2} \end{bmatrix}}. \tag{4.14}$$

Following Part (2) of the Reduction Rule we should now check $n_1^U = 6$. Only the vectors $(6\ 6\ 1_*\ 1)$ and $(6\ 6\ 1_*\ 0)$ are to be considered, for these are the only vectors with $n_1 = 6$ in the promising region for which the inner product with $(26\ -21\ -32\ -16)$ is less than -1. When we proceed in this way we obtain the results that are summarized in Table 1. The procedure consists of 24 rounds and ends when all upper limits have been reduced to the corresponding lower limt. In our example this requires that the Q-values of 65 points be computed, which is of course a very substantial reduction compared with the original of more than 1000.

It will happen from time to time that a certain round leads to a simultaneous reduction of two (or more) upper limits. We shall consider one such case as a final illustration. At the end of Round 10, where

$$-5 \leq n_1 \leq 2,\ -6 \leq n_2 \leq 1,\ -1 \leq n_3 \leq 0,\ -1 \leq n_4 \leq 1,$$

we have the following scheme:

TABLE 1 List of Exceptional points

Round	Check for	Exceptional points to be considered	Number of points	Conclude
1	$n^u_2 = 7$	(6 7 0 − 1), (6 7 0 0), (6 7 0 1)	3	$n^u_2 = 6$
2	$n^u_1 = 6$	(6 6 1 1), (6 6 1 0)	2	$n^u_1 = 5$
3	$n^u_2 = 6$	(5 6 0 − 1), (5 6 0 0), (5 6 0 1)	3	$n^u_2 = 5$
4	$n^u_2 = 5$	(5 5 0 − 1), (5 5 0 0), (5 5 0 1), (4 5 0 − 1), (4 5 0 0), (4 5 0 1)	6	$n^u_2 = 4$
5	$n^u_1 = 5$	(5 4 1 1)	1	$n^u_1 = 4$
6	$n^u_2 = 4$	(4 4 0 − 1), (4 4 0 0), (4 4 0 1), (3 4 0 − 1), (3 4 0 0), (3 4 0 1)	6	$n^u_2 = 3$
7	$n^u_1 = 4$	(4 3 1 1)	1	$n^u_1 = 3$
8	$n^u_2 = 3$	(3 3 0 − 1), (3 3 0 0), (3 3 0 1), (2 3 0 − 1), (2 3 0 0), (2 3 0 1)	6	$n^u_2 = 2$
9	$n^u_1 = 3$	(3 2 1 1)	1	$n^u_1 = 2$
10	$n^u_2 = 2$	(2 2 0 − 1), (2 2 0 0), (2 2 0 1), (1 2 0 − 1), (1 2 0 0), (1 2 0 1)	6	$n^u_2 = 1$
11	$n^u_1 = 2$	(2 1 1 1), (2 1 1 0)	2	$n^u_1 = 1$, $n^u_4 = 0$
12	$n^u_2 = 1$	(1 1 0 − 1), (1 1 0 0), (0 1 0 − 1), (0 1 0 0)	4	$n^u_2 = 0$
13	$n^u_1 = 1$	(1 0 1 0)	1	$n^u_1 = 0$
14	$n^u_2 = 0$	(0 0 0 − 1), (0 0 0 0), (− 1 0 0 − 1), (− 1 0 0 0)	4	$n^u_2 = -1$
15	$n^u_1 = 0$	(0 − 1 1 0)	1	$n^u_1 = -1$
16	$n^u_2 = -1$	(− 1 − 1 0 − 1), (− 1 − 1 0 0), (− 2 − 1 0 − 1), (− 2 − 1 0 0)	4	$n^u_2 = -2$
17	$n^u_1 = -1$	(− 1 2 1 0)	1	$n^u_1 = -2$
18	$n^u_2 = -2$	(− 2 − 2 0 − 1), (− 2 − 2 0 0), (− 3 − 2 0 − 1), (− 3 − 2 0 0)	4	$n^u_2 = -3$
19	$n^u_1 = -2$	(− 2 − 3 1 0), (− 2 − 3 1 − 1)	2	$n^u_1 = -3$, $n^u_4 = -1 = n_4$
20	$n^u_2 = -3$	(− 3 − 3 0 − 1), (− 4 − 3 0 − 1)	2	$n^u_2 = -4$
21	$n^u_1 = -3$	(− 3 − 4 1 − 1)	1	$n^u_1 = -4$
22	$n^u_2 = -4$	(− 4 − 4 0 − 1), (− 5 − 4 0 − 1)	2	$n^u_2 = -5$, $n^u_3 = -1 = n_3$
23	$n^u_2 = -5$	(− 4 − 5 − 1 − 1)	1	$n^u_2 = -6 = n_2^L$, $n^u_1 = -5 = n_1^L$
24		(− 5 − 6 − 1 − 1) (lower limit)	1	
Total			65	

$$a_h + \tfrac{1}{2}b_{hh} \quad \text{Difference}$$

$$\begin{bmatrix} 26 & -21 & -32 & \underline{-16} \\ \underline{-21} & 21 & -35 & 0 \\ -32 & -35 & 83 & \underline{-3} \\ -16 & 0 & -3 & 61 \end{bmatrix} \begin{bmatrix} 2 & 2 & 5_{*} & 2 \\ 1 & 1 & 1 & - \\ 1_{*} & 0 & 0 & 0 \\ 1 & - & 1 & 1 \end{bmatrix} \overset{D}{=} \begin{bmatrix} -17 \\ -21 \\ -198 \\ 29 \end{bmatrix} ; \begin{bmatrix} -1 \\ 24\frac{1}{2} \\ 6\frac{1}{2} \\ 37\frac{1}{2} \end{bmatrix} ; \begin{bmatrix} 16 \\ 45\frac{1}{2} \\ 204\frac{1}{2} \\ 8\frac{1}{2} \end{bmatrix} . \tag{4.15}$$

The Reduction Rule requires that $n_1^U = 2$ be checked in Round 11. The only vectors to be considered are (2 1 1 1) and (2 1 1 0), the latter leading to an exact equality (i.e., to a zero difference). The new scheme then becomes:

$$a_h + \tfrac{1}{2}b_{hh} \quad \text{Difference}$$

$$\begin{bmatrix} 26 & -21 & -32 & \underline{-16} \\ \underline{-21} & 21 & -35 & 0 \\ -32 & -35 & 83 & \underline{-3} \\ -16 & 0 & \underline{-3} & 61 \end{bmatrix} \begin{bmatrix} 1 & 1 & 5_{*} & 1 \\ 1 & 1 & 1 & - \\ 1_{*} & 0 & 0 & 0 \\ 1 & - & 1 & 1 \end{bmatrix} \overset{D}{=} \begin{bmatrix} -43 \\ 0 \\ -198 \\ 45 \end{bmatrix} ; \begin{bmatrix} -1 \\ 24\frac{1}{2} \\ 6\frac{1}{2} \\ 37\frac{1}{2} \end{bmatrix} ; \begin{bmatrix} 42 \\ 24\frac{1}{2} \\ 204\frac{1}{2} \\ -7\frac{1}{2} \end{bmatrix} . \tag{4.16}$$

The last component of the difference is negative. The conclusion is therefore that not only n_1^U changes from 2 to 1 but also that n_4^U changes from 1 to 0. The scheme is then modified as follows:

$$a_h + \tfrac{1}{2}b_{hh} \quad \text{Difference}$$

$$\begin{bmatrix} 26 & -21 & -32 & \underline{-16} \\ \underline{-21} & 21 & -35 & 0 \\ -32 & -35 & 83 & \underline{-3} \\ -16 & 0 & \underline{-3} & 61 \end{bmatrix} \begin{bmatrix} 1 & 1 & 5_{*} & 1 \\ 1 & 1 & 1 & - \\ 1_{*} & 0 & 0 & 0 \\ 0 & - & 0 & 0 \end{bmatrix} \overset{D}{=} \begin{bmatrix} -27 \\ 0 \\ -195 \\ -16 \end{bmatrix} ; \begin{bmatrix} -1 \\ 24\frac{1}{2} \\ 6\frac{1}{2} \\ 37\frac{1}{2} \end{bmatrix} ; \begin{bmatrix} 26 \\ 24\frac{1}{2} \\ 201\frac{1}{2} \\ 53\frac{1}{2} \end{bmatrix} . \tag{4.17}$$

From here we proceed as usual (testing for $n_2^U = 1$ in Round 12).

Fourth Step (Computing the Q-values)

For all vectors x which need to be considered, determine the sign of $a'x$. If this is positive determine $Q(x) = a'x - \frac{1}{2}x'Bx$ and pick out the vector(s) with the largest Q-value.

We have $Q(x) \leq a'x$ because B is positive-definite. It follows that it is not necessary to compute Q for all 65 vectors x; we can confine ourselves to those for which the linear part of the objective function, $a'x$, is positive. This applies to 34 vectors as Table 2 shows, of which only 10 give $Q > 0$. There are two solutions to the discrete maximization problem: (3 4 0 1) and (-4 -5 -1 -1), both with a Q of $\frac{11}{14}$. When reformulated in terms of (3.1) and (4.1) these solutions are

$$\left(557 \;\; 708 \;\; 90 \;\; 152 \;\; - \;\; 1188\tfrac{2}{7}\right) \text{ and } \left(550 \;\; 699 \;\; 89 \;\; 150 \;\; - \;\; 1173\tfrac{2}{7}\right)$$

with a Q-value according to (3.1) of $4845\frac{2}{7}$. If we would apply a linear transformation to Q such that the value of the continuous maximum becomes 1 and that the lattice point which is closest to the vector of this maximum 0, the discrete maximum becomes 0.71.

Discussion

Pigot (France):
Does the problem discussed come from practical work, or does it concern a theoretical question only?

Answer:

As yet, it is a purely theoretical problem; it will become of practical value when linear inequality constraints can be incorporated in the formulation and solution techniques.

TABLE 2 Computation of Q-Values

Round	Vector	*Q*-value (multiplied by 7)	Round	Vector	*Q*-value (multiplied by 7)
1	(6 7 0 − 1)	7 − ½.454	11	(2 1 1 1)	LPN
	(6 7 0 0)	14 − ½.201		(2 1 1 0)	LPN
	(6 7 0 1)	21 − ½.70	12	(1 1 0 −1)	LPN
2	(6 6 1 1)	LPN		(1 1 0 0)	LPN
	(6 6 1 0)	LPN		(0 1 0 −1)	7 − ½.84
3	(5 6 0 − 1)	7 − ½.367		(0 1 0 0)	14 − ½.21 = 3½
	(5 6 0 0)	14 − ½.146	13	(1 0 1 0)	LPN
	(5 6 0 1)	21 − ½.47	14	(0 0 0 −1)	LPN
4	(5 5 0 − 1)	LPN		(0 0 0 0)	LPN
	(5 5 0 0)	LPN		(−1 0 0 −1)	7 − ½.55
	(5 5 0 1)	7 − ½.26		*(−1 0 0 0)	14 − ½.26 = 1
	(4 5 0 − 1)	7 − ½.200	15	(0 −1 1 0)	LPN
	(4 5 0 0)	14 − ½.101	16	(−1 −1 0 −1)	LPN
	*(4 5 0 1)	21 − ½.34 = 4		(−1 −1 0 0)	LPN
5	(5 4 1 1)	LPN		(−2 −1 0 −1)	7 − ½.38
6	(4 4 0 − 1)	LPN		(−2 −1 0 0)	14 − ½.41
	(4 4 0 0)	LPN	17	(−1 −2 1 0)	LPN
	*(4 4 0 1)	7 − ½.13 = ½	18	(−2 −2 0 −1)	LPN
	(3 4 0 − 1)	7 − ½.223		(−2 −2 0 0)	LPN
	(3 4 0 0)	14 − ½.66		(−3 −2 0 −1)	7 − ½.31
	**(3 4 0 1)	21 − ½.31 = 5½		(−3 −2 0 0)	14 − ½.150
7	(4 3 1 1)	LPN	19	(−2 −3 1 0)	LPN
8	(3 3 0 − 1)	LPN		(−2 −3 1 −1)	LPN
	(3 3 0 0)	LPN	20	(−3 −3 0 −1)	LPN
	*(3 3 0 1)	7 − ½.10 = 2		(−4 −3 0 −1)	7 − ½.34
	(2 3 0 − 1)	7 − ½.166	21	(−3 −4 1 −1)	LPN
	(2 3 0 0)	14 − ½.44	22	(−4 −4 0 −1)	LPN
	*(2 3 0 1)	21 − ½.38 = 2		(−5 −4 0 −1)	7 − ½.47
9	(3 2 1 1)	LPN	23	**(−4 −5 −1 −1)	14 − ½.17 = 5½
10	(2 2 0 − 1)	LPN	24	*(−5 −6 −1 −1)	14 − ½.24 = 2
	(2 2 0 0)	LPN			
	(2 2 0 1)	7 − ½.17			
	(1 2 0 − 1)	7 − ½.119			
	*(1 2 0 0)	14 − ½.26 = 1			
	(1 2 0 1)	21 − ½.55			

Notes. LPN means that the linear part is negative or zero. Vectors with a positive Q-value are marked with a star, the two solutions by two stars.

CHAPTER 76

SUBSTITUTION EFFECTS IN GEOMETRIC PROGRAMMING*

HENRI THEIL
University of Chicago,
Chicago, Illinois, U.S.A.

ABSTRACT. The impact of price changes in geometric programming is analyzed in terms of technological substitution relationships. The method can also be applied to sensitivity analysis, which is illustrated by means of a numerical example.

Introduction

Geometric programming as developed by Zener, Duffin, Peterson, and others is a mathematical method of cost minimization for a particular class of cost structures. In its simplest form, the method is concerned with a system consisting of m components, and the total cost of the system is equal to the sum of the costs of the components. The cost of the ith component equals $p_i f_i(x)$, where p_i is the cost coefficient of the component (basically its price) and $f_i(x)$ is a function whose logarithm is linear in n decision variables, written in vector form $[x_1 \cdots x_n]' = x$:

$$C(x) = \sum_{i=1}^{m} p_i f_i(x) , \tag{1}$$

where $\log f_i(x) = \Sigma_{j=1}^{n} a_{ij} x_j$. This is a very special mathematical structure, but it appears to have a rather wide applicability to engineering systems.[1]

To minimize $C(\,)$ for variations in x we equate its n first-order derivatives to zero:

* Reprinted by permission, "Substitution Effects in Geometric Programming," Henri Theil, *Management Science*, 19 (1972), 25-30. Copyright 1972, The Institute of Management Sciences, 290 Westminster Street, Providence, Rhode Island, 02903. The author is indebted to Professor Elmer L. Peterson for his helpful comments on an earlier draft of this article.

[1] Wilde and Beightler (1967, p. 130) make the following comments: " . . . most systems can be decomposed into components, each with its own cost . . .. Component behaviour in most engineering systems can usually be expressed as products of powers of the design variables, as is testified by the frequency of logarithmic graphics in the technical literature. The effect of scale of the operation is often expressed by such approximations as the 'six-tenths' rule, which states that the cost of a piece of equipment varies as the $^6/_{10}$ power of its rate capacity." The decision variables in this article (the x's) are to be interpreted as logarithms of design variables.

$$\frac{\partial C}{\partial x_j} = \sum_{i=1}^{m} p_i \frac{\partial f_i}{\partial x_j} = \sum_{i=1}^{m} p_i f_i \frac{\partial(\log f_i)}{\partial x_j} = \sum_{i=1}^{m} p_i f_i a_{ij} = 0 .$$

The function f_i that occurs before the last equality sign should be interpreted as being evaluated at the minimum. By dividing by the minimum value of total cost we obtain

$$\sum_{i=1}^{m} a_{ij} w_i = 0 , \qquad j = 1, \ldots, n, \tag{2}$$

where w_i is the ith component's share of minimum total cost or, for short, the cost share of the ith component. These shares obviously satisfy

$$\sum_{i=1}^{m} w_i = 1 . \tag{3}$$

Equations (2) and (3) are linear in the cost shares and they are exactly sufficient in number to determine these shares in the special case $m = n + 1$. In that case the cost shares are completely independent of the p's. This is very convenient, because it amounts to a separation of the economic factors (the p's) from the technical factors (the a_{ij}'s). It can be shown that the minimum value of total cost is given by[2]

$$\log C_{\min} = -\sum_{i=1}^{m} \hat{w}_i \log(\hat{w}_i / p_i) , \tag{4}$$

where $\hat{w}_1, \ldots, \hat{w}_n$ is the solution obtained from (2) and (3). Then, by multiplying each $\hat{w}_i$ by $C_{\min}$ we get $p_i f_i(\hat{x})$, from which the minimum cost decision vector $\hat{x}$ can be determined.

The approach is not quite so simple for $m > n + 1$, because the constraints (2) and (3) are then insufficient to determine the $\hat{w}$'s. It can be shown that the optimal cost shares can in that case be found by minimizing, for variations in the w's subject to these constraints, the function

$$\sum_{i=1}^{m} w_i \log(w_i / p_i) . \tag{5}$$

The optimal cost shares are then no longer independent of the p's, so that there is a problem of the price sensitivity of these shares. The objective of this note is to prove a simple theoretical result on this price sensitivity. It concerns technological substitution due

---

[2] For proofs of the statements concerning (4) and (5) see the sources quoted at the end of this article.

to price changes and it can also be used for a simple numerical determination of the displacement of the optimum caused by changes in prices.[3]

Analysis of Infinitesimal Changes

Consider the Lagrangian function

$$\sum_{i=1}^{m} w_i \log \frac{w_i}{p_i} - \lambda\left(\sum_{i=1}^{m} w_i - 1\right) - \sum_{j=1}^{n} \mu_j \sum_{i=1}^{m} a_{ij} w_i \ , \tag{6}$$

where $\lambda, \mu_1, \ldots, \mu_n$ are Lagrangian multipliers. We differentiate (6) with respect to w_i and equate the result to zero.[4]

$$1 + \log w_i - \log p_i - \lambda - \sum_{j=1}^{n} \mu_j a_{ij} = 0 \ . \tag{7}$$

Imagine now that the prices are changed infinitesimally so that they become $p_1 + dp_1, \ldots, p_m + dp_m$. Equation (7) then becomes

$$1 + \log (w_i + d w_i) - \log (p_i + d p_i) - (\lambda + d\lambda) - \sum_{j=1}^{n} (\mu_j + d\mu_j)\, a_{ij} = 0 \ , \tag{8}$$

where $w_i + dw_i$, $\lambda + d\lambda$ and $\mu_j + d\mu_j$ are the values at the constrained minimum that corresponds to the new price situation.

By subtracting (7) from (8) we obtain

$$d w_i / w_i - d(\log p_i) - d\lambda - \sum_{j=1}^{n} a_{ij}\, d\mu_j = 0 \, . \tag{9}$$

Next multiply both sides by w_i and sum over i, using $\sum_i dw_i = 0$ and $\sum_i w_i a_{ij} = 0$:

$$-\sum_{i=1}^{m} w_i\, d(\log p_i) - d\lambda = 0$$

after which substitution into (9) gives

[3] Reference should also be made to Duffin, Peterson and Zener (1967, Appendix B) for other results in sensitivity analysis.

[4] All logarithms in this article are natural logarithms.

$$dw_i/w_i - \sum_{j=1}^{n} a_{ij}\,d\mu_j = d(\log \bar{p}_i) \,, \tag{10}$$

where $d(\log \bar{p}_i)$ stands for the change in the logarithm of the ith deflated price:

$$d(\log \bar{p}_i) = d(\log p_i) - \sum_{k=1}^{n} w_k\, d(\log p_k) \,. \tag{11}$$

We can write equation (10) for $i = 1, \cdots, m$ together with the n equations (2) in the following matrix form:

$$\begin{bmatrix} 1/w_i & 0 & \cdots & 0 & a_{11} & a_{12} & \cdots & a_{1n} \\ 0 & 1/w_2 & \cdots & 0 & a_{21} & a_{22} & \cdots & a_{2n} \\ \vdots & \vdots & & \vdots & \vdots & \vdots & & \vdots \\ 0 & 0 & \cdots & 1/w_m & a_{m1} & a_{m2} & \cdots & a_{mn} \\ a_{11} & a_{21} & \cdots & a_{m1} & 0 & 0 & \cdots & 0 \\ a_{12} & a_{22} & \cdots & a_{m2} & 0 & 0 & \cdots & 0 \\ \vdots & \vdots & & \vdots & \vdots & \vdots & & \vdots \\ a_{1n} & a_{2n} & \cdots & a_{mn} & 0 & 0 & \cdots & 0 \end{bmatrix} \begin{bmatrix} dw_1 \\ dw_2 \\ \vdots \\ dw_m \\ -d\mu_1 \\ -d\mu_2 \\ \vdots \\ -d\mu_n \end{bmatrix} = \begin{bmatrix} d(\log \bar{p}_1) \\ d(\log \bar{p}_2) \\ \vdots \\ d(\log \bar{p}_m) \\ 0 \\ 0 \\ \vdots \\ 0 \end{bmatrix} . \tag{12}$$

The square matrix on the left may be written as

$$\begin{bmatrix} W^{-1} & A \\ A' & 0 \end{bmatrix}, \tag{13}$$

where W is the $m \times m$ diagonal matrix whose ith diagonal element is w_i and A is the $m \times n$ matrix $[a_{ij}]$. The inverse of (13) is, under the condition that A has full column rank,

$$\begin{bmatrix} W - WA(A'WA)^{-1}A'W & WA(A'WA)^{-1} \\ (A'WA)^{-1}A'W & -(A'WA)^{-1} \end{bmatrix} . \tag{14}$$

This may be verified by multiplying the two matrices, which gives the required unit matrix of order $m + n$.

Using the inverse (14), we can solve (12) for the changes in the cost shares:

$$\begin{bmatrix} dw_1 \\ \vdots \\ dw_m \end{bmatrix} = [\,W - WA\,(A'WA\,)^{-1}A'W\,] \begin{bmatrix} d\,(\log \overline{p}_1) \\ \vdots \\ d\,(\log \overline{p}_m) \end{bmatrix} . \tag{15}$$

For the ith share this amounts to

$$dw_i = w_i\, d\,(\log \overline{p}_i) - \sum_{j=1}^{n} s_{ij}\, d\,(\log \overline{p}_j) \ , \tag{16}$$

where s_{ij} is the (i, j)th element of the matrix

$$S = WA\,(\,A'WA\,)^{-1}A'W \ . \tag{17}$$

The first term in the right-hand side of (16) describes the "direct" effect of a change in the relative price of the ith component on this component's cost share. It states that if the relative price goes up by 1 per cent, say, the corresponding cost share will increase by a fraction of 1 per cent which is equal to the value of this share. The second term of (16) describes the technological substitution. Since S is a positive semi-definite matrix, this term implies that an increase in the relative price of the ith component will lead to a smaller increase of the ith cost share than the increase that would be materialized if there were no substitution. The symmetry of S implies that the substitution effect of an increase of the logarithm of the ith deflated price on the cost share of the jth component is equal to that of the same increase of the logarithm of the jth deflated price on the cost share of the ith component.

Further Comments

(i) In the substitution term of (16) we may replace $d(\log \overline{p}_j)$ by the change in the logarithm of the undeflated jth price, $d(\log p_j)$. To prove this we note that the vector of price changes in (15) can be written as

$$\begin{bmatrix} d(\log p_1) \\ \vdots \\ d(\log p_m) \end{bmatrix} - \left[\sum_{k=1}^{m} w_k\, d\,(\log p_k)\right]\iota$$

where ι is a column vector consisting of m unit elements. The proposition is then proved by noting that $A'W\iota$ is a zero vector in view of equation (2).

(ii) The matrix by which the deflated price log-changes are premultiplied in (15) may be written as

$$W^{1/2}[I - W^{1/2}A(A'WA)^{-1}A'W^{1/2}]W^{1/2} ,$$

where $W^{1/2}$ is the $m \times m$ matrix whose elements are the positive square roots of the corresponding elements of W. The unit matrix inside square brackets is of order $m \times m$ and the matrix which is subtracted from this unit matrix is idempotent with rank and trace equal to n. This suggests that, as far as the cost shares are concerned, technological substitution declines in importance when the number of decision variables is smaller relative to the number of components of the system.

(iii) We know that the cost shares are completely independent of the prices in the special case $m = n + 1$. The easiest way to verify this in the present approach is by writing (3) in the form $\sum_i a_{i0} w_i = 1$ and λ of (6) as μ_0. It is then readily seen that (9) becomes

$$dw_i/w_i - d(\log p_i) - \sum_{j=0}^{n} a_{ij}\,d\mu_j = 0$$

which is equivalent to (10) except that the ith price is not deflated and that the summation over j includes $j = 0$. This implies corresponding changes in (15); in particular, the matrix A is replaced by $B = [\iota A]$, which is a nonsingular $m \times m$ matrix in this case. Hence,

$$W - WB(B'WB)^{-1}B'W = W - WBB^{-1}W^{-1}(B')^{-1}B'W = 0$$

which proves that the cost shares are independent of the prices.

A Numerical Illustration

To illustrate the above results we consider the hypothetical chemical plant described by Wilde and Beightler (1967, pp. 11-12, 102-103). It consists of a main compressor, a mixer, a reactor, a separator, a recirculating compressor, and a purifier. There are two design variables: the operating pressure of the raw material gases, to be denoted by X_1, and the recycle ratio X_2. The associated annual cost in dollars is shown below. Note that the cost of the mixer is fixed and hence irrelevant from the viewpoint of minimization. Note also that the separator and the recirculating compressor may be combined because their costs are of identical mathematical form.

main compressor	$1000\,X_1$,
mixer	10^4,
reactor	$4 \times 10^9/X_1X_2$,

separator	$10^5 X_2$,
recirculating compressor	$1.5 \times 10^5 X_2$,
purifier	$9000\ X_1 X_2$.

The cost function is thus

$$p_1 X_1 + p_2 / X_1 X_2 + p_3 X_2 + p_4 X_1 X_2 \tag{18}$$

where

$$p_1 = 1000, \qquad p_2 = 4 \times 10^9, \qquad p_3 = 2.5 \times 10^5, \qquad p_4 = 9000. \tag{19}$$

When we write $x_j = \log X_j$ for $j = 1$ and 2, we may conclude that (18) falls under (1) with $m = 4$ and $n = 2$. The technology matrix $[a_{ij}]$ has the following form:

$$A = \begin{bmatrix} 1 & 0 \\ -1 & -1 \\ 0 & 1 \\ 1 & 1 \end{bmatrix}. \tag{20}$$

It is readily verified that the four cost shares in the price situation (19) are

$$w_1 = 0.0313, \qquad w_2 = 0.4843, \qquad w_3 = 0.0313, \qquad w_4 = 0.4530. \tag{21}$$

Suppose now that the price of the purifier increases by 10 per cent, p_4 going up from 9000 to 9900, while the three other prices remain at their original levels. A 10 per cent increase is equivalent to a change in the natural logarithm equal to 0.09531, so that the log-change in the price index of (11) is

$$\sum_{k=1}^{4} w_k\, d \log (p_k) = (0.4530)(0.09531) = 0.04318 .$$

Hence the log-changes in the deflated prices are

$$\begin{aligned} d(\log \bar{p}_i) &= -0.04318 \quad \text{for} \quad i = 1,\ 2,\ 3, \\ d(\log \bar{p}_4) &= 0.05213 , \end{aligned}$$

which implies the following direct effects of the change in p_4 on the four cost shares:

$$
\begin{aligned}
w_i\, d(\log \bar{p}_i) &= -0.0014 \qquad (i=1)\\
&= -0.0209 \qquad (i=2)\\
&= -0.0014 \qquad (i=3)\\
&= \ \ 0.0236 \qquad (i=4).
\end{aligned}
\tag{22}
$$

To compute the substitution effects we need $A'WA$ and its inverse. Using the A of (20), we have

$$
A'WA = \begin{bmatrix} 1-w_3 & w_2+w_4 \\ w_2+w_4 & 1-w_1 \end{bmatrix},
$$

$$
(A'WA)^{-1} = \frac{1}{D}\begin{bmatrix} 1-w_1 & -w_2-w_4 \\ -w_2-w_4 & 1-w_3 \end{bmatrix},
$$

$$
S = WA(A'WA)^{-1}A'W \tag{23}
$$

$$
= \frac{1}{D}\begin{bmatrix}
w_1^2(1-w_1) & -w_1w_2w_3 & -w_1w_3(w_2+w_4) & w_1w_3w_4 \\
-w_1w_2w_3 & w_2^2(w_1+w_3) & -w_1w_2w_3 & -w_2w_4(w_4+w_3) \\
-w_1w_3(w_2+w_4) & -w_1w_2w_3 & w_3^2(1-w_3) & w_1w_3w_4 \\
w_1w_3w_4 & -w_2w_4(w_1+w_3) & w_1w_3w_4 & w_4^2(w_1+w_3)
\end{bmatrix},
$$

where D is the (positive) determinant value of $A'WA$:

$$
D = w_1 + w_3 - w_1^2 - w_3^2 - w_1w_3 \,.
$$

All diagonal elements of S are positive. In addition, the technology considered here is such that the substitution interactions are all negative with the exception of the two which relate the purifier to the main compressor and the separator/recirculating compressor combination. Substitution of the numerical values (21) gives

$$
S = \begin{bmatrix}
0.016 & -0.008 & -0.015 & 0.007 \\
-0.008 & 0.246 & -0.008 & -0.230 \\
-0.015 & -0.008 & 0.016 & 0.007 \\
0.007 & -0.230 & 0.007 & 0.215
\end{bmatrix}. \tag{24}
$$

This shows that the elements s_{22}, s_{24}, and s_{44} take large numerical values, which is mainly due to the large cost shares of the reactor and the purifier.

We obtain the substitution component of (16) by postmultiplying $-S$ by the vector of the deflated price log-changes. In this case, when only one price changes, it is actually more convenient to multiply by the undeflated log-changes [see the above discussion under (i)]. The result is

$$\begin{aligned} -s_{i4}\, d(\log p_4) &= -0.0007 \qquad (i=1) \\ &= 0.0219 \qquad (i=2) \\ &= -0.0007 \qquad (i=3) \\ &= -0.0205 \qquad (i=4)\ . \end{aligned} \tag{25}$$

These values are to be added to those of (22), which leads to rather small net changes in the cost shares. It seems plausible that this approximate compensation of the direct effects by the substitution effects is due to the small excess of the number of components over the number of variables. The cost shares in the new price situation are then computed as

$$w_1 = 0.0293, \qquad w_2 = 0.4853, \qquad w_3 = 0.0293, \qquad w_4 = 0.4561, \tag{26}$$

which deviate from the correct values by an amount of the order of 10^{-4}. When the price changes are larger than those considered here, one may want to obtain additional precision by making successive computations based on a series of smaller price changes.

References

Duffin, R.J., E.L. Peterson, and C. Zener: 1967, *Geometric Programming*, John Wiley and Sons, Inc., New York.

Wilde, D.J. and C.S. Beightler: 1967, *Foundations of Optimization*, Prentice-Hall, Inc., Englewood Cliffs, N.J.

SECTION 6.3: QUANTITATIVE ANALYSIS

CHAPTER 77

QUANTITATIVE ECONOMICS IN THE NETHERLANDS*

J. TINBERGEN
Netherlands School of Economics
(Now Erasmus University)
Rotterdam, The Netherlands

H. THEIL
Netherlands School of Economics
(Now Erasmus University)
Rotterdam, The Netherlands

Model Building for Economic Policy

INTRODUCTORY

A considerable part of recent research as well as of teaching in the field of quantitative economics in the Netherlands has been grouped around the objective of supplying tools for economic policy. This applies to short-term as well as to long-term economic policy and to policies for developed as well as for under-developed economies. The elements needed for such research cover most of the subjects traditionally included in teaching programmes of this kind, but give them a certain twist and direction. It is the intention of this article to give a brief survey of teaching and research activities as they now exist in this country, more particularly at the Netherlands School of Economics, while indicating the links with practical activities in the field of economic policy.

Teaching programmes at the Netherlands School of Economics are more comprehensive than those in other Dutch schools or universities but the main subjects are taught at the latter as well, i.e. at the Municipal University of Amsterdam, the Roman Catholic School of Economics at Tilburg, at the State University at Groningen and at the Free (Reformed) University of Amsterdam.

In the 'twenties' the Rotterdam School included only three courses bearing on quantitative research methods in its programme, one statistics course, one mathematics course and one course called statistical analysis. The statistics course was obligatory for all students, and dealt with administrative statistics and some elementary methodology. Statistical analysis was a subject taken by a few students only and this group was obliged to take mathematics also. Roughly speaking, the subject covered Yule's textbook and was taught by an insurance mathematician. The three courses were taken over by the present author in 1933 and adapted rather more fully to the needs of economic research at that time. It was soon recognized that some specialization among the teachers was necessary and in the late 'thirties' an additional professor was charged with a course in mathematical statistics. Elementary statistics was transferred to a lecturer and the subject of statistical analysis divided into two subjects, mathematical economics and

* This article first appeared in *Higher Education and Research in the Netherlands*, **2** (1958), 2-16. Reprinted here with the permission of the Netherlands Organization for International Cooperation in Higher Education.

econometrics. Although, in principle, the latter subject could have covered the former too, the practical set-up was to give one course in pure mathematical economics and another in the various phases involved in any piece of concrete econometric research covering mathematical economics and statistical inference, both applied to concrete research problems.

Immediately after the war, the mathematical approach to economics was made an obligatory subject for all students, which means that they now have to follow a mathematics course and that the general course in economic theory is based on some mathematical knowledge.

A few years ago a major improvement in the training facilities in quantitative economic research was introduced, consisting of the creation of a department of quantitative economics and the appointment of Professor Henri Theil, who also heads the newly-created Econometric Institute.

Finally, the subject of development planning (or programming) has quite recently been added to the other subjects taught at the Netherlands School of Economics. It is the successor to what was previously called "oriental economics" and the change of name also indicates a change in approach, supposed to be in line with world developments.

The total number of teachers in the field of quantitative research is now 11, distributed over the various subjects in the following way:

3 professors for (1) mathematical economics and development programming;
(2) econometrics;
(3) market analysis and business statistics;
2 lecturers for (1) mathematics and statistical analysis;
(2) statistics;
1 teacher for mathematics; and
5 "assistants" for these subjects.

A detailed survey of the subjects taught is given in Professor Theil's article in this bulletin.

TEACHING

Of the courses having some relationship to quantitative research on behalf of economic policy mention may be made of the following.

1. *Mathematical economics*. Courses in general economic theory followed by all students are based on some knowledge of mathematics, taught in the first year and covering some infinitesimal calculus, some analytical geometry and some simple algebra of linear equations. A special course in mathematical economics is available for those who choose quantitative research as their special subject. It is a two-year course of two hours weekly and its main purpose is to discuss the various types of equations composing a complete economic model. In the first year, the various types of equations are discussed and illustrated, special attention being paid to behaviour equations. The subject matter is subdivided into static and dynamic theories, into "psychological" and "calculatory" behaviour equations and distinguishes between demand for and supply of the factors of

production in addition to products. The importance of using measurable phenomena, if only as dummy variables, is emphasized with a view to application to concrete situations. In the second year, complete models and their implications are treated, geared as far as possible to policy applications, such as anti-cylical policies, social policy and development policy.

2. *Econometrics*. As has already been stated, the successive courses given under this heading have concentrated on the practical side of econometric work, emphasizing the links between the elements of mathematical economics and statistical inference to be applied to the same concrete research subject. With the development of econometric methods, the subject has expanded considerably and nowadays requires a thorough knowledge of mathematical statistics. Accordingly, the number of auxiliary courses has also been increased.

3. *Statistical inference*. Courses on this subject began, in the 'twenties', with curve-fitting and correlation. At present, such subjects as the testing of hypotheses, estimation of a set of simultaneous equations and problems of aggregation are taught in fairly extensive detail. Students are provided with a solid background in the probability theory of multidimensional distributions.

Applications are to a large extent chosen in the field of model building for policy purposes, as practised in the Central Planning Bureau of the Dutch Government.

4. *Development programming*. In this course some of the recent models of a growing economy are discussed and analyzed, with a view to their application in development programming. To start with, the simplest versions of Domar-Harrod models are treated and the following complications are introduced one by one: a finite gestation period, the existence of several sectors (including foreign countries), the existence of inter-sector deliveries (as represented by input-output analysis) and the existence of several technologies to produce the same product. In this course, the emphasis has to be laid on practical matters, requiring, among other things, an understanding of the sociological background to a development policy, the appplication of simplified methods, such as the appraisal of individual investment projects according to some practical method, and the translation of findings into a concrete policy.

Apart from the courses mentioned by Professor Theil and in this article there are several others in the Netherlands School of Economics dealing with quantitative aspects of economic policy; in particular, the courses in monetary phenomena and policies and in public finance.

RESEARCH

In the Netherlands there is a very close connection between teaching and research. This also applies to research undertaken elsewhere than in university institutes, resulting to a large extent from personal ties between university teaching staff and research workers in the non-university institutes. Several part-time professors hold important functions in government institutions and thereby form immediate links. Quite a few of the full-time professors were formerly members of the research staff of non-university institutes and are often still consultants. The small size of the Dutch community therefore results in a slighter degree of separation of, or division of labour between, pure theory and practical research than seems to be customary in some of the larger countries.

Some of the main centres for quantitative economic research with a bearing on policy problems are, in decreasing order of ties with teaching, the Econometric Institute at the Netherlands School of Economics; the Netherlands Economic Institute[1] and comparable institutes at the Municipal University of Amsterdam and the Catholic School of Economics at Tilburg; the Central Planning Bureau of the Netherlands Government, the Central Bureau of Statistics and various research departments at the Ministries (e.g. of the Treasury and of the Ministry of Economic Affairs) and the Central Bank (De Nederlandse Bank N.V.). Finally, a number of technical departments in government ministries should be mentioned. The largest according to the numbers actually engaged in research are probably The Central Planning Bureau, headed by Professor P. de Wolff of the Municipal University of Amsterdam (whose deputy is Professor P.J. Verdoorn of the Netherlands School of Economics) and the Netherlands Economic Institute. According to total manpower, however, the Central Bureau of Statistics, headed by Professor Ph.J. Idenburg, is by far the largest.

The type of research undertaken at the Central Planning Bureau is determined by its task, i.e. to advise the government and the Social Economic Council on all matters concerned with the co-ordination of general economic policy. This means that whenever the general interdependence of the various sectors of the economy is at stake, advice will be sought from this Bureau. It has therefore specialized in illustrating, in numerical form, this interdependence, using both short-term and long-term economic models based on the Dutch economy. In so far as export markets are analyzed, some work on foreign economies has also been undertaken. The models used by the Bureau have been frequently published and also comparisons between the forecasts made and the results actually achieved (cf. Professor Theil's article in this issue). The models do not only aim at making forecasts, but also at calculating alternative developments to be expected from policy changes. During the last few years a considerable amount of research has been invested into a new short-term model, in co-operation with the Central Bureau of Statistics, the Netherlands Economic Institute and the Mathematical Centre at Amsterdam. The model itself constitutes, as did its predecessors, a macro-model with some 30 variables, but its results are tested with the aid of a multi-sector model, distinguishing eleven sectors. Its predecessors have been used for the annual "Central Economic Plans" and for a considerable number of recommendations by the Social Economic Council, covering such subjects as social insurance reforms, wage policy, rent policy, employment policy and industrialization policy. The long-term models have been used mainly to provide a background to the last-mentioned policy. In co-operation with the Central Bank's Research Division a considerable amount of work has also been devoted to the elaboration of financial accounts for the national economy.

Most of the staff of the Netherlands Economic Institute are engaged in research for municipalities and private firms; the former type, of course, often implies policy

[1] See the "Institutions" section in the Chronicle of this Bulletin.

questions also, mainly town or regional development policy. A small group works on problems concerning the development of underdeveloped countries. Models for general programming as well as for the appraisal of individual projects have been constructed. In addition, detailed studies of the availability of alternative methods of production in well-defined industries are made in co-operation with a research institute of the Technological University at Delft.

OPPORTUNITIES OFFERED TO FOREIGN STUDENTS

Teaching at the Dutch universities has so far been done, with very few exceptions, in the Dutch language. This limits the opportunities for foreign students to follow their courses. It was formerly the tradition that a number of Indonesian students formed part of the student body, but this has been brought to an end by the Indonesian Government. Participation in research by foreign scholars and students has been more frequent, since each member of the staff of the research institutes speaks English and contacts are easily made there. In fact, a considerable number of foreigners have worked at the Central Planning Bureau and the Netherlands Economic Institute.

Shortly after World War II, the Institute of Social Studies was founded in a common effort by all Dutch universities to open up new opportunities to foreign students.

This institute offers courses and facilities for research in English and the overwhelming majority of its students come from abroad. Its subjects do not cover much of the subject matter discussed in this article, with the exception of part of the work done in the Six-month Course in Economic Planning. This course, which is open to those who have practical experience and responsibility in the subject, includes quantitative economic analysis together with a number of practical subjects, but does not specialize in the direction of mathematical statistics. It is intended for those responsible for planning work rather than for experts specialized in some of the mathematical techniques.

At present, plans are being considered to offer research facilities in quantitative economics to foreign post-graduate students, sponsored jointly by the Division of Balanced International Growth of the Netherlands Economic Institute and by the Econometric Institute of the Netherlands School of Economics. Research could be undertaken in one of the following subjects:

(1) Development programming by means of economic models;
(2) Appraisal of investment projects;
(3) Statistical inference in economics;
(4) Economic forecasts and rational decision-making.

Whether these plans materialize will depend on the interest shown by prospective participants.

J. Tinbergen

Economic Forecasts and the Problems Involved in Decision-making Under Conditions of Uncertainty

INTRODUCTION

For many decades now both economists and laymen concerned with economic affairs have been interested in economic forecasts. Their interest is sometimes rather cynical, sometimes constructive; but whatever the case, a whole series of questions looms up. Is it at all possible to make forecasts of reasonable reliability? Is it really necessary to make forecasts at all — cannot one just as well base one's decisions on what is happening at the moment? Is it true that forecasts of changes within a short-term period (e.g. a month or a quarter) are usually more reliable than long-term forecasts? Must one apply very modest standards in judging the quality of forecasts and even, perhaps, be content if they differ less markedly from what really happens than do simpler methods of extrapolation? And how is one to measure their quality? When what is forecast can be represented by a single figure, this seems easy enough (one simply takes the difference between forecast and reality); but how is one to set to work when the merits of a whole series of forecasts requires assessment? Is this merely a question of calculating individual forecasting errors and then taking an average, or is it advisable to take account explicitly of the importance of the various things that are forecasted? And as regards this last point, would it perhaps be advisable to take into account the policy based on the forecasts? As one will have seen, here the problems referred to in the second part of the title of this article come into play.

I hope that the reader does not expect me to supply an exhaustive answer in a nutshell to all these and similar questions. One of the difficulties in the way of doing so is that forecasting on anything resembling a systematic basis is only of recent origin in economics. It is not possible, therefore, to draw on a rich fund of experience as it is in other fields, for example, in meteorology. Naturally, there have been forerunners, like the famous (perhaps I should say notorious) Harvard barometer, which enjoyed a certain prestige, particularly in the nineteen-twenties. This barometer consisted of three component time-series, one related to the Stock Exchange, one to trade in commodities, and one to the money market. It was hoped that the first would always be in advance of the other two (as it had been, more or less, for some time), so that it would be possible to make forecasts of changes in production and employment. The barometer did not, however, prove a very successful device, particularly not during the depression in the 'thirties'. Looking back, we need hardly feel any surprise at this, for the barometer was a pretty primitive affair. It should be said in its defence, however, that thirty years ago the possibilities of arriving at successful forecasts were not abundant. In the first place, few economic statistics were recorded and those that were available were often of poor quality. In the second place, mathematical statistics were still in their swaddling clothes, while, finally, economic science has also come further along the road since those days.

It is natural, therefore, that the greater part of the results obtained in the field of economic forecasts should refer to the period subsequent to the Second World War. It is the intention of this article to give a brief account of these, in doing which I shall be confining myself mainly to the work done by the Econometric Institute of the Netherlands School of Economics. The final section contains a short survey of the specialized study of quantitative economics at this school.

THE CENTRAL ECONOMIC PLANS, 1949-1956

The serious economic problems of the 'thirties' and the dislocation of the war years have induced the governments of several western countries in the post-war period to extend the statistical data on economics at their disposal in two ways; in the first place, the records that were already being compiled relating to past periods became more detailed, while, in the second place, a beginning was made with the compilation of forecasts of the national income, total consumption and investment, the price level, the level of employment and the balance of payments, etc. In most cases these forecasts relate to anticipated changes in these variables during the coming calendar year, and it is to these that I shall be confining my remarks in what follows; forecasts have been made for longer periods as well, while at the moment of writing[2] the unemployment trend is of such a nature that a close watch is being kept on the changes from month to month by government circles and in the daily press. Macro-economic forecasts are published every year by the Netherlands Central Planning Bureau under the title of "The Central Economic Plan". The term "plan" in this connection should not, however, be taken at its face value, since it results from a mistaken forecast of the political situation shortly after the war and suggests — as it should not — a relationship to the economic plans drawn up in the countries of Eastern Europe. In actual fact, the Central Economic Plan is nothing other than a well-arranged collection of forecasts for the coming year, comparable in all respects to the forecasts that have been drawn up for years now by large business firms for the benefit of the directors, and comparable also to what the meteorologists do every day for the benefit of the general public. The only remarkable thing about the matter in my view is that it took such a long time before anything was done to arrive at the compilation of "economic weather reports" of this kind.

The compilation was very primitive in the first, difficult years after the war, the work being done by "trial and error" methods. A change soon came about in this state of affairs, however; that is to say, the technique of forecasting was rendered more systematic by making use of a system of econometric equations which describes the diverse relationships in a simplified algebraic form, whereby relevant economic variables are related the one to the other. For instance, the Central Economic Plan for 1955 was based on a system of 27 equations describing 27 endogenous variables in their dependence upon a large number of exogenous variables.[3] Among the items included in the first category are the total consumption, investment and the level of employment; the last-mentioned category consists of two groups, viz., "government variables", such as government expenditure on wages and salaries, on goods and services, rates of taxation and the like,

[2] May 1958.

[3] Central Economic Plan, 1955, Appendix. The Hague, 1955.

and other exogenous (particularly foreign) variables, such as the level of import prices. If one then makes forecasts of the probable trend of the last-mentioned group and, in addition, assumptions as to the government's behaviour with regard to its own variables in the coming period, it is possible, on the basis of the system of equations, to calculate the corresponding forecasts of the endogenous variables. By making alternative suppositions as to the behaviour of the government, it is possible to estimate the consequences of various measures with respect to the trend of employment, the balance of payments and the like, so that in this way this forecasting technique is turned into a serviceable instrument for use in coming to rational decisions in the field of macroeconomic policy.

The degree to which it actually proves useful for the above-mentioned purpose is largely determined, of course, by its accuracy. Some idea of this is provided by Fig. 1, in which forecast and actual changes with respect to a number of variables in the period 1949-1956 are shown side by side.[4] The information provided here relates to changes from year to year, all measured as percentage deviations from the value of the relevant variable in the preceding year.[5] If one had hit the bull's eye every time, all the points would have lain on the upward sloping line running through the origin (the "perfect forecasts line"). Of course, this is not the case, though it should be said that the errors in the forecasts are not of such a nature as to cause any alarm in the circles of professional economic forecasters. This is, perhaps, modesty forced upon us by sheer necessity. One notices, moreover, that a large majority of the points to the right of the vertical axis lies below the perfect forecasts line. This points to a bias in the direction of the underestimation of mutations, a feature often met with in forecasts in the economic field (and probably in other fields as well).[6] I must add to this that the forecasts discussed above are all "final" forecasts which in some cases were published several months after the beginning of the forecast year. Naturally, this delay has an effect on the quality of the forecasts, since when some months of the year concerned have passed, one can make use of information which has become available in the meantime. It is, indeed, true that on the average the forecasts based on the provisional versions of the Central Economic Plans

[4] The year 1952 has been omitted, since alternative forecasts only were made for that year. Thus the dots drawn in Fig. 1 relate to six years and to about twenty variables. The data in Figs. 1 and 2 have been taken from the work of Mr. C. van de Panne.

[5] The actual changes are measured as deviations from actual values in the previous year, according to the latest data. The forecast changes, on the other hand, are measured as deviations from the "provisional" actual values in the previous year, according to the information available when the forecasts were made. This distinction is made so as to prevent imperfect knowledge of the recent past from obscuring the picture presented by the forecasts. Naturally, a completely exact picture is out of the question, since any statistical representation of reality is liable to errors of measurement.

[6] The forecasts mentioned in this paragraph refer to both exogenous and endogenous variables. The "conditional" forecasts of endogenous changes can also be studied; these are calculated by substituting the actual changes in the exogenous variables in the system of equations used. The forecasts dealt with in the text show the ultimate result of the forecasting technique, actually quite apart from the method followed; the conditional method is more appropriate for assessing the quality of the equation system. The latter forecasts are of higher quality; generally speaking, underestimation of changes does not occur in them.

display wider divergences than the final versions; in the majority of cases, that is to say, the revisions brought the forecasts into closer proximity to the actual changes which were the goal of prediction. One must certainly not, on the other hand, overestimate the success of these revisions. This is illustrated in Fig. 2, which shows the frequency distribution of over 200 "revision ratios". For example, let us assume that total consumption in a given year is first expected to rise by 3%, that this figure is later revised and put at 4% and that the actual increase proves to be 8%. The revision amounted to 1% (from 3% to 4%), whereas it ought to have been 5% in order to have arrived at a perfect forecast, and in this case the revision ratio is 1/5. As long as this ratio is positive and less than 1, the revision was in the right direction; if it lies above 1, the revision was greater than it should have been, though the new forecast will be nearer to reality as long as the ratio is less than 2. If the ratio is negative, the adjustment was in the wrong direction. Fig. 2 shows that most revised forecasts are, in fact, in the right direction but that the large majority of them did not go far enough, while in a fairly considerable minority of the cases the revision was still in the wrong direction.[7]

ANALYSIS OF SURVEY DATA

Surveys have become very popular since the Second World War. The best known are those involving the consumer, who nowadays gets asked when he was last in a cinema, if he is planning to buy a car next year, if he expects to be earning more next year, if he thinks prices will be going up, going down or staying the same in the next six months, etc., etc. But surveys are also being held fairly extensively in the field of business nowadays, enquiries with regard to investment, in particular, having acquired a certain reputation.

In this section I shall have something to say about a certain form of survey to do with the plans and expectations of entrepreneurs. It may at first sight seem strange that plans and expectations (which are often rather vague!) should be placed under the heading of "forecasts". But if we interpret the word forecasts to mean statements, in any form, relating to events in the future, we may certainly include plans and expectations within the meaning of the term. Expectations are, then, statements regarding future events not controlled by the forecaster himself (such as anticipated sales, anticipated purchasing prices); and plans are statements regarding the forecaster's own future actions (investment plans, sales prices plans, etc.). The following problem, however, is of a more substantial nature: if one seeks information from the firms' leading men, one practically always finds that they have little time to spare; the questions asked must accordingly be neither too numerous nor — and this is more important — too detailed. For this reason the *IFO-Institut für Wirtschaftsforschung* at Munich has limited itself in its enquiries to obtaining information on trends — i.e. the entrepreneur is asked whether he expects the purchasing

[7] The distribution in Fig. 2 is limited to the interval -2 to +3. In fact, one should imagine a total frequency of 6% to the left of -2 and a frequency of 3% to the right of +3. Revision ratios such as these, very large in absolute value, occur fairly frequently when the original (revised) forecast was very close to the actual figure.

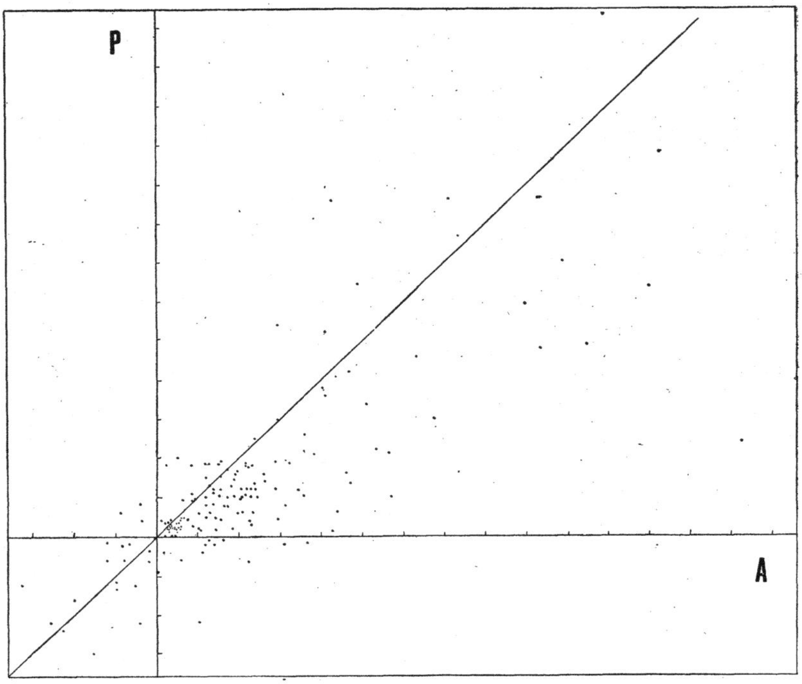

Figure 1. Predicted (P) and Actual (A) changes according to the Central Economic Plans, 1949-1956

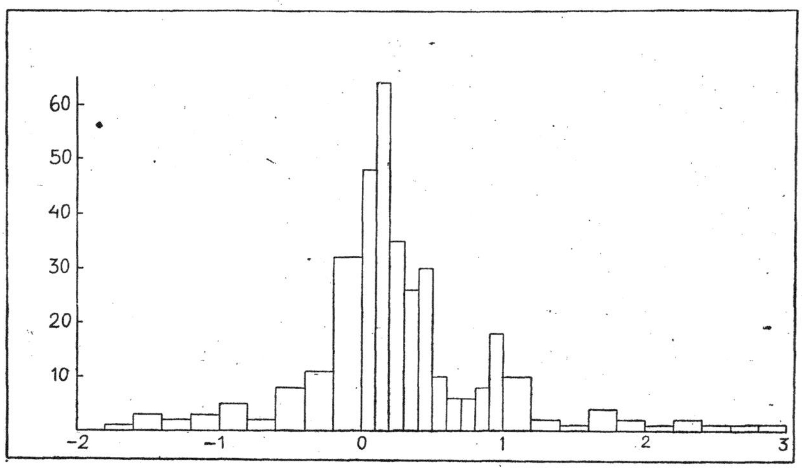

Figure 2. Frequency distribution of revision ratios

price of a certain raw material to rise, fall or remain the same in the coming month, but he is not asked to quote the percentage by which he expects the price to rise or fall. Such questions relate also to actual, in contrast to forecast, developments (Has the price risen, fallen or remained the same since last month?) and to a large number of economic variables (prices, sales, production, stocks, etc.) and to a fairly large number of sectors of industrial and commercial activity. This method, devised in Germany in 1949, has undergone rapid development since and is being applied at the moment in many other countries, including the Netherlands, Sweden, Austria, South Africa and Japan.

This set-up involves many problems — among them those to do with survey technique — and I certainly cannot say that all of them have been solved. I shall confine myself here to a single aspect of what can be done with this material, with special reference to the fairly extensive body of economic theories which have something to say, in one way or another, about the plans and expectations of "economic subjects". A weak point about these theories was always the fact that there was no real means of testing them out; the traditional statistical material — as published by official bureaux of statistics — relates, that is, exclusively to actual, not forecast, developments. The survey data referred to above do, therefore, offer some opportunity of improving on this.

An example will be found in Figs. 3 and 4.[8] Let us first take a look at the left-hand side of Fig. 3, which refers to the monthly development of the selling price plans of Western German leather tanners in the years 1951-1953. The upper curve indicates this development as reported in the survey; the punctuated line, which corresponds fairly closely to the first curve, represents a combination of factors which determine this development (approximately, at least). In this case three such factors come into play, the monthly development of which is indicated under the two curves mentioned above. The first factor is related to the development of the hide dealers' selling price a month before. It is only to be expected, of course, that if the price the tanners have to pay for their raw material rises, there will be a tendency for them to plan an increase in their selling price the following month to cover the resultant rise in their costs. The second factor concerns the tanners' actual selling price the previous month; this is not quite so interesting.[9] The third factor concerns the appraisal of stocks; if the entrepreneur considers his stock of products too large, he tends to plan a lower selling price for the following month in order to reduce the level of his stocks. The shaded area below indicates the degree to which

[8] Source: *Econonomic Forecasts and Policy*, the North-Holland Publishing Company, Amsterdam, 1958.

[9] It would be preferable to work on the basis of the actual purchasing prices here instead of the selling prices. The survey does not provide any data on these prices, however, so that it is necessary to work with a substitute. This is one of the difficulties with which the econometrician has to contend fairly often.

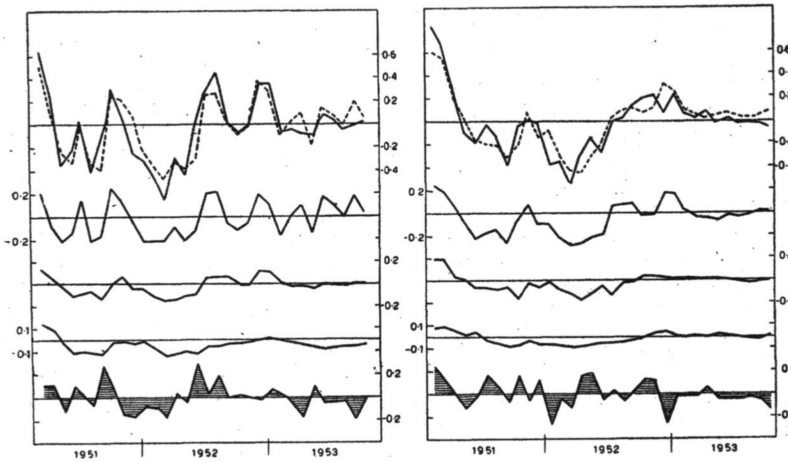

Figure 3. The selling price plans of leather tanners and shoe manufacturers in Western Germany and the factors determining these plans, 1951-1953

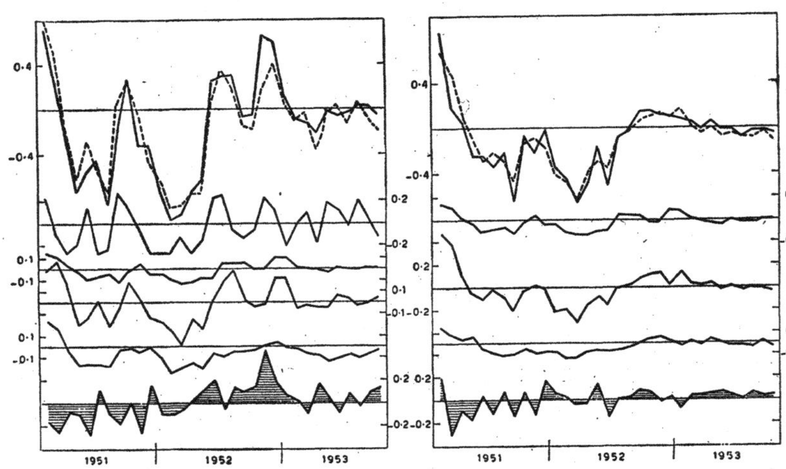

Figure 4. The actual selling prices of leather tanners and shoe manufacturers in Western Germany and the factors determining these prices, 1951-1953

these three factors proved insufficient for the "explanation" of the monthly development of the planned selling prices which form the object of the analysis.[10]

The right side of Fig. 3 deals with the planned selling prices of the Western German shoe manufacturers in an analogous manner; these prices depend, *inter alia*, on the actual development of the tanners' selling prices in the same way as the planned selling prices of this latter group are dependent upon the actual development of the hide dealers' selling prices. Finally, Fig. 4 deals with the determination of the actual selling prices of both groups of manufacturers. Interesting features here are that the appraisal of the stocks play a rôle here as well (without a time-lag this time) and, further, that the planned selling prices also bring an influence to bear. It is evidently difficult for these firms to deviate from plans made, even if the actual circumstances differ from those anticipated when the plan was devised.

DECISION-MAKING IN UNCERTAIN SITUATIONS

The analysis of forecasts of various type as roughly outlined in the foregoing sections is interesting, of course, from the academic point of view; it acquires real practical significance, however, only when applied to the problem of endeavouring to arrive at rational decisions in uncertain situations. Thus, as regards the present-day economic policy of the western countries, the matters particularly concerned are the forecasting of the employment situation and of the consequences of measures to stimulate employment. It is also important that the trend of the balance of payments should be estimated and possibly also the effects of measures to improve the balance of payments position. It often happens that these measures conflict with those desirable to combat unemployment, in which case they should be weighed, the one against the other.

The above is no more than a sample of a whole series of conceivable situations in which one is confronted with a decision which has consequences during a certain period, whereas one cannot clearly foresee what these consequences or the accompanying circumstances will be. One is therefore obliged to make forecasts. Even if one did not accept this and simply based one's decision on the present state of affairs, one would still really be acting on the basis of a forecast, viz., that there will be no change — and this forecast is not always the best. The question then arises as to how one can come to the best decisions in view of the customary flaws in forecasting — which actually amounts to bringing about an improvement in forecasting technique. This is a subject related to what is known in statistics as "decision theory" and one that is difficult to describe without resort to mathematics. On two points, however, I shall endeavour to elucidate a few of the results achieved.

---

[10] For a more precise understanding of these figures, it should be known that the numerical values have been arrived at as follows. The firms taking part in the enquiry are weighted according to size, after which the percentages are calculated (per month) of those which report (or predict) a rise or fall or no change. The lines drawn in the figure indicate the monthly differences of the fractions of those reporting a rise and the corresponding fractions of those reporting a fall. If, therefore, the curve lies above its horizontal axis, the reports of a rise predominate. For more details, cf *Economic Forecasts and Policy*, quoted in footnote 8.

In the second section of the present article, it was stated that the underestimation of changes was a regularly-occurring error in economic forecasts. It will be readily understood that this very often leads to inadequate measures being taken. Suppose, for instance, that employment is predicted to decline by 5%, whereas it afterwards proves to decline by 10%. It is then evident that the policy-maker concerned, basing himself on the forecast, will have decided on less forceful measures than he afterwards feels were necessary. One can then ask oneself whether it is not advisable to correct the forecasts in respect of this systematic error; for instance, if one has noticed in the past that, on the average, the changes forecast are equal to half the actual changes that take place, whether one should not in future act on the assumption that the changes will be double those forecasts. On the whole, such a correction — as can be demonstrated in certain circumstances — is too drastic; it exceeds the optimum. It would, it is true, be a correct adjustment if the underestimation of changes lies at a uniform percentage on all fronts of significance to the policy-maker (employment, balance of payments, etc.); but this is not generally the case and the correction to be made is consequently smaller than the average underestimation. Thus Dutch economic policy in the past years would have done better to base itself on the expectation of greater fluctuations from year to year than those indicated in Fig. 1, though the correction involved is not of dramatic size.

Another aspect of this figure of consequence for decision-making has to do with the unequal variance of the points observed, dependent upon their distance from the vertical axis. If, that is, one considers those dots which correspond with large actual changes, one notices a greater dispersion in the vertical direction than is the case with the dots lying close to the vertical axis. Nevertheless, despite the greater dispersion (and consequently the larger prediction errors), the forecast of large changes is precisely the forecast that is the most valuable. That is to say, in the case of these changes there is an obvious numerical relationship between forecast and what actually takes place, while this relationship is much weaker in the case of slight changes. For example, if a policy-maker bases his decisions on three forecast changes (unemployment, balance of payments, etc.) and these forecasts are 3, 2 and 5% respectively, while the actual changes turn out to be 2, -2, and 4% respectively, then the errors in the forecasts are, indeed, all less than 5%,[11] but the two series actually display very little resemblance. In such a case, it is advisable to act on the assumption that there will be no change (as can be shown in certain circumstances); thus the forecasts 3, 2 and 5% are simply substituted by 0% in each case. Hence, here the increase of the forecast changes referred to in the preceding paragraph is not applicable: if the forecast changes are small, it is advisable to reduce them to nil; if, however, they are large, it may be advisable to increase them still further.

[11] If a 5% change is to be regarded as small or not depends, of course, on the variable in question. In the case of unemployment, for instance, a change of this magnitude is small; in the case of employment it is not.

SPECIALIZATION IN QUANTITATIVE ECONOMICS AT THE NETHERLANDS SCHOOL OF ECONOMICS

When, some years ago, we were considering the matter of adding specialization in quantitative economics to the courses at the Netherlands School of Economics, the general impression was that by so doing we would not be anticipating a small change, but rather that we were, in fact, called upon to respond to large changes which had already taken place, and which could be expected to continue in the future. That is to say, many journals of economics had gradually acquired a fairly pronounced mathematical bias as a result of which a not inconsiderable portion of the articles they published could only be followed by those possessing the necessary knowledge of mathematics. As Professor Tinbergen has already said in the foregoing article, this situation was met shortly after the war by putting mathematics on the first year's syllabus. A few years later, however, this measure was felt to be insufficient, so that it was decided to institute a special series of courses in quantitative economics extending over both undergraduate and graduate study. The accompanying table gives details of these courses. Both the undergraduate and the graduate section of the study cover a period of two academic years; generally speaking, however, the work for the various examinations requires about one year's extra study for each of the two sections, the total period of study consequently lasting for about six years. The first year of undergraduate study is the same as in all the other specialized branches of study at the School of Economics, specialization beginning during the second year. Even then more than 75% of the total number of lecture hours are still shared with students in the other branches, the rest being devoted to mathematics and statistics. Specialization goes further, of course, in the graduate section of the study, more than 60% of the time then being spent on lectures and research, specially organized for this group. Generally speaking the quality of the results achieved is very satisfactory, a favourable feature being the tendency of Dutch students not to regard their study as completed after finishing the undergraduate section. The number of students who have shown interest in the course is also reasonably high, i.e., 10 to 20 every year, though this number is, of course, considerably less than the number studying business economics.

H. Theil

Survey of Specialization in Quantitative Economics at the Netherlands School of Economics at Rotterdam

	Courses in Quantitative Subjects	Other courses
Under-graduate courses (2 years)	Mathematics: 150 hours (differential and integral calculus, introduction to matrix algebra) Statistics: 150 hours (economic statistics, regression analysis and time series analysis, introduction to mathematical statistics)	Economics: 350 hours (introduction to economics, money and banking) Other courses: approx. 500 hours (business economics, introduction to accounting, economic history, *either* economic geography *or* law)
Graduate courses (2 years)	Mathematics: 120 hours (matrix algebra, differential and difference equations, set theory and special subjects) Statistics: 150 hours (probability calculus and mathematical statistics, statistical problems of econometrics, special subjects) Mathematical economics and econometrics: 240 hours Research: 200 hours	Economics: 360 hours (economic theory, money and banking, trade-cycle theory and economic policy, institutional economics, international trade) Other courses: 60 hours (Logic and methodology)

CHAPTER 78

ON THE OPTIMAL MANAGEMENT OF RESEARCH: A MATHEMATICAL APPROACH*

H. THEIL[1]
Econometric Institute,
Netherlands School of Economics
(Now Erasmus University) and
the International Centre for Management Science
Rotterdam, The Netherlands

ABSTRACT. This article considers the interplay of a decision-maker and a research manager in case the former's goal is to maximize a quadratic objective function subject to linear constraints. The analysis is carried out in a dynamic context, which implies that the decision-maker's behaviour pattern is derived from a strategy (decision rule).
The research manager's task is to set up investigations in such a manner that the decision-maker's objective is approached as well as possible. The approach is elaborated in some detail for an illustrative production-inventory example.

1. Introduction

This paper deals with an allocation problem of a research manager whose position can be described as follows. He is in the service of a decision-maker, who has a well-defined objective function which he wishes to maximize subject to certain constraints. This decision-maker may be an entrepreneur who wants to maximize profits over time, or a factory manager who wishes to minimize factory costs, or a government policy-maker who maximizes a social welfare function. Now either the objective function or the constraints or both depend on certain parameters which are not known perfectly. For example, the entrepreneur just-mentioned may have limited knowledge of the price elasticity of demand, the factory manager is not completely aware of the shape of his cost function, etc. It is the research manager's task to set up investigations in such a manner, given a limited budget per time period, that the decision-maker's objective is approached as well as possible. Also, it is his task to formulate a budget proposal which is optimal with respect to the same aim.

---

[1] The author is indebted to Mr. Thomas Rothenberg, Fulbright Visitor of the Econometric Institute and the International Center for Management Science in 1961-1962, for his comments on an earlier draft of this paper.

In this article we shall consider the case of a quadratic objective function which is maximized subject to a set of constraints consisting of linear equations. Generalizations are possible but not pursued here. The order of discussion is as follows. In Section 2 the decision problem will be formulated in dynamic terms and in Section 3 we will go into the effects of given errors in the basic parameters. It will be assumed in Section 4 that the research manager has some probabilistic notion of these errors, either 'subjective' or 'objective,' which enables him to evaluate the expected loss associated with the uncertain knowledge. Section 5 introduces a research production function by which the allocation problem is solved in such a way that the expectation of the decision-maker's objective function is maximized. Each of these sections is divided into a part which describes the general set-up and a part which contains an illustrative production-inventory example. The last paragraph of Section 5.2 summarizes the findings with respect to this example.

2. The Optimal First-Period Decision

2.1. GENERAL[2]

The decision-maker's horizon is supposed to consist of T consecutive periods, in each of which he has certain real-valued controlled variables (instruments) $x_h(t)$ at his disposal, where $h = 1, ..., m$ and $t = 1, ..., T$. He is also interested in a number of noncontrolled variables, $y_i(t)$ where $i = 1, ..., n$. In time-partitioned form these variables can be arranged in the following vectors:

$$x = \begin{bmatrix} x_1 \\ \cdot \\ \cdot \\ \cdot \\ x_T \end{bmatrix}; \quad x_t = \begin{bmatrix} x_1(t) \\ \cdot \\ \cdot \\ \cdot \\ x_m(t) \end{bmatrix}; \quad y = \begin{bmatrix} y_1 \\ \cdot \\ \cdot \\ \cdot \\ y_T \end{bmatrix}; \quad y_t = \begin{bmatrix} y_1(t) \\ \cdot \\ \cdot \\ \cdot \\ y_n(t) \end{bmatrix}. \tag{2.1}$$

The preference function is quadratic:

$$w(x,y) = a'x + b'y + \frac{1}{2}(x'Ax + y'By + x'Cy + y'C'x), \tag{2.2}$$

where a, b, A, .. are matrices of appropriate order. The decision-maker's objective is to maximize (2.2) subject to

$$y = Rx + s, \tag{2.3}$$

[2] For an exposition of the general framework of quadratic maximization see (Theil, 1961, chap. 8).

which is a system of nT constraints, each of which describes a non-controlled variable linearly in terms of instrument values.

If the decision-maker would know all coefficient matrices $a, b, .., R, s$ the maximization problem is a matter of straightforward algebra and the optimal x turns out to be a unique function of these matrices.[3] This holds in particular for the first-period decision, x_1 (the first subvector of x). In what follows it will prove convenient to write π for the column vector of basic parameters (which may amount to a complete enumeration of all elements of $a, b, ..., R, s$), in which case we may write for the optimal first-period decision:

$$x_1^0 = h(\pi) , \tag{2.4}$$

where $h(\ )$ stands for an m-element vector of functions and where the superscript ^{0} indicates that it is the optimal first-period decision.

2.2. A PRODUCTION-INVENTORY EXAMPLE

Our decision-maker is now supposed to be a factory manager for whom production (P_1, ..., P_T) is the only instrument. End-of-period inventories (I_1, ..., I_T) are not controlled, and production and inventory costs in each (t^{th}) period are supposed to be quadratic:

$$c_1 P_t + c_2 P_t^2 \quad \text{and} \quad c_3 I_t + c_4 I_t^2 ,$$

the (irrelevant) constant terms in the cost functions being disregarded. The objective is to minimize total costs, so that we have a special case of the problem of Section 2.1 with

$$x = \begin{bmatrix} P_1 \\ \cdot \\ \cdot \\ \cdot \\ P_T \end{bmatrix}; \quad y = \begin{bmatrix} I_1 \\ \cdot \\ \cdot \\ \cdot \\ I_T \end{bmatrix}; \quad a = -\begin{bmatrix} c_1 \\ \cdot \\ \cdot \\ \cdot \\ c_1 \end{bmatrix}; \quad b = -\begin{bmatrix} c_3 \\ \cdot \\ \cdot \\ \cdot \\ c_3 \end{bmatrix}; \tag{2.5}$$
$$A = -2c_2 I ; \quad B = -2c_4 I ; \quad C = 0 ,$$

where all matrices are of order $T \times 1$ or $T \times T$. Minimization should take place subject to the constraints $I_t - I_{t-1} = P_t - V_t$ where V_t is sales in period t. By successive backward elimination of I_{t-1} we obtain

[3] Provided that a unique maximum does exist. A sufficient condition is that the Hessian of (2.2) be negative-definite.

$$I_1 = P_1 + (I_0 - V_1)$$
$$I_2 = P_1 + P_2 + (I_0 - V_1 - V_2)$$

so that the coefficient matrices of the constraints (2.3) take the special form

$$R = \begin{bmatrix} 1 & 0 & \dots & 0 \\ 1 & 1 & \dots & 0 \\ \cdot & \cdot & & \cdot \\ \cdot & \cdot & & \cdot \\ \cdot & \cdot & & \cdot \\ 1 & 1 & \dots & 1 \end{bmatrix}; \quad s = -Rv\,; \quad v = \begin{bmatrix} V_1 - I_0 \\ V_2 \\ \cdot \\ \cdot \\ \cdot \\ V_T \end{bmatrix}. \tag{2.6}$$

In the present case the first-period decision, x_1, is a scalar, viz., the first-period production decision (P_1). It is shown in the Appendix (Section A) that in the limit for $T \rightarrow \infty$ we have

$$P_1^0 = (1 - \theta)\left[\sum_{t=1}^{\infty} \theta^{t-1} V_t - (c + I_0)\right], \tag{2.7}$$

where

$$c = \frac{c_3}{2c_4}; \quad \theta = 1 - \frac{1}{2c_2}\{- c_4 + \sqrt{4c_2c_4 + c_4^2}\}. \tag{2.8}$$

We assume

$$c_1, c_2, c_3, c_4 > 0, \tag{2.9}$$

in which case $c > 0$ and $0 < \theta < 1$.

Equation (2.7) is the present specific form of the general first-period expression (2.4). Now c_1, ..., c_4 appear to be relevant only in the two forms c and θ, whence it follows that the vector of basic parameters can be written as

$$\pi = \begin{bmatrix} \theta \\ c \\ v \end{bmatrix}. \tag{2.10}$$

Research dedicated to a better specification of θ and c falls under *cost analysis*, research devoted to v under *market analysis*. In most cases these activities are carried out by different departments and one of the interesting features of the present analysis is that it enables us to judge under which conditions this division of labour is justified.

3. The Effects of Given Specification Errors

3.1. GENERAL

Suppose now that the decision-maker is imperfectly informed and acts as if $\pi + \Delta\pi$ is the vector of basic parameters, $\Delta\pi$ being the vector of specification errors. The first-period decision x_1 will then deviate from the optimal x_1^0 and the decision error is

$$\Delta x_1 \equiv x_1 - x_1^0 = h(\pi + \Delta\pi) - h(\pi) = H\Delta\pi , \tag{3.1}$$

where H is the matrix of first-order derivatives of the vector function h with respect to π evaluated at the point of the 'true' π. The last equality sign of (3.1) is based on linearization in case h is nonlinear in π. (It is easily seen that x_1^0 is linear in the coefficient vectors a, b, s but nonlinear in the matrices A, B, C, R).

If the decision taken deviates from the optimal one, the utility level reached will be below the maximum attainable. To explore this in more detail we substitute the constraints (2.3) into the preference function (2.2). Since the constraints are linear and the preference function quadratic, we then obtain another quadratic function in instruments only; and some minor algebraic rearrangements are sufficient to see that the latter function can be written as

$$w_x = (x - x^0)'K(x - x^0) \tag{3.2}$$

(the irrelevant constant term being disregarded), where

$$K = A + R'BR + CR + R'C'. \tag{3.3}$$

It is assumed that K, which is an $mT \times mT$ matrix, is negative-definite[4], in which case x^0 is the optimal decision vector as its notation indicates.[5]

By substituting $x = x^0$ in (3.2) we obtain $w_x = 0$ and by substituting any $x \neq x^0$ we find $w_x < 0$, so that it is natural to interpret the utility reduction $-w_x$ as the *loss* due to the decision error $x - x^0$. But (3.1) specifies only a first-period decision error, $x_1 - x_1^0$, and leaves open what happens in later periods. The *first-period loss* associated with any given first-period decision error is then defined as the *minimum* utility reduction due to this error. A straightforward Lagrangean multiplier technique shows that this first-period loss is $-\frac{1}{2}(\Delta x_1)'K_1(\Delta x_1)$, where K_1 is an $m \times m$ matrix whose inverse, K_1^{-1}, is the leading submatrix of K^{-1} with K as defined in (3.3).[6] On combining this with (3.1) we obtain the first-period loss associated with any given specification error $\Delta\pi$:

$$L(\Delta\pi) = (\Delta\pi)'Q(\Delta\pi) \text{ with } Q = -\frac{1}{2}H'K_1H\,, \tag{3.4}$$

which is a quadratic form in the specification error with Q as (positive semi-definite) matrix.

3.2. THE PRODUCTION-INVENTORY EXAMPLE

We return to the production-inventory example and conclude from (2.7) that the matrix H of (3.1) is now a row vector. Its first element is the derivative of P_1^0 with respect to θ, which is

$$c + I_0 - \sum_{t=1}^{\infty} \theta^{t-2}\{1 - (1-\theta)t\}V_t\,. \tag{3.5}$$

The second element is the derivative with respect to c, which is $-(1-\theta)$; and the $(2+t)^{th}$ element is the derivative with respect to V_t, viz., $(1-\theta)\theta^{t-1}$. The dependence of (3.5) on all future sales values is awkward and it is therefore not unreasonable to assume that the research manager decides to proceed under the assumption that sales are constant at some 'normal' level, $\bar{V}$ say. In that case (3.5) is simplified to $c + I_0$, so that

$$H = \begin{bmatrix} c + I_0 & -(1-\theta) & 1-\theta & (1-\theta)\theta & (1-\theta)\theta^2 \ldots \end{bmatrix} \tag{3.6}$$

---

[4] This assumption is automatically satisfied if the Hessian of the previous footnote is negative-definite.

[5] The full expression of x^0 is $-K^{-1}k$, where K and k are defined in equations (A.2) of the Appendix.

[6] See section B of the Appendix.

and the first-period decision error becomes:

$$\Delta P_1 = (c + I_0)\Delta\theta + (1-\theta)(-\Delta c + \sum_{t=1}^{\infty} \theta^{t-1}\Delta V_t), \tag{3.7}$$

where $\Delta\theta$, Δc, ΔV_t are specification errors in the basic parameters. To interpret the coefficient of the first term, $c + I_0$, we notice that the decision rule (2.7) specifies

$$P_1^0 = \bar{V} - (1 - \theta)(c + I_0)$$

in case it is indeed true that $V_t = \bar{V}$ for all t. The implied optimal change in inventories is then

$$I_1^0 - I_0 = P_1^0 - V_1 = P_1^0 - \bar{V} = -(1-\theta)(c + I_0),$$

whence it follows that under constant-sales conditions $c + I_0$ stands for $1/(1\text{-}\theta)$ times the optimal first-period inventory reduction.

To find the first-period loss we need the leading $m \times m$ submatrix of K^{-1}, which in the present case amounts to the leading element of K^{-1} since $m = 1$. This element is $-\theta/2c_2$ as is shown in Appendix A and its reciprocal, $-2c_2/\theta$, is then K_1. The first-period loss can be written as the sum of three terms, one of which is a quadratic form in cost coefficient errors:

$$L_1(\Delta\theta,\Delta c) = \frac{c_2}{\theta}\{(c + I_0)^2(\Delta\theta)^2 + (1 - \theta)^2(\Delta c)^2 \\ -2(1 - \theta)(c + I_0)\Delta\theta\Delta c\}, \tag{3.8}$$

while the second is a quadratic form in sales prediction errors:

$$L_2(\Delta v) = \frac{(1 - \theta)^2 c_2}{\theta} \sum_{t=1}^{\infty} \sum_{t'=1}^{\infty} \theta^{t+t'-2} \Delta V_t \Delta V_{t'}, \tag{3.9}$$

and the third a bilinear form:

$$L_3(\Delta\theta,\Delta c,\Delta v) =$$

$$\frac{2(1-\theta)c_2(c+I_0)}{\theta}\Delta\theta\sum_{t=1}^{\infty}\theta^{t-1}\Delta V_t - \frac{2(1-\theta)^2 c_2}{\theta}\Delta c\sum_{t=1}^{\infty}\theta^{t-1}\Delta V_t\,. \tag{3.10}$$

4. The Expected First-Period Loss

4.1. GENERAL

Our next step implies that we assume that the research manager is able to formulate probabilistic statements on the specification error $\Delta\pi$ and that he is interested in minimizing the expected first-period loss:

$$\Lambda(\Delta\pi) \equiv E\{L(\Delta\pi)\} = \text{tr}\, QS\,, \tag{4.1}$$

where tr QS (the trace of QS) stands for the sum of the diagonal elements of the (square) matrix QS, and where S is the matrix of second-order moments of $\Delta\pi$:

$$S = E[(\Delta\pi)(\Delta\pi)']\,. \tag{4.2}$$

It follows from (4.1) that minimizing the expected first-period loss due to $\Delta\pi$ amounts to minimization of a linear combination of the second moments of $\Delta\pi$.

4.2. THE PRODUCTION-INVENTORY EXAMPLE

Following (3.8)-(3.10), we shall write the expected first-period loss in the production-inventory example as the sum of three terms. First, we have the part dealing with cost coefficient errors:

$$\Lambda_1(\Delta\theta,\Delta c) = \frac{c_2}{\theta}\{(c+I_0)^2\sigma_{\theta\theta} + (1-\theta)^2\sigma_{cc} - 2(1-\theta)(c+I_0)\sigma_{\theta c},\} \tag{4.3}$$

where the σ's are expected squares and an expected product:

$$\sigma_{\theta\theta} = E(\Delta\theta)^2\,;\quad \sigma_{cc} = E(\Delta c)^2\,;\quad \sigma_{\theta c} = E(\Delta\theta\Delta c)\,. \tag{4.4}$$

To evaluate the second term and to keep things simple, we shall assume that the prediction errors ΔV_t have zero mean and are uncorrelated over time. In that case the expectation of (3.9) involves only a single sum. Further, it is reasonable to assume that the variance of a prediction error is larger when the forecast refers to a point of time which is far in the future than to one in the immediate future. We shall specify this linearly:

$$E(\Delta V_t)^2 = \sigma_0^2\{1 + \delta(t-1)\}, \tag{4.5}$$

in which case the expectation of $L_2(\Delta v)$ becomes

$$\Lambda_2(\Delta v) = \frac{c_2\sigma_0^2\{1-(1-\delta)\theta^2\}}{\theta(1+\theta)^2}. \tag{4.6}$$

The expectation of $L_3(\Delta\theta, \Delta c, \Delta v)$ vanishes if it is assumed, as will be done here, that Δv has zero expectation and is uncorrelated with the cost coefficient errors.

5. The Management of Research

5.1. THE CASE OF FEW RESEARCH PROJECTS: A COMBINATORIAL APPROACH

Let us write μ for the vector of resources available to the research manager: money, specialized labour (which is not easily available for money), etc. In the first instance it will be assumed that these resources are given and that their costs are fixed, so that these have no effect on the research manager's decisions. Suppose then that a limited number of research projects, P_1, P_2, ..., is being considered. Each such project, P_r say, requires certain amounts of resources, which can be arranged in a vector μ_r. If some set U of projects is carried out the total requirements is the sum of all vectors μ_r, which is constrained by availability conditions:

$$\sum_{r \in U} \mu_r \leqq \mu . \tag{5.1}$$

The best set of projects is that U which minimizes tr QS (see (4.1)) subject to (5.1). Now Q is given by the decision-maker's preferences and constraints, and S is the matrix which is to be changed by the research manager's actions. The problem would be very simple if it could be assumed that the various projects have an independent additive influence on the elements of S, but this will be unrealistic in most cases. For example, if we wish to make better sales predictions in the sense that $\Lambda_2(\Delta v)$ as defined in (4.6) is reduced in zero direction, we may spend money on an analysis of the autoregressive nature and the seasonal structure of past sales data, or on a survey of various markets, or do both. We may expect that the first project (P_1) reduces (4.6), that the same is true for the second (P_2), and also that the combination (P_1P_2) will reduce (4.6) still further; but it seems unlikely that the additional reduction obtained by P_1 P_2 compared with the P_1-reduction is as large as the P_2-reduction is by itself. What one has to do, therefore, is to estimate tr QS for each set of projects U which satisfies (5.1) and to select the set with the smallest tr QS. This procedure is of course laborious in the case of a large number of projects, but not when the number is small. There will often be a considerable amount of uncertainty with respect to the precise value of tr QS, but this is simply in the nature of the problem. The application of these ideas to the production-inventory example is in principle straightforward, but it makes little sense to be specific in algebraic terms. Some general statements are possible, however. For example, if θ is small (which according to (2.8) means that the coefficient measuring the curvilinearity of the production cost function, c_2, is small compared with that of the inventory cost function, c_4), then it will usually not pay to devote considerable resources on a reduction of δ (see (4.6)). And if θ is close to 1, it will generally not pay to work very hard on a better specification of c, see (4.3).

Up till now we confined ourselves in this section to the case in which the resources available to the research manager are limited by the vector μ. But it is also conceivable that he wishes to consider sets of projects which violate the constraint (5.1) and to apply for the necessary additional resources. In that case it is appropriate to take account of the costs of research. That is, the research manager's original objective function, tr QS, which is linear in the second moments of $\Delta\pi$, is then modified to the extent that it includes also a linear combination of the components of μ, where the prices of these components act as weights of this combination. Constraint (5.1) is then dropped or at least modified such that it refers to the limit at which the resources can be purchased.

5.2. MANY PROJECTS: THE RESEARCH PRODUCTION FUNCTION

It was just noted that the research manager's objective function is either linear in the elements of S or linear in the elements of both S and μ, depending on whether the resources are considered fixed or not. In both cases the objective function can therefore be written as $p'z$, where z is a column vector containing the diagonal elements of S and those above the diagonal (those below the diagonal are of course equal to their transpose) plus possibly the elements of μ. The vector p, which can be regarded as a vector of 'prices,' consists of the elements of Q (on and above the diagonal) and possibly also the prices of the μ-elements. The problem is then to minimize $p'z$ subject to the constraints which are implied by the technology of research. Suppose now, contrary to the case considered in Section 5.1, that many alternative projects are available such that one can sacrifice any resource practically continuously in favour of expected squares and products of the elements of $\Delta\pi$. It will be necessary to take account of decreasing marginal returns and a simple form of the research production function[7] which can satisfy this requirement is the quadratic:

$$g_0 + g'z + z'Gz = 0 . \tag{5.2}$$

Minimizing $p'z$ subject to (5.2) can be performed conveniently by the Lagrangean technique, which leads to the following first-order minimum conditions:

$$p - \lambda(g + Gz) = 0 , \tag{5.3}$$

λ being a (scalar) Lagrangean multiplier. On the assumption that G is non-singular we find

$$z = \frac{1}{\lambda} G^{-1}p - G^{-1}g , \tag{5.4}$$

from which we can determine z as soon as λ has been found. On premultiplying (5.4) by p' we obtain:

$$p'z = \frac{1}{\lambda} p'G^{-1}p - p'G^{-1}g . \tag{5.5}$$

To find λ we substitute (5.4) into (5.2), which leads to

$$\frac{1}{\lambda^2} = \frac{g'G^{-1}g - 2g_0}{p'G^{-1}p} \tag{5.6}$$

It follows from (5.5) that $1/\lambda$ is that square root of the ratio (5.6) that minimizes $p'G^{-1}p/\lambda$.

We conclude by applying these ideas to the production-inventory example. To keep the algebra simple, we shall assume that θ is close to 1 and/or that the c-errors are small, in which case the σ_{cc} and $\sigma_{\theta c}$-terms in (4.3) can be neglected. We shall also use only one resource, μ (the research budget per time period). The research manager's objective function is then:

---

[7] It will be clear that the analysis can be regarded as a special case of the classical theory of the firm under perfect competition; see e.g. Hicks (1946, Appendix), and Allen (1956, pp. 608-618).

$$\frac{c_2 (c + I_0)^2}{\theta} \sigma_{\theta\theta} + \frac{c_2}{\theta (1 + \theta)^2} \sigma_{\nu\nu} + \mu , \tag{5.7}$$

where

$$\sigma_{\nu\nu} = \sigma_0^2 \{ 1 - (1 - \delta) \theta^2 \} . \tag{5.8}$$

It will prove slightly more convenient to write the expression to be minimized in the form

$$p_\theta (\sigma_{\theta\theta} - \bar{\sigma}_{\theta\theta}) + p_\nu (\sigma_{\nu\nu} - \bar{\sigma}_{\nu\nu}) + \mu , \tag{5.9}$$

where $\bar{\sigma}_{\theta\theta}$ and $\bar{\sigma}_{\nu\nu}$ represent the present precision (before any research is undertaken) and

$$p_\theta = \frac{c_2 (c + I_0)^2}{\theta} ; \quad p_\nu = \frac{c_2}{\theta (1 + \theta)^2} . \tag{5.10}$$

It will be clear that the objective functions (5.7) and (5.9) are equivalent, since they differ only by a constant term, $-(p_\theta \bar{\sigma}_{\theta\theta} + p_\nu \bar{\sigma}_{\nu\nu})$. It will also be clear that if the budget is taken as given without costs, μ acts only as a constant term in (5.9).

Our task is to minimize (5.9) subject to a research production function. This is carried out conveniently in the following four steps:

(*i*) First, assume that the production function takes the linear form

$$d_\theta (\sigma_{\theta\theta} - \bar{\sigma}_{\theta\theta}) + d_\nu (\sigma_{\nu\nu} - \bar{\sigma}_{\nu\nu}) + \mu = 0 , \tag{5.11}$$

where the *d*'s (as well as all further *d*'s which will appear in this section) are fixed positive coefficients. Minimization of (5.9) subject to (5.11) should of course take place subject to the constraints

$$0 \leqq \sigma_{\theta\theta} \leqq \bar{\sigma}_{\theta\theta} ; \quad 0 \leqq \sigma_{\nu\nu} \leqq \bar{\sigma}_{\nu\nu} ; \quad \mu \geqq 0 . \tag{5.12}$$

This is evidently a linear programming problem and the result is that the optimal budget is zero if p_θ/d_θ and p_ν/d_ν are both less than 1; that if one of these ratios is above 1 and the other below 1, the optimal budget is such that perfect knowledge is obtained with respect to the parameter which corresponds with the former ratio while nothing is done with respect to the other parameter; and that if both ratios are above 1, money should be spent such that both $\sigma_{\theta\theta}$ and σ_{vv} are exactly zero. Clearly, the linear production function is unrealistic.

(*ii*) Next, suppose that the research production function is quadratic (in accordance with (5.2)). We shall be restrictive by assuming that the production function is separable without bilinear terms:

$$d_\theta(\sigma_{\theta\theta} - \bar{\sigma}_{\theta\theta}) + \mu_\theta + \tfrac{1}{2}[-d_{\theta\theta}(\sigma_{\theta\theta} - \bar{\sigma}_{\theta\theta})^2 + d'_{\theta\theta}\mu_\theta^2] = 0\,; \tag{5.13}$$

$$d_v(\sigma_{vv} - \bar{\sigma}_{vv}) + \mu_v + \tfrac{1}{2}[-d_{vv}(\sigma_{vv} - \bar{\sigma}_{vv})^2 + d'_{vv}\mu_v^2] = 0\,, \tag{5.14}$$

where μ_θ and μ_v are the research budgets for cost analysis and for market analysis respectively. The positive terms $\frac{1}{2}d'_{\theta\theta}\,\mu_\theta^2$ and $\frac{1}{2}d'_{vv}\,\mu_v^2$ should be interpreted as representing economies of scale in research, the negative squared terms (with coefficients $-\frac{1}{2}d_{\theta\theta}$ and $-\frac{1}{2}d_{vv}$) as representing decreasing returns with respect to further reductions of $\sigma_{\theta\theta}$ and σ_{vv}. It will be clear that in this case of separability we have to solve two separate problems: that of minimizing $p_\theta(\sigma_{\theta\theta} - \bar{\sigma}_{\theta\theta}) + \mu_\theta$ subject to (5.13) and that of minimizing $p_v(\sigma_{vv} - \bar{\sigma}_{vv}) + \mu_v$ subject to (5.14). We can confine ourselves to one of them (say $\sigma_{\theta\theta}$), since the two are algebraically equivalent.

Consider first the case in which the resources μ_θ and μ_v are taken as given without costs. Then, if we translate this case into the language of the general theory, we have $z = [\sigma_{\theta\theta} - \bar{\sigma}_{\theta\theta}]$, $p = [p_\theta]$, $g_0 = \mu_\theta + \frac{1}{2}d'_{\theta\theta}\,\mu_\theta^2$, $g = [d_\theta]$ and $G = [-d_{\theta\theta}]$, so that (5.6) gives

$$\frac{1}{\lambda^2} = \frac{1}{p_\theta^2}\,(d_\theta^2 + 2d_{\theta\theta}\,\mu_\theta + d_{\theta\theta}\,d'_{\theta\theta}\,\mu_\theta^2)\,; \tag{5.15}$$

$1/\lambda$ is the positive square root of (5.15), because this is the root which minimizes $p'G^{-1}p/\lambda$. Furthermore, (5.4) leads to the following optimal improvement of the θ-knowledge:

$$\sigma_{\theta\theta} - \bar{\sigma}_{\theta\theta} = \frac{d_\theta}{d_{\theta\theta}}\,(1 - \sqrt{1 + \alpha\mu_\theta + \beta\mu_\theta^2}\,)\,, \tag{5.16}$$

where

$$\alpha = \frac{2d_{\theta\theta}}{d_\theta^2}\ ; \quad \beta = \frac{d_{\theta\theta}\, d'_{\theta\theta}}{d_\theta^2}\ . \tag{5.17}$$

Hence the optimal $\sigma_{\theta\theta}$-reduction is exclusively determined by the parameters of the production function and the available resources;[8] it is a linear function of the square root of a quadratic expression in the latter variable. It is particularly interesting to note that this optimal reduction is independent of the 'price' p_θ.[9] This is due to the fact that μ_θ is considered as being available without costs, so that minimizing $p_\theta(\sigma_{\theta\theta} - \bar{\sigma}_{\theta\theta}) + \mu_\theta$ is equivalent to minimizing $\sigma_{\theta\theta} - \bar{\sigma}_{\theta\theta}$. For the optimal σ_{vv}-reduction the results are identical except that θ should be replaced throughout by v.

(*iii*) Suppose now that the resources are not fixed without costs, the technology of research being given by (5.13)-(5.14) as before. Then our interpretation becomes:

$$z = \begin{bmatrix} \sigma_{\theta\theta} - \bar{\sigma}_{\theta\theta} \\ \mu_\theta \end{bmatrix}; \quad p = \begin{bmatrix} p_\theta \\ 1 \end{bmatrix}; \quad g_0 = 0\ ;$$
$$g = \begin{bmatrix} d_\theta \\ 1 \end{bmatrix}; \quad G = \begin{bmatrix} -d_{\theta\theta} & 0 \\ 0 & d'_{\theta\theta} \end{bmatrix}, \tag{5.18}$$

so that (5.6) gives in this case:

$$\frac{1}{\lambda^2} = \frac{d_\theta^2 - d_{\theta\theta}/d'_{\theta\theta}}{p_\theta^2 - d_{\theta\theta}/d'_{\theta\theta}}\ , \tag{5.19}$$

while (5.4) specifies:

$$\begin{bmatrix} \sigma_{\theta\theta} - \bar{\sigma}_{\theta\theta} \\ \mu_\theta \end{bmatrix} = \begin{bmatrix} (d_\theta - p_\theta/\lambda)\, d_{\theta\theta} \\ (1/\lambda - 1)/d'_{\theta\theta} \end{bmatrix}. \tag{5.20}$$

---

8 The result (5.16) is of course subject to the constraint $\sigma_{\theta\theta} \geq 0$, (see 5.12). [The other constraint, $\sigma_{\theta\theta} \leq \bar{\sigma}_{\theta\theta}$, is automatically satisfied for $\mu_\theta > 0$, because the square root in (5.16) is always larger than 1.]

9 Note that this 'price' depends on the initial inventory level I_0, which varies over time. Hence it is in order to replace p_θ by an appropriate expectation.

The second component of (5.20) shows that the optimal budget depends (via λ) on the price p_θ and all coefficients of the production function. In order that the optimal μ_θ be positive it is necessary that $1/\lambda > 1$, which given (5.19) means that p_θ should lie between d_θ and $(d_{\theta\theta}/d'_{\theta\theta})^{\frac{1}{2}}$. Furthermore, the optimal $\sigma_{\theta\theta}$-reduction is no longer independent of p_θ.

(*iv*) These results can be extended for the case in which the production function is not separable. The derivations are straightforward and we shall therefore give some results without proof. If there are no bilinear terms, the production function takes the form:

$$\begin{aligned} & d_\theta(\sigma_{\theta\theta} - \bar{\sigma}_{\theta\theta}) + d_\nu(\sigma_{\nu\nu} - \bar{\sigma}_{\nu\nu}) + \mu \\ & + \tfrac{1}{2}[-d_{\theta\theta}(\sigma_{\theta\theta} - \bar{\sigma}_{\theta\theta})^2 - d_{\nu\nu}(\sigma_{\nu\nu} - \bar{\sigma}_{\nu\nu})^2 + d_{\mu\mu}\mu^2] = 0\,, \end{aligned} \tag{5.21}$$

so that z has now three components: $\sigma_{\theta\theta} - \bar{\sigma}_{\theta\theta}$, $\sigma_{\nu\nu} - \bar{\sigma}_{\nu\nu}$, and μ. The last component is to be deleted if the research budget is taken as fixed without costs, in which case we have

$$\frac{1}{\lambda^2} = \frac{\dfrac{d_\theta^2}{d_{\theta\theta}} + \dfrac{d_\nu^2}{d_{\nu\nu}} + 2\mu + d_{\mu\mu}\,\mu^2}{\dfrac{p_\theta^2}{d_{\theta\theta}} + \dfrac{p_\nu^2}{d_{\nu\nu}}} \tag{5.22}$$

and

$$\begin{bmatrix} \sigma_{\theta\theta} - \bar{\sigma}_{\theta\theta} \\ \sigma_{\nu\nu} - \bar{\sigma}_{\nu\nu} \end{bmatrix} = \begin{bmatrix} (d_\theta - p_\theta/\lambda)/d_{\theta\theta} \\ (d_\nu - p_\nu/\lambda)/d_{\nu\nu} \end{bmatrix}. \tag{5.23}$$

We must conclude that it is no longer true that the optimal $\sigma_{\theta\theta}$-reduction (and similarly for $\sigma_{\nu\nu}$, *mutatis mutandis*) is exclusively determined by cost analysis considerations. Equation (5.23) shows that this reduction depends on λ and (5.22) shows that λ depends, given the available budget, on p_ν, d_ν and $d_{\nu\nu}$ which deal with market analysis. If the research budget is not taken as fixed without costs, we have

$$\frac{1}{\lambda^2} = \frac{\dfrac{d_\theta^2}{d_{\theta\theta}} + \dfrac{d_\nu^2}{d_{\nu\nu}} - \dfrac{1}{d_{\mu\mu}}}{\dfrac{p_\theta^2}{d_{\theta\theta}} + \dfrac{p_\nu^2}{d_{\nu\nu}} - \dfrac{1}{d_{\mu\mu}}} \tag{5.24}$$

and

$$\begin{bmatrix} \sigma_{\theta\theta} - \bar{\sigma}_{\theta\theta} \\ \sigma_{\nu\nu} - \bar{\sigma}_{\nu\nu} \\ \mu \end{bmatrix} = \begin{bmatrix} (d_\theta - p_\theta/\lambda)/d_{\theta\theta} \\ (d_\nu - p_\nu/\lambda)/d_{\nu\nu} \\ (1/\lambda - 1)/d_{\mu\mu} \end{bmatrix}. \tag{5.25}$$

In this case λ is completely determined by prices and coefficients of the production function, while the optimal budget has a form similar to (5.20); but now, of course, it deals with the aggregate expenses on cost and market analysis as a whole.

Suppose finally that the production function (5.21) has to be modified to the extent that

$$2d_{\theta\nu}(\sigma_{\theta\theta} - \bar{\sigma}_{\theta\theta})(\sigma_{\nu\nu} - \bar{\sigma}_{\nu\nu})$$

is added between the square brackets. This implies economies in the 'joint production' of $\sigma_{\theta\theta}$ and $\sigma_{\nu\nu}$-reductions, which is realistic when e.g. statisticians can be hired for both cost and market analysis. If the research budget is taken as fixed without costs, we have

$$\frac{1}{\lambda^2} = \frac{d_{\nu\nu}d_\theta^2 + 2d_{\theta\nu}d_\theta d_\nu + d_{\theta\theta}d_\nu^2 + D(2\mu + d_{\mu\mu}\mu^2)}{d_{\nu\nu}p_\theta^2 + 2d_{\theta\nu}p_\theta p_\nu + d_{\theta\theta}p_\nu^2}, \tag{5.26}$$

where $D = d_{\theta\theta}d_{\nu\nu} - d_{\theta\nu}^2$, and

$$\begin{bmatrix} \sigma_{\theta\theta} - \bar{\sigma}_{\theta\theta} \\ \sigma_{\nu\nu} - \bar{\sigma}_{\nu\nu} \end{bmatrix} = \frac{1}{D}\begin{bmatrix} (d_{\nu\nu}d_\theta + d_{\theta\nu}d_\nu) - (d_{\nu\nu}p_\theta + d_{\theta\nu}p_\nu)/\lambda \\ (d_{\theta\nu}d_\theta + d_{\theta\theta}d_\nu) - (d_{\theta\nu}p_\theta + d_{\theta\theta}p_\nu)/\lambda \end{bmatrix}. \tag{5.27}$$

This shows that the optimal $\sigma_{\theta\theta}$-reduction depends on 'alien' coefficients (p_ν, d_ν, ...) even apart from its dependence on λ which in turn depends on all coefficients as is the case of the preceding paragraph. If the budget is not taken as fixed without costs, we obtain

$$\frac{1}{\lambda^2} = \frac{d_{vv}d_\theta^2 + 2d_{\theta v}d_\theta d_v + d_{\theta\theta}d_v^2 - D/d_{\mu\mu}}{d_{vv}p_\theta^2 + 2d_{\theta v}p_\theta p_v + d_{\theta\theta}p_v^2 - D/d_{\mu\mu}}. \tag{5.28}$$

The optimal σ-reductions are the same as those of (5.27) except that λ should be interpreted according to (5.28). The optimal budget is $(1/\lambda - 1)d_{\mu\mu}$ as in (5.25) except that again λ is to be derived from (5.28).

Our *conclusions* can be summarized as follows. The analysis of case (i) shows that if one decides to use a research production function to describe the transformation of research resources into better parameter specifications, one should not use a linear function. Cases (*ii*) and (*iii*) are based on two separate quadratic production functions, one for cost analysis and one for market analysis, each of which has a weighted sum of squares as its homogeneous quadratic part. If the research budgets are fixed and if cost considerations with respect to the budget are not supposed to affect the research manager's decisions, the optimal increase in cost and market knowledge appears to be solely determined by the available budget and by the technology of research (i.e., the coefficients of the research production functions). In particular, the optimal increase is independent of the 'price' of the imperfect knowledge (i.e., of the coefficient by which the relevant expected squared specification error is multiplied in the decision-maker's loss). In addition to this, the decisions with respect to cost analysis are determined by two disjoint sets of factors, which can be regarded as a justification of the procedure of two independently operating cost analysis and market analysis departments. The latter feature holds also in case the budget is variable and if its costs are taken into consideration, but it is then no longer true that the optimal reduction of uncertainty is independent of the price of uncertainty. More complicated situations arise when we analyze, as was done under (*iv*), the case of a research production function which is not separable with respect to cost analysis and to market analysis. If this function is quadratic without bilinear terms, there is one quantity (the Lagrangean multiplier λ) which has to be computed before and which depends on the available resources — if these are taken as fixed without costs — as well as on all coefficients of the objective function and of the production function. Once this λ has been determined, the optimal improvement in the field of cost analysis and in that of market analysis is determined by two disjoint sets of factors. Clearly, the presence of λ as a common determining factor suggests that some co-ordination of the cost analysis department and of the market analysis department is then necessary. The same is true if the research budget is variable and if we take account of its costs, but the Lagrangean λ takes a different value in that case. It is then determined by the coefficients of the objective function and the production function; in turn, it is one of the determinants of the optimal budget. The situation becomes still more complicated if there are economies in joint production as represented by a bilinear term in the research production function. It is then no longer true that, given λ, the optimal improvement of the cost coefficient knowledge and that of future sales are determined by disjoint sets of factors. In other words, still more co-ordination between the two research departments — perhaps even one single department — is then necessary.

References

Allen, R.G.D.: 1956, *Mathematical Economics*, MacMillan & Co Ltd., London.

Hicks, J.R.: 1946, *Value and Capital*, 2nd ed. At the Clarendon Press, Oxford.

Theil, H.: 1961, *Economic Forecasts and Policy*, 2nd ed. North-Holland Publishing Company, Amsterdam.

Appendix

A. THE OPTIMAL FIRST-PERIOD DECISION IN THE PRODUCTION-INVENTORY EXAMPLE

By substituting the constraints (2.3) into the preference function (2.2) we obtain the utility level w_x which is attained if the instruments are fixed at any given level x. This utility level is

$$w_x = w(x, Rx + s) = k_0 + k'x + \tfrac{1}{2}x'Kx\,, \tag{A.1}$$

where

$$\begin{aligned} k_0 &= b's + \tfrac{1}{2}s'Bs \\ k &= a + R'b + (C + R'B)s \\ K &= A + R'BR + CR + R'C'\,. \end{aligned} \tag{A.2}$$

The optimal decision is then $x^0 = -K^{-1}k$ and the optimal first-period decision consists of the first m components of this vector.

In the production-inventory example $m = 1$ and

$$K = -2(c_2 I + c_4 R'R) = -2c_2 R'\left(R'^{-1}R^{-1} + \frac{c_4}{c_2}I\right)R\,, \tag{A.3}$$

see (2.5); R is as specified in (2.6). To find the optimal first-period decision we should postmultiply the first row of K^{-1} by k, and k is in the present case:

$$k = -\begin{bmatrix} c_1 \\ c_1 \\ \cdot \\ \cdot \\ \cdot \\ c_1 \end{bmatrix} - R' \begin{bmatrix} c_3 \\ c_3 \\ \cdot \\ \cdot \\ \cdot \\ c_3 \end{bmatrix} + 2c_4 R'R \begin{bmatrix} V_1 - I_0 \\ V_2 \\ \cdot \\ \cdot \\ \cdot \\ V_T \end{bmatrix}. \tag{A.4}$$

Our task is therefore to find the first row of

$$K^{-1} = \frac{-1}{2c_2} R^{-1} \left(R'^{-1}R^{-1} + \frac{c_4}{c_2} I \right)^{-1} R'^{-1}, \tag{A.5}$$

where

$$R^{-1} = \begin{bmatrix} 1 & 0 & 0 & \dots & 0 & 0 \\ -1 & 1 & 0 & \dots & 0 & 0 \\ 0 & -1 & 1 & \dots & 0 & 0 \\ \cdot & \cdot & \cdot & & \cdot & \cdot \\ \cdot & \cdot & \cdot & & \cdot & \cdot \\ \cdot & \cdot & \cdot & & \cdot & \cdot \\ 0 & 0 & 0 & \dots & 1 & 0 \\ 0 & 0 & 0 & \dots & -1 & 1 \end{bmatrix}; \; R'^{-1}R^{-1} = \begin{bmatrix} 2 & -1 & 0 & & 0 & 0 \\ -1 & 2 & -1 & \dots & 0 & 0 \\ 0 & -1 & 2 & \dots & 0 & 0 \\ \cdot & \cdot & \cdot & & \cdot & \cdot \\ \cdot & \cdot & \cdot & & \cdot & \cdot \\ \cdot & \cdot & \cdot & & \cdot & \cdot \\ 0 & 0 & 0 & \dots & 2 & -1 \\ 0 & 0 & 0 & \dots & -1 & 1 \end{bmatrix}. \tag{A.6}$$

It follows that the middle inverse on the right of (A.5) is the inverse of

$$\begin{bmatrix} 2+\frac{c_4}{c_2} & -1 & 0 & \dots & 0 & 0 \\ -1 & 2+\frac{c_4}{c_2} & -1 & \dots & 0 & 0 \\ 0 & -1 & 2+\frac{c_4}{c_2} & \dots & 0 & 0 \\ \cdot & \cdot & \cdot & & \cdot & \cdot \\ \cdot & \cdot & \cdot & & \cdot & \cdot \\ \cdot & \cdot & \cdot & & \cdot & \cdot \\ 0 & 0 & 0 & \dots & 2+\frac{c_4}{c_2} & -1 \\ 0 & 0 & 0 & \dots & -1 & 1+\frac{c_4}{c_2} \end{bmatrix} \tag{A.7}$$

which is a band matrix whose diagonal elements are all equal and whose elements immediately above and below the diagonal are all -1, all other elements being zero. There is a terminal effect implying that the last diagonal element is 1 less than the other diagonal elements, but this is immaterial when we consider an infinite horizon. To derive the first row of K^{-1} we should postmultiply the first row of R^{-1} by the inverse of (A.7), and then postmultiply by R'^{-1}. But the first row of R^{-1} consists of a 1 on the leading place and zeros on all other places; hence the first row of K^{-1} is simply obtained by postmultiplying the first row of the inverse of (A.7) by R'^{-1}. The latter row is, in the infinite-horizon case,

$$g_1 = [\,\theta,\ \theta^2,\ \theta^3,\ \dots\,] \tag{A.8}$$

with θ as specified in (2.8); this is easily verified by postmultiplying g_1 by (A.7), leading to [1, 0, 0, ...]. Finally, on postmultiplying g_1 by R'^{-1} and taking account of the factor -1/2c_2 in (A.5), we obtain for the first row of K^{-1}:

$$g_2 = \frac{-1}{2c_2}\,[\,\theta,\ -\theta(1-\theta),\ -\theta^2(1-\theta),\ \dots\,]\,.$$

It will be noted that the first element of g_2, $-\theta/2c_2$, is also the leading element of K^{-1}, so that $K_1 = -2c_2/\theta$. This is used in Section 3.2.

The optimal first-period decision is then $-g_2 k$ with k as given in (A.4). This is a matter of adding geometric series and using the θ-definition of (2.8); it leads directly to (2.7).

B. THE FIRST-PERIOD LOSS

Let the m-element vector x_1^* stand for any given first-period decision. Then the first-period loss, being the minimum utility reduction associated with x_1^*, is found by computing the conditional maximum of (A.1) under the condition $x_1 = x_1^*$ and subtracting this conditional maximum from the unconditional maximum. Consider then the Lagrangean expression

$$k_0 + k'x + \tfrac{1}{2}x'Kx - \lambda'(x_1 - x_1^*),$$

λ being an m-element column vector of multipliers. Differentiating, we obtain

$$k + Kx - \begin{bmatrix} \lambda \\ 0 \end{bmatrix} = 0 \tag{B.1}$$

where the 0 of the partitioned column contains $m(T - 1)$ elements and the right-hand 0 consists of mT zeros. Solving (B.1) for x, we find

$$x = -K^{-1}k + K^{-1}\begin{bmatrix} \lambda \\ \\ \\ 0 \end{bmatrix} = x^0 + \begin{bmatrix} K^{11} \\ \cdot \\ \cdot \\ \cdot \\ K^{T1} \end{bmatrix}\lambda \tag{B.2}$$

where $x^0 = -K^{-1}k$ is the vector which maximizes (A.1) unconditionally and K^{11}, ..., K^{T1} stand for $m \times m$ submatrices of K^{-1}; $K^{11} = K_1^{-1}$ as defined in Section 3.1. We conclude from (B.2) and the side condition $x_1 = x_1^*$ that

$$\lambda = (K^{11})^{-1}(x_1^* - x_1^0) = K_1 \Delta x_1$$

where Δx_1 is the first-period decision error. Hence

$$x - x^0 = \begin{bmatrix} K^{11} \\ \cdot \\ \cdot \\ K^{TI} \end{bmatrix} (K^{11})^{-1} \Delta x_1 \tag{B.3}$$

and the minimum utility reduction due to Δx_1 is then found by applying (3.2) which gives $-(\Delta x_1)' K_1 (\Delta x_1)$ as mentioned in the last paragraph of Section 3.1.

CHAPTER 79

CAN ECONOMISTS CONTRIBUTE TO MARKETING RESEARCH?*

HENRI THEIL
University of Chicago
Chicago, Illinois, U.S.A.

ABSTRACT. An extensive economic literature on consumer demand theory has not been adequately applied to marketing research. Marketing research tends to use sophisticated econometric tools without adopting underlying economic models. The author draws upon his own research for a non-technical analysis of this problem.

I have felt for a long time that there ought to be useful connections between the economist's approaches to consumption theory and the work done by market researchers for consumer goods. There is, of course, a difference; economists usually consider broad product classes, and market researchers tend to look at more narrowly defined goods or even brands of goods. However, this difference can be handled under appropriate conditions.

Consumer Utility and Demand Functions

During a number of weeks last autumn I did a lot of reading in the *Journal of Marketing Research* and other journals, partly in an effort to educate myself, and partly in order to find out whether my own work in consumption theory is or can be made useful for the problems considered in these articles. What I found in many articles in the marketing journals is very econometric but also very uneconomic. These articles are very econometric in the sense that there are numerous Durbin-Watson statistics, Koyck distributed lags, and even simultaneous equation systems. Yet, the articles are very uneconomic in the sense that they say very little about consumer utility.

Whenever an economist thinks about a consumer, he does so in terms of utility maximization subject to a budget constraint, or some mathematically equivalent version of this idea. The economist postulates that the consumer has certain preferences which can be described by a utility function. The budget constraint describes the consumer's financial limitations. By maximizing the utility function subject to the budget constraint, the consumer finds the optimal quantities to be bought of the various goods and services

---

* This article first appeared in the *Sloan Management Review*, **20** (Summer 1979) 19-29. Reprinted here with the permission of the Sloan Management Review Association. This article is adapted from the closing address delivered before the meeting of the European Academy for Advanced Research in Marketing in Groningen, the Netherlands on April 12, 1979.

(optimal in the sense that they are best according to his tastes without violating his budget constraint). These optimal quantities depend on the amount of income which is at the consumer's disposal and on the prices which he has to pay for the goods and services. This dependence is formalized in terms of a set of demand functions, each of which describes the demand for a good or service in terms of income and prices.

The numerical specification of demand functions is a useful scientific project. We want to know the numerical values of income and price elasticities of demand. This kind of work has been going on for more than a century: Engel's Law, proposed in 1857, states that when income increases, the amount spent on food also increases, but that the proportion of income allocated to food becomes smaller. (This amounts to an income elasticity of the demand for food which is positive but less than one). In 1943, Holbrook Working used family budget data for a further specification of this relation; he found that the proportion of income allocated to food could be closely approximated by a decreasing linear function of the logarithm of income.[1] Recently, Kenneth Clements and I found that this relation also applies, in a cross-country context, to per capita food expenditure in fifteen countries at different states of economic development, ranging from India to the United States.[2]

When I speak about expenditure on food, I recognize that I am far from the level of detail in which most marketing researchers are interested. Nevertheless, such a discussion provides perspective; I want to use this argument to engage in a short digression on parallel developments in the theory of the firm.

Whereas consumption theory is based on the notion of utility maximization subject to a budget constraint, the theory of the cost-minimizing firm assumes that this firm minimizes the total amount spent on production factors (or inputs) subject to a technological constraint in the form of a production function. This constrained minimum problem is equivalent to the dual problem of maximizing output subject to a budget constraint, in the sense that a fixed total amount is spent on the inputs. Note that maximizing output subject to a budget constraint for a firm is comparable to maximizing utility subject to a budget constraint for a consumer. This similarity is one reason for this digression. A second reason is that there is an important difference: the output of a firm can be measured (at least in principle), whereas utility is a more abstract concept.

Consumer Demand Equations in Marketing Research

How can we make this abstract concept useful in marketing research? Let me list a number of problems that are important in marketing research for consumer goods. The

---

[1] See H. Working: 1943, "Statistical Laws of Family Expenditure," *Journal of the American Statistical Association*, **38**, 43-56.

[2] See K.W. Clements and H. Theil: 1979, "A Cross-Country Tabulation of Income Elasticities of Demand," *Economics Letters*, **3**, 199-202. The data used are from I.B. Kravis, A.W. Heston, and R. Summers: 1978, *International Comparisons of Real Product and Purchasing Power*, Johns Hopkins University Press, Baltimore, MD.

list is my own and probably reflects my biases, although I had the benefit of discussions and correspondence with others.[3] In this article I will make a distinction between a product or product class, such as coffee, detergents, or soap, and a particular brand sold by one firm within that product class. Here are the problems:

- How sensitive are the sales of the product to a change in economic conditions, such as an increase or decrease in the consumer's real disposable income?
- How does this affect the market share of my brand?
- How sensitive are the sales of my brand to a change in my price and to changes in the prices of my competitors?
- How effective are promotional techniques in inducing consumers to buy the product?
- How effective are my promotional techniques in inducing consumers to buy my brand?
- How effective in this regard are the promotional techniques of my competitors?
- If such techniques have a lagged effect on demand, what is the form of the lag?
- What is the effect of shelf space, package design, etc., on the market share of my brand?
- To what extent are the purchasers of my brand loyal, in the sense that they keep buying it?
- What kind of people are loyal to my brand and what kind are not?
- Why are some people loyal to my brand and others not?
- How can I create more brand loyalty?
- How can I change the composition of my brand and the package design to make it more salable?
- Should I design my brand to target on particular market segments and, if so, which ones?
- Should I introduce new brands in order to capture market segments which are not covered by present brands?

I presume that you do not expect me to provide an answer to all of these questions. I listed them approximately in the order of increasing difficulty which I face when I try to answer them.

Some of these problems can be solved when we use certain recent developments in the economic theory of systems of consumer demand equations. There is a gap between these developments and the current marketing research literature on the price and advertising effects on the demand for narrowly defined goods. The existence of such a gap is understandable, because most of the economists' attempts to model consumer behavior in a system-wide manner refer to the consumer's total expenditure, not to the expenditure on a particular product class. This necessitates the use of broad groups of consumer goods. However, it is possible to formulate subsystems for more narrowly defined goods under appropriate separability conditions on the consumer's preferences. When such a subsystem refers to the brands of a particular product, it contains only the prices and quantities of these brands, not of the goods outside the product class under

---

[3] I am particularly indebted to Professor Robert Ferber of the University of Illinois, who sent me a long letter.

consideration. This is an attractive feature from the viewpoint of a marketing researcher who is particularly interested in this product and its brands.

The Specification of Demand Equation Systems

I will now describe the way in which this separability procedure works. The literature on separability is substantial, and much of it is in rather abstract mathematical terms,[4] which is probably one reason why it has not penetrated much into marketing research. The simplest way to proceed is by postponing separability until the next stage.

The first stage in estimating consumer demand functions is to maximize the utility function subject to the budget constraint. This yields equilibrium conditions in the form of the familiar proportionality of marginal utilities and prices. We can then obtain algebraically specified demand functions by specifying a particular algebraic form of the consumer's utility function. The best-known specification is the Klein-Rubin utility function.[5] This function implies the so-called linear expenditure system; that is, the expenditure on each good is described as a linear function of total expenditure and the prices of all goods. This model has become particularly popular since Richard Stone applied it to British data in 1954.[6] Note that the model provides a complete system of consumer demand equations. This is shown by terms such as the system-wide approach or the equation systems approach. It should be contrasted with the older approach, which estimates demand equations individually rather than as a system.[7]

The linear expenditure system is obtained from an algebraic specification of the consumer's utility function. There are several other ways in which demand systems can be derived. For example, we can provide an algebraic specification of the so-called indirect utility function, which describes the maximum utility level that is attainable for given values of income and prices. We can also algebraically specify the consumer's cost

---

[4] See C. Blackorby, D. Primont, and R.R. Russell: 1978, *Duality, Separability, and Functional Structure*, Elsevier North-Holland, New York.

[5] See L.R. Klein and H. Rubin: 1948, " A Constant-Utility Index of the Cost of Living," *The Review of Economic Studies*, **15**, 84-87.

[6] See R. Stone: 1954, "Linear Expenditure Systems and Demand Analysis: An Application to the Pattern of British Demand," *Economic Journal*, **64**, 511-527.

[7] For a recent survey of the new approach, see: A.P. Barten: 1977, "The Systems of Consumer Demand Functions Approach: A Review," *Econometrica*, **45**, 23-51; For an earlier survey, see: A. Brown and A. Deaton: 1972, "Surveys in Applied Economics: Models of Consumer Behaviour," *Economic Journal*, **82**, 1145-1236; L. Solarí: 1971, *Théorie des Choix et Fonctions de Consommation Semi-agrégées*, Librairie Droz, Geneva; A.A. Powell: 1974, *Empirical Analytics of Demand Systems*, D.C. Heath and Co., Lexington MA; L. Phlips: 1974, *Applied Consumption Analysis*, North-Holland, Amsterdam; A.S. Deaton: 1975, *Models and Projections of Demand in Post-War Britain*, Chapman and Hall, London; H. Theil: 1975-76, *Theory and Measurement of Consumer Demand*, 2 vols., North-Holland, Amsterdam; L. Solarí and J.-N. Du Pasquier, eds.: 1976, *Private and Enlarged Consumption*, North-Holland, Amsterdam; C. Lluch, A.A. Powell, and R.A. Williams: 1977, *Patterns in Household Demand and Saving*, Oxford University Press, New York.

function, which describes the smallest amount of expenditure needed to attain a given utility level at given prices. The cost function is of particular importance in the theory of the cost-of-living index and the real-income index. This theory is also relevant in marketing research, because price and volume indexes are important when we consider a set of closely related, narrowly defined goods, such as brands of the same product class.

Differential Consumption Theory

The differential approach postpones the matter of algebraic specification. Noting the prominence of partial derivatives in demand theory will put this approach in appropriate perspective. The income elasticity of demand for a good is a logarithmic derivative with respect to income. The Slutsky equations decompose price effects into income and substitution effects. Slutsky negativity amounts to a negative derivative of the demand for each good with respect to its own price, provided that an appropriate correction is made for the fact that a price increase makes the consumer poorer. There is also Slutsky symmetry, which relates the derivative of the demand for good A with respect to the price of good B to the derivative of the demand for B with respect to the price of A (after similar corrections).

The differential approach to consumption theory goes one step further by collecting these income and price derivatives in the form of differentials; that is, the differential of the demand for each good is written as a weighted sum of the differentials of income and prices, with weights equal to the corresponding derivatives. Most applications of the differential approach use time series data, in which case the differentials are simply changes over time. But this is an unnecessary restriction; there are also applications in a cross-country context, in which case the differentials are interpreted as moves from any country to any other country.[8]

What can we learn from the differential approach to consumption theory? Does it enable us to statistically test and impose Slutsky symmetry? Does it tell us something about the form of price indexes which transform money income into real income and absolute prices into relative prices? The answer is yes; to clarify this optimistic statement, I will proceed under the assumption that we work with time series data, so that the abstract differentials take the more familiar form of changes over time.

Effects of Price Changes on Demand

An important result is that when the price of any good changes, the demand for this good, and also for any other good, is affected in three distinct ways. One of the three components of the effect of a price increase on demand reflects a reduced affluence, or a decline in real income. This is the income effect of a price change on demand, which

---

[8] See Clements and Theil (1979).

can be conveniently visualized as a deflation procedure which transforms money income into real income. The deflator used is the Divisia price index, which is obtained by weighting the logarithmic price changes of the individual goods proportionally to the amounts spent on these goods.[9]

The two other components of the effect of a price change on demand reflect a change in relative prices, or of price substitution. There are good reasons for a separation of the substitution effect into two components. One reason is that whereas all goods compete with each other for an extra dollar of the consumer's income, there are usually certain pairs of goods which compete with each other because they are closely related, such as different brands of the same kind of product. Also, other pairs of goods, such as cars and gasoline, complement each other. The general competition of all goods for an extra dollar of the consumer's income results from the consumer's budget constraint; this component of the substitution effect is known as the general component of the substitution effect or, more shortly, the general substitution effect. The other component results from the interaction of the two goods in the consumer's utility evaluation and is known as the specific substitution effect. The distinction between these two components is from Houthakker.[10]

Price Deflators

The most straightforward way to handle the two components of the substitution effect (also from the viewpoint of the application to narrowly defined goods, such as different brands of the same product) is to use the general substitution effect as a deflator of the specific effect. This yields the following picture of the differential demand system. First, the change in the demand for each good depends on the change in money income. Next, the change in demand depends on the income effects of the price changes. This is formulated in terms of a deflator which transforms money income into real income; the deflator used is the Divisia price index. Further, the change in demand depends on the changes in relative prices. This is formulated in terms of changes in prices deflated by a price index. The price changes that are deflated represent the specific substitution effect, and their deflator represents the general substitution effect.

This deflator is not identical to the Divisia price index which transforms money income into real income. Most price indexes, including the Laspeyres and Paasche indexes (which date back to the nineteenth century), can be viewed as approximations of one kind or other to the Divisia index. The Divisia index weights the logarithmic changes in the prices of the individual goods with their budget shares, which are the proportions of income allocated to the individual goods. By contrast, the price index which represents the general substitution effect as the deflator of the specific substitution effect is the

---

[9] See F. Divisia: 1925, "L'Indice Monétaire et la Théorie de la Monnaie," *Revue d'Economie Politique*, **39**, 980-1008.

[10] See H.S. Houthakker: 1962, "Additive Preferences," *Econometrica*, **28**, 244-257; errata, **30**, 633.

Frisch price index.[11] This index weights the logarithmic changes in the prices of the individual goods with their marginal shares.

These marginal shares answer the following question: Suppose that income increases by one dollar; what is the additional amount spent on each of the goods? In general, the answer will differ from the budget share. In fact, it is not difficult to show that the ratio of the marginal share of a good to its budget share is equal to the income elasticity of demand for this good. It is only under the unrealistic assumption that all goods have unitary income elasticities that the marginal and budget shares are pairwise all equal. Such an assumption is particularly unattractive when we are interested in brands of the same product, because high-quality brands will have higher income elasticities than low-quality brands.

The existence of two different price deflators (Divisia and Frisch) is one of the interesting features of the differential approach to consumption theory. This approach yields a demand system which describes the change in demand in terms of the income change deflated by the Divisia price index and the Frisch-deflated price changes of all goods. However, this result does not yet enable the market researcher to analyze the market of his interest conveniently. The problem is that the Frisch-deflated price changes of all goods include prices of goods outside the market in which he is interested. To solve this problem, we turn to separability conditions on the consumer's preferences.

Separability and Preference Independence

The simplest and most drastic separability condition states that the consumer's preferences can be described by a utility function which is the sum of a number of functions, one for each good. This implies that the marginal utility of each good is independent of the consumption of all other goods; accordingly, this preference structure is frequently referred to as preference independence. The Klein-Rubin utility function which underlies the linear expenditure system belongs to this category, since it may be written in additive form.

If the consumer is preference independent, we can write the differential demand equations in a particularly simple form, viz., so that the substitution component of the change in the demand for each good depends only on the change in its own Frisch-deflated price. In addition, the own-price elasticities, i.e., the elasticities of the demand for the goods with respect to their own Frisch-deflated prices, are then proportional to their income elasticities. A rudimentary version of this proportionality was discussed by Pigou many years ago.[12]

There are several other interesting features of preference independence, particularly regarding the behavior of the proportionality coefficient in the relation between income

---

[11] See R. Frisch: 1932, *New Methods of Measuring Marginal Utility*, J.C.B. Mohr, Tübingen, West Germany.

[12] See A.S. Deaton: 1974, "A Reconsideration of the Empirical Implications of Additive Preferences," *Economic Journal*, **84**, 338-348.

and own-price elasticities,[13] but I will ignore these matters here, because preference independence is too restrictive for narrowly defined goods. It is simply not realistic to assume that the marginal utility of a dollar spent on brand A is independent of the consumption of brand B when we consider brands of the same kind of product. However, a weaker version of preference independence, called block-independence, is more promising.

Block-Independence

Let us divide the consumer goods into a number of groups, and assume that one of these groups consists of certain more narrowly defined goods in which the market researcher is interested. Also assume that the consumer's preferences can be represented by a utility function which is additive, not in the individual goods, but in the groups; that is, utility is the sum of a number of group utility functions. This implies that the marginal utility of each good is independent of the consumption of all goods that belong to different groups. It also implies that the change in the demand for each good is independent of the changes in the Frisch-deflated prices of all goods belonging to different groups.

The most interesting features of this block-independence specification become apparent when we consider the composite demand equations for the groups and the conditional demand equations for individual goods within their group. The composite demand equation for a group is obtained by simply adding the demand equations for its constituent goods. The form of a group demand equation under block-independence resembles the individual demand equations under preference independence. The change in the quantity consumed is now measured by the Divisia volume index of the group; this index is obtained by weighting the logarithmic quantity changes of the goods of the group in proportion to the amounts spent on these goods. This volume index contains a substitution component which depends only on the Frisch-deflated price index of the group, and this index is itself a Frisch price index. Price substitution at the group level can be expressed in terms of own-price elasticities, which are proportional to the income elasticities of the groups. All these features are simply group extensions of the corresponding properties of the demand equations for individual goods under preference independence.

Conditional Demand Equations

Next, by appropriately combining the demand equation for one good of a group with the corresponding group demand equation, we obtain the so-called conditional demand equation for this good within its group. This version is, in my view, one of the more

[13] For interesting conjectures on the dependence of the value of this proportionality coefficient on the level of real income, see R. Frisch: 1959, "A Complete Scheme for Computing All Direct and Cross Demand Elasticities in a Model with Many Sectors," *Econometrica*, **27**, 177-196.

promising developments of modern consumption theory for application in marketing research. A system of conditional demand equations enables the analyst to concentrate his attention on a group of related goods.

For example, we may consider beef, pork, chicken, and lamb. Each of these meats has a conditional demand equation within the group of all four meats jointly. Such an equation describes the change in the demand for a meat in terms of the Divisia volume index of meat and the changes in the four meat prices; no prices of other goods enter into the picture. Application of this model to U.S. data for the period 1950-1972 yields the result that beef and lamb are the most luxurious among the four meats.[14] The luxury character of such goods is measured, as usual, by their income elasticities; when we use conditional demand equations, we can obtain statistical estimates of the ratios of income elasticities of individual goods to the income elasticity of the group.

The picture that emerges from the previous paragraphs can be most easily visualized as a decision hierarchy. In the first stage, the consumer considers groups of goods, not individual goods; he decides how to allocate his income to these groups. In the second stage, he decides how much to spend on each good within its group. That second stage, represented by conditional demand equations, is completely confined to the group, as far as price changes of individual goods are concerned.

This is a very convenient feature, but note the underlying assumption of block-independence: utility equals the sum of group utility functions. This assumption can be somewhat relaxed; utility may be some increasing function (rather than the sum) of the group utility functions. The conditional demand equations take the same form under this weaker assumption.[15] Nevertheless, we have to make some separability assumption on the consumer's preferences in order to justify the absence of prices of goods outside the group in which we are interested.

The analysis of conditional demand systems also requires a statistical assumption. Demand equations do not hold exactly: a random disturbance is added to the right-hand side. Thus, a conditional demand equation describes the change in the demand for a good in terms of the Divisia volume index of the group, the price changes of the goods of the group, and a random disturbance. It is typically assumed that this disturbance is stochastically independent of the Divisia volume index; we run into serious statistical difficulties when this assumption is not true.

There is a problem because the Divisia volume index is a random variable in the composite demand equation for the group. The random component of the Divisia volume index is the disturbance in the group demand equation. Therefore, me must assume that the group disturbance is stochastically independent of the disturbances of all conditional demand equations. Is this realistic? A casual look at this problem suggests that there is no reason why this should be so but a more extensive analysis based on the theory of rational random behavior provides an affirmative answer. This theory also implies

---

[14] See Theil (1975-76), chap. 7.

[15] The group demand equations take a different form under the weaker assumption because they now involve Frisch price indexes of all groups. See Theil (1975-76), chap. 8.

interesting and testable restrictions on the variances and contemporaneous covariances of the disturbances. One of the major features of the theory of rational random behavior is that it pays more explicit attention than standard economic theory does to second-order derivatives so as to analyze situations surrounding the optimum.[16]

Conditional Demand Systems and Marketing Research

There are several features of conditional demand systems which can be conveniently discussed in conjunction with certain questions raised in marketing research. For example, what are the positive features of a brand which induce customers to buy it? (We should also ask whether there are any negative features which induce customers not to buy it.) One possible answer to these questions is based on the preference independence transformation. Recall that preference independence implies that the consumer's tastes can be represented by a utility function which is additive in the individual goods. This is an unrealistic assumption for narrowly defined goods, but it is always possible to transform goods so that preference independence prevails after the transformation. This procedure yields transformed goods, each of which has a marginal utility that is independent of the consumption of all other transformed goods. This means that the consumer's utility function becomes additive after the transformation, which can be interpreted in the sense that each transformed good is associated with one of the consumer's basic wants. Statistically, the transformation can be viewed as a constrained principal component transformation; the constraint results from the fact that the transformed goods are required to satisfy the budget constraint, and that the Divisia price and volume indexes are required to be invariant.

For example, when we apply the transformation to U.S. data on the consumption of beef, pork, and chicken, we obtain three transformed meats. One of these dominates the two others in terms of the amount spent on it, and it also has the lowest income elasticity, suggesting that this transformed meat is associated with the consumer's basic want for affordable meat. A second transformed meat represents beef positively, pork negatively, and chicken hardly at all, implying that it is associated with the consumer's desire to have beef rather than pork. This transformed meat is the most luxurious of the three; it has the highest income elasticity. The income elasticities of transformed goods are obtained from the latent roots of the principal component transformation which is associated with the preference independence transformation.

The preference independence transformation, in contrast to the principal component transformation, is unique. Principal components are not unique; they change in value when the original variables are measured in different units. The preference independence transformation does not have this problem because of the constraints which it is required to satisfy. From a more economic point of view, the transformation

[16] For details on the theory of rational random behavior, see H. Theil: 1979, *The System-Wide Approach to Microeconomics*, University of Chicago Press, Chicago, chaps. 7-9.

resembles Lancaster's work[17] on basic characteristics of consumer goods, but it has the advantage of being more directly applicable on the basis of the estimated price coefficients of differential demand systems.[18]

The estimation of these price coefficients requires consideration of the size of the demand system. There are no great problems when we analyze three or four meats, but problems do arise and increase in complexity when we consider larger models. The number of price coefficients tends to increase almost proportionally to the square of the number of goods. When we impose constraints across equations such as Slutsky symmetry, it becomes necessary to estimate all equations jointly rather than individually. The problem is not that our computers are not big enough; rather, our data base is insufficient relative to the number of coefficients to be estimated.[19]

Equicorrelated Substitutes

The most satisfactory solution to this problem is the formulation of plausible constraints on these coefficients. I attempted to do this for a set of brands which can be viewed as variations of the same theme.[20] The underlying assumption refers to the impact on the marginal utility of a dollar spent on a brand or an extra dollar spent on a different brand. Such effects are treated in a uniform manner for all pairs of brands; the result is that the relevant submatrix of the Hessian matrix of the utility function resembles the covariance matrix of a random vector of a special form, viz., so that all pairs of elements of this vector have the same correlation coefficient. Accordingly, brands which satisfy this preference structure may be called equicorrelated substitutes. This statistical formulation will sound a bit unusual to those who are not accustomed to merging economics and statistics, but it does have an interesting precedent. As early as 1932, Harold Hotelling proposed correlation-type measures for the description of the effects of price changes on demand.[21]

Conditional demand systems for equicorrelated substitutes satisfy the requirement of a modest number of unknown coefficients. Whether this specification is realistic for the brands of a particular product is a matter that can be decided only on the basis of statistical data. It may well be the case that it is more realistic to introduce different

---

[17] See K.J. Lancaster: 1971, *Consumer Demand: A New Approach*, Columbia University Press, New York.

[18] For further details on the preference independence transformation and the analogous input and output independence transformations in the theory of the firm, see Theil (1975-76), chaps. 10-13.

[19] A related problem is that of the use of an asymptotic test in a finite-sample context. For an article showing that such tests may be seriously biased against the null hypothesis, particularly for demand homogeneity and the absence of trends, see K. Laitinen: 1978, "Why Is Demand Homogeneity So Often Rejected?" *Economics Letters*, **1**, 187-191.

[20] H. Theil: 1980, *System-Wide Explorations in International Economics, Input-Output Analysis, and Marketing Research*, North-Holland, Amsterdam.

[21] See H. Hotelling: 1932, "Edgeworth's Taxation Paradox and the Nature of Demand and Supply Functions," *Journal of Political Economy*, **40**, 577-616.

correlations for subgroups, such as domestic brands and imported brands. If the model or some extension of this model appears acceptable, it would be interesting to verify whether the implied income elasticities of the brands are positively associated with their prices. Such a relation could be used to obtain more accurate coefficient estimates.

Quality

It is worthwhile to pursue this matter a little further, because a high income elasticity of a brand may be viewed as an indication that consumers consider this brand to be of relatively high quality. The measurement of the quality of consumption is a hot topic these days which can be approached from various angles. For example, we can consider certain desirable characteristics, such as the length, weight, and engine horsepower of an automobile. This approach is used in the theory of hedonic price indexes, on which there is an extensive literature,[22] but it faces difficulties when it tries to handle subjective characteristics.

An alternative procedure is to let the consumer decide what is high quality and what is low quality. Since income elasticities are behavioral characteristics, one way of doing this is by registering a shift to high income-elastic goods away from low income-elastic goods as a quality increase, and a shift to low income-elastic goods as a quality decrease. This can be done very elegantly in terms of the weighted covariance of the income elasticities and the logarithmic quantity changes, using the budget shares as weights. This formulation has the advantage that the income and substitution components of the change in quality can be easily established. It appears that the income elasticity of the demand for quality is equal to the variance of the income elasticities of the individual goods.

Clements and I applied these ideas in a cross-country context to consumption patterns of fifteen countries.[23] We estimated the pairwise quality differences for these countries and their real-income and substitution components, and found that the differences in real income and relative prices account for 88 percent of the quality differences. These computations are based on broad product classes, but the results should be inspiring for those whose interest is in more narrowly defined goods.

Closely Related Products and the Effects of Advertising

There are several problems regarding these narrowly defined goods which must still be discussed. Frequently the prices of goods which are brands of the same product move up and down more or less proportionately. How can we estimate price substitution among

[22] For example, see Z. Griliches, ed.: 1971, *Price Indexes and Quality Change*, Harvard University Press, Cambridge, MA.

[23] See Clements and Theil (1979).

such goods when there is little or no change in their relative prices? How can we estimate the effect on the demand for these goods of various forms of promotion, such as advertising?

It will be convenient to start with the second question, because under certain conditions the answer also provides a solution for the first. Let us model the effect of advertising in terms of an assumed effect on the marginal utility of the promoted brand. If this is done judiciously, only one additional parameter is needed to describe the advertising effects on demand in a full system of conditional demand equations.[24] Basically, advertising effects are absorbed into the substitution terms; what counts is the changes in relative advertising for the goods involved, in the same way that price substitution involves changes in relative prices. Since the substitution terms contain advertising effects, we can estimate the coefficients of these terms even when there are no changes in relative prices; it is sufficient that there be changes in relative advertising (which provides an answer to the first question raised above). Also, it is possible to link this approach to the Dorfman-Steiner theorem on price and advertising elasticities.[25]

These results look promising and perhaps even exciting, but several qualifications are in order. This approach, in the tradition of comparative statics, ignores the possibility of lagged effects of advertising on demand. This shortcoming can be remedied by adding lagged terms in the style of the Nerlove-Arrow approach to optimal advertising under dynamic conditions.[26]

A more fundamental question concerns the assumption that an increase in advertising affects demand via an increased marginal utility of the brand which is advertised. This is an obvious approach within the utility framework, but it is not obvious that this is always a satisfactory assumption. Suppose that we extend the advertising concept so that it includes shelf space. Does an increase in shelf space raise the marginal utility of a brand? Probably not, since shelf space is not an attribute of the brand.

Professor Robert Ferber, the editor of the *Journal of Consumer Research*, and a former editor of the *Journal of Marketing Research*, as well as the *Journal of the American Statistical Association*, suggested that I make a distinction between objective and subjective attributes. Objective attributes are inherent in the brands, while subjective attributes are external to the brand and are created by marketing strategy. For objective attributes we could expect a relationship with the consumer's marginal utility, whereas subjective attributes would require a different treatment. One possibility would be the application of Stigler's theory of the economics of information to advertising, but the integration of this theory and the differential approach is still a task for the future.[27]

---

[24] See Theil (1980).

[25] See R. Dorfman and P.O. Steiner: 1954, "Optimal Advertising and Optimal Quality," *American Economic Review*, **44**, 826-836.

[26] See M. Nerlove and K.J. Arrow: 1962, "Optimal Advertising Policy under Dynamic Conditions," *Econometrica*, **29**, 129-142.

[27] See G.J. Stigler: 1961, "The Economics of Information," *Journal of Political Economy*, **69**, 213-225.

Conclusions

The differential approach has proved to be applicable to areas other than consumption theory, such as the theories of the cost-minimizing and profit-maximizing firms.[28] This has led to:

- Differential input demand systems and output supply systems;
- An interesting independence property of input demand disturbances and output supply disturbances under rational random behavior;
- An input independence transformation and an output independence transformation which may be viewed as the firm's version of the consumer's preference independence transformation;
- An intriguing picture, based on Shephard's lemma, of the consumer as a profit-maximizing firm which sells utility to itself.[29]

The theory of the cost-minimizing firm can be used to endow Leontief's input-output relations with substitution terms.[30] This theory has also been applied to international trade for the estimation of systems of import demand equations.[31] Such applications require strong assumptions. For example, the international trade application proceeds under the heroic assumption that a nation can be viewed as a cost-minimizing producer of its gross national product, with a technology that is appropriately separable in terms of domestic and foreign inputs. By contrast, the application to marketing research is a matter of paying attention to detail. It is the respect for detail that gives marketing research an advantage relative to macroeconomics.

[28] See K. Laitinen and H. Theil: 1978, "Supply and Demand of the Multiproduct Firm," *European Economic Review*, **11**, 107-154; Theil (1979).

[29] This intriguing picture is from Gorman. See Theil (1979), chap. 6.

[30] See Theil (1980).

[31] See K.W. Clements and H. Theil: 1978, "A Simple Method of Estimating Price Elasticities in International Trade," *Economics Letters*, **1**, 133-137; H. Theil and K.W. Clements: 1978, "A Differential Approach to U.S. Import Demand," *Economics Letters*, **1**, 249-252.

CHAPTER 80

THE CUBE LAW REVISITED*

HENRI THEIL
University of Chicago,
Chicago, Illinois, U.S.A.

ABSTRACT. The cube law, which has a history of several decades,[1] may be stated as follows. Consider a two-party system and suppose that the representatives of the two parties are elected according to a single-member district system. Then the ratio of the numbers of representatives elected is approximately equal to the third power of the ratio of the national votes obtained by the two parties. The objective of this note is to provide a theoretical argument which predicts the mathematical form of this relationship.

1. Votes in the Districts and in the Nation

1.1 A LOGIT MODEL FOR VOTES IN A DISTRICT

Let there be n districts and write P_{it} for the proportion of the valid votes obtained by Party 1 in the ith district at the tth election, so that $1 - P_{it}$ is the corresponding proportion of the other party. It is well known that the changes in these proportions from one election to the next are, for most of the districts, in the same direction and of roughly the same order of magnitude. One way of formalizing this is by means of a linear equation of the form $P_{it} = A_i + B_t$, where A_i is a district parameter and B_t an election parameter. However, such a specification may imply proportions P_{it} outside the range from zero to one, which is not attractive. The specification also neglects the fact that it is typically much harder to convince the hard-core party members to vote for the other party than those who are not so much committed. As an example, take two districts (the ith and the jth) with $A_i = .5$ and $A_j = .7$; hence the jth district leans toward Party 1 whereas the ith is "neutral". Take $B_t = .2$, so that $P_{it} = .7$ and $P_{jt} = .9$. Suppose that at the next election $B_{t+1} = .25$, so that $P_{i,t+1} = .75$ and $P_{j,t+1} = .95$. Assume, for simplicity's sake, that the same voters participated in both elections and that no voters shifted from Party 1 to Party 2. Then in the ith district we have five out of every 30 Party 2 voters at the tth election who shifted toward Party 1 at the $(t + 1)$st, whereas it is five out of every ten in the jth district. This does not seem plausible. The ten percent Party 2 voters at the tth election

* This article first appeared in the *Journal of The American Statistical Association*, **65** (1970), 1213-1219. Reprinted with the permission of The American Statistical Association. Henri Theil is a university professor and director of the Center for Mathematical Studies in Business and Economics, University of Chicago.

[1] See (March, 1957-58) and the earlier articles quoted there, which include (Kendall and Stuart, 1950). The author's interest in the subject was stimulated by an article (MacRaw, 1969) written by his colleague.

in the jth district are at least as likely to be hard core as the 30 percent of the ith district, yet one-half of the former group changes its alliance and only one-sixth of the latter.

Both disadvantages are avoided when we modify the specification as follows:

$$\log \frac{P_{it}}{1 - P_{it}} = \alpha_i + \beta_t \ . \tag{1.1}$$

The left-hand side is the natural logarithm of the ratio $P_{it}/(1 - P_{it})$, the "odds" favoring Party 1. This logarithm is the logit corresponding to the proportion P_{it}; it increases monotonically from $-\infty$ to ∞ as P_{it} increases from 0 to 1. The parameters α_i and β_t refer to the district and the election, respectively, and an algebraically large value of α_i (β_t) indicates that the ith district (the tth election) is in favor of Party 1. These parameters may take any real values without violating the zero-unit bounds on P_{it}, simply because the logit in the left-hand side of (1.1) has an infinite range. Also, when P_{it} is close to either limit, a change in β_t which pushes P_{it} even further toward the limit has only a small effect on the value of P_{it}. This is so, because a change in β_t (given α_i) is identical with the change in the logit, and a change in the logit when it is very large in absolute value leads to a small change in the corresponding proportion. This can be illustrated conveniently by means of two graphs, one of which describes the logit as a function of the proportion and a second which proceeds in the opposite way (see the figure). The algebraic forms corresponding to these two curves are

$$L = \log \frac{p}{1 - p} \quad \text{and} \quad p = (1 + e^{-L})^{-1} \tag{1.2}$$

and the second curve is the familiar logistic.

1.2 THE NATIONAL VOTE

Write w_{it} for the proportion of the ith district in the national vote at the tth election. The national proportion of the votes obtained by Party 1 is then

$$P_t = \sum_{i=1}^{n} w_{it} P_{it} \tag{1.3}$$

and the corresponding proportion for Party 2 is $\Sigma_i \, w_{it}(1 - P_{it}) = 1 - P_t$.

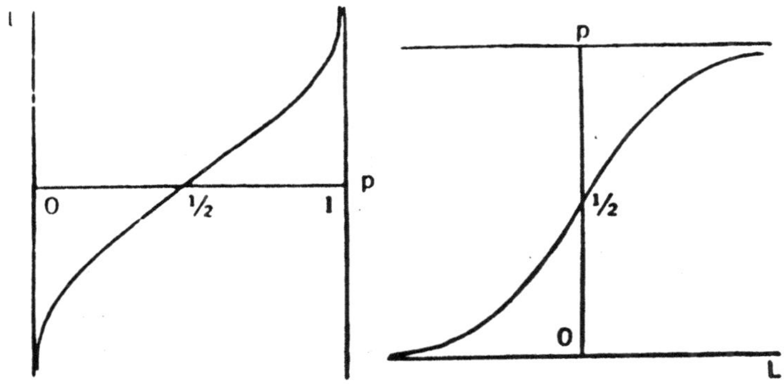

Figure 1. The logit (L) as a function of the proportion (p) and vice versa.

One could attempt to express P_t as a function of the parameters $\alpha_1, \ldots, \alpha_n, B_t$, using the relation between P_{it} and the logit given in (1.2), but doing so directly does not lead to attractive results. Instead, we shall make use of the fact that in a considerable proportion of the districts the political distribution is not very far from 50-50, so that a Taylor approximation around P_{it} = 1/2 leads to a sufficiently accurate result. Consider then p as a function of L as given in (1.2), and in particular the first three derivatives of this function:

$$\frac{dp}{dL} = p^2 e^{-L} \qquad \frac{d^2p}{dL^2} = -p^2 e^{-L}(1 - 2pe^{-L})$$

$$\frac{d^3p}{dL^3} = p^2 e^{-L}(1 - 6pe^{-L} + 6p^2 e^{-2L}) .$$

For L = 0 we have $p(L) = p(0)$ = 1/2. When the derivatives are evaluated at L = 0 we thus obtain:

$$p(0) = 1/2 \qquad p'(0)=1/4 \qquad p''(0)=0 \qquad p'''(0)=-(1/8) . \tag{1.4}$$

A linear Taylor approximation thus implies

$$p \approx p(0) + p'(0)L = (1/2) + (1/4)L \tag{1.5}$$

and it should be noted that it is actually a quadratic approximation because the second derivative vanishes at $L = 0$. For the cubic approximation we obtain:

$$p \approx p(0) + p'(0)L + (1/2!)p''(0)L^2 + (1/3!)p'''(0)L^3 = (1/2) + (1/4)L - (1/48)L^3 \ . \tag{1.6}$$

Below is a list of p values which enables us to evaluate the accuracy of these approximations. For $p = .7$ (the majority party being more than twice as large as the minority party) we obtain a linear approximation of .712, which amounts to an error of less than two percent. For $p = .8$ this error has become six percent, but the error of the cubic approximation is still only about one percent. The errors become relatively large only when p is close to its bounds.

	Linear	*Cubic*
$p = .6$	.601	.600
.7	.712	.699
.8	.847	.791
.9	1.049	.828

We shall use the cubic approximation in order to keep the erros under control. We identify L of (1.6) with the logit of (1.1) and hence p with P_{it}:

$$P_{it} \approx (1/2) + (1/4)(\alpha_i + \beta_t) - (1/48)(\alpha_i + \beta_t)^3 \ . \tag{1.7}$$

Next apply (1.3) to obtain the national proportion of Party 1:

$$P_t \approx (1/2) + (1/4)\sum_{i=1}^{n} w_{it}\alpha_i + (1/4)\beta_t - (1/48)\sum_{i=1}^{n} w_{it}(\alpha_i + \beta_t)^3 \ . \tag{1.8}$$

Now go back to (1.1) and note that one may raise the α's of all districts by an arbitrary constant and reduce the β's of all elections by the same constant without affecting the right-hand side of (1.1) for any pair (i, t). This means that the model (1.1) has one additive degree of freedom, which we shall exploit as follows. Write $\overline{w}_i$ for the average over t (over all elections under consideration) of the district proportions w_{it}. Then impose:

$$\sum_{i=1}^{n} \overline{w}_i \alpha_i = 0 \tag{1.9}$$

so that (1.8) can be written as

$$P_t \approx (1/2) + (1/4)(\beta_t + \varepsilon_t) , \tag{1.10}$$

where

$$\varepsilon_t = \sum_{i=1}^{n} (w_{it} - \overline{w}_i)\, \alpha_i - (1/12) \sum_{i=1}^{n} w_{it} (\alpha_i + \beta_t)^3 . \tag{1.11}$$

The national proportion $1 - P_t$ of Party 2 then becomes $(1/2) - (1/4)(\beta_t + \varepsilon_t)$, and the logit of the national vote:

$$\log \frac{P_t}{1 - P_t} \approx \log \frac{(1/2) + (1/4)(\beta_t + \varepsilon_t)}{(1/2) - (1/4)(\beta_t + \varepsilon_t)} = \log \frac{1 + (1/2)(\beta_t + \varepsilon_t)}{1 - (1/2)(\beta_t + \varepsilon_t)} . \tag{1.12}$$

Using the expansion of the natural log of $1 + x$, we obtain the following third-order approximation:

$$\begin{aligned} \log \frac{P_t}{1 - P_t} &\approx (1/2)(\beta_t + \varepsilon_t) - (1/8)(\beta_t + \varepsilon_t)^2 + (1/24)(\beta_t + \varepsilon_t)^3 \\ &\quad - \left[-(1/2)(\beta_t + \varepsilon_t) - (1/8)(\beta_t + \varepsilon_t)^2 - (1/24)(\beta_t + \varepsilon_t)^3 \right] \\ &= \beta_t + \varepsilon_t + (1/12)(\beta_t + \varepsilon_t)^3 . \end{aligned} \tag{1.13}$$

This result implies:

$$\log \frac{P_t}{1 - P_t} \approx \beta_t \tag{1.14}$$

when ε_t is small relative to β_t in absolute value and β_t^3 small relative to β_t (i.e., β_t^2 is small relative to 1). This is a very convenient result, because it enables us to identify the election parameter β_t as the logit of the national vote. To evaluate the validity of this rule it is appropriate to review the various approximations under which it is derived:

1. Note first of all that the $\approx$ signs in all equations up to and including (1.12) are due to the fact that in (1.6) fourth and higher-order terms are neglected. It was shown in the discussion below that equation that the cubic approximation is adequate at least up to $p = .8$. There will be a small number of districts with larger p values, and the cubic approximation then uses a p which is too small. However, there will also be a (small)

number of districts with $p < .2$, and the approximation error has then a different sign. This leads to partial cancellation of such errors in the national proportion $P_t = \Sigma_i w_{it} P_{it}$.

2. The first component of ε_t is

$$\sum_{i=1}^{n} (w_{it} - \bar{w}_i)\, \alpha_i \,. \tag{1.15}$$

If the number of voters in each district changes proportionally with the national total, we have $w_{it} = \bar{w}_i$ for each pair (i, t), so that the expression (1.15) vanishes. This will be a satisfactory approximation for many districts, but it is of course the case that there are fast-growing districts and others which do not grow at all or even decline. For such districts we may have values of $w_{it} - \bar{w}_i$ that are relatively large absolutely, particularly for the earliest and the latest elections. Yet, this does not mean that the expression (1.15) must be large for any given t. The expression vanishes when the α's are uncorrelated with the w's and although they may be correlated, there does not seem to be any reason why the correlation should be high.

3. The second component of ε_t is -(1/12) times a weighted average of the third powers of the logits (1.1). If it is neglected, we return to the approximation (1.5). Note that these third powers are of either sign, so that in the weighted average there is at least partial cancellation. Neither component of ε_t has a sign which is predictable *a priori*.

4. If we neglect ε_t in (1.13), the logit of the national vote becomes $\beta_t(1 + (1/12)\beta_t^2)$. Typically, P_t varies between .4 and .6, which corresponds to a maximum logit of about .4. Neglecting the relative error of $(1.12)\beta_t^2$, as we do in (1.14), then amounts to an error of about (.16)/12 or a little over one percent.

We may summarize these considerations by stating that, if the logit model (1.1) is applicable, the approximation (1.14) will usually be sufficiently accurate although one can conceive of circumstances under which this accuracy leaves something to be desired. Further progress will have to be based on an analysis of district election data, but this is beyond the scope of the present note.

2. The Candidates Elected

The Party 1 candidate of the ith district is elected if and only if $P_{it} > 1/2$; that is if and only if the logit (1.1) is positive, which amounts to $\alpha_i > \beta_i$. Arrange the districts so that the α's are in ascending order: $\alpha_1 \leq \alpha_2 \leq \ldots \leq \alpha_n$, with the districts that are Party 2 oriented taking values of the subscript and those which are Party 1 oriented taking large values. Write $F(\,)$ for the cumulated distribution function of the α's. Then the proportions of Party 1 and Party 2 candidates elected at the tth election are $1 - F(-\beta_t)$ and $F(-\beta_t)$, respectively. Hence the logit of the representatives elected is

$$\log \frac{1 - F(-\beta_t)}{F(-\beta_t)} . \tag{2.1}$$

To evaluate this expression it will prove convenient to approximate $F(\ )$ by a function with continuous first and second-order derivatives. Write f for the first and g for the second derivative, both evaluated at zero. Then a quadratic Taylor expansion of $F(-\beta_t)$ around zero gives

$$F(-\beta_t) \approx F(0) - f\beta_t + (1/2)g\beta_t^2 . \tag{2.2}$$

For the interpretation of $F(0)$ we go back to (1.9), which shows that the argument 0 is nothing but the weighted mean of the α's. It will typically be the case that this weighted mean is not far from the median, and it will be advantageous to express this as follows:

$$F(0) = (1/2)(1 - \eta) . \tag{2.3}$$

If the weighted mean coincides with the median, we have $\eta = 0$; in general, η will be a number small compared with 1 in absolute value. Using (2.2) and (2.3), we can write the logit (2.1) in the following form:

$$\log \frac{1 - F(-\beta_t)}{F(-\beta_t)} \approx \log \frac{1 + \eta + 2f\beta_t - g\beta_t^2}{1 - \eta - 2f\beta_t + g\beta_t^2} . \tag{2.4}$$

The f on the right-hand side is the density of the continuous approximation of the distribution of the α's at their weighted mean, and g is the rate of change of this density function at the same point. Suppose now that the distribution of the α's is unimodal and that the mode coincides with the weighted mean. The rate of change g is then zero, and we may conclude that g is close to zero when the mode is not too far from the weighted mean.

3. The Cube Law

Equation (1.14) states that the logit of the national vote is approximately equal to β_t. The cube law states that the ratio of the representatives elected is equal to the third power of the national vote ratio, or equivalently that the logit of the representatives elected is three times the logit of the national vote. This means that the logit (2.4) should be approximately equal to $3\beta_t$. Suppose now that the median, the mode and the weighted mean of the distribution of the α's all coincide, so that η and g of (2.4) are not only small but actually zero. Then the logit (2.4) may be further simplified to

$$\log \frac{1 - F(-\beta_t)}{F(-\beta_t)} \approx 4f\beta_t \tag{3.1}$$

with an approximation error of order β_t^3. Thus, the cube law implies $f = 3/4$. To interpret this value, assume that the distribution of the α's is normal with variance σ^2, so that the density at the mean is $f = 1/\sigma\sqrt{2\pi}$. When equating this to 3/4 we obtain a σ of about 1/2. Then go back to (1.1), which shows that the standard deviation of the α's is identical with that of the n logits at the tth election, and to $p'(0) = 1/4$ in (1.4), which shows that when the logits are in the neighborhood of zero (and hence the vote proportions in the neighborhood of 1/2) the variations in the proportions are one quarter of those of the logits. This suggests that at each election the standard deviation of the vote proportions across districts must be about one quarter of the σ of the α's. This gives $(1/4) \times (1/2) = (1/8)$, which is in satisfactory agreement with numerical results described in earlier publications on the basis of a normal distribution of the vote proportions across districts.[2]

It is important to note that the proportionality constant $4f$ in (3.1) is formulated in terms of the rate of change of the cumulated distribution function of the α's at their weighted mean. This is a characteristic of the *central part* of the distribution of the α's. It is of course true that this rate of change is determined uniquely by the standard deviation if the distribution is normal, but it is also true that the standard deviation itself is a measure of dispersion rather than a characteristic of the central part of the distribution. When the α's have a leptokurtic or platykurtic distribution, the rate of change of the cumulated distribution at the mean may take quite different values even when the standard deviation is fixed.

References

Kendall, M.G. and A. Stuart: 1950, "The Law of Cubic Proportions in Election Results," *British Journal of Sociology*, **1**, 183-197.

MacRae, Duncan, Jr.: 1969, "Models on Legislative Representation," University of Chicago, Illinois (mimeographed).

March, James G.: 1957-58, "Party Legislative Representation as a Function of Election Results," *Public Opinion Quarterly*, **21**, 521-542.

[2] See Kendall and Stuart (1950) and March (1957-58), where a normal distribution with variance .0187 (standard deviation .137) is discussed.

CHAPTER 81

THE APPORTIONMENT PROBLEM AND THE EUROPEAN PARLIAMENT*

HENRI THEIL
University of Chicago,
Chicago, Illinois, U.S.A.

LINUS SCHRAGE
University of Chicago,
Chicago, Illinois, U.S.A.

ABSTRACT: A class of allocation rules is introduced for allocating votes in a parliament to parties based on population. A unique feature of the class is that a well-defined objective function is associated with each allocation rule in the class. It is shown that the objective function corresponding to the "square root" allocation rule is of particular interest. This rule attempts to give each party a number of votes proportional to the square root of its size. Also described is an allocation *procedure* which takes care of the typical situation when the allocation *rule* results in fractional votes being allocated whereas in fact one allows only whole number votes to be allocated. Allocations for the European Parliament using the above class of rules are compared with the currently proposed allocations for that body.

1. Introduction

Recently a decision was made to elect the European Parliament by direct universal suffrage. Several proposals were formulated, listed in columns (2) to (5) of Table 1, to solve the problem of how many seats must be allocated to the participating countries. Efforts were made to apply general principles, such as "the highest degree of proportionality should be achieved between the number of inhabitants of a State and the number of its representatives . . ." but a comparison with column (1) shows that the apportionments proposed are far from proportional to the population. Nevertheless, the idea that an apportionment should be based on general principles, rather than ad hoc negotiations of the parties involved, is a sound one. The objective of this paper is to discuss such a principle and to apply it to the European Parliament.

2. A Class of Representation Systems

We write n for the number of participating countries, P_i for the population of the ith country, and N for the total number of Parliament members. We consider the representation system

* This article first appeared in the *European Economic Review*, **9** (1977), 247-263. Reprinted with the permission of Elsevier Science Publishers B.V. (North-Holland). Research supported in part by NSF Grant GS-41319X.

TABLE 1. Populations and Apportionment Proposals

	Population (thousands) (1)	First EEC proposal (2)	French proposal (3)	Irish proposal (4)	German proposal (5)
W. Germany	62,041	72	66	75	81
United Kingdom	56,056	68	60	71	81
Italy	55,361	67	59	70	81
France	53,780	66	57	69	81
Netherlands	13,450	27	17	30	25
Belgium	9,772	23	13	26	24
Denmark	5,052	17	9	20	16
Ireland	3,086	13	7	18	15
Luxembourg	357	6	3	9	6
Total	258,955	359	291	388	410

$$[N_i(\alpha)/N] = \left(\frac{P_i^\alpha}{\sum_{j=1}^{n} P_j^\alpha} \right), \qquad i = 1, \ldots, n, \tag{1}$$

where $N_i(\alpha)$ is the number of seats allocated to the ith country. This number depends on α, which is non-negative:

$$\alpha \geq 0 . \tag{2}$$

Eq. (1) defines a class of representation systems, the number of which are obtained by selecting a particular numerical value of α. This system has been used or suggested in various contexts on a substantial scale. Proportionate representation corresponds to $\alpha = 1$. A smaller α reduces the representation of large units relative to smaller units. The International Federation of Operational Research Societies (IFORS) selected $\alpha = ½$: each national member society has a vote in IFORS which is proportional to the square root of its membership. For $\alpha = 0$ each unit has the same representation: $N_i(0)/N = 1/n$ for each i. This is applied in the U.S. Senate, where each State is represented by two Senators irrespective of its population. When $\alpha > 1$ is selected, the representation of the larger units is increased relative to the smaller ones. Grosfeld (1967) proposed $\alpha = 2$ for the Dutch Parliament by assigning to each party a number of seats proportional to the square of the number of votes which it received in the election. This proposal is based on the large number of political parties, none of which receives a majority of the votes; the use of the square rule may enable the largest party to obtain a majority of seats in the Parliament. Finally, there is the so-called cube law (Kendall-Stuart, 1950; Theil, 1972, pp.

204-217) which states that, in a two-party system with single-member constituencies, the ratio of the number of seats obtained by the two parties is approximately equal to the cube of the ratio of the number of votes. This corresponds to $\alpha = 3$ and $n = 2$ in (1).

The class of representation systems (1) can be justified by means of the principle of *weak proportionality* (Theil, 1969; Theil, 1972, pp. 96-97). Strict proportionality implies that the seat ratio N_i/N_j equals the population (or vote) ratio P_i/P_j for all pairs (i, j). Weak proportionality means that, for all pairs (i, j) the seat ratio N_i/N_j is determined uniquely as a function of the ratio P_i/P_j

$$N_i/N_j = f(P_i/P_j) \ , \qquad i, j = 1, \ldots, n \ , \tag{3}$$

where $f(\ )$ is a continuous non-decreasing function which takes positive values for all positive values of the argument. Consider then the identities

$$N_i/N_k = (N_i/N_j)/(N_j/N_k) \quad \text{and} \quad P_i/P_k = (P_i/P_j)/(P_j/P_k) \ ,$$

which imply $f(P_i/P_k) = f(P_i/P_j)\, f(P_j/P_k)$ in view of (3). Since this result holds identically for all values of the argument, we may write it in the general form

$$f(x,y) = f(x) f(y) \ , \qquad x, y > 0 \ . \tag{4}$$

When we take logarithms in (4) and then antilogs, it appears that $f(x)$ must be of the form x^{α} for some $\alpha \geq 0$. Hence, the right-hand side of (3) equals $(P_i/P_j)^{\alpha}$; after which we obtain (1) from the requirement that the N_i's add up to N.

The weak proportionality criterion is one justification of the class of representation systems (1). Another justification is based on concepts from information theory, with the entropy used as a measure of dividedness. Details are provided in Appendix A, also on the logarithmic transformation mentioned below eq. (4).

The above results suggest that it is worthwhile to check whether the proposals of Table 1 are in approximate agreement with (1) for some value of α. Figure 1 answers this question with the population size measured horizontally and the proposed number of representatives vertically, both on a logarithmic scale.[1] The slopes of the straight lines fitted through the four sets of points (the $\hat{\alpha}$'s indicated on the right) vary between just under 0.5 and just over 0.6 except that of the French proposal, which takes a larger value. The method of fitting is described in Appendix B.

---

[1] The four large countries (W. Germany, United Kingdom, Italy and France) are represented by points that are very close to each other. These countries are jointly indicated by L below the horizontal axis.

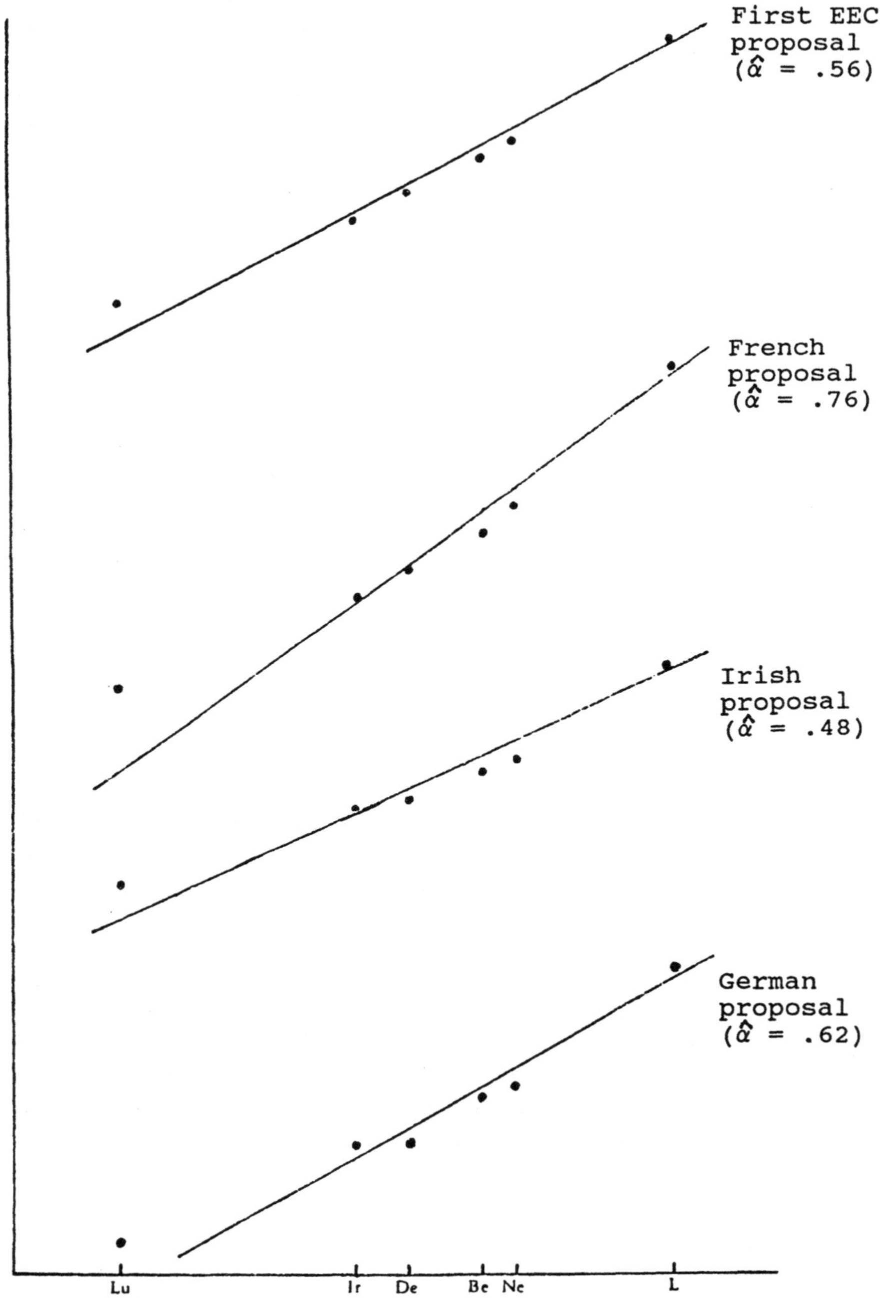

Figure 1. Double-log illustration of the apportionment proposals.

3. The Square-Root Representation System

Given that most of the $\hat{\alpha}$'s discussed above are close to the value ½ which IFORS selected for an adequate representation of its member societies of various sizes, an obvious question is whether this specific member of the class (1) has particular merits.[2] Penrose (1946, 1952) advocated this representation system on the basis of the assumption that a large majority of people tend to vote in a random manner. An alternative approach, suggested in Theil (1971) uses a particular criterion function. We define p_i as the population share of the ith country and w_i as its representation share in the European Parliament,

$$p_i = P_i/P \quad \text{and} \quad w_i = N_i/N \ , \quad i = 1, \ldots, n \ , \tag{5}$$

where $P = P_1 + \cdots + P_n$. Each citizen of the ith country thus has a proportion equal to w_i of Parliament members of his own nationality. So let us assume that when such a citizen expresses a desire, the chance is w_i that he meets a willing ear. This implies that, in a long series of such expressed desires, the number of efforts per successful effort is $1/w_i$. Obviously, the larger this number, the worse the Parliament is from this individual's point of view. Our criterion is to minimize its expectation over the combined population of all n countries,

$$\sum_{i=1}^{n} (p_i/w_i) \ , \tag{6}$$

subject to the constraint $\Sigma_i \, w_i = 1$. So we construct the Lagrangean function $\Sigma_i \, (p_i/w_i) - \lambda(\Sigma_i \, w_i - 1)$ and equate its derivative with respect to w_i equal to zero. This gives $-p_i/w_i^2 - \lambda = 0$, which shows that w_i is proportional to the square root of p_i. Using $\Sigma_i \, w_i = 1$, we thus obtain

---

[2] It is also instructive to compare this number with the bicameral system of the U.S. with respect to the individual States. The U.S. Senate uses $\alpha = 0$; the U.S. House of Representatives is based on districts with about equal populations and thus corresponds approximately to $\alpha = 1$. Hence $\alpha = 1/2$ may be viewed as the average of the α values of the two components of the American bicameral system. We should add that the square-root representation is related, although not very precisely, to concepts of voting power in weighted voting schemes. The various ideas of voting power, such as described by Lucas (1974), generally indicate that voting power is more than proportional to the number of votes directly controlled. Thus, if power should be proportional to population size, then votes should be less than proportional to population.

$$w_i = \left(\frac{p_i^{1/2}}{\sum_{j=1}^{n} p_j^{1/2}} \right) , \qquad i = 1 , \ . \ . \ . \ , n \ , \tag{7}$$

which is equivalent to (1) for $\alpha = ½$. Substitution of (7) in (6) shows that

$$\left(\sum_{i=1}^{n} p_i^{1/2} \right)^2 \tag{8}$$

is the minimum value of the criterion function (6).

We conclude that the case $\alpha = ½$ results from minimizing the expectation of the number of efforts per successful effort over all individual citizens of all countries. Other members of the class (1) can also be justified by means of a particular criterion function, but the interpretation of this function is not as straightforward as that of (6).

The general criterion function is that of a minimum of

$$\sum_{i=1}^{n} p_i w_i^{(\alpha - 1)/\alpha} \ , \tag{9}$$

if $\alpha < 1$, and a maximum of (9) if $\alpha > 1$, in both cases subject to $\Sigma_i \ w_i = 1$. For $\alpha = 1$, (9) does not apply and must be replaced by a maximum of

$$\sum_{i=1}^{n} p_i \log w_i \ , \tag{10}$$

which has a simple interpretation in terms of concepts from information theory. Further details are provided in Appendix C.

The above developments are all in terms of the viewpoints of the individuals. We proceed to a more macroscopic approach by considering the ratio P_i/N_i, which is the average number by citizens represented by the Parliament members from the ith country. Obviously, each country would like to minimize this ratio, so that we may want to consider the criterion of a minimum of

$$(1/n) \sum_{i=1}^{n} (P_i/N_i) \ , \tag{11}$$

subject to $\Sigma_i N_i = N$. But it follows from (5) that minimizing (11) is equivalent to minimizing (6). Therefore, the square-root representation system minimizes the average (over all countries) of the average numbers of citizens represented by the Parliament members from their own countries. An alternative analysis in terms of the reciprocal ratios (N_i/P_i), which is mathematically equivalent to consumer demand analysis, is discussed in Appendix D.

4. Geometric Analysis of the Representation Systems

A geometric picture of the class of representation systems (1) in the n-dimensional Euclidean space has considerable clarifying value. Figure 2 illustrates the case $n = 2$, with the characteristics of the countries 1 and 2 measured along the axes. The points A_1 and A_2 are at unit distance from the origin; hence A_1A_2 is the locus of all points whose coordinates are positive and add up to 1. Let P and C be the points whose i^{th} coordinates equal p_i and 1, respectively. The curve between P and C is the locus of all points with ith coordinate equal to p_i^{α} for α decreasing from 1 to 0; hence the points on this curve have coordinates that are proportional to the right-hand numerator of (1). When α increases from 1 to ∞, the points whose i^{th} coordinates equal p_i^{α} move from P toward the origin. This part of the curve is not shown in the figure.

The curve through A_1, S and A_2 is the unit circle in the positive quadrant. This circle is the locus of all points for which the sum of the squares of the coordinates equals 1. Consequently, the ith coordinate of the intersection point S of the circle and the curve through P and C equals $\sqrt{p_i}$. Further, the intersection point W of the lines OS and A_1A_2 has an ith coordinate equal to

$$\frac{p_i^{1/2}}{\sum_{j=1}^{n} p_j^{1/2}}, \tag{12}$$

which is identical to the representation share (7). The squared length of the vector OW is

$$\frac{\sum_{j=1}^{n} p_i}{\left(\sum_{j=1}^{n} p_j^{1/2}\right)^2} = \frac{1}{\left(\sum_{j=1}^{n} p_j^{1/2}\right)^2}, \tag{13}$$

so that $(OW)^2$ is simply the reciprocal of the minimum (8) of the criterion function (6). It is also easily verified that the "representation point" W is always closer to the midpoint of A_1A_2 than is the "population point" P.

In the general case we have n axes, one for each country, and n points $A_1, \ldots,$ A_n on these axes at unit distance from the origin. The line A_1A_2 is replaced by the $(n-1)$-dimensional plane through $A_1, \ldots, A_n$ and the unit circle becomes the n-dimensional unit sphere. The construction of the points P, S and W is then a straightforward extension of the case $n = 2$.

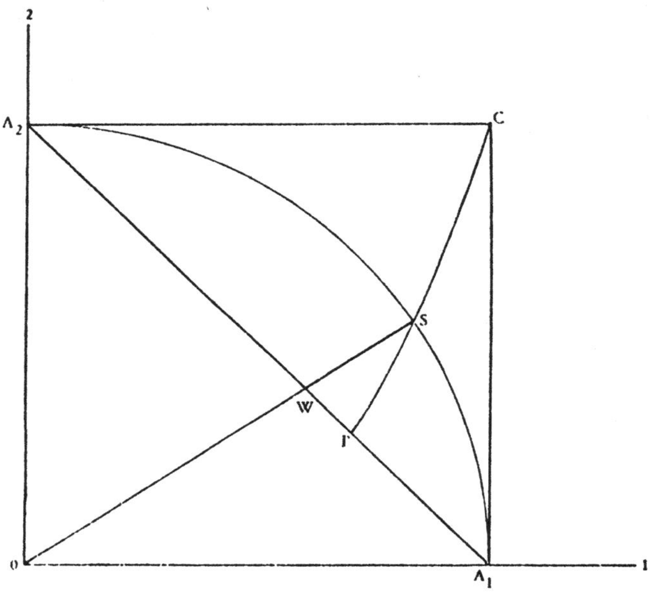

Figure 2. The geometry of the representation system (1).

5. Finding the Integer Solution

So far we have ignored the fact that the number of representatives of each country must be an integer. This problem arises in all representation systems and is solved in various ways, but these methods have the disadvantage of being much more explicit about *how* an integer solution is obtained than about *why* this particular solution is selected. However, when we have the well-defined criterion of a minimum value of (6), the problem can be solved satisfactorily. It is not a matter of rounding the representation obtained from the square-root rule; rather, it is a matter of minimizing (6) over the set of representations that correspond to integer values.

We use (5) to write the criterion (6) in the form

$$\min_{N_i} \sum_{i=1}^{n} \frac{p_i}{N_i/N} \quad \text{subject to} \quad \sum_{i=1}^{n} N_i = N \ , \tag{14}$$

and subject to the additional constraint that the N_i's be non-negative integers. Note that $N_i = 0$ for some i implies that the function to be minimized becomes infinitely large; hence the additional constraint can be strengthened to that of positive integer values of all N_i's. Therefore, our criterion implies that each country has at least one representative; it is unnecessary to impose this as a constraint. This result also implies that the problem is solved for $N = n$, since each of the n countries must then have one representative in the Parliament.

Given that the problem has been solved for $N = n$, we may want to ask what the solution is for $N = n + 1$. Indeed this is a fruitful approach to the problem, because it can be shown (see Appendix E) that there always exist optimal integer solutions of the minimizing problem (14) for which $N_1, \ldots, N_n$ are non-decreasing functions of N.[3] Therefore, if we raise the size of the Parliament by one seat, no country will lose a seat and, hence, exactly one country will obtain one additional seat. It is a simple matter to identify that one country which, when assigned the additional seat, causes the greatest improvement in the criterion function. So, in the case of the European Parliament with nine countries represented, we start with $N = 9$ and assign one seat to each country. Next we take $N = 10$; it will cause no surprise that this yields a second seat for Germany. We continue in this way for successive larger values of N, yielding second seats for the United Kingdom ($N = 11$), Italy ($N = 12$) and France ($N = 13$), followed by third seats for Germany ($N = 14$), the United Kingdom ($N = 15$), Italy ($N = 16$) and France ($N = 17$), after which the Netherlands obtains a second seat ($N = 18$) and Germany a fourth ($N = 19$) and Belgium a second ($N = 20$). Denmark obtains a second seat at $N = 28$, Ireland at $N = 35$, and Luxembourg at $N = 99$.

The mathematical rule behind these numerical results is straightforward. Suppose that the allocation $(N_1, \ldots, N_n)$ for some N has been obtained. It follows from (14) that this allocation minimizes $\Sigma_i\ (p_i/N_i)$ subject to $\Sigma_i\ N_i = N$. We raise N to $N + 1$ and allocate the new seat to the jth country ($j = 1, \ldots, n$), which, yields the following expression which is to be minimized:

---

[3] This non-decreasing property excludes the so-called Alabama paradox; see, for example, Balinski and Young (1976). These authors propose an apportionment in which each county is assigned a certain minimum number of seats. One disadvantage of this proposal is that there is no rule for the value of this minimum. Another is that countries whose population entitles them to no more than the minimum are equally represented irrespective of their populations ('you are so small that it doesn't matter how small you are') and that these countries tend to be overrrepresented relative to those just above the minimum. For example, for N between 300 and 400 and a minimum number of seats between three and six, Ireland and Luxembourg are about equally represented in spite of the fact that Luxembourg's population is only about one-ninth that of Ireland's. The eight apportionments in Table II all assign to Luxembourg a number of seats between one-third and one-half of that of Ireland.

$$\sum_{i \neq j} \frac{p_i}{N_i} + \frac{p_j}{N_j + 1} = \sum_{i=1}^{n} \frac{p_i}{N_i} - \left(\frac{p_j}{N_j} - \frac{p_j}{N_j + 1} \right). \tag{15}$$

The first term on the right is a fixed number, obtained from the previous step. Therefore, the jth country that will obtain the additional seat is that for which the expression in parentheses in (15) takes the largest value. An extension is discussed in Appendix E.

Table 2 contains the results for the four proposed values of N (see Table 1). Columns (1a), (2a), (3a) and (4a) are the apportionment proposals; they are reproduced from Table 1. Columns (1b) to (4b) show the result of the criterion (14) applied to the same value of N. As is to be expected, corresponding apportionments are characterized by some minor and some not-so-minor differences. Note the three entries marked by an asterisk; they are the number of French seats according to the French proposal, that of the Irish seats according to the Irish proposal, and that of the German seats according to the German proposal. These proposed numbers are all larger than the corresponding numbers based on (14), which illustrates the danger of relying on proposals made by interested parties. In contrast to this, the criterion (14) yields a straightforward solution of the apportionment problem once the decision on the total number of seats (N) has been made. It does not require further negotiations when other nations join the European Parliament, nor when the population shares change over time.

TABLE 2. Apportionment Proposals Compared with Those Based on (14)

	French total		EEC total		Irish total		German total	
	(1a)	(1b)	(2a)	(2b)	(3a)	(3b)	(4a)	(4b)
W. Germany	66	55	72	68	75	74	81*	78
United Kingdom	60	53	68	65	71	70	81	74
Italy	59	52	67	64	70	69	81	74
France	57*	51	66	64	69	69	81	72
Netherlands	17	26	27	32	30	34	25	36
Belgium	13	22	23	27	26	29	24	31
Denmark	9	16	17	19	20	21	16	22
Ireland	7	12	13	15	18*	16	15	17
Luxembourg	3	4	6	5	9	6	6	6
Total	291	291	359	359	388	388	410	410

Appendix A: Further Details on the Class of Representation Systems

We introduce $\xi = \log x$ and $\eta = \log y$,[4] so that $\log f(x) = \log f(e^{\xi}) = \phi(\xi)$ say. Next we take logarithms of both sides of (4),

$$\phi(\xi + \eta) = \phi(\xi) + \phi(\eta) \ . \tag{A.1}$$

Since (4) holds for all positive values of x and y, (A.1) holds for all values of ξ and η in $(-\infty, \infty)$. Given that $f(\ )$ and hence $\phi(\ )$ are continuous nondecreasing functions, (A.1) implies that $\phi(\xi)$ must be of the form $\alpha\xi$ for some non-negative constant α. Therefore, $f(x) = e^{\phi(\xi)} = (e^{\xi})^{\alpha} = x^{\alpha}$.

Consider the entropy of the representation shares $w_1 = N_1/N, \ldots, w_n = N_n/N$,

$$H_w = -\sum_{i=1}^{n} w_i \log w_i \ . \tag{A.2}$$

This entropy is a measure of dividedness of the representation; it vanishes when only one country is represented ($w_i = 1$ for some i and $w_j = 0$ for all $j \neq i$) and it takes its maximum value when all proportions are equal ($w_1 = \ldots = w_n = 1/n$). The proposals listed in Table 1 all have in common that the representation entropy (A.2) exceeds the entropy based on population shares; they assign more (fewer) seats to small (large) countries than is in accordance with the population shares.

Imagine that it is decided to select representation shares $w_1, \ldots, w_n$ which are as close as possible to the corresponding population shares $p_1 = P_1/P, \ldots, p_n = P_n/P$ (P = the combined population of the n countries) subject to the condition that the representation entropy H_w takes a given numerical value. The following is our criterion of closeness:

$$I(w{:}p) = \sum_{i=1}^{n} w_i \log (w_i/p_i) \ . \tag{A.3}$$

In the language of information theory, $I(w{:}p)$ is the expected information of the message which transforms the p_i's into the w_i's. We have $I(w{:}p) = 0$ if $p_i = w_i$ for each i, and $I(w{:}p) > 0$ otherwise.

The criterion stated in the discussion preceding (A.3) amounts to the selection of the w_i's which minimizes (A.3) subject to $\Sigma_i \, w_i = 1$ and to the condition that the right-hand side of (A.2) takes a given value. This can be performed by differentiating an appropriate Lagrangean function, which leads to the result that w_i is proportional to p_i^{α}

---

[4] All logarithms used are natural logarithms.

for some $\alpha \geq 0$, and hence N_i proportional to p_i^α in agreement with (1), with some minor provisos. For details see Theil (1972, pp. 91-96).

Appendix B: Fitting the Proposed Apportionments

We write (1) in the equivalent form

$$w_i(\alpha) = \frac{p_i^\alpha}{\sum_{j=1}^{n} p_j^\alpha}, \qquad i = 1, \cdots, n. \tag{B.1}$$

For any of the columns (2) to (5) in Table 1, write $\overline{w}_i$ for the proposed number of seats of the ith country divided by the proposed total number of seats. As a criterion of fit for the class (B.1) we use

$$I(\overline{w}:w_\alpha) = \sum_{i=1}^{n} \overline{w}_i \log\left(\overline{w}_i / w_i(\alpha)\right), \tag{B.2}$$

which is to be minimized by varying α. This is equivalent to maximizing

$$\sum_{i=1}^{n} \overline{w}_i \log w_i(\alpha) = \alpha \sum_{i=1}^{n} \overline{w}_i \log p_i - \log\left(\sum_{i=1}^{n} p_i^\alpha\right). \tag{B.3}$$

The first-order derivative of the right-hand side of (B.3) with respect to α is

$$\sum_{i=1}^{n} \overline{w}_i \log p_i - \left(\frac{\sum_{i=1}^{n} p_i^\alpha \log p_i}{\sum_{i=1}^{n} p_i^\alpha}\right) = \sum_{i=1}^{n} \left[\overline{w}_i - w_i(\alpha)\right] \log p_i, \tag{B.4}$$

and the second-order derivative can be written as

$$-\sum_{i=1}^{n} w_i(\alpha)\left[\log p_i - \sum_{j=1}^{n} w_j(\alpha)\log p_j\right]^2 . \tag{B.5}$$

Using a quadratic approximation of (B.3) based on (B.4) and (B.5) [which is equivalent to applying the Newton-Rapheson method to (B.4)], we can find the optimal value of α iteratively. This value, $\hat{\alpha}$, and the minimum value $I(\bar{w}:w_{\hat{\alpha}})$ of (B.2) are shown below for each proposal. The convergence is very rapid in each case.

	EEC	French	Irish	German
$\hat{\alpha}$	0.56	0.76	0.48	0.62
$I(\bar{w}:w_{\hat{\alpha}})$	0.0021	0.0048	0.0036	0.0057

Appendix C: Alternative Criterion Functions

To obtain the extremum of (9) subject to $\Sigma_i\, w_i = 1$ we construct the Lagrangean function

$$\sum_{i=1}^{n} p_i w_i^{(\alpha-1)/\alpha} - \mu\left(\sum_{i=1}^{n} w_i - 1\right), \tag{C.1}$$

which we differentiate with respect to w_i:

$$\frac{\alpha-1}{\alpha} p_i\, w_i^{-1/\alpha} - \mu . \tag{C.2}$$

By equating this to zero we find that w_i is proportional to p_i^{α}, which yields the class of representative systems (1). A sufficient condition for a constrained maximum (minimum) of (9) subject to $\Sigma_i\, w_i = 1$ is that the second-order derivatives of the Lagrangean function (C.1) with respect to $w_1, \ldots, w_n$ form a negative (positive) definite matrix. So we differentiate (C.2) with respect to w_j, which gives zero for $i \neq j$ and

$$-\frac{\alpha-1}{\alpha^2} p_i\, w_i^{-(1+\alpha)/\alpha} \tag{C.3}$$

for $i = j$. Since the expression (C.3) is positive for $\alpha < 1$ and negative for $\alpha > 1$, this shows that we minimize (9) for $\alpha < 1$ and maximize for $\alpha > 1$.

When we proceed for (10) as in (C.1) and differentiate with respect to w_i, we obtain $p_i/w_i - \mu = 0$, which yields proportionate representation [(1) for $\alpha = 1$]. Note that maximizing (10) is equivalent to minimizing the information expectation

$$I(p{:}w) = \sum_{i=1}^{n} p_i \log(p_i/w_i) \; . \tag{C.4}$$

Appendix D: Representation Ratios

We define $x_i = N_i/P_i$ as the representation ratio of the ith country: the number of representatives per inhabitant. Each country would like to have as high a representation ratio as possible. To express these desires, we formulate a utility function,

$$u = u(x_1, \ldots, x_n) \; , \tag{D.1}$$

which is to be maximized subject to $\Sigma_i N_i = N$ and hence, in view of $x_i = N_i/P_i$, to

$$\sum_{i=1}^{n} P_i x_i = N \; . \tag{D.2}$$

The problem of maximizing (D.1) subject to (D.2) is mathematically equivalent to that of the consumer who maximizes a utility function subject to a budget constraint. For the consumer, x_i is the quantity of the ith good, P_i its price, and N the given total amount available for spending. Note that, in the apportionment problem, the population size P_i thus plays the role of the price of the representation ratio x_i.[5]

A simple symmetric additive specification of (D.1) is

$$u(x_1, \ldots, x_n) = -\sum_{i=1}^{n} \frac{1}{x_i} \; . \tag{D.3}$$

It follows from (5) and $x_i = N_i/P_i$ that maximizing (D.3) is equivalent to minimizing (6). Also, since (D.3) and

[5] Similarly, the representation share w_i plays the role of the budget share of the ith good in consumption theory. It would be interesting to compare the geometric analysis of section 4 with the orthogonal transformation of square roots of budget shares which is implied by the preference independence transformation of consumption theory (Theil, 1975/6, sect. 12.4).

$$\left(\frac{1}{n}\sum_{i=1}^{n}\frac{1}{x_i}\right)^{-1} \tag{D.4}$$

are monotonically increasing functions of each other, maximizing (D.3) is equivalent to maximizing (D.4). Since (D.4) is the harmonic mean of the x_i's, the square-root representation system thus maximizes the harmonic mean of the representation ratios of the n countries.

Appendix E: The Integer Solutions of the Class of Representation Systems

We can write the criteria (9) and (10) as

$$\min_{N_i} h(N) + k(N)\sum_{i=1}^{n} g_i(N_i) \ , \tag{E.1}$$

where, in the case of (9) for $0 < \alpha < 1$,

$$h(N)=0, \quad k(N) = N^{(1-\alpha)/\alpha}, \quad g_i(N_i) = p_i N_i^{(\alpha-1)/\alpha} \ ,$$

while for $\alpha = 1$ [the case (10)]:

$$h(N) = \log N, \quad k(N) = 1, \quad g_i(N_i) = -p_i \log N_i \ .$$

Since $h(N)$ and $k(N)$ are constants with regard to the optimization over the N_i's, and since $k(N)$ is positive, we can simplify (E.1) to the problem

$$\min_{N_i}\sum_{i=1}^{n} g_i(N_i) \ , \tag{E.2}$$

subject to

$$\sum_{i=1}^{n} N_i = N \ ,$$

and

$$N_i = \text{positive integer.}$$

Note that $g_i(\ )$ is a convex function, i.e.,

$$g_i(x) - g_i(x - 1) \text{ is an increasing function of } x. \tag{E.3}$$

This is the only property of $g_i(\ )$ that will be used in the next three paragraphs.

For given N, let $(N_1^*, \ldots, N_n^*)$ be an integer solution which minimizes $\Sigma_i\ g_i(N_i)$ subject to $\Sigma_i\ N_i = N$. We define the left and right differences,

$$L_i(N) = g_i(N_i^* - 1) - g_i(N_i^*) , \tag{E.4}$$

and

$$R_i(N) = g_i(N_i^*) - g_i(N_i^* + 1) , \tag{E.5}$$

where the insertion of N in parentheses after L_i and R_i indicates that N_i^* and hence also $g_i(N_i^* - 1)$, $g_i(N_i^*)$ and $g_i(N_i^* + 1)$ depend on N. Suppose that we raise N_i^* by 1 and lower N_j^* by 1 ($i \neq j$), so that $\Sigma_i\ g_i(N_i)$ increases by

$$g_i(N_i^* + 1) + g_j(N_j^* - 1) - \left[g_i(N_i^*) + g_j(N_j^*)\right] = L_j(N) - R_i(N) .$$

This must be non-negative, because otherwise $(N_1^*, \ldots, N_n^*)$ does not minimize $\Sigma_i\ g_i(N_i)$. Therefore,

$$L_j(N) \geq R_i(N), \quad \text{for} \quad i \neq j . \tag{E.6}$$

Next we raise N by 1. At least one of the values $N_1^*, \ldots, N_n^*$ must then increase; let this be N_i^*, which becomes $N_i^* + r$, where r is a positive integer, so that (E.4) yields

$$L_i(N + 1) = g_i(N_i^* + r - 1) - g_i(N_i^* + r) . \tag{E.7}$$

The right-hand side equals $R_i(N)$ given in (E.5) if $r = 1$, and it is smaller than $R_i(N)$ if $r > 1$ in view of the convexity property (E.3). Therefore,

$$L_i(N + 1) \leq R_i(N) . \tag{E.8}$$

Suppose that the increase of N by 1 lowers N_j^*; we proceed to prove that this possibility can be ignored. If N_j^* becomes $N_j^* - s$, where s is a positive integer, (E.5) yields

$$R_j(N+1) = g_j(N_j^* - s) - g_j(N_j^* - s + 1) \ , \tag{E.9}$$

which equals $L_j(N)$ if $s = 1$ and exceeds $L_j(N)$ if $s > 1$ in view of (E.3). Therefore,

$$R_j(N+1) \geq L_j(N) \ . \tag{E.10}$$

We proceed to combine (E.10), (E.6) and (E.8):

$$R_j(N+1) \geq L_j(N) \geq R_i(N) \geq L_i(N+1) \ .$$

Specifically, $R_j(N+1) \geq L_i(N+1)$. It follows from (E.7) and (E.9) that this can be written as

$$g_i(N_i^* + r) + g_j(N_j^* - s) \geq g_i(N_i^* + r - 1) + g_j(N_j^* - s + 1) \ ,$$

which shows that we can lower $N_i^* + r$ and raise $N_j^* - s$ by 1 without damaging the criterion (E.2). When we move from a Parliament of size N to one of size $N + 1$, the number of increases in representation must exceed the number of decreases by 1. So, whenever we find a country j with fewer representatives under $N + 1$ than under N, we can always find a country i with more representatives and engage in a transfer from i to j with at worst no improvement in the criterion (E.2). These transfers, none of which raises $\Sigma_i\, g_i(N_i)$, can be repeated until each country has at least as many representatives under $N + 1$ as it had under N, which completes the proof.

For $\alpha > 1$, similar arguments apply if we minimize the negation of (9). One must, however, start at $N = 1$. Once the apportionment problem has been solved for a particular value of N, we assign the $(N + 1)^{st}$ seat to the country j which maximizes

$$p_j N_j^{(\alpha-1)/\alpha} - p_j(N_j+1)^{(\alpha-1)/\alpha} \ , \quad \text{if} \quad 0<\alpha<1 \ , \tag{E.11}$$

$$p_j \log\left([N_j+1]/N_j\right) \ , \quad \text{if} \quad \alpha = 1 \ , \tag{E.12}$$

$$p_j(N_j+1)^{(\alpha-1)/\alpha} - p_j N_j^{(\alpha-1)/\alpha} \ , \quad \text{if} \quad \alpha>1 \ . \tag{E.13}$$

The assignment discussed below (15) corresponds to (E.11) for $\alpha = ½$.

References

Balinski, M.L. and H.P. Young: 1976, "A Problem of Fair Division: Apportioning the European Parliament," Research Memorandum RM-76-55, International Institute for Applied Systems Analysis, Laxenburg, Austria.

Grosfeld, F.: 1967, "De kwadratuur van de democratische cirkelgang," *Vrij Nederland,* December 30, 4.

Kendall, M.G. and A. Stuart: 1950, "The Law of Cubic Proportion in Election Results," *British Journal of Sociology* **1**, 183-196.

Lucas, W.F.: 1974, "Measuring Power in Weighted Voting Schemes," Technical Report no. 227, Department of Operations Research, Cornell University, Ithaca, New York.

Penrose, L.S.: 1946, "The Elementary Statistics of Majority Voting," *Journal of the Royal Statistical Society* **109**, 53-57.

Penrose, L.S.: 1952, *On the Objective Study of Crowd Behaviour*, H.K. Lewis, London.

Theil, H.: 1969, "The Desired Political Entropy," *The American Political Science Review* **63**, 521-525.

Theil, H.: 1971, "The Allocation of Power that Minimizes Tension," *Operations Research* **19**, 977-982.

Theil, H.: 1972, *Statistical Decomposition Analysis with Applications in the Social and Administrative Sciences*, North-Holland, Amsterdam.

Theil, H.: 1975/6, *Theory and Measurement of Consumer Demand,* (2 vols.), North Holland, Amsterdam.

INDEX

Advanced Studies in Theoretical and Applied Econometrics

1. J.H.P. Paelinck (ed.): *Qualitative and Quantitative Mathematical Economics.* 1982 ISBN 90-247-2623-9
2. J.P. Ancot (ed.): *Analysing the Structure of Econometric Models.* 1984 ISBN 90-247-2894-0
3. A.J. Hughes Hallet (ed.): *Applied Decision Analysis and Economic Behaviour.* 1984 ISBN 90-247-2968-8
4. J.K. Sengupta: *Information and Efficiency in Economic Decision.* 1985 ISBN 90-247-3072-4
5. P. Artus and O. Guvenen (eds.), in collaboration with F. Gagey: *International Macroeconomic Modelling for Policy Decisions.* 1986 ISBN 90-247-3201-8
6. M.J. Vilares: *Structural Change in Macroeconomic Models.* Theory and Estimation. 1986 ISBN 90-247-3277-8
7. C. Carraro and D. Sartore (eds.): *Development of Control Theory for Economic Analysis.* 1987 ISBN 90-247-3345-6
8. D.P. Broer: *Neoclassical Theory and Empirical Models of Aggregate Firm Behaviour.* 1987 ISBN 90-247-3412-6
9. A. Italianer: *Theory and Practice of International Trade Linkage Models.* 1986 ISBN 90-247-3407-X
10. D.A. Kendrick: *Feedback.* A New Framework for Macroeconomic Policy. 1988 ISBN 90-247-3593-9; Pb: 90-247-3650-1
11. J.K. Sengupta and G.K. Kadekodi (eds.): *Econometrics of Planning and Efficiency.* 1988 ISBN 90-247-3602-1
12. D.A. Griffith: *Advanced Spatial Statistics.* Special Topics in the Exploration of Quantitative Spatial Data Series. 1988 ISBN 90-247-3627-7
13. O. Guvenen (ed.): *International Commodity Market Models and Policy Analysis.* 1988 ISBN 90-247-3768-0
14. G. Arbia: *Spatial Data Configuration in Statistical Analysis of Regional Economic and Related Problems.* 1989 ISBN 0-7923-0284-2
15. B. Raj (ed.): *Advances in Econometrics and Modelling.* 1989 ISBN 0-7923-0299-0
16. A. Aznar Grasa: *Econometric Model Selection.* A New Approach. 1989 ISBN 0-7923-0321-0
17. L.R. Klein and J. Marquez (eds.): *Economics in Theory and Practice.* An Eclectic Approach. Essays in Honor of F. G. Adams. 1989 ISBN 0-7923-0410-1
18. D.A. Kendrick: *Models for Analyzing Comparative Advantage.* 1990 ISBN 0-7923-0528-0
19. P. Artus and Y. Barroux (eds.): *Monetary Policy.* A Theoretical and Econometric Approach. 1990 ISBN 0-7923-0626-0

Advanced Studies in Theoretical and Applied Econometrics

20. G. Duru and J.H.P. Paelinck (eds.): *Econometrics of Health Care.* 1990
ISBN 0-7923-0766-6
21. L. Phlips (ed.): *Commodity, Futures and Financial Markets.* 1991
ISBN 0-7923-1043-8
22. H.M. Amman, D.A. Belsley and L.F. Pau (eds.): *Computational Economics and Econometrics.* 1992
ISBN 0-7923-1287-2
23. B. Raj and J. Koerts (eds.): *Henri Theil's Contributions to Economics and Econometrics.* Vol. I: Econometric Theory and Methodology. 1992
ISBN 0-7923-1548-0; Set ISBN 0-7923-1666-5
24. B. Raj and J. Koerts (eds.): *Henri Theil's Contributions to Economics and Econometrics.* Vol. II: Consumer Demand Analysis and Information Theory. 1992
ISBN 0-7923-1664-9; Set ISBN 0-7923-1666-5
25. B. Raj and J. Koerts (eds.): *Henri Theil's Contributions to Economics and Econometrics.* Vol. III: Economic Policy and Forecasts, and Management Science. 1992
ISBN 0-7923-1665-7; Set ISBN 0-7923-1666-5

Kluwer Academic Publishers – Dordrecht / Boston / London

MIX
Papier aus verantwortungsvollen Quellen
Paper from responsible sources
FSC® C105338

If you have any concerns about our products,
you can contact us on
ProductSafety@springernature.com

In case Publisher is established outside the EU,
the EU authorized representative is:
Springer Nature Customer Service Center GmbH
Europaplatz 3, 69115 Heidelberg, Germany

Printed by Libri Plureos GmbH
in Hamburg, Germany